RISK AND THE REGULATION OF UNCERTAINTY IN INTERNATIONAL LAW

Risk and the Regulation of Uncertainty in International Law

Edited by
MÓNIKA AMBRUS
ROSEMARY RAYFUSE
WOUTER WERNER

OXFORD
UNIVERSITY PRESS

OXFORD
UNIVERSITY PRESS

Great Clarendon Street, Oxford, OX2 6DP,
United Kingdom

Oxford University Press is a department of the University of Oxford. It furthers the University's objective of excellence in research, scholarship, and education by publishing worldwide. Oxford is a registered trade mark of Oxford University Press in the UK and in certain other countries

First Edition published in 2017
Impression: 1

Published in the United States of America by Oxford University Press
198 Madison Avenue, New York, NY 10016, United States of America

British Library Cataloguing in Publication Data
Data available

Library of Congress Control Number: 2017934733

ISBN 978–0–19–879589–6

Printed and bound by
CPI Group (UK) Ltd, Croydon, CR0 4YY

Preface

This book has its origins in a small 'exploratory workshop' which was held at the Faculty of Law at Lund University in May 2011 on 'Imagining the Future Climate Regime'. At the time our interest revolved around the 'clash of precautions' evident in the international climate regime where the precautionary approach demands, on the one hand, that lack of scientific uncertainty as to the seriousness or irreversibility of damage from climate change should not prevent the taking of protective or mitigation measures while, on the other hand, simultaneously demanding that lack of seriousness or irreversibility of damage from these protective or mitigation measures themselves should not be used as an excuse to prevent their introduction. We foresaw, and wanted to explore, the problem of responding to climate change by introducing mitigation measures despite uncertainty as to both their efficacy and their potential to cause serious or irreversible damage. Although not sure where the topic would take us, we particularly had in mind the then emerging debates relating to global geoengineering as a mitigation strategy, as well as discussions relating to scientific uncertainty in decision-making more generally.

It quickly became apparent that there was much more to the topic than a climate change-centred focus would suggest. Indeed, 'imagining the future' has become an important and influential part of international law in general, with international legal arrangements across the multiple regimes and sub-regimes of international law increasingly imagining future worlds, or creating space for experts to articulate how the future can be conceptualized and managed. In short, science and technology have made it possible to imagine different possible futures in all areas of international law, be they in the form of promises, or threats, or of radical uncertainty. Examination of the various imageries, vocabularies, expert knowledge, and rules developed within these different areas of international law seemed, at its core, a worthy pursuit, and one which might lay the groundwork for future comparisons between the values articulated and methodologies or practices developed in different international legal regimes for anticipating future regime stress and allocating preference for one imagined future over another.

In a second workshop held in 2013 at the Vrije Universiteit (VU) Amsterdam, a group of scholars from a range of substantive areas across international law mapped out the way forward for the more ambitious project which eventually became this book. At a further workshop hosted by the Institute for Legal Studies at the Centre for Social Sciences of the Hungarian Academy of Sciences in October 2014, participants exchanged papers and ideas on the theme, which have now been transformed into the chapters of this book.

As is inevitable in a project of this breadth and ambition, not everyone who participated in the workshops was able, ultimately, to contribute to this book and not everyone who has contributed to this book was able to attend the workshops. Thus, in addition to thanking the authors represented here for their contributions and for their forbearance with the project, we would also like to thank the numerous other colleagues who, over the years, participated in and contributed to the project at various stages and in various ways. Their contributions have been equally valuable in shaping the direction, contours, and content of this book.

In terms of institutional and financial support we are extremely grateful to the Law Faculty at Lund University for providing seed funding for this project and hosting the exploratory workshop from which this book arose. Thanks are also due to the Law Faculty at VU Amsterdam and the Hungarian Institute for Legal Studies, and in particular, Dr Tamás Hoffmann, for kindly hosting our two main workshops. We are also grateful for the financial support provided by the European Cooperation in Science and Technology (COST) programme, an intergovernmental framework aimed at facilitating the collaboration and networking of scientists and researchers at the European level. COST is supported by the European Union Seventh Framework Programme (EUFP7) through a dedicated Coordination and Support Action (CSA) and is funded by the European Commission. For more information on COST, see <http://www.cost.eu>. This volume was prepared within the context of COST Action IS1003 (*International Law between Constitutionalisation and Fragmentation: The Role of Law in the Post-national Constellation*).

Finally we are grateful to Oxford University Press, and in particular to Nicole Leyland, for putting the publication of this book on track and to Emma Endean-Mills for seeing the publication through to fruition.

Mónika Ambrus, Rosemary Rayfuse, and Wouter Werner
Groningen/Budapest, Sydney/Lund, and Amsterdam
September 2016

Contents

List of Tables

Table of Cases

ERITREA-ETHIOPIA CLAIMS COMMISSION

EUROPEAN COURT OF HUMAN RIGHTS (ECTHR)

EUROPEAN COURT OF JUSTICE (ECJ)

INTER-AMERICAN COMMISSION ON HUMAN RIGHTS (IACHR)

INTERNATIONAL CENTRE FOR SETTLEMENT OF INVESTMENT DISPUTES (ICSID)

INTERNATIONAL COURT OF JUSTICE (ICJ)

INTERNATIONAL CRIMINAL TRIBUNAL FOR THE FORMER YUGOSLAVIA (ICTY)

LONDON COURT OF INTERNATIONAL ARBITRATION (LCIA)

PERMANENT COURT OF ARBITRATION (PCA)

UNITED NATIONS COMMISSION ON INTERNATIONAL TRADE LAW (UNCITRAL)

WTO/GATT

OTHER ARBITRATIONS

Table of Treaties

List of Abbreviations

AIEA	International Atomic Energy Agency
ARTs	Assisted reproductive technologies
BECCS	Bio-energy carbon capture and storage
BEINGS	Biotechnology and the Ethical Imagination: A Global Summit
BIT	Bilateral Investment Treaty
CBD	Convention on Biological Diversity
CBDRRC	Common but differentiated responsibilities and respective capabilities
CDR	Carbon dioxide removal
CE	Climate engineering
C-EENRG	Cambridge Centre for Environment, Energy and Natural Resource Governance
CoC	Code of Conduct for Outer Space Activities
COP	Conference of the Parties (Paris Agreement to the United Nations Framework Convention on Climate Change)
COST	Cooperation in science and technology
CSA	Coordination and support action
CTLD	Center for Transboundary Legal Development
ECHR	European Convention on Human Rights
ECtHR	European Court of Human Rights
ESA	European Space Agency
EUFP7	European Union Seventh Framework Programme
FDI	Foreign direct investment
FET	Fair and equitable treatment
GATT	General Agreement on Tariffs and Trade
GDP	Gross domestic product
GHG	Greenhouse gas
GMO	Genetically modified organism
IADC	Inter-Agency Space Debris Coordination Committee
IASS	Institute for Advanced Sustainability Studies
ICES	International Council for the Exploration of the Sea
ICISS	International Commission on Intervention and State Sovereignty
ICJ	International Court of Justice
ICRC	International Committee of the Red Cross
ICSID	International Centre for Settlement of Investment Disputes
ICTY	International Criminal Tribunal for the former Yugoslavia
IEA	International Energy Agency
IIAs	International Investment Agreements
ILC	International Law Commission
ILO	International Labour Organization
IMO	International Maritime Organization
Intelsat	International Telecommunications Satellite Organization
IPCC	Intergovernmental Panel on Climate Change
ISA	International Seabed Authority

ISPS Code	International Ship and Port Facility Security Code
ISS	International space station
LDC	Least developed countries
LOSC	Law of the Sea Convention
MA	Moon Agreement
MFN	Most-favoured-nation
MIDAS	Managing Impacts of Deep-seA reSource exploitation
NATO	North Atlantic Treaty Organization
NDC	Nationally determined contributions
NGO	Non-governmental organization
NPCs	Nationally determined contributions
NPMs	Non-precluded measures
NRC	National Research Council
OST	Outer Space Treaty
PAROS	Prevention of an arms race in outer space
PCASP	Privately contracted armed security personnel
PPMs	Process and production methods
PPWT	Draft Treaty on the Prevention of the Placement of Weapons in Outer Space and of the Threat or Use of Force Against Outer Space Objects
R2P	Responsibility to protect
RCP	Representative concentration pathway
SDG	Sustainable development goal
SID	Seafarer identification documents
SOGI	Sexual orientation and gender identity
SOLAS	International Convention for the Safety of Life at Sea
SRM	Solar radiation management
TCBMs	Transparency and confidence-building measures
TILT	Tilburg institute for Law, Technology and Society
TOA	Technology options analysis
TSC	Tilburg Sustainability Center
UNC	Charter of the United Nations
UNCOPUOS	United Nations Committee on the Peaceful Uses of Outer Space
UNDOALOS	UN Division for Ocean Affairs and the Law of the Sea
UNEP	United Nations Environment Programme
UNESCO	The United Nations Educational, Scientific and Cultural Organization
UNFCCC	United Nations Framework Convention on Climate Change
UNGA	United Nations General Assembly
UNSCOM	United Nations Special Commission
UNSW	University of New South Wales
UNTS	United Nations Treaty Series
USNSS	National Security Strategy of the United States of America
VCLT	Vienna Convention on the Law of Treaties
WMD	Weapons of mass destruction
WTO	World Trade Organization

List of Contributors

Mónika Ambrus is a Senior Researcher in Public International Law at the Institute for Legal Sciences at the Hungarian Academy of Sciences in Budapest. Earlier she worked as a lecturer in public international law at the Department of Public International Law at the University of Groningen and as Assistant Professor at the Department of Public International Law at the Erasmus University Rotterdam, the Netherlands. She obtained her PhD in 2010, focusing on European anti-discrimination law and its enforcement mechanisms. Her current research focuses on the discourse analysis relating to the legitimacy of international adjudication and legal designs in international water law. Between 2010 and 2016 she was the managing editor of the *Netherlands Yearbook of International Law*, and the editor with RA Wessel of *Between Pragmatism and Predictability: Temporariness in International Law* (45 Netherlands Yearbook of International Law, TMC Asser Press 2014).

Azernoosh Bazrafkan joined the Globalization and International Economic Law program of the University of Antwerp in partnership with the World Trade Institute. Her doctoral research focuses on international investment law from the perspective of development. Currently, she is engaged as a part-time consultant for the World Bank on a project analysing pro-development provisions in international investment agreements. She holds an LLM degree in International and European Law from the Vrije Universiteit Amsterdam and a Bachelor's degree in Law and Economics from Leiden University.

Lianne Boer is Assistant Professor of Public International Law at VU University, Amsterdam, and Research Fellow of the Centre for the Politics of Transnational Law. Her research focuses on academic practices, such as the construction of legal knowledge in international humanitarian law, approaching these from the perspectives of inter alia linguistics and the sociology of science. She has been a visiting scholar at the Lauterpacht Centre for International Law in Cambridge, as well as at the Faculty of Law at Lund University, Sweden.

Leslie-Anne Duvic-Paoli is a Philomathia Postdoctoral Research Associate at the University of Cambridge and a Fellow of the Cambridge Centre for Environment, Energy and Natural Resource Governance (C-EENRG). She holds a PhD in international law from the Graduate Institute of International and Development Studies (Geneva) and Master's degrees from Sciences Po Paris and the University of Panthéon-Sorbonne. She teaches and researches international environmental law and international energy law. Her current research focuses on the legal aspects of the energy transition to a low-carbon economy. She is also interested in investigating the nature and content of the fundamental principles of international environmental law, in particular the principle of prevention.

Floor M Fleurke is Assistant Professor of European Environmental Law at Tilburg Law School, the Netherlands, where she is member of three research schools within Tilburg University, namely the Center for Transboundary Legal Development (CTLD), the multidisciplinary Tilburg Sustainability Center (TSC) and the Tilburg Institute for Law, Technology and Society (TILT). Her research focuses on European environmental law, with a specific interest in the relationship between science, technology, and environmental law. She holds a PhD (*cum laude*) from the University of Amsterdam for a thesis on the application of the precautionary principle in the European Union and has published several peer-reviewed articles.

Steven Freeland is Professor of International Law at Western Sydney University, Australia and Permanent Visiting Professor at the iCourts Centre of Excellence for International Courts. His main teaching and research interests are in the fields of international criminal law, commercial aspects of space law, public international law, and human rights law. He is a Visiting Professor at the University of Vienna; a member of Faculty at the London Institute of Space Policy and Law; Director of the International Institute of Space Law; a member of the Space Law Committee of the International Law Association; a member of the Advisory Board at the Australian Centre for Space Engineering Research; and a member of the European Centre for Space Law. He sits on the editorial board of a number of international journals, including the *Australian International Law Journal*, the *Annals of Air and Space Law*, the *German Journal of Air and Space Law*, and the *Space Law Review*, and is Co-Editor of *Annotated Leading Cases of the International Criminal Tribunals.*

Douglas Guilfoyle is an Associate Professor in the Faculty of Law at Monash University. He was previously a Reader at University College London. He is the author of *Shipping Interdiction and the Law of the Sea* (Cambridge University Press, 2009) and *International Criminal Law* (Cambridge University Press, 2016) and numerous articles on Somali piracy, and maritime security and law enforcement. He has acted as a consultant on piracy and maritime security issues to the Contact Group on Piracy off the Coast of Somalia (Working Group 2), the Foreign Affairs Committee of the House of Commons and the UN Office on Drugs and Crime, among other organizations. He holds a PhD and LLM from the University of Cambridge, where he was a Chevening and a Gates Scholar, and undergraduate degrees in law and history from the Australian National University.

Alexia Herwig is Assistant Professor in International Economic Law at the University of Antwerp. Prior to joining the Faculty of Law, she held a personal post-doctoral fellowship from the Flemish Research Foundation and was a post-doctoral Research Fellow at the University of Bremen, Germany in a project on social regulation and trade. She holds a doctoral degree and an LLM in International Legal Studies from New York University and a Bachelor of Science from the London School of Economics. Her research interests focus on risk regulation in international economic law, as well as more philosophical thought about matters of human rights, distributive justice, and democracy in the context of economic globalization.

Aline Jaeckel is a Postdoctoral Research Fellow at Macquarie Law School, where she is a recipient of the Macquarie University Research Fellowship. Her work focuses on the regulation of deep seabed mineral mining in areas beyond national jurisdiction. She is the author of *The International Seabed Authority and the Precautionary Principle* (Martinus Nijhoff, 2017) as well as articles and book chapters in the fields of law of the sea, international law, and international environmental law. Previously, she worked for the Institute for Advanced Sustainability Studies (IASS) in Potsdam and taught international law and law of the sea at the University of New South Wales (UNSW), Australia. Aline holds a PhD from UNSW, an LLM from Leiden University, and an LLB from UWE Bristol.

Jacqueline Peel is a Professor at the Melbourne Law School. Her research interests are in the areas of environmental law (domestic and international), risk regulation, and the role of science and climate change law. She has published numerous articles and several books on these topics, including *Australian Climate Law in a Global Context* (with A Zahar and L Godden) (Cambridge University Press Melbourne, 2013); *Principles of International Environmental Law* (with P Sands) (3rd edn, Cambridge University Press, 2012); *Environmental Law: Scientific, Policy and Regulatory Dimensions* (with L Godden) (Oxford

University Press, 2010); *Science and Risk Regulation in International Law* (Cambridge University Press, 2010); and *The Precautionary Principle in Practice* (Federation Press, 2005). She holds a BSc and an LLB from the University of Queensland, an LLM from New York University, where she was a Fulbright scholar, and a PhD from the University of Melbourne. She has been Hauser Research Scholar and Emile Noël Fellow at NYU Law School and a Visiting Scholar at the Berkeley Law School's Centre for Law, Energy and Environment and Stanford Water in the West, Stanford University.

Rosemary Rayfuse is Scientia Professor of Public International Law at UNSW, Australia, Conjoint Professor in the Faculty of Law at Lund University, and Visiting Professor at the University of Gothenburg. Her research focuses on the law of the sea and international environmental law, with particular emphasis on protection of the marine environment in areas beyond national jurisdiction. Her publications include the edited *Research Handbook on International Marine Environmental Law* (Edward Elgar, 2015) *Protection of the Environment in Relation to Armed Conflict* (Martinus Nijhoff, 2014), and *International Law in the Era of Climate Change* (with Shirley Scott) (Edward Elgar, 2012). She is on the editorial board of the *International Journal of Marine and Coastal Law* and is Chair's Nominee on the International Law Association's Committee on International Law and Sea-Level Rise.

David Sifonios is attorney at law and in-house lawyer with an energy and telecommunication company in Switzerland. His forthcoming PhD thesis presented at the University of Lausanne analyses the issue of environmental processes and production methods (PPMs) in World Trade Organization (WTO) law.

Nicholas Tsagourias is Professor of International Law at the University of Sheffield. His main teaching and research interests are in the fields of international law and the use of force, international humanitarian law, and international criminal law. He sits on the editorial board for the *Journal of Conflict and Security Law* (Oxford University Press) and he is a member of the Cyberterrorism Study Group of the International Law Association. Among his recent publications are the edited book *Research Handbook on International Law and Cyberspace* (with Dr Russell Buchan) (Edward Elgar, 2015) and the co-authored book *Collective Security: Theory, Law and Practice* (with Professor Nigel White) (Cambridge University Press, 2013).

Britta van Beers is Associate Professor at the Department of Legal Theory of VU University, Amsterdam, the Netherlands. Her research involves the legal-philosophical aspects of the regulation of medical biotechnology. She has degrees in philosophy (*cum laude*) and law from the University of Amsterdam and New York University School of Law and a PhD from the VU, for which she received the CJ Goudsmit prize from the Dutch Health Law Association and the Praemium Erasmium Research Prize from the Praemium Erasmianum Foundation in 2011. Since 2011, she has been a member of several advisory committees of the Dutch Health Council. Recent publications include the volume *Humanity across International Law and Biolaw* (co-edited with Wouter Werner and Luigi Corrias) (Cambridge University Press, 2014) and *Symbolic Legislation and Developments in Biolaw* (co-edited with Bart van Klink and Lonneke Poort) (Springer, 2016).

Wouter Werner is Professor of Public International Law at VU University, Amsterdam. His main fields of interest are international legal theory, conflict and security law, international criminal law, and the interplay between international law and international politics. In his recent publications, Werner has focused on audio-visual representations of international criminal law. Werner is Co-Director of the Centre for the Politics of Transnational Law and editor of the *Netherlands Yearbook of International Law*. In 2010, he received a grant of approximately €550,000 from Cooperation in Science and Technology (COST) for the establishment of a pan-European, interdisciplinary research network on foundational changes in international law. This volume is one of the publications that has emerged from the COST research network.

Andreas R Ziegler is currently a Professor of International Law and the Director of the LLM Program in International and European Economic and Commercial Law at the University of Lausanne. Previously he was a civil servant working for several Swiss Ministries and international organizations. He has published widely on European law, public international law, on international courts and tribunals, and on sexual orientation and gender identity (SOGI), as well as trade and investment. He regularly advises governments, international organizations, non-governmental organizations (NGOs), and private clients and has represented them before various domestic and international courts and arbitral tribunals. He is counsel with a law firm specializing in economic and business law (Blum & Grob Attorneys-at-law, Zurich), is on the permanent roster of panelists of the World Trade Organization (WTO) and the International Centre for Settlement of Investment Disputes (ICSID), and is a SOGI expert for the Council of Europe.

PART I

INTRODUCTION

1

Risk and International Law

Mónika Ambrus, Rosemary Rayfuse, and Wouter Werner

1.1 The Relevance of Risk to International Law

Some fifteen years ago, the sociologist François Ewald signalled the 'return of Descartes's malicious demon' in legal and political decision-making.[1] As may be recalled, René Descartes hypothesized the existence of a malicious demon as a means of exploring the boundaries of that which can be known with certainty. If we assume there could be a malicious demon interfering with our senses and our ability to obtain objective knowledge, we are left with radical uncertainty as to the outside world. Today, legal and political decision-makers do not even need to *hypothesize* the existence of such a demon. Whether malicious or not, there is radical doubt all around. In many contexts, our ability to know the outside world is limited by both an over- and an underproduction of (scientific) knowledge. In several fields, we lack the knowledge necessary to be able to establish, for example, exact chains of cause and effect. Yet, for the application of law, such knowledge is often indispensable. In other fields, there is an abundance of scientific knowledge, but experts come to diametrically opposed conclusions. Doubt is produced not through philosophical reflection, but through the attempt to apply legal rules to a world that can be read and known in many different ways. In other words, legal and political decision-makers have to apply rules and take decisions in the face of sometimes radically uncertain futures. In this volume, we explore what this means for different fields of international law. How is uncertainty imagined across different fields of international law? What do lawyers recognize as 'certain' and 'uncertain' and through which mechanisms do they cope with uncertainty? What is the role of law in the imagination of uncertainty?

To a large extent the return of radical uncertainty is the result of the developments that challenge the boundaries of traditional risk management. As Ulrich Beck, Anthony Giddens, and many others have argued, 'risk' has long been a useful category to absorb and manage uncertainty.[2] Instead of attributing undesired

[1] F Ewald, 'The Return of Descartes's Malicious Demon: An Outline of a Philosophy of Precaution' in T Baker and J Simon (eds), *Embracing Risk* (University of Chicago Press 2002) 273–98.

[2] The literature on risk and 'risk society' is vast. See among (many) others: U Beck, *Risk Society, Towards a New Modernity* (Sage Publishing 1992); U Beck, 'Living in the World Risk Society' (2006) 35(3)

events to aggrieved deities or to previous norm violations by individuals, the logic of risk sets out how an individual event is part of a larger pattern that can be known and mastered intellectually. Although it may be impossible to predict the occurrence of specific, individual events, the logic of risk makes it possible to predict that on average we can expect a certain number of occurrences over a certain period of time. This, in turn, enables the development of technologies such as insurance, which combines a probabilistic logic with a scheme of compensation. In addition, it makes it possible to develop preventative measures. A good example is the way in which the application of 'risk' transformed the regulation of work-place safety in the nineteenth century. Accidents at work were, for a long time, treated as a matter of individual responsibility, where the main question was 'Who bears responsibility for violating a norm in the past?' During the course of the nineteenth century, however, the notion of individual responsibility was supplemented by a more collectivist strategy of dealing with undesired events. Crucial in this respect was the further development of probabilistic and statistical thinking, as well as the development of the concept of professional risk. As mentioned at the first French Congress on accidents at work, statistics showed the operation of a mysterious law: '[T]aking a large number of workers in the same occupation, one finds a constant level of accidents year by year. It follows from this that accidents, just when they may seem to be due to pure chance, are governed by a mysterious law.'[3]

The progress of science and technology, however, has produced possible dangers that escape the logic of probabilistic risk. An example is what Ewald has called the two infinities of risk: the infinitely small-scale risks (biological, natural, food-related risks) and the infinitely large-scale risks, such as nuclear risks.[4] In a similar fashion, Ulrich Beck has contrasted the archetypical risks in industrial society (ie, the accident at work or in traffic) with what he calls the icons of destruction: nuclear power, environmental despoliation, and gentechnology.[5] These types of risk transcend temporal, spatial, and social boundaries and challenge established institutions dealing with risk, such as insurance companies or the welfare state. In order to deal with these risks, it is necessary to develop alternative, or at least supplementary, forms of imagination, together with principles informing decision-makers as to how they should relate to uncertainty. A prime example is the precautionary principle as it has been developed in environmental law. While formulations of the principle differ, its core message is that, in cases of possible serious or irreversible damage, lack of full scientific certainty shall not be used as a reason for postponing preventative

Economy and Society 329; A Giddens, 'Risk and Responsibility' (1999) 62(1) *Modern Law Review* 1–10; A Giddens, *Modernity and Self-Identity: Self and Society in the Late Modern Age* (Polity Press 1991); U Beck, A Giddens, and S Lash (eds), *Reflexive Modernization: Politics, Tradition and Aesthetics in the Modern Social Order* (Polity Press 1994).

[3] O Keller, *Premier Congrès International des Accidents du Travail* (April 1889), as quoted by F Ewald, 'Insurance and Risk' in G Burchell, C Gordon, and P Miller (eds), *The Foucault Effect, Studies in Governmentality* (University of Chicago Press 1991) 197, 202.

[4] F Ewald, 'Two Infinities of Risk' in B Massumi (ed), *The Politics of Everyday Fear* (University of Minnesota Press 1993) 221.

[5] Beck, *Risk Society* (n 2).

measures.[6] The principle thus aims to guide decision-making while recognizing the existence of sometimes radical uncertainty and ambiguous and contestable scientific knowledge. Indeed, so powerful is the allure of the precautionary principle that its underlying logic is beginning to figure prominently in other areas of international law.

As the example of the precautionary principle indicates, there is a dialectical relation between uncertainty and the law. On the one hand, law is confronted with social, technological, and scientific developments that call for new normative answers. However, law is not just a passive receptor of changes in science, technology, and society; it also plays an active role in the development and design of such changes. What counts as uncertainty, how uncertainty is framed, and which policy-options are available in dealing with uncertainty are all, to a large extent, determined by the laws in place. Lawyers are thus not just the people applying rules to rapidly changing and uncertain environments; they are also the ones co-producing the uncertainties they seek to regulate.

How the dialectical relation between law and uncertainty takes form may vary from one legal field to another. In the past decades international law has undergone a process of ever-growing specialization, often referred to as the fragmentation of international law.[7] International law today consists of a series of sometimes highly specialized regimes, each with their own rationality, rules and procedures, and expert vocabularies. What is taken for granted in, for example, environmental law circles may seem strange to an audience of international criminal lawyers, and vice versa. Even within functional fields one may find several sub-regimes, each with their own rules, politics, biases, and expertise. The development of these specialized regimes unavoidably results in different ways in which uncertainties are imaged, experienced, articulated, and regulated. This volume contains an overview of these imaginations, articulations, and regulations of uncertainties across international law, with particular focus on environmental law, human rights law, the regulation of the use of force, economic law, and investment law.

1.2 Imagining Risk in Various Functional Fields of International Law

While the chapters in this book differ in terms of the functional fields examined, they all deal with the question how international law imagines, or helps to imagine, the future. In this way, they all treat the politics of international law as a politics of framing. After all, legal imaginaries of the future have very real consequences for

[6] Rio Declaration on Environment and Development, *Report of the United Nations Conference on Environment and Development*, I (1992) UN Doc A/CONF.151/26; (1992) 31 *International Legal Materials* 874, Principle 15.

[7] One example out of the vast literature on this topic is the report by the Study Group of the International Law Commission, *Fragmentation of International Law: Difficulties Arising from the Diversification and Expansion of International Law*, UN Doc A/CN.4/L.682, 13 April 2006.

the present; they come with particular rights, duties, and powers, with distributions of risk and costs, with positions of authority, and with alternative framings that are pushed to the margin. In other words, the chapters all deal with essentially three basic questions:

1. How is the future imagined in a particular legal field? This question also covers the questions pertaining to thresholds of application, standards of evidence, and the burden of proof.
2. How are these imaginings translated into legal rights, duties, and competences operating in the present?
3. How does the distribution of rights, duties, and competences affect the distribution of risks, costs, and benefits?

The chapter by Nicholas Tsagourias (Chapter 2) takes up these questions in the context of self-defence. Tsagourias sets out how the law on self-defence has increasingly been affected by a logic of anticipation and what he calls a 'risk calculus'. This implies a shift towards images of possible future attacks against (powerful) states, at the expense of images of the future that focus on the dangers of stretching exceptions to the prohibition on the use of force. The turn towards a logic of anticipation thus comes with a profound redistribution of legal powers, combined with a redistribution of the risks of being the victim of political violence. What is more, Tsagourias argues, the adoption of the 'risk calculus' in the *ius ad bellum* facilitates the 'transnational security state' (a point also made in Guilfoyle's chapter), refocuses legal provisions towards the future, and brings with it a deformalizition of international law.

The chapter by Wouter Werner and Lianne Boer (Chapter 3) studies images of the future in the so-called *Tallinn Manual* on cyberwar. More specifically, they focus on the specific way in which legal experts involved in the drafting of the *Manual* have imagined the future. This way, they argue, is distinctively different from the way in which social scientists or policy advisors have imagined the future of cyberwar. Where the latter have mainly dealt with the probability or likelihood of cyberwar and its possible consequences, the *Tallinn Manual* imagines the future through the lens of already existing legal provisions. In other words: for the legal experts involved, the future is framed in terms of the content of legal rules drafted in the past. This, in turn, has consequences for the kind of questions that can be posed, the sort of problems that can be articulated, and the distributional effects that can be put on the agenda.

Douglas Guilfoyle's chapter (Chapter 4) examines how the field of maritime security has come to be dominated by two imaginaries of the future: (i) imaginaries based on worst-case scenarios for states, predominantly in the area of counterterrorism; and (ii) portrayals of existential threats to states pertaining to issues of transboundary migration. Taken together, these imaginaries have facilitated the rise of a 'transnational security state'; a state projecting its power to define and fight threats beyond its own borders. In addition, the images of danger to states have affected the use and interpretation of some core provisions of the law of the sea. The costs of this particular way of framing the future are borne by vulnerable groups such as seafarers and illegal migrants.

The contribution by Steven Freeland (Chapter 5) explores a topic that recurs in several chapters in this volume, the interplay between technology and international law in the framing and regulation of uncertainty. Freeland analyses how the rapid development of technologies in outer space challenged long-standing legal categories. In a short period of time both the legal status of outer space and the limits of state territory were re-defined, and international law was called to deal with the possible consequences of newly developing unknown technologies and activities in outer space. However, the way in which international law has sought to imagine and regulate these risks leaves many questions unanswered, particularly when it comes to non-sovereign claims to outer space and the regulation of debris. Freeland discusses several initiatives to deal with the mismatch between the categories of formal international law and the risks created by space activities.

The chapter by Mónika Ambrus (Chapter 6) discusses the role of courts, in particular that of the European Court of Human Rights, in the governance of future scenarios. Ambrus focuses on the way in which this governance affects the rights and duties enshrined in the European Convention on Human Rights, and the role the Court thus attributes itself in this context. Although the Court does not impose obligations on states regarding future scenarios which include uncertainty, relying on the concept of governmentality as defined by Foucault, Ambrus concludes that the Court can still be regarded as a governor of risk.

Similarly, the impact of imageries of the future on legal rights and duties is one of the central topics in the chapter by Britta van Beers (Chapter 7), who examines the way in which bio-law tends to rely on dystopian imageries of the future, to the effect that the field is dominated by prohibitions and restrictions on the development or application of new technologies. The emphasis on dystopian imageries should be understood in the context of what is at stake in debates on biotechnology and its regulation; the future of mankind and the human being as such. Traditional risk approaches have failed to do justice to what van Beers calls the 'political and metaphysical nature' of the regulation of biotechnologies. Building on Jonas's work on technological risks, she advocates a sense of responsibility that includes imagination and the use of (legal) fictions.

The specific way in which law facilitates imaginaries of the future is also central to the chapter on international environmental law by Leslie-Anne Duvic-Paoli (Chapter 8). International environmental law, she argues, is intrinsically bound up with images of the future because of its anticipatory and preventative nature. At the same time, international law contains rules and procedures that determine how futures are to be imagined. This is reflected in the material scope of the duty to prevent (which risks should be included and which excluded?), the temporal scope (which time frames count as relevant for imagined futures?), and the potential beneficiaries (whose futures are imagined, and whose futures fall outside the scope of law?). The chapter provides an answer to these questions and thereby to the question of how international environmental law structures the way in which the future is brought into the present.

Bringing the future into the present is a theme in the chapter by Aline Jaeckel and Rosemary Rayfuse (Chapter 9) on the still-yet-to-occur deep seabed mining. With advances in scientific knowledge contributing to rather than resolving competing imageries of the environmental risks and uncertainties associated with deep seabed mining, the chapter explores the extent to which the approach to regulating and managing these risks has both influenced and been influenced by institutional choices. Characterizing the establishment of the International Seabed Authority as a 'precautionary moment', they examine the way in which the imagined future of perceived economic riches is being balanced against the present requirement to protect the marine environment and how the collectivization of these benefits and risks is being translated into legal rights and duties.

Jacqueline Peel's chapter (Chapter 10) deals with the question of how international law has framed the 'unimaginable effects' of climate change. Peel analyses how international law initially followed scientific imageries of the future, which emphasized the need of emission reductions. Gradually, alternative conceptions of the future emerged, which centred on questions of adaptation and loss and damages. International climate law followed suit, which resulted in the development of different sets of rules and principles. The focus shifted towards the broader causes of climate change and considerations of equity. Yet, these shifts could not do away with dystopian imageries of the future, including fears that climate change presents existential threats to human life as we know it. This has led to the consideration of more radical technologies such as climate engineering, technologies that give rise to new imageries of the future, and calls for their legal regulation.

Precisely these technologies are the topic of the chapter by Floor Fleurke (Chapter 11), who discusses how climate engineering, biotechnology, and synthetic technology give rise to competing imageries of the future in the area of climate change. As a consequence, regulators are called upon to deal with the 'risk/risk dilemma'; whereas new technologies may help to fight existential risks of climate change, they may also pose new, equally threatening dangers themselves. Fleurke argues that the precautionary principle, although often critiqued for its debilitating consequences, offers a fruitful starting point to deal with the problem of risk trade-offs in the field of climate change. While the precautionary principle does not dictate any outcomes, it does facilitate decision-making and deliberative processes. In terms of this volume as a whole, the precautionary principle may assist deliberations on the prioritization of particular framings of the future and the rights, duties, and powers that come with it, and on the corresponding distribution of costs and benefits to be incurred when relating the present to particular images of the future.

The chapter by Andreas R Ziegler and David Sifonios (Chapter 12) provides an example of the politics of framing in international law. Their chapter studies the assessment of environmental risks in international trade law, with a focus on the regulation of process and product methods (PPMs). For trade law, environmental concerns appear not as primary objects for regulation, but first and foremost as possible exceptions to free trade rules or as threats to the regime as a whole. Yet, international trade law leaves room for images of the future that emphasize ecological protection. Such images compete with more established images of the future in trade law which stress the need for free trade and economic prosperity. The more ecologically oriented images, Ziegler and Sifonios demonstrate, give rise to new interpretations of positive rules of trade law and novel conceptions of economic growth, captured in the idea of 'sustainable development'.

In the final chapter of this volume (Chapter 13), Azernoosh Bazrafkan and Alexia Herwig conceptualize international investment agreements as a way to allocate and manage risk. Through investment treaties, investors seek to secure return on investment in the face of uncertain future decisions by the host state. This requires a balance between, on the one hand, the need to tie future decision-making to norms agreed upon in the present and, on the other hand, the need to retain political freedom and self-determination for the host state. In this context, arbitral awards have been pivotal. In the 1990s, they contributed to a shift in favour of foreign investors, relegating risks of unmitigated externalities shifted towards host states and their populations. In response, investment treaties have sought to create more regulatory space for host countries. Subsequent case law, however, has failed to develop consistent interpretations on the allocation of risk among host states and investors. In order to remedy the shortcomings in current investment law, Bazrafkan and Herwig propose an approach to risk allocation derived from theories of fairness and equity.

Returning to the three basic questions addressed in this book, it is apparent that there are numerous ways in which the future can be imagined and thus construed, including through the social construction of uncertainty, the definition of public values that are or might be endangered, the relation between expertise and lay persons in the construction of uncertainty and danger, the production of consensus around uncertainty and danger, the limits of scientific constructions of risk and danger, and qualitative and/or quantitative instruments of risk projection. While modern society has attempted to articulate and deal with uncertainty through 'risk management', traditional forms of risk management have increasingly come under strain, resulting in debates about the individualization or collectivization of risk; the relationship between sovereignty and risk; the territorial dimensions of risk, risk regulation, risk assessment, and risk management; and the management of clashing imperatives that follow from the use of the precautionary approach. It has been suggested that 'a world incapable of imagining a future is unlikely to have one'.[8] As the chapters in this book demonstrate, international law is deeply involved in debates about future imaginings, the reconfiguration of risk, and the impact of those future imaginings, be they utopian or dystopian, on present and future subjects of international law.

[8] R Rayfuse and S Scott, 'Mapping the Impact of Climate Change on International Law' in R Rayfuse and S Scott (eds), *International Law in the Era of Climate Change* (Edward Elgar 2012) 3–25, 25.

PART II

RISK AND SECURITY

2

Risk and the Use of Force

Nicholas Tsagourias

2.1 Introduction

Risk was treated as a feature of modernity by Ulrich Beck in his book *Risk Society*. According to him '[*r*]*isk* may be defined as a *systematic way of dealing with hazards and insecurities induced and introduced by modernization itself*'.[1] For Tony Blair, the former Prime Minister of the United Kingdom, 'risk seems to matter more than ever, partly because we are so much more aware of the risks we face, and partly because of the sheer speed of change in science and technology'.[2] Due to the omnipresence of risks, governments are preoccupied with risk management.[3]

In a globalized world, risks are not contained within state borders, but cross them to create a world risk society.[4] A world risk society is characterized by unbounded risks in spatial, temporal, and social terms.[5] Risks not only transgress state boundaries but also affect individuals directly.[6] Moreover, their latency challenges time frames and no single individual or event can be identified as their cause. Thus, world risk society preoccupies itself with '*how to feign control over the uncontrollable*—in politics, law, science, technology, economy and everyday life'.[7]

Inevitably, the concept of risk has entered the discipline and practice of international security because risk and security are closely connected.[8] Risk, implying

[1] U Beck, *Risk Society: Towards a New Modernity* (Sage 1992) 21. He continues by saying 'Risks, as opposed to older dangers, are consequences which relate to the threatening force of modernization and to its globalization of doubt. They are *politically reflexive*' (italics in the original).

[2] UK Government Cabinet Office: Strategy Unit, Summary Report, *Risk: Improving Government's Capability to Handle Risk and Uncertainty* (November 2002) 2.

[3] Beck, *Risk Society* (n 1) 19.

[4] U Beck, *World Risk Society* (Polity Press 1999).

[5] U Beck, 'The Terrorist Threat: World Risk Society Revisited' (2002) 19 *Theory, Culture and Society* 39, 41.

[6] Giddens named them 'high consequence risks'. According to Giddens, 'high consequence risks by definition are remote from the individual agent, although—again, by definition—they impinge directly on each individual's life chances'. A Giddens, *Modernity and Self-Identity: Self and Society in the Late Modern Age* (Stanford University Press 1991) 121.

[7] Beck, 'The Terrorist Threat' (n 5) 41.

[8] MV Rasmussen, *The Risk Society at War: Terror, Technology and Strategy in the Twenty-First Century* (CUP 2006); Y-K Heng, *War as Risk Management: Strategy and Conflict in an Age of Globalised Risks* (Routledge 2006).

a danger, is a component of the concept of security, which is about safety and protection from dangers. Moreover, since security is central to states as well as to the international society, the conceptualization of security in terms of risks reoriented its theory and practice to focus on the identification and assessment of security risks and on methods or actions to prevent, deter, mitigate, or generally manage risks.

This turn to risk is evident in the security policies of states or of international security organizations. For example, the North Atlantic Treaty Organization's (NATO's) first *Strategic Concept* following the end of the Cold War stated that 'a great deal of uncertainty about the future and risks to the security of the Alliance remain', and stressed that 'in contrast with the predominant threat of the past, the risks to Allied security that remain are multifaceted in nature and multidirectional, which makes them hard to predict and assess'.[9] The 2001 US Quadrennial Defense Review likewise stated that 'managing risks is a central element of the defense strategy'.[10] The 2013 French White Paper on Defence and National Security similarly opined that

> [i]n the complex, interconnected world in which we live, it is unrealistic to think that absence of risk is possible. The concept of national security expresses an intention to adopt a holistic approach to identifying risks and threats, as well as to the response required, using a combination of tools including knowledge and foresight, protection, prevention, deterrence and intervention.[11]

The language of risk reached its peak in 2002–2003 with regard to Iraq. After the first Gulf War following Iraq's invasion and annexation of Kuwait, the United States and other Western states embarked on a policy of containment which included sanctions and limited military action to enforce Iraqi disarmament.[12] The 9/11 attacks and the advent of global terrorism, however, changed the perception of the security challenges that Iraq posed to the world. It was the risk of renewed Iraqi aggression, the risk to international security of Iraq possessing weapons of mass destruction (WMD) and of supporting terrorism and the risk of egregious human rights violations being committed by the Iraqi regime[13] that preoccupied decision-makers in Washington and London, and justified military action to avert them.

In this chapter, I focus on the actualization of the concept of risk in the international law regime concerning the use of force. More specifically, I explore the

[9] NATO, *The Alliance's New Strategic Concept* (8 November 1991) paras 5 and 8. The 1999 *Strategic Concept* similarly observed that the Alliance was 'subject to a wide variety of military and non-military risks which are multi-directional and often difficult to predict'. NATO, *The Alliance's Strategic Concept*, Approved by the Heads of State and Government participating in the meeting of the North Atlantic Council in Washington, DC, on 23 and 24 April 1999 (NATO Office of Information and Press 1999) para 20.

[10] US Department of Defense, *Quadrennial Defense Review Report* (30 September 2001) 57.

[11] French White Paper on Defence and National Security 2013 (July 2013) 10–11.

[12] UNSC Res 687 (8 April 1991) UN Doc S/RES/687.

[13] UK Government, 'Iraq's Weapons of Mass Destruction: The Assessment of the British Government' (2002) <http://news.bbc.co.uk/nol/shared/spl/hi/middle_east/02/uk_dossier_on_iraq/pdf/iraqdossier.pdf> accessed 30 June 2015.

normative consequences for the law governing the use of force when a risk calculus is included within its body of rules. For this reason, I first explain the concept of risk and the characteristics of risk-oriented decisions relating to security. The central contention of this section is that the inclusion of a risk calculus to security invites prospectivism in decision-making. I then go on to consider the place of prospectivism in the international regime governing the use of force. Thus, section 2.3 examines the place of anticipatory self-defence in international law. Since decision-making is critical in matters of security because it involves choices about action or inaction that have political and legal consequences, in section 2.4 I examine in relation to anticipatory action the merits of institutional and unilateral decision-making processes and of decision-making standards whereas, in section 2.5, I examine issues of evidence. Overall, the chapter uses insights from international relations theory on risk and security in order to study the rules of international law governing the use of force under a risk rationale.

2.2 The Concept of Risk and the Characteristics of Risk-Oriented Decisions

As noted above, security is currently conceptualized in terms of risks, whereas traditionally security was conceptualized in terms of threats. Threats and risks share a common property in that they are both reference dependent and contextual, and they both refer to a danger or a peril.[14] A risk or a threat is, in other words, a danger that is conceptualized and categorized as such by a referent subject, for example by a state, in a particular context.[15] Where the concepts of risk and threat differ, however, is in their constitutive elements. The constitutive elements of a threat are capabilities and intention. If an actor has capabilities and intends to use them against another actor to achieve a certain goal, there is a threat to that latter actor. Threats are thus calculable dangers falling in a 'means-end rational framework'.[16] Risks are constructed instead around the elements of harm and probability.[17] Harm refers to an adverse consequence and probability refers to likelihood. As stated in the 2013 French White Paper: '[t]he term "risk" refers to any danger that does not include any hostile intent but which might impact on ... security'.[18]

[14] JA Bradbury, 'The Policy Implications of Differing Concepts of Risk' (1989) 4 *Science Technology Human Values* 380.

[15] Beck, *World Risk Society* (n 4) 136.

[16] Rasmussen, *The Risk Society at War* (n 8) 1–2.

[17] 'Risk is defined as the probability that a substance or situation will produce harm under specified conditions. Risk is a combination of two factors: [t]he probability that an adverse event will occur (such as a specific disease or type of injury) and [t]he consequences of the adverse event.' The Presidential/Congressional Commission on Risk Assessment and Risk Management, 'Risk Assessment and Risk Management In Regulatory Decision-Making', Final Report Volume 2, 1997 <http://www.corpsriskanalysisgateway.us/data/docs/ref/Explore%20Resources/vol_2_comm_rpt.pdf> accessed 30 June 2015.

[18] French White Paper on Defence and National Security 2013 (n 11) 10.

The 2002 National Security Strategy of the United States of America (USNSS) implicitly distinguished between risks and threats when it categorized terrorism and the possession of WMD by 'rogue states' as risk because

> Rogue states and terrorists do not seek to attack us using conventional means. They know such attacks would fail. Instead, they rely on acts of terror and, potentially, the use of weapons of mass destruction—weapons that can be easily concealed, delivered covertly, and used without warning.[19]

What the Strategy alluded to is that terrorists and rogue states, in themselves, do not constitute a threat because, even if they have the intention to attack, their capabilities are not comparable to those of the United States. Rather, they constitute a risk because of the harm that any possible attack will cause and because of the unpredictability of the attack.

In sum, it can be said that risk is the composite of the probable harmful effects of probable events or situations and security risks, more specifically, are the composite of the probable harmful effects of probable security challenges. These two elements—harm and probability—need not, however, be in a symmetrical relationship, but may rather be counterbalanced; for example, a less probable but very harmful event amounts to a risk, as does a more probable but less harmful event.

What, however, differentiates security risks from risks in other areas—for example, insurance risks—is that there are no broad aggregate data to predict security risks; security risks operate within a broad and unstable environment with many variables—political, economic, religious, social—at play; and evidence is imperfect, inconclusive, or fragmented.[20] Moreover, security risks are future projections of the existence of a danger and, therefore, they are essentially 'virtual'. Rasmussen put it aptly when he said '[a] risk is never a present danger: it only becomes a danger because of what it is expected to cause in the future'.[21] All of the above imply that risks include an element of uncertainty, expressed in degrees of 'knowns' and 'unknowns'.[22]

The condition of uncertainty inherent in risks brings to the fore the importance of decision-making.[23] Since the primary task of governments or decision-makers

[19] The White House, *The National Security Strategy of the United States of America* (September 2002) 15 (USNSS).

[20] As Condoleezza Rice said with regard to evidence preceding the 9/11 attacks: 'But they don't tell us when; they don't tell us where; they don't tell us who; and they don't tell us how.' Dr C Rice, Assistant to the President for National Security Affairs, 'Remarks to the Hearing of the National Commission on Terrorist Attacks Upon the United States' (Washington, 8 April 2004) <http://govinfo.library.unt.edu/911/archive/hearing9/9-11Commission_Hearing_2004-04-08.pdf> accessed 20 June 2015.

[21] Rasmussen, *The Risk Society at War* (n 8) 115; Beck, *World Risk Society* (n 4) 137; Beck, *Risk Society* (n 1) 33–34. In Adams' view, '"Risk" is defined, by most of those who seek to measure it, as the product of the probability and utility of some *future* event. The future is uncertain and inescapably subjective; it does not exist except in the minds of people attempting to anticipate it. Our anticipations are formed by projecting past experience into the future. Our behaviour is guided by our anticipations. If we anticipate harm, we take avoiding action.' J Adams, *Risk* (Routledge 1995) 30.

[22] J Adams, 'Risk and Morality: Three Framing Devices', in R Ericson and A Doyle (eds), *Risk and Morality* (University of Toronto Press 2003) 91. In his view, 'risk is a close relation to uncertainty'. See also Beck, *World Risk Society* (n 4) 140–41; Heng, *War as Risk Management* (n 8) 44–45.

[23] 'Handling risk is at heart about judgement.' Cabinet Office, *Risk: Improving Government's Capability* (n 2) 6.

generally is to provide security for people, the state, or the international society,[24] in the absence of an algorithm to calculate danger and to determine action, decision-makers need to assess the probability and the potential of risks, decide which security risks need to be acted upon, what measures need to be taken and, even more importantly, when measures should be taken. Decision-makers will then be held accountable to their people or to the international community for the decisions they make.

Because of the conditions under which decisions in relation to risks are made and because of the amorphous, interconnected, and globalized nature of risks, such decisions exhibit certain characteristics. One such characteristic is that they have a global perspective. Security risks merge national and international security needs and perceptions and thus extend the scope of national decisions to cover remote risks in geographic or other terms. At the same time, such decisions have global consequences because it is not only the acting state but also other states or the international society as a whole that benefit or, conversely, that are negatively affected by such decisions. For example, the risk of terrorism merges national and international security concerns leading to decisions having global perspective and scope, such as decisions to curb terrorist financing, monitor terrorist activities, or even use force against terrorists anywhere in the world. At the same time, such decisions may have beneficial or detrimental consequences on individuals, states, or the international society as a whole.

Another characteristic of decisions relating to risk is their prospective-orientedness; decisions are proactive and anticipatory. Because of the gaps in knowledge, decisions in relation to risk affect the present by anticipating—preventing or preempting—future dangers.[25] In Beck's words, 'risk presumes decision-making' for 'colonising the future'.[26] This is because with risks, the present state of affairs is assessed against a future that looms menacing and needs to be tamed before it becomes real or, alternatively, needs to be prevented from becoming real. To put this slightly differently, risks as projected dangers or as prognosticated dangers become real here and now, and a cause for immediate action to anticipate them.[27] For example, President Kennedy said with regard to the construction of facilities in Cuba to host Soviet ballistic missiles that were not at the time assembled and did not represent a proximate danger to the United States, that they were a 'clear and present danger'.[28] In contrast, threats as calculable dangers based on capabilities and

[24] See President GW Bush, 'President Bush Addresses the Nation' (Washington, 17 March 2003) <http://georgewbush-whitehouse.archives.gov/news/releases/2003/03/20030319-17.html> accessed 30 June 2015.

[25] Rasmussen, *The Risk Society at War* (n 8) 115. As the 2002 USNSS makes it clear, 'The United States can no longer solely rely on a reactive posture as we have in the past. The inability to deter a potential attacker, the immediacy of today's threats, and the magnitude of potential harm that could be caused by our adversaries' choice of weapons, do not permit that option. We cannot let our enemies strike first.' USNSS (n 19) 15.

[26] Beck, 'The Terrorist Threat' (n 5) 40.

[27] The thought trail has been described by Adams in a different context but very accurately as 'He begins with a *possibility,* proceeds by an *if,* via doubts about *how soon,* to the *imperative for urgent action.*' Adams, *Risk* (n 21) 168 (italics in the original).

[28] President JF Kennedy, 'Radio and Television Report to the American People on the Soviet Arms Buildup in Cuba' (22 October 1962) <www.presidency.ucsb.edu/ws/index.php?pid=8986> accessed 30 June 2015.

intent, invite reactive action[29] either through counter-action or counter-threats.[30] The immediate question is whether anticipation has any place in the international law regime regulating the use of force.

2.3 Anticipatory Self-Defence

Anticipation in the use of force regime revolves around the concept of anticipatory self-defence. Before examining the place of anticipatory self-defence in contemporary international law, it is important to explain first the main features of this regime. The contemporary international law regime on the use of force as defined by the Charter of the United Nations (UNC) is centralized and institutional. On the one hand, it prohibits unilateral uses of force and, on the other, it endows the Security Council, the central security organ of the UN system, with the power to determine the existence of a threat to the peace, a breach of the peace, or an act of aggression and then use force, or authorize others to do so, in order to restore or maintain international peace and security.[31] The only exception to the centralized and institutional use of force is self-defence, which is a unilateral forcible reaction to an armed attack.[32] As the Eritrea–Ethiopia Claims Commission observed, 'the predicate for a valid claim of self-defence under the Charter is that the party resorting to force has been subjected to an armed attack'.[33] The aim of the UNC regime on the use of force is to protect states from security dangers and to maintain international peace and security through institutional or, in exceptional circumstances, through individual action. That said, the UN regime is more attuned to calculable security dangers where causes, intentions, and effects can be confidently measured than to amorphous and potential dangers. This is evident in the case of self-defence which, for the Charter, is triggered when there is an armed attack; that is, when the hostile intention and the capability to cause harm are apparent. Under this reading, anticipatory self-defence has no place in the UNC regime.

Whether this is an accurate reflection of the law has been debated. Anticipatory action has not been alien to international law, in particular in the pre-Charter period. As Vattel, one of the 'fathers' of international law opined,

[29] B Heurlin, *The Threat as a Concept in International Politics* (The Information and Welfare Service of the Danish Defence 1977) 16–21.

[30] Heng, *War as Risk Management* (n 8) 50.

[31] The Charter of the United Nations (adopted 26 June 1945, entered into force 24 October 1945) 1 UNTS) XVI, Chapter VII (UNC).

[32] ibid, art 51; *Case Concerning Military and Paramilitary Activities In and Against Nicaragua (Nicaragua v United States of America)* (Merits) [1986] ICJ Rep 14, paras 194–200, 229; *Legality of the Threat or Use of Nuclear Weapons* (Advisory Opinion) [1996] ICJ Rep 226, para 41; *Case Concerning Oil Platforms (Islamic Republic of Iran v United States of America)* [2003] ICJ Rep 161, paras 51, 57, 71–72; *Legal Consequences of the Construction of a Wall in the Occupied Palestinian Territory* (Advisory opinion) [2004] ICJ Rep 136, para 139; *Case Concerning Armed Activities on the Territory of the Congo (Democratic Republic of the Congo v Uganda)* [2005] ICJ Rep 168, paras 143–47.

[33] *Partial Award: Jus Ad Bellum—Ethiopia's Claims 1–8* (2005) XXVI RIAA 457, 465.

to forestall an injury which it is about to inflict upon him, and avert a danger which seems to threaten him ... one is justified in forestalling a danger in direct ratio to the degree of probability attending it, and to the seriousness of the evil with which one is threatened.[34]

Moreover, ever since the adoption of the UNC, legal commentators and states have often invoked a right to anticipatory self-defence by appealing to: the continuous relevance of the customary law on self-defence;[35] the different type of security environment within which states have operated in the years following the adoption of the Charter;[36] and the structural failings of the UN collective security system, which have prevented it from acting in a timely and effective manner when states were faced with security dangers. However, it was the 9/11 attacks and the post-9/11 United States National Security Strategy[37] that mainstreamed anticipation in the use of force regime.

Anticipatory self-defence includes two forms of self-defence: pre-emptive and preventive self-defence. The former refers to the use of defensive force prior to an actual armed attack but against an imminent armed attack, whereas the latter refers to the use of defensive force against a distant armed attack.[38] The criteria for pre-emptive self-defence were set out in the *Caroline* case as a 'necessity of self-defence, instant, overwhelming, leaving no choice of means and no moment of deliberation'.[39] Since then, the *Caroline test* has become part of the international law *aquis* concerning pre-emptive self-defence. It is interesting, however, to also recall the preventive element in the British thinking. As the Law Officers wrote to the Foreign Secretary,

the grounds on which we consider the conduct of the British Authorities to be justified is that it was absolutely necessary as a measure of precaution for the future and not as a measure of retaliation for the past. What has been done previously is only important as affording irresistible evidence of what would occur afterwards.[40]

[34] E de Vattel, *Le Droit des Gens ou Principes de la Loi Naturelle, appliqués à la Conduite et aux Affaires des Nations et des Souverains* (CG Fenwick trans, Carnegie Institution of Washington 1916) Bk III, Ch I, para 5 and Ch 3 paras 42 and 44. Gentilli argues that 'No one ought to wait to be struck, unless he is a fool. One ought to provide not only against an offense which is being committed, but also against one which may possibly be committed. Force must be repelled and kept aloof by force.' A Gentilli, *On the Laws of War* (JC Rolfe trans, Clarendon Press 1933) Bk I, Ch 14.

[35] DW Bowett, *Self-Defence in International Law* (Manchester University Press 1958) 188–91; TM Franck, *Recourse to Force: State Action against Threats and Armed Attacks* (CUP 2002) 97–107.

[36] MS McDougal and FP Feliciano, *Law and Minimum World Public Order: The Legal Regulation and International Coercion* (Yale University Press 1961) 222.

[37] USNSS (n 19) 15. It should be noted that previous US administrations have also taken this view. See WJ Clinton, 'Address to the Nation by the President' (Washington, 20 August 1998) 16; W Perry and A Carter, *Preventive Defense: A New Security Strategy for America* (The Brookings Institution 1999); The White House, *United States National Security Strategy for a New Century* (White House 2008).

[38] Although the use of these terms is not always clear, I use the term anticipatory self-defence to describe actions prior to an actual armed attack. For the distinction between pre-emption (against an imminent attack) and prevention (against a remote attack) see M Walzer, *Just and Unjust Wars: A Moral Argument with Historical Illustrations* (Basic Books 1977) 74–85.

[39] Lord Ashburton, 'Correspondence with United States, Relative to the Destruction of American Steam-boat "Caroline"' (1841/1842) 30 *British and Foreign State Papers* 196–98.

[40] Quoted in RY Jennings, 'The Caroline and McLeod Cases' (1938) 32 *American Journal of International Law* 82, 87.

Today, there is broad consensus that there exists a right of pre-emptive self-defence in international law. As the UN High-Level Panel on Threats, Challenges and Change admitted in its 2004 report, 'a threatened State, according to long-established customary international law, can take military action as long as the threatened attack is imminent, no other means would deflect it, and the action is proportionate'.[41]

Any remaining controversy surrounds the concept of preventive self-defence,[42] because of its supposed arbitrariness and the fear of abuse in the absence of concrete evidence to prove the danger of an attack. As Strachan notes, 'preventive war … is a political choice to start a war.'[43]

Yet, the distinction between pre-emption and prevention 'was one of the many casualties of September 11'.[44] This is evident in the 2002 and 2006 USNSS. Although both documents employ the language of pre-emption, the thrust of their argument is anchored in prevention. According to the 2002 USNSS,

> We cannot let our enemies strike first … [but must take] anticipatory action to defend ourselves, even if uncertainty remains as to the time and place of the enemy's attack. To forestall or prevent such hostile acts by our adversaries, the United States will, if necessary, act pre-emptively.[45]

The 2006 USNSS states that 'under long-standing principles of self-defense, we do not rule out the use of force before attacks occur, even if uncertainty remains as to the time and place of the enemy's attack.'[46] In the same vein, the 2003 EU Security Strategy invokes self-defence but adds that the European Union 'should be ready to act before a crisis occurs. Conflict prevention and threat prevention cannot start too early.'[47]

Where the two forms of self-defence merge is in the interpretation of 'imminence'. Traditionally, imminence has been interpreted in temporal terms, referring to the proximity of a specific attack. In this context, both the attack and the hostile intention should be relatively determinable in order for a state to use force by way of self-defence. That approach to imminence is, however, difficult to maintain under contemporary security conditions, if it ever was.[48] Indeed, as one commentator

[41] United Nations, 'A More Secure World: Our Shared Responsibility', Report of the Secretary-General's High-Level Panel on Threats, Challenges and Change (United Nations 2004) paras 188 and 189–92; United Nations Secretary General, 'In Larger Freedom: Towards Development, Security and Human Rights for All' (2005) UN Doc A/59/2005, para 124.

[42] CD Gray, *International Law and the Use of Force* (3rd edn, OUP 2008) 212.

[43] H Strachan, 'Preemption and Prevention in Historical Perspective' in H Shue and D Rodin (eds), *Preemption: Military Action and Moral Justification* (OUP 2007) 27.

[44] JL Gaddis, 'Grand Strategy in the Second Term', [2005] January/February Foreign Affairs 84, 5 <www.foreignaffairs.com/articles/2005-01-01/grand-strategy-second-term> accessed 30 June 2015.

[45] USNSS (n 19) 15.

[46] The White House, *The National Security Strategy of the United States of America* (March 2006) 23.

[47] European Union, *A Secure Europe in a Better World: European Security Strategy* (December 2003) 11.

[48] 'If applied literally to the world of modern weapons, the *Caroline* test would be a suicidal pact.' J Yoo, *Point of Attack: Preventive War, International Law and Global Welfare* (OUP 2014) 87.

noted after studying state practice, 'I have not found one example of *Caroline* rules clearly validating an act of pre-emption.'[49]

Contemporary security conditions characterized by the destructiveness and speed of modern weaponry;[50] the non-physicality and non-concreteness of dangers; the overlapping types of enmity, be it national, social, religious, or economic; the unconventional, latent, and diffuse nature of dangers; the proliferation of hostile non-state actors operating from within states but having global access, all indicate that the pre-emptive notion of imminence does not provide states with sufficient room to forestall a threat or to defend themselves against an attack whenever it matures. It is under-inclusive; and this was picked up by the 2002 USNSS, which stressed the need to adapt the concept of imminent attack to the capabilities and objectives of today's adversaries.[51] For this reason, a broader interpretation of imminence has been proposed: one that goes beyond temporal probability to use qualitative criteria to assess the probability of an attack. Accordingly, assessments of imminence take into account the underlying conditions that define the danger of an attack as well as the state's capacity to defend itself against the prospective attack. As the Chatham House Principles of International Law on the Use of Force in Self-Defence state:

> Factors that may be taken into account include: the gravity of the threatened attack—whether what is threatened is a catastrophic use of WMD; capability—for example, whether the relevant state or terrorist organisation is in possession of WMD, or merely of material or component parts to be used in its manufacture; and the nature of the attack —including the possible risks of making a wrong assessment of the danger. Other factors may also be relevant, such as the geographical situation of the victim state, and the past record of attacks by the state concerned.[52]

Imminence thus interpreted permits self-defence action against attacks, which are still relatively amorphous but quite grave if they materialize, as well as against non-immediate attacks if any delay would make a state's self-defence action ineffective.

The 2003 action against Iraq and the rationales offered at the time by the United States and the United Kingdom[53] to justify their use of force offer a glimpse into the legal actualization of anticipatory self-defence. Certain risks emanating from Iraq were presented as being imminent, such as the risk of the United Kingdom being attacked by Iraq with WMD within forty-five minutes.[54] Other risks, such as the

[49] MW Doyle, *Striking First: Preemption and Prevention in International Conflict* (Princeton University Press 2008) 28.

[50] *Legality of the Threat or Use of Nuclear Weapons* (n 32) 244.

[51] USNSS (n 19) 15.

[52] E Wilmshurst, 'The Chatham House Principles of International Law on the Use of Force in Self-Defence' (2006) 55 *International Comparative Law Quarterly* 963; USNSS (n 19) 15; V Lowe, 'Clear and Present Danger: Responses to Terrorism' (2004) 54 *International Comparative Law Quarterly* 185, 192; D Bethlehem, 'Self Defence Against an Imminent or Actual Armed Attack by Nonstate Actors' (2012) 106 *American Journal of International Law* 769, principle 8; D Akande and T Liefländer, 'Clarifying Necessity, Imminence, and Proportionality in the Law of Self-Defence' (2013) 107 *American Journal of International Law* 563, 564–65.

[53] UK Government, 'Iraq's Weapons of Mass Destruction' (n 13).

[54] Lord Butler et al., 'Review of Intelligence on Weapons of Mass Destruction' (14 July 2004) <http://news.bbc.co.uk/nol/shared/bsp/hi/pdfs/14_07_04_butler.pdf> accessed 30 June 2015.

risk of aggression against Iraq's neighbouring states or the risk of supplying WMD to terrorists, were more distant. Faced with such risk, the UK Government relied on pre-emptive self-defence to justify its action against Iraq. According to the Legal Advice of Lord Goldsmith, the Attorney General:

> Force may be used in self-defence if there is an actual or imminent threat of an armed attack ... It is now widely accepted that an imminent armed attack will justify the use of force if the other conditions are met.
>
> The concept of what is imminent may depend on the circumstances. Different considerations may apply, for example, where the risk is of attack from terrorists sponsored or harboured by a particular State, or where there is a threat of an attack by nuclear weapons.
>
> However, in my opinion there must be some degree of imminence. I am aware that the USA has been arguing for recognition of a broad doctrine of a right to use force to pre-empt danger in the future. If this means more than a right to respond proportionately to an imminent attack (and I understand that the doctrine is intended to carry that connotation) this is not a doctrine which, in my opinion, exists or is recognised in international law.[55]

Although the United States did not rely on preventive self-defence formally, the preceding statement indicates that prevention underpinned the US action.[56] The US action was also in line with the 2002 USNSS and, in the words of President Bush, 'instead of drifting along towards tragedy by waiting, it is better to set a course towards safety'.[57]

2.4 Decision-Making Processes and Standards

The 2003 war on Iraq also brought to the fore the question of who decides to use anticipatory force and according to what standards. International law provides two decision-making processes in relation to the use of force: a unilateral one, according to which states make their own decisions to use force, and an institutional one, according to which the Security Council determines whether force is warranted. According to the UN High-Level Panel on Threats, Challenges and Change, for example, the best forum to authorize preventive self-defence is the Security Council.[58] In the case of Iraq, France, as well as other states, recognized the risk

[55] P Goldsmith, 'The Attorney General's Advice on the Iraq War. Iraq: Resolution 1441' (2005) 54 *International Comparative Law Quarterly* 767. See also C Greenwood 'The Legality of Using Force Against Iraq', Select Committee on Foreign Affairs Minutes of Evidence (24 October 2002) <http://goo.gl/LPd1Is> accessed 30 June 2015.

[56] Authorization for Use of Military Force Against Iraq Resolution of 2002 (HJ Res 114, 107th Congress, 2001–2002) <https://www.govtrack.us/congress/bills/107/hjres114/text> accessed 30 June 2015; 'Letter dated 20 March 2003 from the Permanent Representative of the United States of America to the United Nations addressed to the President of the Security Council' (21 March 2003) UN Doc S/2003/351.

[57] G Jaffe and N King Jr, 'Bush Gives Hussein 48 Hours to Leave Iraq or Face War', *The Wall Street Journal* (Washington, 18 March 2003) <http://www.wsj.com/articles/SB104789804716311080> accessed 30 January 2016.

[58] United Nations, 'A More Secure World' (n 41) para 190.

posed by Iraq and were not adverse to the use of force but preferred the institutional process,[59] whereas the United States and the United Kingdom tried initially, albeit very reluctantly, the institutional process, but eventually opted for the unilateral process. This warrants a discussion of the merits and de-merits of each decision-making process and of the standards attached to each process.[60]

With respect to the advantages of the institutional process, it should first be recalled that the Security Council has broad legal and political competences in relation to peace and security and can authorize the use of force, including anticipatory force, to maintain or restore peace and security.[61] Second, the Security Council has the power to collect information through inspections or through other mechanisms, as it did in relation to Iraq. Third, the deliberative process within the Security Council can, in principle, produce better assessments of the evidence and better decisions.[62] Finally, the Security Council is in a better position to place any decision involving the use of force or the use of anticipatory force within the broader context of peace and security and thus minimize consequential risks.

Against these advantages, it can be argued that the decision-making process in the Security Council is politicized and is mainly driven by the national interests of its members. The Security Council does not have independent expertise to evaluate information.[63] In addition, member states do not provide fully reasoned opinions for their decisions. Moreover, the Security Council does not apply a consistent set of evidentiary standards and of decision-making variables in order to make its decisions predicable.[64] Finally, the Security Council may err on the side of caution in order not to disturb peace and security, with devastating results for the affected states.

As far as the unilateral process is concerned, it must first be remembered that self-defence is an inherent right that has not been subjected to institutional authorization, even within the UN regime.[65] Second, the aim of self-defence is to protect the particular security interests of the affected state, whereas such interests are diluted in the institutional process. Third, security is the primary purpose of the state and failure to provide security will delegitimize the state. Fourth, assessments of evidence and of risks are better performed by affected states that have the relevant expertise and experience. Fifth, in order to be accepted by the international community, unilateral judgements and decisions need to satisfy higher criteria of probity than Security Council decisions. Sixth, the risks inherent in any unilateral anticipatory action demand a higher degree of prudence and circumspection than institutional decisions.

[59] UNSC 4707th Meeting (14 February 2003) S/PV.4707, 11–13.

[60] MC Waxman, 'The Use of Force Against States That *Might* Have Weapons of Mass Destruction' (2009) 31 *Michigan Journal of International Law* 1, 31–47.

[61] UNC, Chapter VII.

[62] I Johnstone, 'Security Council Deliberations: The Power of the Better Argument' (2003) 14 *European Journal of International Law* 437, 453.

[63] With regard to Iraq, for example, almost all reports produced by the inspectors and their evidence were contested by one party or the other.

[64] United Nations, 'A More Secure World' (n 41) 66.

[65] See UNC, art 51.

In terms of the disadvantages of the unilateral process, first, individual states may not possess adequate evidence and may not be able to acquire such evidence to allow them to make informed decisions, particularly if the accused state fails to cooperate. Second, states may politicize the evidence and assessments to satisfy domestic audiences, pressure groups, or other interests.[66] Third, there is a possibility of 'group think' among national decision-makers that disregards alternatives. Fourth, harms may be exaggerated and decisions may be triggered by fear. Fifth, the legitimacy of the action may be easily challenged in the absence of institutional backing.[67] Sixth, and finally, unilateral actions may destabilize world order.[68]

It is evident from the preceding exposition that both processes have advantages and disadvantages, but the main reason why states are reluctant to use the institutional process represented by the Security Council in cases where their security is at risk seems to be its haphazard decisions in the absence of consistent decision-making standards. In order to improve the quality of institutional decisions concerning anticipatory action and engender trust and confidence in the institutional process, a number of decision-making standards have been proposed by commentators and policy makers.

Doyle, for example, has proposed four standards according to which the Security Council can authorize anticipatory action. The first standard is lethality, which seeks to identify the likely loss of life if the threat is not eliminated; the second, likelihood, assesses the probability that the threat will occur; the third, legitimacy, covers the traditional just war criteria of proportionality, necessity, and deliberativeness of proposed responses; and the fourth, legality, asks whether the threatening situation is itself produced by legal or illegal actions, and whether the proposed remedy is more or less legal.[69]

Similar standards were suggested by the former UN Secretary-General Kofi Annan:

> When considering whether to authorize or endorse the use of military force, the Council should come to a common view on how to weigh the seriousness of the threat; the proper purpose of the proposed military action; whether means short of the use of force might plausibly succeed in stopping the threat; whether the military option is proportional to the threat at hand; and whether there is a reasonable chance of success.[70]

[66] As for the failings of intelligence with regard to Iraq, see Lord Butler et al, 'Review of Intelligence on Weapons of Mass Destruction' (n 54); J Cirincione et al, 'WMD in Iraq: Evidence and Implications' (Carnegie Institute for International Peace 2004) <http://www.carnegieendowment.org/files/Iraq3FullText.pdf> accessed 30 June 2015; United States Senate Select Committee on Intelligence, 'Report on the US Intelligence Community's Prewar Intelligence Assessments on Iraq' (7 July 2004) <https://fas.org/irp/congress/2004_rpt/ssci_iraq.pdf > accessed 29 June 2015.

[67] TM Franck, 'The Power of Legitimacy and the Legitimacy of Power: International Law in an Age of Power Disequilibrium' (2006) 100 *American Journal of International Law* 88, 102.

[68] According to the UN High-Level Panel, 'in a world full of perceived potential threats, the risk to the global order and the norm of non-intervention on which it continues to be based is simply too great for the legality of unilateral preventive action, as distinct from collectively endorsed action, to be accepted.' United Nations, 'A More Secure World' (n 41) para 191.

[69] Doyle, *Striking First* (n 49) 48.

[70] United Nations Secretary General, 'In Larger Freedom' (n 41) para 126.

Although having clearly articulated decision-making standards goes some way towards alleviating states' anxieties with the institutional process, there is no guarantee that the Security Council will adopt or follow them. As the Responsibility to Protect (R2P) doctrine demonstrates, the Security Council did not follow, and did not even note, the proposed standards for authorizing the use of force for humanitarian purposes.[71] Moreover, even in the unlikely event such standards are adopted, they do not cure the other defects of the Security Council process. In addition, any standards will always be open to interpretation, with the Security Council's interpretation being challenged by concerned states, which may eventually resort to unilateral action notwithstanding the Security Council process. Indeed, as both Doyle and Annan recognize, these same standards can be used to justify unilateral uses of preventive force if the Security Council is not able to decide. Likewise, previous iterations of the R2P provided for regional action without Security Council authorization, or even for unilateral action.[72] All proposals for improved institutional decision-making thus accept, at least as a last resort, that which they initially exorcise.

We thus come full circle, with the unilateral process being the most reassuring option. This is because when it comes to decisions concerning security and the use of force, the merits of the decision-making process need to be reconciled with the merits of the action, which in the case of anticipatory self-defence is to protect the concerned state from dangers. For this reason, states are less inclined to entrust their security to a process which is unpredictable, too politicized, and over which they have little control. They instead prefer the unilateral process, notwithstanding its pitfalls. Yet unilateral decision-making needs to follow certain standards in order for decisions to use anticipatory force to be predictable, well-reasoned, and justified. In this respect, Dershowitz has constructed a jurisprudence of decision-making concerning pre-emption and prevention, which is based on complexification, qualification, quantification, and simplification of relevant factors. These factors refer to: the nature of the harm; the likelihood that the harm will occur in the absence of pre-emption; the source of the harm; the possibility that the contemplated pre-emption will fail; the costs of a successful pre-emption; the costs of a failed pre-emption; the nature and quality of the information on which these decisions are based; the ratio of successful to unsuccessful pre-emption; the legality, morality, and potential political consequences of the pre-emptive steps; the incentivizing of others to act pre-emptively; and the recoverability or irrevocability of the harms caused by the feared event or the contemplated pre-emption, as well as other facts such as the inevitability of unanticipated outcomes.[73] Of course, as

[71] See United Nations, 'A More Secure World' (n 41). The International Commission on Intervention and State Sovereignty (ICISS) Report laid down six criteria according to which coercive intervention can be undertaken: right authority; just cause; right intention; last resort; proportionality; and reasonable prospects for success. ICISS, *The Responsibility to Protect* (International Development Research Centre 2001) vii.

[72] ICISS, *The Responsibility to Protect* (n 71) 6.28–6.40.

[73] AM Dershowitz, *Preemption: A Knife that Cuts Both Ways* (WW Norton 2007) 12–13 and 237–50.

Dershowitz concedes, this formula is just a starting point, whereas actual decisions will be more nuanced.[74] Nevertheless, it cannot be denied that this framework provides a prudent basis upon which unilateral decisions to use anticipatory force can be made.

2.5 Evidence, Standard of Proof, and Burden of Proof

In section 2.4, I examined the merits of available decision-making processes and concluded that the unilateral process offers better guarantees to states when it comes to the anticipatory use of force. An important element in decision-making, albeit not the only element, is evidence. This section will thus discuss the evidentiary basis upon which anticipatory action can be taken.

Evidence is important in decision-making because it can justify decisions and actions. In this respect, political and legal approaches to evidence share the same rationale, notwithstanding any differences they may have. Furthermore, legal and political approaches to evidence intersect in that decisions and actions by policy makers which are underpinned and justified by evidence have legal implications. In other words, evidence can validate such decisions and actions in law.[75] In sum, evidence is important because of its function in explaining and justifying decisions and actions, and because it underwrites political as well as legal accountability.[76]

That said, issues of evidence are complicated in situations calling for anticipatory action because the status of knowledge about the risk of attack is provisional and imperfect, and evidence may not be factual, concrete, or explicit. It is therefore important to consider what types of evidence and what standard of proof can be accepted in the context of anticipatory self-defence, and also who bears the burden of proving the existence of a risk of an attack. In this respect, legal approaches to evidence will provide useful insights on these issues.

2.5.1 The type of evidence

With regard to the type of evidence, in cases concerning the use of force, the International Court of Justice (ICJ) has accepted material evidence such as documents, statements, satellite pictures, testimonies, as well as forensic, visual, and digital evidence. Because such evidence is often collected from confidential sources and is protected, the ICJ has been less demanding in not requesting its production.[77] The ICJ has also recognized that it may be difficult to collect evidence when

[74] ibid.

[75] *Case Concerning Armed Activities on the Territory of the Congo* (n 32) para 105.

[76] Wilmshurst, 'The Chatham House Principles' (n 52) Principle D.

[77] *Case Concerning Application of the Convention on the Prevention and Punishment of Genocide (Bosnia and Herzegovina v Serbia and Montenegro)* [2007] ICJ Rep 241, Dissenting Opinion of Vice-President Al-Khasawhen, para 35.

such evidence is controlled by another state and therefore it has taken 'a more liberal recourse to inferences of fact and circumstantial evidence'.[78] Circumstantial evidence includes surrounding facts or political, technical, economic, or other considerations that can lead to reasonable—albeit rebuttable—inferences being drawn as to the existence of a fact.[79] This is particularly important in relation to risks because, as noted previously, risks are constructed on the basis of many indices not always amounting to direct, material, or concrete evidence. To give an example, whereas the development or acquisition of WMD by a state may not, in itself, prove the existence of a risk of an attack, past aggressive conduct by the particular state may allow reasonable inferences to be drawn of the existence of a present risk of an attack, if that is also corroborated by other facts such as hostile relations or hostile statements.[80]

Political processes of decision-making use the same type of evidence in order to prove the existence of a risk. One should recall in this respect the US Ambassador Adlai Stevenson's presentation during a dramatic session of the Security Council in 1962, where he used satellite pictures to prove the construction of missile installations in Cuba and the transportation of equipment by the Soviet Union.[81] The evidence produced was not contradicted by the USSR with its own evidence, which gave credence to the US claim, exposed the Soviet deception, and swayed international public opinion. In this vein is also Secretary of State Colin Powell's PowerPoint presentation to the Security Council on 5 February 2003 in an attempt to prove Iraq's duplicity, its possession of biological and nuclear capabilities, its links to terrorism, and its hostile intent. The presentation contained satellite images of Iraqi facilities allegedly developing WMD, recordings, documents, interviews with Iraqi officials, and reports by inspectors.[82]

Extrapolations from previous conduct were also critical in proving the risk that the Iraqi regime posed. More specifically, Iraq's aggressive propensities were proven by recalling its previous wars against Iran and Kuwait, whereas its use of chemical weapons against internal and external 'enemies' of the regime was sufficient to

[78] *Corfu Channel Case* (*United Kingdom of Great Britain and Northern Ireland v Albania*) (Merits) [1949] ICJ Rep 4, 18; A Riddell and B Plant, *Evidence before the International Court of Justice* (British Institute of International and Comparative Law 2009) 112–13.

[79] *Corfu Channel Case* (n 78), Dissenting Opinion of Judge Badawi Pasha, para 59. See also *Case Concerning Application of the Convention on the Prevention and Punishment of Genocide* (n 77), Dissenting Opinion of Vice-President Al-Khasawhen, para 51; *Velasquez Rodriguez Case*, 1988 IACHR, Series C: Decisions and Judgments No 4, 135, para 130.

[80] Waxman, 'The Use of Force Against States That *Might* Have Weapons of Mass Destruction' (n 60), 57–75; MC Waxman, 'Self-defence and the Limits of WMD Intelligence (May 2010)' in Peter Berkowitz (ed), *Future Challenges in National Security and Law* 16–18 <http://www.hoover.org/sites/default/files/research/docs/futurechallenges_waxman.pdf> accessed 17 November 2016.

[81] Ambassador A Stevenson, 'Statement to the United Nations Security Council' (New York, 25 October 1962) <https://www.mtholyoke.edu/acad/intrel/adlai.htm> accessed 30 January 2016. A Chayes, *The Cuban Missile Crisis: International Crisis and the Role of Law* (OUP 1974) 84–85.

[82] CL Powell, Secretary of State, 'Remarks to the United Nations Security Council' (New York, 5 February 2003) <http://2001-2009.state.gov/secretary/former/powell/remarks/2003/17300.htm> accessed 30 January 2016.

prove its ability and willingness to use WMD. As Secretary of State Colin Powell pointed out:

Given Saddam Hussein's history of aggression, given what we know of his grandiose plans, given what we know of his terrorist associations, and given his determination to exact revenge on those who oppose him, should we take the risk that he will not someday use these weapons at a time and a place and in a manner of his choosing, at a time when the world is in a much weaker position to respond? The United States will not and cannot run that risk for the American people. Leaving Saddam Hussein in possession of weapons of mass destruction for a few more months or years is not an option, not in a post-September 11th world. When we confront a regime that harbors ambitions for regional domination, hides weapons of mass destruction, and provides haven and active support for terrorists, we are not confronting the past; we are confronting the present. And unless we act, we are confronting an even more frightening future.[83]

Another critical element in the Iraqi saga is that both the United States and the United Kingdom drew adverse inferences from Iraq's failure to provide them with the requested evidence or its failure to cooperate with the UN inspectors. Although the ICJ is quite cautious when it comes to drawing adverse consequences,[84] it is quite a common practice in political settings. For example, in 1998, the United States and the United Kingdom took military action against Iraq following the United Nations Special Commission (UNSCOM) report, which accused Iraq of non-cooperation with the inspectors, non-disclosure, and concealment of evidence.[85] According to the report, this made Iraq's claims of compliance with its disarmament obligations under relevant Security Council resolutions unverified. In the Security Council debates, the Iraqi representative asked:

where are the prohibited weapons which they allege that Iraq still has? If UNSCOM has any evidence that Iraq possesses a prohibited weapon or its components, then we challenge them, as we have done in the past, to provide physical evidence to the Security Council. Indeed, some members of the Security Council have requested, time and again, that such evidence be submitted, but UNSCOM has failed to do so.[86]

But for the UK Representative

UNSCOM's report makes clear that Iraq has yet again failed to keep its promises. The report details not merely the obstruction but the fact that it relates directly to documents, sites and personnel that would give a clue as to the whereabouts of WMD and the capabilities to make them. It is not obstruction simply for the sake of it, but a plan of deceit to prevent those WMD from being located and destroyed.[87]

[83] ibid.

[84] *Barcelona Traction, Light and Power Company, Limited* (*Belgium v Spain*) [1970] ICJ Rep 4, 161, but Separate Opinion of Judge Jessup, para 97 and Separate Opinion of Judge Fitzmaurice, para 58; *Case Concerning Application of the Convention on the Prevention and Punishment of Genocide* (n 77), Dissenting Opinion of Vice-President Al-Khasawhen, para 35.

[85] Secretary General, 'Letter Dated 15 December 1998 from the Secretary-General Addressed to the President of the Security Council' (15 December 1998) S/1998/1172.

[86] UNSC 3955th Meeting (16 December 1998) S/PV.3955, 3.

[87] ibid, 6.

Similar arguments were made some years later following Security Council resolution 1441 (2002), which gave Iraq a last opportunity to prove the non-existence of WMD by cooperating with the inspectors.[88] In his Security Council address, Secretary of State Powell drew inferences from Iraq's failure to cooperate. As he said: 'the facts and Iraq's behavior show that Saddam Hussein and his regime are concealing their efforts to produce more weapons of mass destruction'.[89] Likewise, Tony Blair, in his House of Commons address, concluded that Iraq's lack of cooperation with the inspectors is proof that '[h]is weapons of mass destruction programme is active, detailed and growing. The weapons of mass destruction programme is not shut down; it is up and running now.'[90]

From the above it can be safely said that different types of evidence from different sources—national or international—can be used to establish the existence of a risk of an attack, but circumstantial evidence and inferences are inevitably more expedient due to the prospective nature of the attack and the lack of direct and concrete evidence of intentions or facts.

2.5.2 The standard of proof

The second question concerns the standard of proof, that is, the level of persuasiveness required for a particular claim to stand. The ICJ uses different standards or different formulations of the same standard, ranging from 'sufficient'[91] or 'conclusive'[92] to 'beyond a reasonable doubt'.[93] In relation to the use of force it has been claimed, for example, that the ICJ employs the 'clear and convincing'[94] standard. This corresponds to the ICJ's position of aligning standards of proof to the gravity of the charge. As the Court opined in the *Bosnia Genocide* case, for charges of exceptional gravity, evidence needs to be fully conclusive.[95] In that case, the Court

[88] UNSC Res 1441 (8 November 2002) UN Doc S/RES/1441.

[89] Powell, 'Remarks to the United Nations Security Council' (n 82).

[90] T Blair, 24 September 2002, HC Deb (2001–2002), vol 390, col 3.

[91] *Case Concerning Armed Activities on the Territory of the Congo* (n 32) para 172; *Case Concerning Military and Paramilitary Activities In and Against Nicaragua* (n 32) para 110; *Oil Platforms* (n 32) para 57. The Court often uses terms such as 'on the basis of a balance of evidence', 'on a balance of probabilities', 'in all probability', 'consistent with the probabilities', 'with a high degree of probability', see, respectively, *Case Concerning the Land, Island and Maritime Frontier Dispute* (*El Salvador/Honduras: Nicaragua Intervening*) [1992] ICJ Rep 351, paras 121, 155, 248; *Case Concerning Sovereignty over Pulau Ligitan and Pulau Sipadan* (*Indonesia/Malaysia*) [2002] ICJ Rep 625, para 72; *Case Concerning Military and Paramilitary Activities In and Against Nicaragua* (n 32) para 158.

[92] *Case Concerning Armed Activities on the Territory of the Congo* (n 32) para 91; *Oil Platforms* (n 32) para 71; *Case Concerning Application of the Convention for the Prevention and Punishment of Genocide* (n 77) para 209.

[93] The ICJ has also mentioned the 'beyond any doubt' standard. See *Case Concerning Application of the Convention on the Prevention and Punishment of the Crime of Genocide* (n 77) para 422. For the 'no room for reasonable doubt' standard, see *Corfu Channel Case* (n 78) 18.

[94] M O'Connell, 'Rules of Evidence for the Use of Force in International Law's New Era' (2006) 100 *American Society of International Law Proceedings* 44; JA Green, 'Fluctuating Evidentiary Standards for Self-Defence in the International Court of Justice' (2009) 58 *International Comparative Law Quarterly* 165.

[95] *Application of the Convention on the Prevention and Punishment of the Crime of Genocide* (n 77) para 209. In the *Oil Platforms* case, Judge Higgins opined that the 'graver the charge the more

applied a high standard of evidence in relation to genocide and a lower one in relation to the charge of breach of treaty.[96] The Court was, however, criticized for introducing criminal law standards to civil law cases;[97] as Judge ad hoc Lauterpacht stated in his 1993 separate opinion, guilt should not be proven beyond reasonable doubt because the case was not a criminal law case.[98] What becomes evident is that the ICJ does not apply a common standard of proof,[99] but rather shows flexibility, depending on the case at hand.

Similarly, one cannot identify any particular political standard of proof that states apply to justify their uses of force. The United States, for example, claimed to possess 'clear and compelling information'[100] that proved the role of Al-Qaeda in the 9/11 attacks and its links with the Taliban regime in Afghanistan. Although it did not disclose the information and declared that '[t]here is still much we do not know',[101] the Security Council went on to approve the military action in Afghanistan. On another occasion, the United States claimed to possess 'convincing information based on a variety of intelligence sources' to justify its actions in Afghanistan and Sudan in 1998.[102] During the Cuban missile crisis, the United States claimed 'incontrovertible' evidence that proved the existence of missile sites in Cuba.[103] With regard to Iraq or to risks in general, the United States declared that it cannot wait for conclusive evidence before action is taken.[104]

Although such statements may be viewed as part of the political rhetoric, they do demonstrate, however, that there is no established standard of proof in political discourse but, as in the legal setting, the standard is flexible.

According to the present author, the standard of proof applied to evidence in situations calling for anticipatory action needs to fulfil the function of the device of standard of proof, which is to facilitate decision-making when the status of

confidence there must be in the evidence relied on'. *Oil Platforms* (n 32), Separate Opinion of Judge Higgins, para 33. See also *Partial Awards on Prisoners of War between the State of Eritrea and the Federal Democratic Republic of Ethiopia: Eritrea's Claim* [2003] 42 *ILM* 1083, paras 43 et seq.

[96] *Case Concerning the Application of the Convention on the Prevention and Punishment of the Crime of Genocide* (n 77) paras 209–10.

[97] T Meron, 'Major Developments in International Law: A Conversation on the ICJ's Opinion in Bosnia and Herzegovina v Serbia and Montenegro', (2007) 101 *American Society of International Law Proceedings* 215, 216.

[98] *Case Concerning the Application of the Convention on the Prevention and Punishment of the Crime of Genocide (Bosnia and Herzegovina v Serbia and Montenegro)* (Further Requests for the Indication of Provisional Measures Order) [1993] ICJ Rep 407, Separate Opinion of Judge ad hoc Lauterpacht, para 44.

[99] *Oil Platforms* (n 32) para 189; Separate Opinion of Judge Higgins, paras 30–33; and Separate Opinion of Judge Buergenthal, para 41.

[100] 'Letter dated from the Permanent Representative of the United States of America to the United Nations addressed to the President of the Security Council' (7 October 2001) UN Doc S/2001/946.

[101] ibid.

[102] 'DoD News Briefing' (20 August 1998) <http://archive.defense.gov/transcripts/transcript.aspx?transcriptid=1727> accessed 30 January 2016.

[103] Stevenson, 'Statement to the United Nations Security Council' (n 81).

[104] See D Rumsfeld, US Secretary of State, 'Remarks at the Defence Ministers Meeting of the North Atlantic Council' (Brussels, 6 June 2002) <http://www.nato.int/docu/speech/2002/s020606d.htm> accessed 30 January 2016.

knowledge is uncertain.[105] Conversely, the standard of proof should not paralyse decision-making or render the right to anticipatory self-defence redundant. Furthermore, although the standard should not be too low or too high, it should allow evidence with sufficient probative value. As Vattel put it, '[w]e must … have good grounds to think ourselves threatened, before we can lawfully have recourse to arms'.[106] Likewise, the UN High-Level Panel noted that there needs to be good evidence before preventive military action is taken.[107] These considerations, together with the fact that evidence may be conjectural and sensitive, would support a standard of proof resembling that of the 'preponderance of the evidence', according to which the most probable evidence presented by the parties is accepted.[108] For example, if the evidence produced by one party establishes that there is a higher risk of an attack than the evidence produced by the other party to refute such a risk, then the standard of the preponderance of the evidence will support the conclusions made by the former.

This standard balances the amount of confidence decision-makers should have in the probative value of the evidence with the residual uncertainties that exist when they are called upon to decide whether to use force in anticipatory self-defence.

2.5.3 The burden of proof

The burden of proof gives rise to questions as to whether it is the proponent of the anticipatory action that needs to prove the existence of a risk of an attack or, conversely, whether it is the targeted state that needs to prove the non-existence of such risk. Put differently, is it for the accused state to prove that no risk of attack emanating from its territory exists or for the defending state to prove that such risk exists?

International jurisprudence traditionally holds that the burden of proof falls on the party that makes a particular assertion.[109] This rule stems from the principle of fairness and the principle of presumption of compliance with international law,

[105] LB Solum, 'Presumptions and Transcendentalism: You Prove it! Why Should I?' (1994) 17 *Harvard Journal of Law and Public Policy* 691; RJ Allen, 'Burdens of Proof Uncertainty, and Ambiguity in Modem Legal Discourse' (1994) 17 *Harvard Journal of Law and Public Policy* 627, 627; D Walton, 'Burden of Proof' (1988) 2 *Argumentation* 233, 242.

[106] de Vattel, *Les Droits des Gens* (n 33), Book III, para 44.

[107] United Nations, 'A More Secure World' (n 41) paras 189–90.

[108] CE Foster, *Science and the Precautionary Principle in International Courts and Tribunals* (CUP 2011) 227; C Brown, *A Common Law of International Adjudication* (OUP 2007) 19; CF Amerasinghe, *Evidence in International Litigation* (Brill 2005) 245.

[109] *Case Concerning Pulp Mills on the River Uruguay* (*Argentina v Uruguay*) (Request for the Indication of Provisional Measures) [2006] ICJ Rep 113, para 162; *Case Concerning Application of the Convention on the Prevention and Punishment of Genocide* (n 77) para 204; *Case Concerning Military and Paramilitary Activities In and Against Nicaragua* (*Nicaragua v United States of America*) (Jurisdiction of the Court and Admissibility of the Application) [1984] ICJ Rep 392, para 101; *Case Concerning the Temple of Preah Vihear* (*Cambodia v Thailand*) [1962] ICJ Rep 6, 15; *Case Concerning the Frontier Dispute* (*Burkina Faso/Republic of Mali*) [1986] ICJ Rep 554, para 64; S Rosenne, *The Law and Practice of the International Court, 1920–2005* (Brill 2006) 1040; M Kazazi, *Burden of Proof and Related Issues: A Study on Evidence Before International Tribunals* (Martinus Nijhoff Publishers 1996) 54.

which protects states against spurious claims which they are consequently called upon to disprove.[110]

It has been claimed, however, that the burden of proof shifts in cases of uncertainty. International jurisprudence is not clear on this matter. There are instances where shifting the burden of proof has been proposed by parties in judicial proceedings, or opined by individual judges. For example, in the *Nuclear Tests* case (1974), Australia and New Zealand claimed that it was France, the respondent in the proceedings, that should be required to prove the harmlessness of its nuclear activities.[111] The ICJ did not deal with this issue in its 1974 judgment. However, in its 1995 Order concerning the request for a re-examination of the situation, it did require proof of harmlessness from the party that engaged in a possibly harmful activity.[112] More explicit was Judge Weeramantry, who opined that

> [w]here a party complains to the Court of possible environmental damage of an irreversible nature which another party is committing or threatening to commit, the proof or disproof of the matter alleged may present difficulty to the claimant as the necessary information may largely be in the hands of the party causing or threatening the damage. The law cannot function in protection of the environment unless a legal principle is evolved to meet this evidentiary difficulty, and environmental law has responded with what has come to be described as the precautionary principle.[113]

In other cases, such as the *Pulp Mills* case, the ICJ refused to shift the burden of proof, even though it was proposed by one of the parties.[114]

Likewise, in political contexts it is mainly the proponent of the action that needs to prove the risk, although claims to the opposite have also been made. For example, during the Cuban crisis it was the United States, the claimant, that bore the burden of proving the danger to it and to allied security from the prospective installation of missiles in Cuba. With regard to Iraq, the inspections imposed by Security Council resolution 687 in 1991 indicate that the burden of proof had shifted to Iraq; it was Iraq that had to prove that it did not possess WMD and, as was noted above, Iraq's non-cooperation led to negative inferences being drawn and to action being taken. With regard to the 2003 action against Iraq, the burden of proof shifted between Iraq and the proposers of the anticipatory action, the United States and the United Kingdom. For example, Security Council resolution 1441 (2002) demanded that Iraq comply with the inspection regime imposed by the resolution in order to prove its innocence. As Secretary of State Powell said in his Security Council address, '[t]his Council

[110] Kazazi, *Burden of Proof* (n 109) 57–66.

[111] *Nuclear Tests (Australia v France)* (Oral Arguments on Jurisdiction and Admissibility) [1974] ICJ Pleadings, Oral Arguments, Documents Vol I, 43.

[112] *Nuclear Tests (New Zealand v France)* (Order Concerning the Request for an Examination of the Situation in Accordance with Paragraph 63 of the Court's Judgment of 20 December 1974) [1995] ICJ Rep 288, paras 5 and 105.

[113] ibid, Dissenting Opinion of Judge Weeramantry, 342. See also *Legality of the Threat or Use of Nuclear Weapons* (n 32) Dissenting Opinion of Judge Weeramantry, 502–03.

[114] *Case Concerning Pulp Mills on the River Uruguay* (n 109) paras 162–64.

placed the burden on Iraq to comply and disarm, and not on the inspectors to find that which Iraq has gone out of its way to conceal for so long. Inspectors are inspectors; they are not detectives.'[115] The Canadian Foreign Minister Bill Graham commented that the speech 'amounts to a transfer of the burden of proof from the United States to Saddam Hussein'.[116] At the same time, and as Colin Powell's presentation to the Security Council demonstrates, the proposers of the action tried to prove that the Iraqi regime posed a danger to them and to international security. This was lamented by the UK Ambassador to Washington, Christopher Meyer, who said:

> The original genius of the Security Council resolution in November 2002 [resolution 1441] was that it charged Saddam to prove his innocence; then, by becoming obsessed with finding a smoking gun or getting him to do something loony like shoot down a drone [the plan changed]. People suddenly realised that they had to prove him guilty. The onus of proof shifted, which was a serious own goal.[117]

It has been claimed that even if the proposer still bears the burden of proof in situations calling for anticipatory action, the burden is alleviated by accepting inferences, by lowering the standard of proof, or by not requiring proof of certain facts that are 'notorious'.[118] For example, Secretary of State Powell relied on the notoriety of Saddam's actions to prove the regime's mal-intentions and the danger it posed to the United States or to the world at large.[119]

Such techniques are concerned, however, with the type of evidence and the required standard of proof and not with the question of who bears the burden of persuasion. It is for this reason that the question of who bears the burden of proof in cases calling for anticipatory action needs more attention.

The burden of proof together with the standard of proof and, of course, the evidence, assist decision-makers to make decisions under conditions of uncertainty and prevents as far as possible erroneous decisions that may have serious consequences for those making such decisions, their state, or other states. More specifically, a decision to use anticipatory force will be erroneous if it is based on 'false positives', where a risk of an attack is deemed to exist although no such risk exists.[120] The war in Iraq in 2003, for example, was based on 'false positives', where weapons were believed to exist where, in fact, they did not. The Iraqi regime may have also

[115] Powell, 'Remarks to the United Nations Security Council' (n 82); JB Wiener and J Stern, 'Precaution Against Terrorism' (2006) 9 *Journal of Risk Research* 393, 401–02.

[116] Quoted in Wiener and Stern, ibid, 400.

[117] G Hinsliff, P Harris, and J Doward, 'Iraq War Inquiry Could Reveal Secrets, Lies and the Rush to War' *The Guardian* (London, 21 June 2009) <www.theguardian.com/politics/2009/jun/21/iraq-war-inquiry-politics> accessed 30 January 2016.

[118] *Fisheries Case* (*United Kingdom v Norway*) [1951] ICJ Rep 116, 138–39; *Nuclear Tests* (*New Zealand v France*) [1974] ICJ Rep 457, para 17; *Isle of Palmas* (1928) 2 United Nations Reports of the International Arbitral Awards 829, 841–42.

[119] Powell, 'Remarks to the United Nations Security Council' (n 82).

[120] For a discussion of 'false positives' and 'false negatives' in decision-making, see MC Waxman, 'The Use of Force Against States That *Might* Have Weapons of Mass Destruction' (n 60) 7–47; and MC Waxman, 'Self-Defence and the Limits of WMD Intelligence' (n 80) 7–14.

contributed to 'false positives' by boasting of its capabilities for its own purposes, in circumstances in which its previous conduct made these boasts credible.[121]

Conversely, a decision not to take action may also be erroneous if it is based on 'false negatives', where a risk of an attack was deemed not to exist when it actually existed and was eventually realized. For example, the 9/11 attacks were the result of 'false negatives' in the face of evidence to the contrary, for which the Bush Administration was criticized. As the 9/11 Commission put it:

> The most important failure was one of imagination. We do not believe leaders understood the gravity of the threat.... Though top officials all told us that they understood the danger, we believe there was uncertainty among them as to whether this was just a new and especially venomous version of the ordinary terrorist threat the United States had lived with for decades, or it was indeed radically new, posing a threat beyond any yet experienced. As late as September 4, 2001, Richard Clarke, the White House staffer long responsible for counterterrorism policy coordination, asserted that the government had not yet made up its mind how to answer the question: 'Is al Qida a big deal?' A week later came the answer.[122]

If the existence of 'false negatives' is proven wrong, then future exaggeration in the assessment of evidence is also possible. This, perhaps, explains to a large extent the 2003 'false positives'. As the Butler Report noted, '[i]t is a well-known phenomenon within intelligence communities that memory of past failures can cause overestimation next time around'.[123]

By allocating the burden of proof on the proposer of the anticipatory action, law tries to prevent the first type of erroneous decision. In this case, it is the state that proposes to use force that needs to prove the existence of an attack or of a threat that warrants the use of force. Its mantra is to err on the side of caution, also because of the serious consequences a wrong decision may have.

By shifting the burden of proof to the state that allegedly presents a security risk, law tries to prevent the second type of erroneous decision, that based on 'false negatives'. The mantra is to better err by taking action than by not taking action unless the accused state proves that no security risks exist. As Tony Blair explained with regard to Iraq, '[t]his is not a time to err on the side of caution; not a time to weigh the risks to an infinite balance; not a time for the cynicism of the worldly wise who favour playing it long. Their worldly wise cynicism is actually at best naiveté and at worst dereliction.'[124]

[121] MR Gordon and BE Trainor, *Cobra II: The Inside Story of the Invasion and Occupation of Iraq* (Atlantic Books 2006) 65.

[122] The National Commission on Terrorist Attacks Upon the United States, 'The 9/11 Commission Report' (2004) <http://www.9-11commission.gov/> accessed 30 June 2015. As the Commission also commented in the executive summary to the report 'the 9/11 attacks were a shock, but they should not have come as a surprise. Islamist extremists had given plenty of warning that they meant to kill Americans indiscriminately and in large numbers. Although Usama Bin Ladin himself would not emerge as a signal threat until the late 1990s, the threat of Islamist terrorism grew over the decade.'

[123] Lord Butler et al., 'Review of Intelligence on Weapons of Mass Destruction' (n 55).

[124] T Blair, Prime Minister of the United Kingdom, 'PM Warns of Continuing Global Terror Threat' (Sedgefield, 5 March 2004) <http://www.britishpoliticalspeech.org/speech-archive.htm?speech=282> accessed 30 January 2016.

Shifting the burden of proof in such situations can also be justified by the broader aims pursued by the anticipatory action. The state that takes anticipatory action seeks to maintain the status quo of peace and security against a state that challenges it, for example, by developing WMD. It is thus the latter state that needs to provide evidence that its actions and intentions are benign, and not the party that wants to maintain the status quo.

Yet neither scenario can conclusively solve the dilemmas facing decision-makers who need to decide on the right course of action in an environment of inconclusive, positive, or negative evidence; and need to justify their decision and the action to domestic and international audiences, and for which decision and action they may be held accountable in political or even legal terms. The dilemma is evident in Tony Blair's account of the decision to go to war against Iraq:

> Here is the crux. It is possible that even with all of this [evidence of the threat Saddam posed], nothing would have happened. Possible that Saddam would change his ambitions; possible he would develop the WMD but never use it; possible that the terrorists would never get their hands on WMD, whether from Iraq or elsewhere. We cannot be certain. Perhaps we would have found different ways of reducing it. Perhaps this Islamic terrorism would ebb of its own accord. But do we want to take the risk? That is the judgement. And my judgement then and now is that the risk of this new global terrorism and its interaction with states or organisations or individuals proliferating WMD, is one I simply am not prepared to run.[125]

For this reason, the burden of proof in situations calling for anticipatory action should be allocated symmetrically between the parties.[126] In this way, an exchange between the opposing states will be instituted where each state proves or disproves claims and where conclusions reached on the basis of such evidentiary exchange can be defended in domestic or international political or legal fora.

Such balancing also needs to take into account the principles of fairness and presumption of compliance with international law that underpin the burden of proof as well as the broader values of peace and security served by anticipatory action. In this respect, fairness may require the party that holds the evidence to provide it, particularly as this is the party that allegedly poses a risk. For example, Iraq was in control of the evidence relating to its weapons capabilities and therefore in a better position to produce such evidence. Honest production of evidence and cooperation can be induced by the knowledge that non-production of evidence or production of deficient evidence will fail to persuade the other party, and may even lead to adverse conclusions being arrived at. The presumption of compliance with international law, for its part, implies that parties are innocent until proven guilty and thus, in order to prevent wild accusations being made, the proponent of the action needs to furnish plausible evidence to prove the existence of a risk. With regard to Iraq, the 'dodgy' dossier produced by the UK government was an example of implausible evidence and of

[125] ibid.

[126] MC Waxman, 'The Use of Force Against States That *Might* Have Weapons of Mass Destruction' (n 60) 70–75; and MC Waxman, 'Self-Defence and the Limits of WMD Intelligence' (n 80) 16–18.

claims which were quickly challenged.[127] Finally, the broader aim of peace and security means that both parties need to provide evidence that their actions do not pose a risk thereto. The accused party needs to prove that it does not pose such a risk, and the acting party also needs to prove that its action is in response to a risk and does not present an additional risk to peace and security by causing cascading risks, for example by provoking civil strife, refugee waves, or regional conflagration.[128]

In sum, a symmetric allocation of the burden of proof together with the standard of proof can facilitate decision-making and, subsequently, support decisions in situations calling for anticipatory action.

2.6 Conclusion

It is apparent from the preceding discussion that risks have transformed the security debate and have pushed the law on the use of force to adopt an anticipatory dimension. The 9/11 events acted as a catalyst in the reorientation of the use of force regime, whereas the political and legal debates surrounding the 2003 action against Iraq reveal the battle between the new risk-informed approach to the use of force and the older threat-informed approach. More specifically, whereas the United States and the United Kingdom spoke the language of risks and resorted to unilateral and anticipatory action, the opponents of the action spoke the language of threats and resorted to an institutional and reactive response.

What are the broader ramifications of this state of affairs for the international law on the use of force? First, with respect to the temporal trajectory of the law, a risk rationale places the law on the use of force onto a future temporality; in other words, it becomes the law that attempts to regulate future events that have not yet been realized rather than the law that applies retrospectively to past and defined events. Second, the inclusion of a risk calculus and the interconnectedness of risks globalize unilateral uses of force. Whereas, according to the traditional threat calculus, states react with force against identifiable threats to their sovereignty as a kind of 'duel', risks, being amorphous, future-oriented, and interconnected, globalize the security perspective of states, merge national and global security, and globalize the reach of unilateral uses of force.[129] This has been referred to as a culture of 'global unilateralism',[130] which competes with or prevails over the institutional globalism of the UN regime according to which it is only the Security Council that has global competence to use force reactively or proactively.[131] Third,

[127] Federation of American Scientists, 'Iraq—Its Infrastructure of Concealment, Deception and Intimidation' (2002). <https://fas.org/irp/world/iraq/uk0103.pdf> accessed 30 January 2016.

[128] Rasmussen, *The Risk Society at War* (n 8) 91–140.

[129] As Beck puts it, 'these problems endow each country with a common global interest, which means that, to a certain extent, we can already talk about the basis of a global community of fate'. Beck, 'The Terrorist Threat' (n 5) 42.

[130] Beck, 'The Terrorist Threat' (n 5) 49.

[131] N Tsagourias and N White, *Collective Security: Theory, Law and Practice* (CUP 2013) 20–38.

the inclusion of a risk calculus deformalizes the law on the use of force. Law is immersed into decisional prospective-orientedness and loses its distinct, universal, and finite quality. Finally, in the absence of clear end-points in legal regulation, the role of international law as producer of order is affected. International law does not provide closure, but is in a state of anticipation of further risks, even if a particular risk has been acted upon.

3

'It Could Probably Just as Well Be Otherwise': Imageries of Cyberwar

Wouter Werner and Lianne Boer

3.1 Introduction

One of the core insights of Robert Musil's magnum opus *The Man Without Qualities* is that there must be 'a sense of possibility'. For Ulrich, the main character of the book, the world is not just what is out there; it is also what *could* be out there. In other words, alongside a 'sense of reality' there must be a 'sense of possibility':

> To pass freely through open doors, it is necessary to respect the fact that they have solid frames. This principle … is simply a requisite of the sense of reality. But if there is a sense of reality, and no one will doubt that it has its justifications for existing, then there must also be something we can call a sense of possibility.[1]

Whoever has a sense of possibility acknowledges that the world is not only made up of 'real possibilities', as dictated by the laws of nature and probabilistic thinking. In addition, there is such a thing as 'possible realities'; realities which might, could, or should happen:

> Whoever has [a sense of possible realities] does not say, for instance: Here this or that has happened, will happen, must happen; but he invents: Here this or that might, could, or ought to happen. If he is told that something is the way it is, he will think: Well, it could probably just as well be otherwise.[2]

In this chapter we analyse debates on the law applicable to cyberwar, as debates emanating from a sense of possibility. This sense of possibility translates into imageries of the way cyberwar might, could, or ought to happen. More specifically, we will focus on the ways in which possible future realities are construed in these debates. Our analysis is limited to the so-called *Tallinn Manual on the International Law Applicable to Cyber Warfare* (*Tallinn Manual*, or the *Manual*).[3] We would like

[1] R Musil, *The Man Without Qualities* (Picador 2011) 10–11.
[2] ibid, 11; for the phrase 'possible reality', see 12.
[3] MN Schmitt (ed), *Tallinn Manual on the International Law Applicable to Cyber Warfare* (CUP 2013) (*Tallinn Manual*).

to stress, however, that the reasoning applied in the *Tallinn Manual* is representative of the way in which most legal analysis of cyberwar has taken place so far. In a nutshell, the basic point of much legal analysis is to make sense of new phenomena (cyberwar) in terms of pre-existing legal rules, or, to make the unfamiliar familiar.

The *Tallinn Manual* was written by a group of mostly public international lawyers, described by the *Manual* as 'distinguished international law practitioners and scholars' whose task was 'to examine how extant legal norms applied to [cyber] warfare'.[4] Mainly focusing on *jus ad bellum* and *jus in bello*, the *Manual* outlines ninety-five Rules accompanied by explanatory Comments, dealing with issues ranging from the meaning of a 'cyber-armed attack' to what a *levée en masse* might look like in cyberspace.[5] Though the reception of the *Manual* has not been uncritical,[6] one can safely say it represents a new milestone in the debate on international law and cyberwar.

For our present purposes, the *Tallinn Manual* is an interesting case in point for a number of reasons. First, it deals with a 'war' that, so far, has not taken place (with, arguably, one or two exceptions[7]), but primarily belongs to the realm of that which might or could take place, namely cyberwar. Discussing the legal regulation of such virtual wars necessarily comes with attempts to imagine a phenomenon that 'exists in a state of floating, suspended between reality and possibility, past and future'.[8] Second, it constitutes a very structured attempt to imagine possible future realities, with a group of selected experts who spent years deliberating what cyberwar might, could, or ought to look like from the perspective of international law. Third, the *Manual* itself can be considered as an attempt to invent new realities. To be sure, this is not what the *Manual* itself claims to do. Time and again the *Manual* claims that it merely spells out what existing legal rules already require, irrespective of the preferences of the experts involved. However, and as the *Manual* itself explicates, it seeks to apply existing rules to phenomena that could not even be imagined at the time the relevant treaties were drafted.[9] Likewise,

[4] *Tallinn Manual* 1. [5] ibid, Table of Contents, 4.

[6] C Sweet, 'Tallinn Manual on the International Law Applicable to Cyber Warfare' (2014) 66 *Europe-Asia Studies* 669; D Fleck, 'Searching for International Rules Applicable to Cyber Warfare—A Critical First Assessment of the New Tallinn Manual' (2013) 18 *Journal of Conflict and Security Law* 331; N Tsagourias, 'The Tallinn Manual on the International Law Applicable to Cyber Warfare: A Commentary on Chapter II—The Use of Force' in TD Gill et al (eds) (2014) 15 *Yearbook of International Humanitarian Law* 2012 (TMC Asser Press 2014) 19–43; M Roscini, *Cyber Operations and the Use of Force in International Law* (OUP 2014) 30–32.

[7] At least, at the time the *Manual* was published, and as far as 'cyber-only' wars are concerned. *Jus ad bellum* cyber-incidents remain very rare; one incident arguably approaching the use-of-force threshold is the Stuxnet worm, which infiltrated a nuclear power plant in Iran. On Stuxnet, see R Buchan, 'Cyber Attacks: Unlawful Uses of Force or Prohibited Interventions?' (2012) 17 *Journal of Conflict and Security Law* 211. With regard to *jus in bello*, the use of cyber operations during kinetic armed conflict seems to be more common. Eg, (prior to and) during the 2008 Georgia–Russia conflict Georgia suffered cyberattacks; on this conflict, see L Swanson, 'The Era of Cyber Warfare: Applying International Humanitarian Law to the 2008 Russian–Georgian Cyber Conflict' (2010) 32 *Loyola of Los Angeles International and Comparative Law Review* 303.

[8] J Braungardt, *Possibility and Reality in Robert Musil* (2012) <http://braungardt.trialectics.com/literature/german-lit/possibility-and-reality-in-robert-musil/> accessed 24 March 2016.

[9] *Tallinn Manual* 3.

in its application of customary law the *Manual* draws from existing sources, but '[u]ltimately, the professional knowledge, experience, and expertise of the Experts form the basis for the *Tallinn Manual*'s conclusions as to the customary status of a Rule'.[10] In other words, it is impossible *not* to rely on the creative and imaginary faculties of the experts involved.

In this chapter, we contrast the creation of these legal imageries with other, non-legal imageries of cyberwar, as found in military and security studies. We first explore alternative ways in which cyberwar has been conceived in this discipline, before turning to the specific *legal* methods involved in its imagination. The purpose of this exercise is to carve out more clearly what is particular about the way in which international lawyers have imagined the future in this domain. Whereas the *Manual* deals with the legal possibilities of cyberwar, the debate we sketch in section 3.2, revolves around the question whether cyberwar will 'actually' happen.[11] It presents the two opposing sides in this debate on the 'real possibility' of cyberwar, in our case represented by Thomas Rid and William Lynn. The first is known as one of the major sceptics in this particular debate; the other emphasizes 'the scale of cyberwarfare's threat'.[12] These discussions stand in stark contrast to the way in which the *Tallinn Manual* imagines the future of cyberwar. There, the question whether cyberwar has happened, is happening, or will happen, and what form or shape this will assume, is largely irrelevant. Instead, the legal experts are concerned only with those scenarios that can follow from existing legal categories; these categories limit the shape and form of the possible realities of cyberwar. What results, as we show in

[10] ibid, 7, 8 (capitals in original).

[11] In the Introduction to her book on the construction of cyber as a threat, Miriam Dunn Cavelty devotes a section to what she refers to as the 'fact or fiction' question. See MD Cavelty, *Cyber-Security and Threat Politics: US Efforts to Secure the Information Age* (Routledge 2008) 4–5. She furthermore writes that 'despite the fact that cyber-threats have not (yet) actually materialised, the ongoing debate creates considerable pressure for decision-makers....The debate on cyber-threats is therefore not only about predicting the future, but also about how to prepare for possible contingencies in the present ... decisions have to be made based on scenarios and assumptions. The various actors involved ... compete with each other "by means of constructed versions of the future"' (6, citing R Bendrath, 'The American Cyber-Angst and the Real World—Any Link?' in R Latham (ed), *Bombs and Bandwidth: The Emerging Relationship between IT and Security* (The New Press 2003) 51.

[12] WJ Lynn, *Defending a New Domain: The Pentagon's Cyberstrategy* (2010) <https://www.foreignaffairs.com/articles/united-states/2010-09-01/defending-new-domain> accessed 24 March 2016. For a sketch of the two opposing sides, and a possible middle position, see I Duyvesteyn, 'Between Doomsday and Dismissal: Collective Defence, Cyber War and the Parameters of War' (2014) 38 *October Atlantisch Perspectief* 20. On 'threat representations', see MD Cavelty, 'From Cyber-Bombs to Political Fallout: Threat Representations with an Impact in the Cyber-Security Discourse' (2013) 15 *International Studies Review* 105, particularly 116–18. In this respect, the February 2015 *Worldwide Threat Assessment of the US Intelligence Committee* is very interesting; though cyber is the first threat discussed in the report, it says that 'cyber threats to US national and economic security are increasing in frequency, scale, sophistication, and severity of impact. The ranges of cyber threat actors, methods of attack, targeted systems, and victims are also expanding.... *However*, the likelihood of a catastrophic attack from any particular actor is remote at this time. Rather than a "Cyber Armageddon" scenario that debilitates the entire US infrastructure, we ... foresee an ongoing series of low-to-moderate level cyber attacks from a variety of sources over time, which will impose cumulative costs on US economic competitiveness and national security.' JR Clapper, (2015) *Worldwide Threat Assessment of the US Intelligence Community* 1 (emphasis added) <http://www.dni.gov/files/documents/Unclassified_2015_ATA_SFR_-_SASC_FINAL.pdf> accessed 7 April 2016.

section 3.3, is a way of imagining cyberwar based on the cultivation of our sense of possibility; what could, may, or ought to happen.

3.2 On the 'Real Possibility' of Cyberwar

3.2.1 Cyberwar is coming—or not

One of the earliest writings on cyberwar bore the alarming title 'Cyberwar is Coming!'—a much quoted article, published one year after the term was first coined in 1992.[13] The aim of the article was to prepare US policy makers for what the authors envisaged to be the dominant type of war-fighting in the twenty-first century. It sketches a future where armed conflicts revolve around issues of information, communication and, most of all, knowledge.[14] Although the article claims to be speculative and future-oriented, its imageries of what cyberwar may, could, or should look like are firmly rooted in the past. Cyberwar is presented in three different, partly overlapping ways: (i) as the provisional end-point of a long history of 'technological breakthroughs'; (ii) as a break with history, or as a new way of thinking that 'fundamentally alters' the battlefield and constitutes nothing less than an '[assured] ... sea-change ... in the nature of conflict and warfare';[15] and (iii) as part of a cyclical history; as the return of what we have experienced before. The authors here refer to examples such as Mongol warfare in the thirteenth century ('a paradigm for cyber war'[16]) or the Vietnamese forces in the 1960s (who 'may have applied cyber principles more effectively than did the United States'[17]).

The idea that cyberwar is about to come took hold in the (US) military and political establishment.[18] This recognition comes with specific imageries about the nature and consequences of cyberwar. Often, when US state officials go public about the possible realities of cyberwar, they do so by making references to, for instance, 'Hiroshima'[19] or 'the next Pearl Harbor'[20]—invoking images of unpredictability

[13] J Arquilla and D Ronfeldt, 'Cyberwar is Coming!' in J Arquilla and D Ronfeldt (eds), *In Athena's Camp: Preparing for Conflict in the Information Age* (RAND 1997); previously published in (1993) 12 *Comparative Strategy* 141. The term 'cyberwar' was coined in 1992 by EH Arnett, 'Welcome to Hyperwar' (1992) 48 *Bulletin of the Atomic Scientists* 14. For Arnett, however, 'cyberwar' was about automated warfare 'in which robots do much of the killing and destroying without direct instructions from human operators. The weapons would be '"autonomous," to use one of the weapons designers' favorite words' (15).

[14] The scenarios, speculations, and policy advice can be found at Arquilla and Ronfeldt, 'Cyberwar is Coming!' (n 12) 43–47.

[15] Arquilla and Ronfeldt, 'Cyberwar is Coming!' (n 12) 24, 32.

[16] ibid, 37.

[17] ibid, 38.

[18] On 'the development of cyber-threat frames in the military, see MD Cavelty, *Cyber-Security and Threat Politics* (n10) 67.

[19] MJ Gross, *A Declaration of Cyber-War* (2011) <http://www.vanityfair.com/news/2011/03/stuxnet-201104> accessed 7 April 2016.

[20] L Daniel, *Panetta: Intelligence Community Needs to Predict Uprisings* (American Forces Press Service 2011) <http://archive.defense.gov/news/newsarticle.aspx?id=62790> accessed 7 April 2016.

and catastrophic consequences. This picture is aptly captured in a 2010 article in *Foreign Affairs*, written by the then Deputy Secretary of Defense, William Lynn.[21] Although Lynn's article shies away from the catastrophic imageries that characterize some other US writings on the subject,[22] it does repeat many of the common tropes about the nature and future of cyberwar. Let us briefly mention the two main shared tropes.

First, Lynn invokes history as a reminder that, not for the first time, the United States is about to enter a radically new era. The article concludes with the observation that '[t]he daunting challenges of cyber security represent the beginning of a new technological age. In this early hour, the United States' greatest strength is its awareness of the transformation.'[23] The article recalls Albert Einstein's 1939 letter to Roosevelt, which alerted the President to breakthroughs in nuclear fission and the possibility that a new type of bomb could be developed. The invocation of the letter serves several purposes at the same time. It signals that, just like in 1939, we are on the eve of a new technological era—adding a heralding flavour to the article as a whole. Moreover, it contains a warning; we had better act speedily, because otherwise our adversaries may gain the upper hand in a new arms race. Finally, it has a reassuring function. Just as Einstein's warning led to the launch of the Manhattan project, which assured US supremacy in the atomic age, the current US government is securing US supremacy in cyberspace. The article is filled with concrete examples of current policies and new initiatives that show the hands-on approach of the US government in the face of the new technological era that is now upon us.

Second, the article portrays the development of 'cyber' as the emergence of an intangible, fluid sphere that destabilizes established doctrines and categories through which we make sense of war and peace. Simply put, the threat of cyber is presented as omnipresent, disruptive, unpredictable, extremely speedy ('milliseconds could make a difference'), and difficult to attribute. The United States, Lynn argues, is faced with a potentially amorphous enemy that could strike at any time and within no time. This implies that established doctrines based on retaliation and deterrence will not work and that divisions between military and civilian infrastructure no longer hold up; cooperation is sought with allies to protect US infrastructures. The possible reality of a future cyberwar is then brought to the present through a series of policy recommendations and actions that have already been put in place. Uncertainty is here to stay; resilience is required: 'Thus, the US government must be modest about its ability to know where and how this threat might mature; what it needs is a strategy that provides operational flexibility and capabilities that offer maximum adaptability.'[24]

[21] WJ Lynn III, *Defending a New Domain: The Pentagon's Cyberstrategy*, September/October 2010 <http://www.foreignaffairs.com/articles/66552/william-j-lynn-iii/defending-a-new-domain> accessed 7 April 2016.

[22] Compare Lynn's article (ibid, n 20) with a letter sent by several technology experts to President Bush in 2002, warning him of the 'grave risk of a cyber attack that could devastate the [US] national psyche and economy more broadly than did the September 11th attack'. See <http://www.pbs.org/wgbh/pages/frontline/shows/cyberwar/etc/letter.html> accessed 7 April 2016.

[23] Lynn, *Defending a New Domain* (n 20). [24] ibid.

3.2.2 Redefining the past—redefining the future

It was simply a matter of time before the gloomy images of cyberwar would find their sceptics—or at least, those downplaying the idea of imminent disaster.[25] Among the sceptic literature, Thomas Rid's 2013 article 'Cyber War Will Not Take Place' stands out as one of the most conceptually grounded critiques of the idea that we are heading towards a new, virtual domain of warfare.[26] At first sight, Rid's article seems to be informed by what Musil would call a sense of reality, as it claims to be about the past, the present, and the likely future,[27] what cyber offences 'actually are' as well as 'the real world' of war.[28] Moreover, his article departs from the observation that 'the empirical trend is obvious: over the past dozen years, cyber attacks have been steadily on the rise'.[29] However, on closer inspection, the core of the argument revolves around the ways in which we *should* imagine what war is—and what it is not. In other words, the article is not about what is 'actually the case' in the 'real world'; it is about possible ways to make (sense of) reality and construes imageries of the future along those lines.

Rid starts out from the Clausewitzian concept of war as violent, instrumental, and being used for political purposes. It is this concept of war that is equated with 'the real world'[30] and the one relied on to determine whether wars have taken place in the past. Although he starts out from the observation that '[a]ny attempt to answer the question of cyber war has to start conceptually',[31] Rid seems to be unaware of the constitutive functions of concepts; that is, of the institutional nature of the 'real' world he is constructing.[32] The move in the article is from the world of imagination towards the real world—from the concept of war towards those acts and events that count as 'war' to those that should be regarded as something else. This move has an important consequence: it excludes, by definition, the possibility that new developments could unearth the Clausewitzian concept of war—anything that does not fit this particular concept cannot be a war properly called.[33]

The next step in his analysis consists of a debunking of the idea that any cyberattack on record so far has ever amounted to a 'war' in the Clausewitzian sense. Although there have been numerous cyberattacks, Rid contends, none of them was violent, instrumental, and political at the same time. Instead, Rid argues, previous attacks should be viewed as measures short of war, or as measures supportive of other 'real' war efforts. They are either 'sabotage' (attempts to weaken or destroy

[25] See, eg, CS Gray, *Making Strategic Sense of Cyber Power: Why the Sky is Not Falling* (US Army War College Press 2013); T Rid, 'Cyber War Will Not Take Place' (2011) 35 *Journal of Strategic Studies* 5.

[26] Rid, ibid. [27] ibid, 5–6. [28] ibid, 7–8. [29] ibid, 15. [30] ibid, 8.

[31] ibid, 6.

[32] The constitutive function of concepts has been a longstanding topic in the philosophy of language, at least since John Austin published his *How to Do Things With Words: The William James Lectures Delivered at Harvard University in 1955* (Clarendon Press 1962). For an application to the field of legal theory, see D Ruiter, *Institutional Legal Facts, Legal Powers and their Effects* (Kluwer Academic Publishers 1993).

[33] For an opposite argument, see M Kaldor, *New and Old Wars: Organized Violence in a Global Era* (Polity Press 2012). Kaldor argues that the new features of violence render the Clausewitzian understanding of 'war' outdated.

military or economic systems), 'espionage', or 'subversion' (attempts to undermine authorities and order). According to Rid, these are forms of action that should be central to policy makers.

Interestingly, Rid's article ends with what lawyers would call a combination of a rule distributing the burden of proof and a closing rule. The burden of proof is put on the shoulders of those who argue that a cyberwar may, could, or will take place in the future. They can only back up their claim if more public, detailed evidence comes available:

> There was no and there is no Pearl Harbor of cyber war. Unless significantly more evidence and significantly more detail are presented publicly by more than one agency, we have to conclude that there will not be a Pearl Harbor of cyber war in the future either.[34]

The closing rule states that absent examples of cyberwar in the past, we should assume they will not occur in the future. The imagined future is here the result of a re-imaging of the past through Clausewitzian lenses, together with the idea of historical continuity; whatever has happened in the past is likely to occur in the future. The term 'likely' is chosen deliberately here, as the last sentence of the article all of a sudden opens up to the possibility that the world may as well be otherwise. After having spent the whole article explaining that cyberwar will not take place, Rid ends with the Musilian insight that '[n]eedless to say, Cassandra could still have the last word'.[35]

3.3 The *Tallinn Manual*

Section 3.2 has set out how the future of cyberwar has been imagined in the field of security and military studies. Although the articles studied in the previous section differ significantly in tone and argument, they do share two important characteristics. First of all, they both construe imageries of the future in order to defend policies or to effectuate changes *in the present*.[36] Second, they all use *the past* in order to imagine what the future will look like; what cyberwar will look like is construed on the basis of historical examples, earlier revolutions, extrapolation of trends, and so on.

When we turn to the *Tallinn Manual* the picture changes. As was set out in section 3.1, the aim of the *Manual* is to clarify which rules of international conflict and security law are applicable to cyber operations. This implies a thorough re-articulation of the socio-political world of cyber. Cyber operations are not understood in terms of Clauzewitz's concept of war or in terms of fundamental transformations in warfare, but on the basis of existing categories of international law. Whatever the uncertainties that surround issues of cyberwar, the *Tallinn Manual* imagines the future through the lens of '[l]ong-standing international

[34] Rid, 'Cyber War Will Not Take Place' (n 24) 29. [35] ibid.

[36] See also MD Cavelty, *Cyber-Security and Threat Politics* (n 10) Chapter 4.

norms guiding State behavior—in times of peace and conflict—[that] also apply in cyberspace'.[37] The tone here is almost reassuring and comforting; no matter how revolutionary new technologies may be, for international law there is nothing new under the sun.[38] There are only age-old rules that will help us make sense of whatever the future may bring.

In this context, it is not surprising to see that the *Manual* does not contain a discussion of the likelihood of cyberwars in the future. The *Manual* starts with the observation that different states as well as the North Atlantic Treaty Organization (NATO) itself are concerned about cyber threats, only to quickly move on to debates on the law applicable to cyberwar—in case one should occur. Whether cyberwar is *indeed* likely to occur is, in a way, immaterial for the meaning and content of the *Manual*. The fundamental question for the drafters of the *Manual* is whether the law applies in the first place; after all, if the answer is negative, there is no point to their endeavour. This is explicitly acknowledged by the director of the group of experts, Michael Schmitt: 'The *sine qua non* issue for the *Tallinn Manual* was whether international law applies to cyber activities at all, for absent an affirmative response the project would have been pointless.'[39] What counts is which factual situations the experts could imagine in light of potentially applicable legal provisions. The *Manual* is thus the result of an active use of Musil's 'sense of possibility'. It is about what we imagine that may, could, or should happen, if we take age-old legal provisions as our starting point.

The structure within which the *Manual* discusses the Rules we selected for closer scrutiny is one that recurs several times throughout the *Manual*. It takes place by way of three argumentative moves, and is crucial to understanding the different cyberwar 'scenarios' we find here. In the first move, the Rule itself is presented in the shape of the black-letter Rule. The *Manual*'s very first Rule, for example, makes it known that '[a] State may exercise control over cyber infrastructure and activities within its sovereign territory'.[40] These firm openings are then followed by an elaboration on this Rule in the Commentary, which constitutes the second move. This second move involves a discussion of applicable law, where the word 'cyber' is inserted in key places.[41] What this insertion signifies is that the reader of

[37] *Tallinn Manual* 3, citing the US *International Strategy for Cyberspace*.

[38] Other ways of controlling the (future) uncertainty of cyberwar are presented in R Kaiser, 'The Birth of Cyberwar' (2015) 46 *Political Geography* 11. He briefly mentions the *Tallinn Manual* on page 12.

[39] MN Schmitt, 'International Law in Cyberspace: The Koh Speech and Tallinn Manual Juxtaposed' (2012) 54 *Harvard International Law Journal Online* 13, 16. In a conference presentation, Schmitt very briefly addressed this issue, saying 'in most cases issues addressed in the Tallinn Manual are not relevant, because you're not approaching either the armed conflict threshold or in the *ad bellum* sense, the use of force or armed attack threshold'. See MN Schmitt, *CyCon 2012 | Michael Schmitt: Tallinn Manual Part I* (Naval War College 2012) <https://www.youtube.com/watch?v=wY3uEo-Itso> 23:02, accessed 11 April 2016.

[40] *Tallinn Manual* 15.

[41] Roscini, *Cyber Operations and the Use of Force* (n 5) 31: 'Overall, it seems fair to say that the Experts were very cautious to avoid taking any risks when drafting the rules, which are often a mere restatement of existing treaty provisions with the addition of the adjective "cyber"' (capital in original). Roscini here refers to and quotes the *Manual* itself, which states that '[a]t times, the text of a Rule closely resembles that of an existing treaty norm'. *Tallinn Manual* 6.

the *Manual* is now informed that the law, relevant to the discussion of the Rule in question, applies—it soothes any anxieties we might have over the 'inadaptability' of international law to cyber. Only in the third and final move do possible future scenarios of cyberwar enter the Commentary, as the content of the Rule or areas of disagreement and uncertainties regarding that Rule are accounted for.

In other words, the outlook of the law is not determined by more or less likely scenarios; it is the law that determines how the future is imagined.[42] In the following sections we show how this structure functions in the *Manual*, and what its effects are on the manner in which cyberwar is imagined. We do this by way of two of its Rules: the prohibition on the use of force and the *Manual's* treatment of *levée en masse*. We have selected these two as they represent two opposing sides in terms of their continued relevance in international law. *Levée en masse* signifies a spontaneous uprising by a civilian population against an intervening aggressor and is considered to be of 'limited current application'[43] by the International Committee of the Red Cross (ICRC). The prohibition on the use of force, on the other hand, has been described as the 'cornerstone of the United Nations Charter'[44]—the complete opposite of the characterization of *levée en masse*. Our analysis starts with the *Manual's* discussion of the prohibition on the use of force in section 3.3.1. As part of the outline of applicable law in this area, the experts have also included a brief discussion of the non-intervention principle. Contrary to the three-part structure prominent in most of the *Manual*, this treatment of the non-intervention principle follows a different trajectory. We therefore discuss it here separately (section 3.3.1.2), followed by the discussion of *levée en masse* (3.3.2).

3.3.1 Article 2(4) UN Charter

3.3.1.1 Article 2(4) and the use of force

As stated above, the prohibition on the use of force is at the heart of the current international legal system. Its application to cyberwar can be thought of as problematic due to the fact that the attack is performed through cyberspace, rather than by means of traditional weapons. Though some scholars—as well as the experts in the *Tallinn Manual*—argue that the prohibition can be applied to cyberattacks as well, others have argued that cyberattacks do not fit the *jus ad bellum* regime at all, instead arguing for or inquiring into the feasibility of a treaty regulating cyberattacks.[45] Hathaway et al, for example, argue that '[t]he law of war offers a basis for

[42] Although phrased in different wording, the way in which the *Manual* dealt with the law-future nexus was critiqued in DA Wallace and SR Reeves, 'The Law of Armed Conflict's "Wicked" Problem: *Levée en Masse* in Cyber Warfare' (2013) 89 *International Law Studies* 646 <http://papers.ssrn.com/sol3/papers.cfm?abstract_id=2295088> accessed 11 April 2016.

[43] See the ICRC's Customary IHL database <https://www.icrc.org/customary-ihl/eng/docs/v1_cha_chapter1_rule5?OpenDocument&highlight=levee%20en%20masse> accessed 11 April 2016.

[44] *Armed Activities on the Territory of the Congo (Democratic Republic of the Congo v Uganda)*, Judgment, [2005] ICJ Reports 168, para 148.

[45] See for a critique on applying the prohibition, and an argument for an 'international law for information operations', D Hollis, 'Why States Need an International Law for Information Operations'

responding only to those cyber-attacks that amount to an armed attack or that take place in the context of an ongoing armed conflict'; and 'getting at the root of the global cyber-attack challenge will require international solutions'.[46] They propose, therefore, a treaty that contains, inter alia, 'a shared definition of cyber-attack, cyber-crime, and cyber-warfare'.[47] Back in 2002, Daniel Silver argued that 'efforts should be made towards the adoption of an international convention that would bind the parties not to use [computer network attacks] for any military or hostile use'.[48]

The *Manual* argues against the need for such a specialized treaty and instead claims that the *jus ad bellum* regime does apply to it, by reference to the *Nuclear Weapons* Advisory Opinion of the International Court of Justice (ICJ). In this Opinion, the Court advised that the body of law regulating the use of force governs 'any use of force, regardless of the weapons employed'.[49] There is thus no reason for the group of experts, prima facie, to reject the application of the prohibition to cyber operations; 'the mere fact that a computer ... is used during an operation', they write, 'has no bearing on whether that operation amounts to a 'use of force'.[50] Though the experts acknowledge the possibility that the law might develop in a different direction, they are sure of its applicability at the time of writing.[51]

In its first move, the *Manual* adopts the *Nuclear Weapons* Opinion, allowing the experts to postulate the first black-letter Rule on the use of force (Rule 10): '[a] cyber operation that constitutes a threat or use of force ... is unlawful'.[52] The kind of reasoning employed—the use of force is illegal; cyberattacks are potential uses of force, therefore, cyberattacks are potentially illegal—is repeated elsewhere in the commentary.[53] Thus, similarly, by adopting a line of reasoning set out by the ICJ in the *Nicaragua* case,[54] the group's second black-letter Rule (Rule 11) on the use of force reads: '[a] cyber operation constitutes a use of force when its scale and effects are comparable to non-cyber operations rising to the level of a use of force'.[55]

(2007) 11 *Lewis and Clark Law Review* 1023; for an argument in favour of a comprehensive treaty, see OA Hathaway et al, 'The Law of Cyber-Attack' (2012) 100 *California Law Review* 817, particularly 880 et seq; for a more critical analysis of the feasibility of a treaty, see PA Johnson, 'Is It Time for a Treaty on Information Warfare?' in BT O'Donnell and MN Schmitt (eds), *Computer Network Attack and International Law* (Naval War College 2002) vol 76, 439–55; in the same volume, concluding his analysis with an argument for a treaty, DB Silver, 'Computer Network Attack as a Use of Force under Article 2(4) of the United Nations Charter' in MN Schmitt and BT O'Donnell (eds), *Computer Network Attack and International Law* 73–97.

[46] Hathaway et al, ibid, 877. They do point out 'that cyber-attacks that do constitute use of force under the law of war are already covered by *jus in bello* principles, which may be more clearly defined over time in the cyber-attack context through state practice' (880 n 309).

[47] ibid, 881.

[48] Silver, 'Computer Network Attack as a Use of Force' (n 44) 94, adding that 'this is an explicit expression of a policy preference, not a statement about the law as it is'.

[49] *Legality of the Threat or Use of Nuclear Weapons, Advisory Opinion,* [1996] ICJ Reports 226.

[50] *Tallinn Manual* 42. [51] ibid. [52] ibid.

[53] See Hollis, 'Why States Need an International Law for Information Operations' (n 44) for an analysis of the 'translation problems' when applying the prohibition to cyberattacks.

[54] *Military and Paramilitary Activities In and Against Nicaragua (Nicaragua v United States of America).* Merits, Judgment, ICJ Reports 1986, 14, para 195.

[55] *Tallinn Manual* 45.

In the second move, these two black-letter Rules are both followed by similar statements of law, where the word 'cyber' is inserted in key places.[56] For example, setting the parameters for its discussion of force, dealing with the attribution of behaviour of specific actors to the state, the *Manual* states that: '[a]n action qualifying as a "use of force" need not necessarily be undertaken by a State's armed forces'.[57] By analogy, 'a cyber operation that would qualify as a "use of force" if conducted by the armed forces would equally be a "use of force" if undertaken by a State's intelligence agencies or by a private contractor whose conduct is attributable to the State'.[58] Similarly, in distinguishing force from economic and political coercion, the *Manual* provides that: '[a]s an example, non-destructive cyber psychological operations intended solely to undermine confidence in a government or economy do not qualify as uses of force'.[59] Though the experts use this 'as an example', it does not tell us what these 'non-destructive cyber psychological operations' look like, or how their appearance is different from or similar to the kinds of non-destructive operations we are familiar with. The same goes for the permissibility (under Article 2(4), that is) of 'merely funding a hacktivist group'.[60] The word 'hacktivist' in this phrase is no specification whatsoever; the sentence does not lose meaning by eliminating 'cyber-specific words' such as 'hacker'—nor does it gain anything by adding them.[61] One senses that the word 'cyber', to paraphrase the title of our chapter, could just as well be replaced by any other word—we only need to insert the word 'cyber' to know the law in this particular area.

In its third and final move, scenarios as to what the use of force in cyberspace might look like emerge on the final pages of the *Manual*'s discussion of Rule 11,[62] where the experts set out to give more specific meaning to the prohibition. For example, 'a highly invasive operation that causes only inconvenience such as temporary denial of service is unlikely to be classified as a use of force'; conversely, '[c]yber operations that specifically target the domain name of a particular State (eg, 'mil.ee') ... may ... be considered more invasive' and thus are more likely to be regarded as violating the prohibition.[63] Given that '[t]here is no authoritative definition of ... "use of force"', the Commentary to this Rule, after outlining what we *do* know about the meaning of force (present in its second move), proceeds by stating that this still leaves a range of (cyber) operations legally undefined.[64] Therefore, the *Manual* includes a framework for analysing 'less clear cases'.[65] It is here where the legal analysis comes closest to the possible realities of cyberwar. The goal of this approach is to draw parallels between 'conventional' uses of force and those cyberattacks 'analogous' to them.[66] What results is a set of eight factors that can be applied to each individual case; factors that look to 'both the level of harm inflicted

[56] See Roscini, *Cyber Operations and the Use of Force* (n 40). [57] *Tallinn Manual* 43.

[58] ibid. [59] ibid, 46. [60] ibid.

[61] As a final illustration, 'providing an organized group with malware and the training necessary to use it to carry out cyber attacks against another State would also qualify [as a use of force]' is of a similar structure. See *Tallinn Manual* 46.

[62] ibid, 48–52. [63] ibid, 52, 49–50. [64] ibid, 46, 48.

[65] ibid, 48 ('Since other cases are less clear ...'). [66] ibid.

and certain qualitative elements of a particular cyber operation'.[67] These include the level of severity, immediacy, directness, invasiveness, measurability of effects, and military character, state involvement, and presumptive legality, where, for instance, measurability signifies 'a cyber operation that can be evaluated in very specific terms (eg, amount of data corrupted, percentage of servers disabled, number of confidential files exfiltrated)'.[68] The experts provide examples of questions that may be asked with regard to the particular cyberattack under scrutiny. For each factor, two or three questions are asked, such as 'How many people were killed?' (severity), 'Was the locus of the action within the target country?' (invasiveness), 'How certain is the calculation of the effects?' (measurability), and 'Did the military conduct the cyber operation?' (military character). Not all questions are tailored to the specific attack; some clearly originate from the kind of analogous thinking displayed elsewhere in the chapter, such as 'Are the effects of the action distinct from the results of parallel or competing actions?' and 'Are the means qualitatively similar to others presumed legitimate under international law?'[69]

Although these questions seem to allow room for the specifics of cyberattacks, they are still an attempt to fit cyberattacks within existing legal frames. This also highlights the *Manual*'s assumption that there is no room for scenarios other than those that the legal framework allows, because such scenarios, indeed, would 'render the project pointless'. Thus, except for a few glimpses of the legally impossible[70] (as the discussion of non-intervention, discussed below, demonstrates), we are told that there is nothing particular about cyber that the law cannot cover. What the *Manual* sets out to do is to paint a picture of cyberwar that still makes legal sense. This means that, even though in some cases we may not be entirely sure *how* the law applies, apply it does.[71]

3.3.1.2 Article 2(4) and the non-intervention principle

As stated above, the experts' discussion of the non-intervention principle is somewhat differently structured than the 'three moves' we find elsewhere in the *Manual* generally. The *Manual* begins its discussion of the principle by stating that 'The fact that a cyber operation does not rise to the level of a use of force does not necessarily render it lawful under international law … a cyber operation may constitute a violation of the prohibition on intervention.'[72] The Commentary to

[67] ibid.

[68] For the eight factors, see ibid, 48–51. With regard to invasiveness, the experts note this factor should be 'cautiously applied' to cyberattacks, as cyber espionage is very invasive but does not violate the prohibition.

[69] ibid, 51 n 22.

[70] ibid, 50: 'In the cyber realm, consequences may be less apparent'—so states might not be too eager to qualify these as uses of force. What this line truly tells us, is that if cyber operations have non-apparent effects, they probably will not be considered to fit within the 'force' category.

[71] See, for a similar comment, Hollis, 'New Tools, New Rules' (n 44) 1037: 'To say the law of war covers [information operations] does not, of course, tell us *when* and *how* it applies' (emphasis in original).

[72] *Tallinn Manual* 44.

this Rule expresses uncertainty with regard to the 'scope and content of the non-intervention principle'.[73] Pointing out that the ICJ states that a state action needs to be of a coercive nature in order to violate the non-intervention principle, the experts name as an example of a cyber operation that is *not* coercive, and thus not in violation of the principle, 'the breaching of firewalls or the cracking of passwords'.[74] Suddenly, the scope of inquiry turns towards the nature of cyber operations, rather than the application of international law; 'The assessment … becomes complex when it comes to other operations along the broad spectrum of cyber operations.'[75] Identifying the 'element of coercion' in these cases is not so easy, leading to the conclusion that is the last resort and thus the safety net of the kind of reasoning employed, which is that assessing the legality of these operations '[depends] on the circumstances of each individual case'.[76] Pointing out yet again that these kinds of operations 'are more difficult to characterize', the experts conclude their discussion of this Rule by giving some examples of state actions that are known to violate the non-intervention principle, such as 'regime change' and 'coercive political interference'.[77] As a further attempt at 'closing the ranks', we find the word 'cyber' inserted once again: 'When such actions are taken or facilitated by cyber means, they constitute prohibited intervention.'[78] Examples given by the experts are:

> the manipulation by cyber means of elections or of public opinion on the eve of elections, as when online news services are altered in favour of a particular party, false news is spread, or the online services of one party are shut off.[79]

Again, we can remove the words 'cyber' and 'online' and be left with what we already knew to be law; prohibited intervention is, inter alia, 'the manipulation of elections, when news services are altered, or the services of one party are shut off'.

3.3.2 *Levée en masse*

Contrary to the key position held by the prohibition on the use of force, we find the concept of *levée en masse* on the margins of international (humanitarian) law. The term '*levée en masse*' refers to a situation where civilians spontaneously take up arms against an invading power, in order to prevent the enemy army from occupying their land. The idea of the 'people in arms' originates in revolutionary France, where the National Assembly called upon citizens to voluntarily take up arms against invading forces as a form of civic duty.[80] The idea took hold throughout Europe and found its way into the American civil war as well.[81] In that context, *levée en*

[73] ibid. [74] ibid, 44, 45. [75] ibid, 45. [76] ibid. [77] ibid.
[78] ibid. [79] ibid.
[80] For a discussion of the reality and myths of *levée en masse*, see D Moran and A Waldron, *The People in Arms: Military Myth and National Mobilization Since the French Revolution* (CUP 2003).
[81] Wallace and Reeves, 'The Law of Armed Conflict's "Wicked" Problem (n 41) 652, referring to GD Solis, *The Law of Armed Conflict: International Humanitarian Law in War* (CUP 2010) 200.

masse was recognized in the so-called Lieber Code,[82] which granted prisoner-of-war status to the people who, under a duly authorized *levée en masse*, had taken up arms against an invading army in territory that had not yet been occupied.[83] Since then, *levée en masse* has been recognized in an increasing number of international legal instruments regulating international armed conflicts, such as the 1874 Brussels Declaration, the 1899/1907 Hague Conventions, and eventually the Geneva Conventions.[84] In addition, the notion has been incorporated into numerous national military manuals and is considered to be part of customary international law.[85]

Civilians participating in a *levée en masse* enjoy the same privileges (and vulnerabilities) as combatants, including the right to be treated as prisoners of war upon capture. However, the criteria for what counts as a *levée en masse* are very strict. First, there is only a very limited time span available; enemy forces must be approaching, but not yet occupying the homeland. Second, the territorial scope for *levée en masse* is restricted to (national) territory that is not yet occupied. Third, civilians participating in a *levée en masse* have to carry their arms openly and to respect the laws and customs of war.

As a result, the *levée en masse* has become a widely recognized, yet also marginal phenomenon in international law. The ICRC customary law study speaks of *levée en masse* as being of 'limited current application', although 'still repeated in many military manuals, including very recent ones'.[86] Scholars have taken similar positions, describing the *levée en masse* as 'a situation that almost never happens' or something that 'has become less significant'.[87] The *levée en masse* is thus most of all a potentiality; something that almost never takes place, but still *could* happen.[88]

[82] *Instructions for the Government of Armies in the US in the Field, General Orders*, 24 April 1863 (Lieber Code), Yale Law School Avalon Project <http://avalon.law.yale.edu/19th_century/lieber.asp> accessed 12 April 2016.

[83] ibid, arts 51 and 52.

[84] *Project of an International Declaration concerning the Laws and Customs of War*, Brussels 1874 <https://www.icrc.org/ihl/INTRO/135> accessed 12 April 2016; the texts of the 1899 and 1907 Hague Conventions are available at <http://avalon.law.yale.edu/subject_menus/lawwar.asp> accessed 12 April 2016; the Geneva Conventions I–IV of 1949 together with the Additional Protocols of 1977 are available at <https://www.icrc.org/applic/ihl/ihl.nsf/vwTreaties1949.xsp> accessed 12 April 2016.

[85] For an overview, see ICRC, *Customary Humanitarian International Law* (CUP 2005) (ICRC Study), in particular the part relating to civilians <https://www.icrc.org/customary-ihl/eng/docs/v1_cha_chapter1_rule5>, as well as the conditions for prisoners of war status <https://www.icrc.org/customary-ihl/eng/docs/v2_cha_chapter33_rule106_sectionb> accessed 12 April 2016.

[86] ICRC Study, ibid <https://www.icrc.org/customary-ihl/eng/docs/v1_cha_chapter1_rule5> accessed 12 April 2016.

[87] Emily Crawford, '*Levée En Masse*: A Nineteenth-Century Concept in a Twenty-First Century World' (2011) 11/31 *Sydney Law School Research Paper* 14 <http://papers.ssrn.com/sol3/papers.cfm?abstract_id=1851947> accessed 13 April 2016. The second quote is taken from page 14, where she refers to K Ipsen, 'Combatants and Non-Combatants' in D Fleck (ed), *The Handbook of Humanitarian Law* (2nd edn, OUP 2008) 94.

[88] In the *Oric* case, the International Criminal Tribunal for the former Yugoslavia (ICTY) contemplated the existence of a *levée en masse* in Srebrenica in 1992, concluding that there could have been one, but eventually dismissing the qualification because of the lack of organization of the Bosnian forces. *Prosecutor v Naser Oric* (International Criminal Tribunal for the former Yugoslavia), Judgment of 30 June 2006, paras 133, 135, 136, IT-03-68-T.

It is this sense of possibility that is invoked in the *Tallinn Manual.* Referring to military manuals and ICRC studies, the *Tallinn Manual* acknowledges that 'the circumstances under which a *levée en masse* can exist are factually limited', whereas the application of the concept to the cyber context is seen as 'somewhat problematic'.[89] Given the criteria for a *levée en masse*, the latter is somewhat of an understatement. Cyber operations are difficult to square with requirements such as 'carrying arms openly' or limiting the operations to the threatened but not yet occupied parts of the homeland. However, as stated above, the point of the *Tallinn Manual* is not to sketch the *likely* future of cyberwar—in other words, whether it will happen, and if so, how catastrophic it would be; rather, it sketches the *possible* futures of cyberwar, as imagined through the lens of legal provisions. Therefore, the director of the *Manual* project stated in a presentation that 'initially we thought "*levée en masse* has nothing to do with cyber", however, when we thought about it, it did in fact'.[90] This allows for the first move of the *Manual*'s discussion on *levée en masse*, which is the formulation of the Rule itself: 'In an international armed conflict, inhabitants of unoccupied territory who engage in cyber operations as part of a *levée en masse* enjoy combatant immunity and prisoner of war status.'[91] In the first two paragraphs we witness the second move of the discussion; they set out the customary law status of *levée en masse* generally, and expound on what it looks like in traditional armed conflicts. The final sentence of the second paragraph concludes the second move: 'Extension [of the provision] to orders given by cyber means is appropriate.'[92] But trying to paint the picture of *levée en masse* in cyberspace is, as cited above, 'somewhat problematic'. Thus we find, in the third and final move, a discussion that is rife with uncertainty. The *Manual* takes the reader through the criteria set out in the Third Geneva Convention,[93] based on a speculative scenario 'in which members of the population spontaneously begin to mount cyber operations in response to an invasion of their country'.[94] But whereas in traditional armed conflict 'taking up arms' probably involved the use of pitchforks and the like, the *Manual* acknowledges that, in cyberspace, it is not likely that every citizen has 'the means and expertise necessary to engage effectively in cyber operations'.[95] The remainder of the discussion of this Rule is thus filled with expressions of uncertainty: '*It is unclear* whether a *levée en masse* can be comprised solely of a significant portion of the cyber-capable members of the population'; '*it is questionable* whether individuals launching cyber operations against enemy military objectives other than the invading forces can be considered members of a *levée en masse*'; and

> [t]he International Group of Experts *was divided* as to whether the privileges associated with the *levée en masse* concept apply to a civilian population countering a massive cyber attack, the effects of which are comparable to those of a physical invasion by armed forces.[96]

[89] *Tallinn Manual* 102, 103.
[90] Schmitt, *CyCon 2012* (n 38) 19:28.
[91] *Tallinn Manual* 102.
[92] ibid, 103.
[93] Convention (III) relative to the Treatment of Prisoners of War. Geneva, 12 August 1949.
[94] ibid.
[95] ibid. See also Schmitt, *CyCon 2012* (n 38) 20:16 et seq.
[96] *Tallinn Manual* 103 (emphasis added; capitals in original).

Nevertheless, however uncertain we may be as to what *levée en masse* looks like in cyberspace and how, in these specific situations, the law applies, what we *do* know is that 'inhabitants of unoccupied territory who engage in cyber operations as part of a *levée en masse* enjoy combatant immunity and prisoner of war status'.[97] It is hard to ascribe any meaning to this Rule, given the uncertainty expressed by the experts as to its application in concrete situations. What the *Manual* does is to set out what the provisions of the Third Geneva Convention *could* mean and what cyber operations *could* look like. In postulating the Rule, the *Manual* shows that it is possible to apply a concept of limited practical value to a scenario that may never occur, and thus it fulfils a reassuring function. It soothes those who are concerned about the revolutionary implications of cyber for the realm of law. Whatever possible reality will materialize in the future, the *Manual* contends, it remains possible to make sense of the world in terms of existing international law, including some of its most romantic provisions.

Compared to the sense of possibility as expressed by William Lynn and Thomas Rid, a few things stand out. While pointing out the threat faced by the United States, William Lynn argues that the United States has handled these kinds of scenarios before, and that it will do so again. Thus, though the kinds of scenarios portrayed in the *Manual* and those by Lynn are very different, the end result is the same; this is a situation that can be dealt with. Lynn's warning, paired with his pointing out of the measures already taken by the United States to protect itself against the threat, are similar to what the experts describe in the *Manual*. Having pointed out in their introduction the lack of specific rules, the experts conclude that 'This uncertainty does not mean cyber operations exist in a normative void.'[98] 'Yes,' both Lynn and the experts seem to say, 'there is uncertainty, but here are the tools with which to tackle it.' This is completely opposed to Rid's analysis, who—that is, until the last phrase of his article—denies the existence of uncertainty in the first place.

3.4 Conclusion

This chapter has sketched the possible realities of cyberwar, in two very different debates. Whereas those involved in strategic and military studies argue about the 'actual' possibility of cyberwar, imposing their own categories on the world in the attempt, the *Tallinn Manual* discusses these possibilities in legal terms. What these discussions have in common, however, is that both invoke history to make sense of the future of cyberwar. In the case of Lynn and Rid, cyberwar is portrayed as a phenomenon that is part of a familiar pattern; we have seen these major transformations before, so all that is required is preparedness.[99] Alternately, a major break with the past is unlikely; what we have called 'war' before certainly will not suddenly change face.[100]

[97] For a similar critique, see Roscini, *Cyber Operations and the Use of Force* (n 40) and Hollis, 'New Tools, New Rules' (n 44).

[98] *Tallinn Manual* 5.

[99] Lynn, *Defending a New Domain* (n 11).

[100] Rid, 'Cyber War Will Not Take Place' (n 24).

On the one hand, the imagination of the *Tallinn Manual* is not that different from its counterparts in military studies. It also imagines the future through the lens of history, although it should be emphasized that it does so through a very particular reading of the past. It only includes past decisions and practices that have found their way into established international legal sources such as treaties, customary law, judicial decisions, and so on. On the other hand, the *Manual* is radically different in its portrayal of the future. It is not concerned with the likelihood of future events as such, but first and foremost with the applicability of legal provisions. The leading question is not 'What is likely to happen?' but rather 'What would the application of this provision in future cases look like?'

This posture is not unique to the *Manual*. Other writing on cyberwar and international law contains similar conclusions: the way the law is applied might, at the moment, be uncertain, but other existing laws apply; and even if they do not, customary or treaty law will develop to bridge the gap between these different scenarios and the ability of existing law to deal with them properly. 'Fortunately,' one of these works concludes, after having stated that the development of this extra set of rules is 'unlikely', 'the lack of a cyber war addendum to the laws of war does not mean that cyber attacks are unregulated. States may continue to rely on the existing regime of international law to regulate cyber attacks, while they await the international community's response to this modern form of waging battle.'[101] This echoes the way in which the future is imagined in the *Tallinn Manual*; as that which could possibly trigger the applicability of age-old rules. However new and revolutionary cyber technologies may be, imagining their reality through law confirms that, at the end of the day, our futures are covered by pre-existing rules.

[101] M Gervais, 'Cyber Attacks and the Laws of War' (2012) 30 *Berkeley Journal of International Law* 525, 579.

4

Maritime Security

Douglas Guilfoyle

4.1 Introduction

This chapter considers maritime security and how we imagine the future and assess, respond to, and distribute risk as a matter of international law within that field. Maritime security, from the perspective of international law, is principally a question of the international law of the sea. We must therefore begin by considering the relationship of the law of the sea to questions of risk and security and, moreover, questioning whether the law of the sea itself contains a vision of the future, or even the tools for imagining one.

A basic difficulty is the lack of a common definition of 'maritime security'.[1] The term can encompass terrorism, piracy, 'smuggling, counter-proliferation, human food security',[2] military activities at sea, intelligence gathering (or 'maritime domain awareness'),[3] climate change, bio-prospecting, and the vulnerability of submarine communication cables.[4] The list of possible subject matters is inexhaustible and capable of change[5] and they are not necessarily governed by any (or any common) method of risk assessment.

My device for exploring these questions will be that of the 'transnational security state'. My contention is that in an increasingly borderless and de-territorialized, world states are not merely threatened by a growing range of transnational actors whose actions impinge upon their autonomy, but are also able to project power beyond their borders, especially into the maritime domain. In this context the question arises: who assesses which risks should be countered and how is that assessment carried out? The 'who' consists of government decision-makers in maritime affairs and transnational policy networks consisting of such decision-makers, international

[1] N Klein, *Maritime Security and the Law of the Sea* (OUP 2011) 2.

[2] D Guilfoyle, *Shipping Interdiction and the Law of the Sea* (CUP 2009) 24.

[3] Klein, *Maritime Security* (n 1) Chapters 2 and 5; compare D Guilfoyle, 'Maritime Security' in J Barrett and R Barnes (eds), *Law of the Sea: UNCLOS as a Living Instrument* (British Institute of International and Comparative Law 2016) Chapter 12.

[4] General Assembly Resolution on Oceans and the Law of the Sea, UN Doc A/RES/65/37A (7 December 2010).

[5] Klein, *Maritime Security* (n 1) 319–21.

civil servants, academics, and non-governmental organizations and industry representatives. As to the 'how', the simple answer is that there is no generally accepted methodology for assessing maritime security risks. In the maritime domain measures adopted to address perceived threats follow a logic more of securitization than any analysis of the probability of threats or cost–benefit analysis of measures adopted. Risk identification appears driven by worst-case scenarios (as in the case of terrorism) and the reframing of genuine challenges to maritime order as existential threats to state security (such as Somali pirates and maritime mass migration). As a consequence, the very real costs of securitization in the maritime domain are often borne by vulnerable groups such as seafarers and irregular maritime migrants.

This chapter begins by first considering the extent to which the law of the sea contains a vision of the future or risk assessment tools of its own, its relationship to maritime security, and its openness to securitization. It then proceeds by way of a biopsy, selecting a number of case studies from an otherwise broad field. Certain issues in the literature will be omitted. These notably include the field of intelligence gathering and weapons proliferation (including weapons of mass destruction (WMD) and their precursors), which have been extensively discussed (including by the present author) elsewhere.[6] The case studies chosen here will try to illustrate the manner in which maritime security has shifted the burden of risk from states onto humans, especially those people in transnational or liminal spaces. It thus focuses on three themes: seafarers, migrants, and private violence at sea (pirates and private security).

4.2 The Law of the Sea: Future Visions, Risk Assessment, and Securitization

4.2.1 Future-making and change in the law of the sea

At times the law of the sea appears only to have a past. The heroic era of future making in the law of the sea spanned the period from Ambassador Pardo's famous 1967 speech on the common heritage of mankind to the conclusion, after nine years of negotiation, of the Law of the Sea Convention (LOSC) in 1982.[7] The innovations of this era were extraordinary. The concept of the archipelagic state was born, the Exclusive Economic Zone crystallized into custom and, profoundly influenced by the New International Economic Order, a regime for the international management of deep seabed resources was devised. These developments did embody a vision for the future: a comprehensive legal regime for ocean affairs paying equal attention to the concerns of developing states. That vision was not entirely divorced from security. The LOSC's drafters might well have considered that much of the

[6] Klein, *Maritime Security* (n 1); D Guilfoyle, 'Counter Proliferation Activities and Freedom of Navigation' in MH Nordquist et al (eds), *Freedom of Navigation and Globalization* (Brill 2015), Chapter 3; CH Allen, *Maritime Counterproliferation Operations and the Rule of Law* (Prager 2007).

[7] United Nations Convention on the Law of the Sea (adopted 10 December 1982, entered into force 16 November 1994) 1833 UNTS 3 (LOSC).

Convention concerned resource security or the balancing of coastal state security and navigational freedoms.

Even three decades after the LOSC's conclusion its gravitational pull on the international law of the sea remains enormous. With 166 parties and major non-parties such as the United States accepting much of it as custom, it is simply *the* logical starting point for discussion of almost any topic regarding the law of the sea, despite preceding and subsequent legal developments.

The very scale of the LOSC and the length of its negotiation underlines the fact that effective law making as regards the maritime domain requires significant multilateral buy-in. New instruments serving a narrow agenda are unlikely to be widely ratified. Indeed, given the unified character of ocean space, without widespread ratification new treaties will generally be of little use. The International Maritime Organization (IMO) can be an effective forum for legal change, but the very effectiveness of that organization in promoting technical and safety standards may lie in its conservative vision of itself as a facilitative and member-driven organization. The spaces in which to radically re-imagine the law of the sea 'from within' are thus few. The usual view is that the capacity to take an evolutionary view of the LOSC as a 'constitution for the oceans' is, at best, limited.[8]

4.2.2 Risk assessment and securitization in the law of the sea

Certainly, some areas of the law of the sea do involve risk assessment as commonly understood.[9] 'Due diligence' obligations of environmental protection have been found to apply to deep seabed mining and exploration activities occurring beyond national jurisdiction;[10] fisheries law has always acknowledged the risk of over-exploitation of stocks whether through the anthropocentric 'maximum sustainable yield' standard or the more modern application of the precautionary principle.[11] Risk-assessment-oriented rules, however, are not a pervasive feature of the LOSC.

'Maritime security' arose not from within the limited conception of risk assessment found within the law of the sea, but rather from exogenous concerns projected into the maritime domain, principally the perceived threat of terrorism

[8] See, generally, A Boyle, 'Further Development of the 1982 Law of the Sea Convention: Mechanisms for Change' (2005) 54 *International and Comparative Law Quarterly* 563.

[9] As a technical process of risk–benefit analysis that guides societal decision-making, see P Slovic, *The Perception of Risk* (Earthscan 2000) 40–50.

[10] *Responsibilities and Obligations of States with Respect to Activities in the Area, Advisory Opinion*, 1 February 2011, ITLOS Reports 2011, 10, paras 117–20; D French, 'From the Depths: Rich Pickings of Principles of Sustainable Development and General International Law on the Ocean Floor' (2011) 26 *The International Journal of Marine and Coastal Law* 525.

[11] Contrast LOSC art 61(3); and United Nations Agreement for the Implementation of the Provisions of the United Nations Convention on the Law of the Sea of 10 December 1982 relating to the Conservation and Management of Straddling Fish Stocks and Highly Migratory Fish Stocks (adopted 4 December 1995, entered into force 11 December 2001) 2167 UNTS 88, arts 5(c) and 6. See: R Barnes, 'The Convention on the Law of the Sea: An Effective Framework for Domestic Fisheries Conservation?' in D Freestone et al (eds), *The Law of the Sea: Progress and Prospects* (OUP 2006) 233–60.

following 11 September 2001.[12] There is thus no single 'law of maritime security'.[13] Rather, it is an instance of 'securitization' applied across various aspects of the law of the sea.[14] September 11 was taken to reveal the potential vulnerability of global maritime trade and offshore infrastructure to terrorism (infrastructure being seen principally as a target,[15] while shipping could be potentially either a target of or a vector for terrorist attack). This resulted in such measures as the International Ship and Port Facility Security Code (ISPS Code), efforts to counter the threat of proliferation of WMD by sea or the use of ships as 'floating bombs', and reforms to information gathering and sharing about international ship movements.[16]

Maritime security law, in a narrow counter-terrorism sense, has simply evolved in response to projected catastrophic or existential threats detached from any meaningful assessment of their probability, or even technical feasibility.[17] There are good reasons to believe that maritime targets are of little interest to most terrorist groups. The maritime domain is inherently an unstable and uncertain environment requiring specialized skills to bring a complex operation to fruition. Given that terrorist organizations are generally conservative in their methods (in order to maximize their chances of success) and typically favour highly visible targets, the threat of maritime terrorism is generally considered remote.[18] Nonetheless, on the basis of limited evidence that catastrophic terrorist attacks on port facilities are likely, considerable changes have been made to the international port security regime, as discussed below.

If there is no good answer to 'how' risk assessment is performed in the field of maritime security, the next question to address is 'who' is doing it and under what conditions.

[12] Terrorism (and maritime terrorism) clearly predate 2001. The *Achille Lauro* incident famously prompted development of the Convention for the Suppression of Unlawful Acts against the Safety of Maritime Navigation (adopted 10 March 1988, entered into force 1 March 1992) 1678 UNTS 201. See: M Halberstam, 'Terrorism on the High Seas: The *Achille Lauro*, Piracy and the IMO Convention on Maritime Safety' (1988) 82 *American Journal of International Law* 269. The term 'maritime security' also predates 2001: see eg the *Merchant Shipping and Maritime Security Act 1997* (UK); and isolated scholarly references, eg 'The Brazilian Slave Traders' (1846) 4 *Law Magazine: Or Quarterly Review of Jurisprudence* 251, 256.

[13] Klein, *Maritime Security* (n 1) 2.

[14] Klein, *Maritime Security* (n 1) 4–11. The classic Copenhagen School work is B Buzan, O Wæver, and J de Wilde, *Security: A New Framework for Analysis* (Lynne Rienner 1998) 25.

[15] On oil platforms, see A Harel, 'Preventing Terrorist Attacks on Offshore Platforms: Do States Have Sufficient Legal Tools?' (2012) 4 *Harvard National Security Journal* 131; and Stuart Kaye, 'International Measures To Protect Oil Platforms, Pipelines, and Submarine Cables from Attack' (2007) 31 *Tulane Maritime Law Journal* 377.

[16] Klein, *Maritime Security* (n 1) 1; Guilfoyle, 'Maritime Security' (n 3).

[17] On worst-case scenarios and probability neglect, see C Sunstein, *Laws of Fear: Beyond the Precautionary Principle* (CUP 2005) Chapter 3.

[18] P Chalk, *The Maritime Dimension of International Security: Terrorism, Piracy, and Challenges for the United States* (Rand 2008) 19–20; Martin Murphy, *Small Boats, Weak States, Dirty Money: Piracy and Maritime Terrorism in the Modern World* (Hurst 2009) 262.

4.3 The Transnational Security State and Maritime Security

A familiar theme in international law scholarship has long been the threat posed by globalization to various 'old' conceptions of sovereignty, principally in the economic sphere.[19,20] More recently it has been common to perceive 'old' territorial and exclusionary sovereignty being challenged by 'new' transnational forces (multinational corporations,[21] transnational terrorism) to which it is poorly adapted to respond. On this account, states face declining economic autonomy on the one hand, while the military might they have amassed to check the ambitions of other states has, on the other, shown only a limited ability to deter and disrupt 'asymetrical' actors such as transnational terrorist groups.[22] Similarly, irregular mass migration can be seen as a form of 'globalization from below', which challenges territorial conceptions of state security.[23] Indeed, the irregular migrant is globalization in human form; a person who moves without regard to formal boundaries and participates in a 'translocal' economy, possibly working in a migrant diaspora abroad and remitting money to a home community.[24]

The security state which must respond to these transnational threats to its autonomy and interests appears to exist in a borderless, de-territorialized world and to be threatened by it. Such concerns might only be thought to be heightened in the maritime domain, which is in many senses the original globalized space and still the principal platform for international trade. However, in the face of such forces the state has not withered away. Rather, in an increasingly porous and transnational world, states, too, are able to project their authority beyond their borders in a range of non-war contexts. We see this in the increasing externalization of US customs/security requirements into foreign ports through the Container Security Initiative,[25] maritime migrant interdiction operations

[19] The 'transnational security state' is further discussed in: D Guilfoyle, 'Transnational Crime and the Rule of Law at Sea: Responses to Maritime Migration and Piracy Compared' in Violeta Moreno-Lax and Efthymios Papastavridis (eds), *'Boat Refugees' and Migrants at Sea: Integrating Maritime Security with Human Rights'* (Brill 2016), Chapter 7.

[20] JH Jackson, 'Sovereignty-Modern: A New Approach to an Outdated Concept' (2003) 97 *American Journal of International Law* 782, 784.

[21] For a literature survey, see SM Tarzi, 'Multinational Corporations and American Foreign Policy: Radical, Sovereignty-at-Bay, and State-Centric Approaches' (1991) 28 *International Studies* 359.

[22] H Behr, 'Political Territoriality and De-Territorialization' (2007) 39 *Area* 112, 113–14.

[23] D Guilfoyle, 'Transnational Criminal Law as a Governance Strategy in the Global Labour Market: Criminalizing Globalization from Below' (2010) 29 *Refugee Survey Quarterly* 185; see also GS Goodwin-Gill, 'The Right to Seek Asylum: Interception at Sea and the Principle of *Non-Refoulement*' (2011) 23 *International Journal of Refugee Law* 443, 447.

[24] S Sassen, *Territory, Authority, Rights: From Medieval to Global Assemblages* (Princeton UP 2008) 1–3.

[25] Klein, *Maritime Security* (n 1) 163–67.

conducted by various developed states, and in the response to Somali (and, increasingly, West African) piracy.

'Transnational' is the term chosen in this chapter to describe state activities in the maritime domain which target the real and perceived 'threats' posed by actors such as pirates, terrorists, migrants, and (seemingly) seafarers. First, the actors targeted themselves are transnational; they move across borders and between states often in manners challenging local authority or control. Second, international law, at least as a formal matter, concerns binding and reciprocal legal commitments between juridically equal states.[26] When powerful states combat transnational threats, the instruments of choice are often non-legal, non-reciprocal, target individuals, or effectively treat other states as subservient.

The survey here begins with measures which may seem, however, most like traditional international law; IMO measures adopted after September 11. However, examining the securitization of ships and ports leads us quite rapidly to the impact of these risk-management measures on a vulnerable and inherently transnational population: seafarers.

4.4 Seafarers and Maritime Security

4.4.1 The International Ship and Port Facility Security Code (ISPS Code)

The ISPS Code should, in theory, be the pre-eminent risk assessment tool in the field of maritime security. In simple terms:

> [The] International Ship and Port Facility Security Code … , adopted in December 2002, entered into force on 1 July 2004, is a comprehensive set of measures to enhance the security of ships and port facilities, developed in response to the perceived threats to ships and port facilities in the wake of the 9/11 attacks in the United States. The ISPS Code is implemented through chapter XI-2 on special measures to enhance maritime security in the International Convention for the Safety of Life at Sea (SOLAS), 1974.[27]

The Code's implementation under the SOLAS Convention benefitted from the IMO's tacit amendment procedure; that is, it binds all parties to the SOLAS Convention unless they specifically objected prior to the Code's entry into force.[28] Thus the Code binds 162 SOLAS parties and covers over ninety-eight per cent of world shipping by tonnage.[29]

[26] S Humphreys, *Theatre of the Rule of Law: Transnational Legal Intervention in Theory and Practice* (CUP 2010) 10.

[27] M Tsamenyi and K-D Ali, 'African States and the Law of the Sea Convention: Have the Benefits Been Realized?' (2012) 26 *Ocean Yearbook* 113, 144 n 168.

[28] J Harrison, *Making the Law of the Sea: A Study in the Development of International Law* (CUP 2011) 161–63.

[29] See <http://www.imo.org/About/Conventions/StatusOfConventions/Pages/Default.aspx> accessed 14 December 2015.

The Code views ship and port security as 'a risk management activity':[30]

> Under the Code Contracting Governments are required to ensure security information is provided to port facilities and ships prior to entering a port .... Three security levels apply. Additionally, ships and owners are required to establish ship security plans and act upon the security levels set by governments. Moreover, a port facility security assessment must be [periodically] undertaken and ... may culminate in the development of a port facility security plan.[31]

The ISPS Code requires ports and ships to take measures according to risk levels set by the contracting government. The Code was, in part, intended 'to provide a methodology for security assessments so as to have in place plans and procedures to react to changing security levels'.[32] It achieves the latter goal better than the former. While stipulating matters to be taken into account in setting a risk level (normal, heightened, or exceptional)[33] and while requiring contracting governments to share relevant information, no particular risk assessment methodology is mandated by the Code. In practice, then, much is left to individual governments.[34] Further, governments may target potentially non-existent or hypothetical threats though measures going beyond the Code. These can transfer significant maritime security costs to the shipping industry and, in particular, seafarers.

4.4.2 The status of seafarers

The status of seafarers is extensively regulated by the IMO and the International Labour Organization (ILO).[35] The ISPS Code and other national security measures set the stage for conflicts between the 'strict and robust implementation of the new [state-centred] security regime' and seafarer interests.[36] There is clearly a risk that seafarers may be 'penalized' by 'excessive concerns about security'.[37]

Seafarers' right to shore-leave is a particular flashpoint. Seafarers may spend long periods at sea and subsequent 'mental and physical exhaustion' can jeopardize seafarer welfare and ship safety.[38] Seafarer and shipping industry organizations all view shore leave 'as an important seafarer right and also a safety and efficiency issue'.[39]

[30] 'IMO 2004: Focus on Maritime Security' [2004] (3) *IMO News* 13, 16.

[31] A McKinnon, 'Administrative Shortcomings and Their Legal Implications in the Context of Safe Ports' (2009) 23 *Australian and New Zealand Maritime Law Journal* 186, 187–88.

[32] Conference Resolution 2: Adoption of the International Code for the Security of Ships and of Port Facilities, IMO Doc SOLAS/CONF.5/34 (17 December 2002) para 1.2.4.

[33] ibid, para 1.8.

[34] See, eg, *Maritime Transport and Offshore Facilities Security Act 2003* (Australia) and its Regulations. Neither stipulates a methodology.

[35] This section draws substantially upon material published in Guilfoyle, 'Maritime Security' (n 3).

[36] R Balkin, 'The International Maritime Organization and Maritime Security' (2006) 30 *Tulane Maritime Law Journal* 1, 32.

[37] ibid. [38] ibid.

[39] US Government Accountability Office, 'Maritime Security: Federal Agencies Have Taken Actions to Address Risks Posed by Seafarers, but Efforts Can Be Strengthened' (January 2011), GAO-11-195, 12 ('GAO Report') 47.

Nonetheless, as a security measure, some port states (especially the United States) have taken measures aimed at limiting visa-free shore leave.

Historically, under the Convention on Facilitation of International Maritime Traffic 1965 (Facilitation Convention)[40] seafarers have been entitled to take shore leave without a visa on production of a passport or a national seafarer's identity document in 115 states.[41] The Annex to the Facilitation Convention expressly provides as a 'standard' that crew members 'shall be allowed ashore' while in port and 'shall not be required to hold a visa for the purpose of shore leave'.[42] States parties are under an obligation to adopt such 'standards'.[43] Limited exceptions apply 'for reasons of public health, public safety or public order'.[44] However, under Article VIII, where a state 'finds it impracticable' to comply and adopts different 'requirements or procedures' it must notify the IMO. Such Article VIII notifications appear, in practice, to function as a derogation procedure.

The United States has taken two initiatives regarding the identification and mobility of seafarers. Unilaterally, it has restricted shore leave in the United States to those who obtain a visa at a US consulate prior to embarkation.[45] Multilaterally, it championed a revised ILO Convention on Seafarer Identification Documents (SID Convention).[46] The former would appear incompatible with the Facilitation Convention; the latter appears unlikely ever to be widely implemented.

Prior to 2004, the United States already required visas for shore leave but had a 'long-standing' system of issuing 'a single "crew list visa" for the entire crew'.[47] This was revoked in 2004 in favour of requiring seafarers to apply for visas in person and prior to departure. However, 'seafarers do not always know in advance' the ports at which their 'vessels may call',[48] making it 'often impractical to obtain visas in advance'.[49] The US visa process now involves: a pre-departure consulate interview; having biometric data (fingerprints) recorded; background checks against US databases; and a US $140 application fee.[50] The United States considers that this process constitutes 'an important layer of border security to prevent terrorists, illegal immigrants, and criminals from gaining entry'.[51] Similarly, Australia now requires maritime crew visas for seafarers to take shore leave.[52]

[40] Convention on Facilitation of International Maritime Traffic (adopted 9 April 1965, entered into force 5 March 1967) 591 UNTS 265 (Facilitation Convention). For member states, see <http://www.imo.org/en/About/Conventions/StatusOfConventions/Pages/Default.aspx> accessed 16 November 2016.

[41] Facilitation Convention, Annex, paras 3.10–3.10.3 and 3.45.

[42] ibid, Annex, para 3.45. [43] ibid, art I and VI(a). [44] ibid, Annex, para 3.44.

[45] ILO, 'Third and Fourth Informal Special Sittings on Improved Security of Seafarers' Identity Documents' (4–5 February 2003), ILO Doc SSSID/2003/1, para 9; and 'Informal Special Sitting on Improved Security of Seafarers' Identity Documents' (25 June 2002), ILO Doc SSSID/2002/1, para 9.

[46] Klein, *Maritime Security* (n 1) 236.

[47] DB Stevenson, 'The Burden that 9-11 Imposed on Seafarers' (2002–2003) 77 *Tulane Law Review* 1407, 1412 (see also Sassen, *Territory, Authority, Rights*, n 24).

[48] Stevenson, ibid.

[49] ILO, 'Consultation Meeting on Improved Security of Seafarers' Identification' (9–10 May 2002), ILO Doc CMISSI/2002, Appendix 3 ('ILO Consultation Meeting 2002').

[50] GAO Report (n 39) 8, 14, and 16. [51] GAO Report (n 39) 40.

[52] IMO Doc FAL.3/Circ 189 (6 June 2007).

Restrictions have also been applied by European Schengen Convention countries, but these may still allow seafarers visa-free shore leave in municipalities in a port's immediate vicinity.[53] The impact of such measures on seafarers is real. As many as 17 per cent of all seafarers are now denied US shore-leave and are confined to their vessels.[54]

The United States also considers it '*imperative* to ensure that *no* seafarer poses a threat to the safety and security of the maritime industry' (emphasis added).[55] Thus it has campaigned for a universal system of 'positive verifiable [seafarers] identification documents' containing biometric data and coupled with background checks.[56] The United States was thus instrumental in the push to negotiate the revised 2003 SID Convention.[57] Historically, in the ILO's experience, numerous immigration authorities worldwide are frequently unable to determine if any particular nationally issued SID 'is genuine or counterfeit'.[58] The SID Convention requires member states to issue biometric SIDs and maintain a national database capable of responding to other member states' enquiries regarding the 'authenticity and validity' of SID documents.[59] This would obviously be a significant improvement in the security of SIDs.

However, the SID Convention also provides that holders of such a biometric SID *must* be admitted by port states without a visa.[60] In contrast to Facilitation Convention obligations, this obligation is non-derogable. This acknowledges both the importance of shore leave and the enhanced security provided by biometric SIDs. However, if a member state cannot give effect to this no-visa requirement, seafarers may be admitted under 'substantially equivalent' arrangements.[61] This provision was intended to accommodate the United States.[62] Nonetheless, the visa-free shore leave requirement has proven an obstacle to the United States ratifying the SID Convention.[63]

4.4.3 Conclusion

While the SID Convention appears to strike an appropriate balance between state security and the interests of seafarers, only twenty-eight states have ratified it.[64]

[53] See, eg, IMO Doc FAL.3/Circ 208 (1 November 2011) (Finland).

[54] Seamen's Church Institute Center for Seafarers' Rights, '2015 Seafarer Shore Leave Survey', 28 July 2015 <http://seamenschurch.org/article/2015-seafarer-shore-leave-survey> accessed 20 December 2016.

[55] United States, 'Consideration of Proposals and Information on Maritime Security Issues: Measures to Improve Maritime Security', IMO Doc MSC 75/ISWG/5/7 (15 January 2002) para 13.

[56] ibid.

[57] Seafarers' Identity Documents Convention (Revised) 2003 (adopted 19 June 2003, entered into force 9 February 2005) 2304 UNTS 121 (SID Convention).

[58] ILO, 'Consultation Meeting on Improved Security of Seafarers' Identification: Briefing Paper', ILO Doc CMISSI/2002/BR (9–10 May 2002) para 7.

[59] SID Convention, art 3(8). [60] ibid, art 6(4) and (6). [61] ibid, Art 6(6).

[62] GAO Report (n 39) 40. [63] ibid.

[64] See ILO, 'Ratifications of C185—Seafarers' Identity Documents Convention (Revised) 2003 (No 185) <http://www.ilo.org/dyn/normlex/en/f?p=1000:11300:0::NO:11300:P11300_INSTRUMENT_ID:312330> accessed 20 December 2016.

The reasons for this include the expense (especially for developing countries) of implementing a biometric SID system[65] as well as problems of compatibility with national privacy laws.[66] Further, unless major port states are willing to provide visa-free shore leave, it is hard to see why states with large numbers of seafaring nationals should assume the costs of the SID Convention.[67] Indeed, without this crucial benefit, biometric SID requirements may appear stigmatizing or punitive. While seafarers should be treated as 'partners in the fight against terrorism',[68] they all too often perceive themselves treated as potential terrorists.[69]

4.5 Migrants and Irregular Migration by Sea

4.5.1 Introduction

As discussed above, irregular migration may be seen as a form of 'globalisation from below'.[70] Historically, the evidence is that irregular, undocumented migration provides a host of well-known advantages to a receiving economy and displaces relatively little native labour.[71] Irregular migration thus plays a role in a globalized economy for low-skilled labour and may certainly be seen as a transnational force challenging state autonomy. However, the rhetoric surrounding irregular migration seems increasingly to be less about economic concerns and more a question of the perceived threat to the symbolic integrity of developed states' territorial sovereignty and national borders.[72]

Nonetheless, despite the rhetoric of threat and vulnerability, irregular migration by sea provides a ready theatre for the projection of power by developed states over vulnerable individuals. On the one hand, the best rationale for intercepting overcrowded migrant boats is that it saves lives.[73] On the other, persons intercepted at sea by a foreign government are non-citizens clothed only in the 'abstract nakedness of being human';[74] as such they often enjoy little effective human rights protection.[75] In such situations, there is a temptation for governments to devise legal strategies

[65] See, eg, GAO Report (n 39) 47; ILO, 'Second Informal Special Sitting on Improved Security of Seafarers' Identity Documents' (17 October 2002), ILO Doc SSSID/2002/2, para 18.

[66] GAO Report (n 39) 44.

[67] ILO, 'Consultations on the Seafarers' Identity Documents Convention (Revised), 2003 (No 185)', ILO Doc CSID/C.185/2010/4 (23–24 September 2010) para 11 (statement by Canada, Greece, Indonesia, Malaysia, Namibia, Norway, Korea, and Russia) para 14 (Iran), para 16 (Namibia), para 33 (spokesperson for seafarers), and Appendix I.

[68] Balkin, 'The International Maritime Organisation' (n 36) 33.

[69] ILO, 'Consultation on the Seafarers' Identity Documents Convention' (n 67) para 8.

[70] The following section draws on Guilfoyle, 'Transnational Crime and the Rule of Law at Sea' (n 19).

[71] See the literature reviewed in Guilfoyle, 'Transnational Criminal Law' (n 23).

[72] See, eg, on Australia, T Leslie et al, 'Operation Sovereign Borders: The First Six Months', ABC News, 26 March 2014 <http://www.abc.net.au/news/interactives/operation-sovereign-borders-the-first-6-months/> accessed 20 December 2016.

[73] G Palmer, 'Guarding the Coast: Alien Migrant Interdiction Operations at Sea' (1997) 29 *Connecticut Law Review* 1565, 1572–73.

[74] H Arendt, *The Origins of Totalitarianism* (Harcourt 1973) 297.

[75] A Kesby, *The Right to Have Rights: Citizenship, Humanity and International Law* (OUP 2012) 3.

that fragment or displace human rights protections by insisting only certain rights are engaged or that responsibility for protection lie elsewhere. Intercepted migrants at sea, therefore, risk bearing the full brunt of the security states' powers with minimal effective protections.

The point can be made relatively briefly with reference to Spanish/EU operations since 2007 to prevent migrant departures from Mauritania or Senegal by boat in operation *Hera* and Italian push-back practices in the Mediterranean in 2009 (and both before and since), as challenged in *Hirsi*. The question then arises whether these approaches, at least in Europe, have been modified in response to the case law of the European Court of Human Rights (ECtHR). Of particular note in relation to the present maritime migration crisis in the Mediterranean are the Frontex regulation of 2014, the establishment of EUNAVFOR MED in 2015, and UN Security Council Resolution 2240, adopted in October 2015, which provides additional legal support for interdicting migrant smuggling vessels in the Mediterranean.

4.5.2 Operation *Hera*

Operation *Hera*'s practical significance has declined since the opening up of the migration route through Libya to the Mediterranean; nonetheless, it has a number of notable legal features.[76] First, it involved interceptions in the territorial sea and contiguous zone of the states of migrant departure. These interceptions ostensibly occur under technical agreements concluded in 2007 below the level of treaty law between Spain and Senegal or Mauritania.[77] These agreements were also non-reciprocal; no Senegalese or Mauritanian patrolling in Spanish waters was contemplated. Second, it involved the deployment of personnel/resources from other EU member states to assist Spanish operations under the auspices of the EU border agency Frontex and its Rapid Border Intervention Taskforce regulation. Third, a degree of legal uncertainty surrounds the precise basis for this Frontex participation, given that it is not actually a party to the relevant technical agreements between Spain and its 'partner' states.[78] Finally, the operations involve the participation of coastal state law-enforcement officials ('shipriders'), who apparently direct and control the return of vessels intercepted in a relevant territorial sea or contiguous zone to shore.

Collaborative territorial sea operations might take a variety of forms and may also be conducted under bilateral treaty relationships. In a different context—the practice of joint patrols between Italy and Libya in Libyan waters (discussed further below)—'Italy stress[ed] the joint nature of patrols and the treaty basis for Libya's responsibility for the migrants' while apparently taking care to avoid 'actual physical contact' with intercepted migrants.[79] In territorial sea operations (whatever

[76] See E Papastavridis, *The Interception of Vessels on the High Seas* (Bloomsbury 2013) 286–91; V Moreno-Lax, 'Asylum in the Mediterranean: Against a Fragmentary Reading of EU Member States' Obligations Accruing at Sea' (2011) 23 *International Journal of Refugee Law* 174.

[77] Papastavridis, ibid, 288.

[78] ibid.

[79] Goodwin-Gill, 'The Right to Seek Asylum' (n 23) 453.

their exact legal basis), the question might be thought to arise whether a patrolling state can disclaim responsibility on the basis that all actions are performed under the authority of the coastal state (or an international organization). It is a question capable of a direct answer; unless foreign state assets and personnel have been placed 'at the disposal' of the coastal state,[80] in the sense that the latter 'exercises exclusive command and control',[81] then joint liability may arise.[82] Indeed, as Papastavridis notes, in such operations it is not the patrolling state that is at the disposal of the coastal state, 'rather the opposite is the case'.[83] The basic proposition remains that state organs when acting extraterritorially must refrain from acts or omissions which would violate their duties under international law; and if they act wrongfully, international responsibility arises.[84]

Nonetheless, within the framework of such operations there may be an attempt to 'fragment' the applicable law, through assertions that the relevant duties either do not apply in practice or the duty to ensure compliance rests with another state.[85] On the first issue, the case is sometimes made that rescue operations, especially on the high seas, do not engage further human rights responsibilities, even when the rescue was conducted by government forces. This argument is put either on the basis that the relevant rights do not apply extra-territorially (a proposition that is increasingly untenable in most contexts), or on the basis that the degree of physical control exercised over a rescued person is not such as to bring them within the 'jurisdiction' of a state actor.

On the second point, the argument may be attempted that in joint territorial sea operations any *non-refoulement* obligations bind only the coastal state; the reasoning being that such obligations only apply once an individual has left the territory of a state where he or she faces persecution. The most obvious problem with such reasoning is that it presumes that such persons face no persecution within the coastal state and/or are its nationals and face no danger of being transferred from its territory to a place of persecution. Such a conclusion could only validly be reached in individual cases following a case-by-case status determination.

4.5.3 Italian push-back operations as challenged in *Hirsi*

The *Hirsi* case involved the rescue on the high seas of a group of Somali and Eritrean migrants who were transferred onto Italian warships and returned to Tripoli.[86] As in other cases (such as US practice in the Caribbean), the duty of rescue was used de facto as a means of intercepting migrants.[87] No consideration was given in the planning of the operation to *non-refoulement* obligations under Article 3 of the

[80] Article 6, International Law Commission (ILC) Articles on Responsibility of States for Internationally Wrongful Acts, 53 UN GAOR Supp. (No 10), 43; UN Doc A/56/83 (2001) (ILC Articles).

[81] E Papastavridis, '"Fortress Europe" and FRONTEX: Within or Without International Law?' (2010) 79 *Nordic Journal of International Law* 75, 107.

[82] ILC Articles, art 47.

[83] Papastavridis, 'Fortress Europe' (n 81) 107.

[84] Goodwin-Gill, 'The Right to Seek Asylum' (n 23) 447.

[85] Moreno-Lax, 'Asylum in the Mediterranean' (n 76).

[86] *Hirsi Jamaa and Others v Italy* App No 27765/09 (ECHR 23 February 2012) paras 9–10.

[87] Guilfoyle, *Shipping Interdiction* (n 2) 195.

European Convention on Human Rights (ECHR); and the ECtHR also found a violation of Article 4 of Protocol 4 on collective expulsions, as well as a failure to provide access to a remedy with automatic suspensive effect as required under Article 13.

Italy's position was that it did not owe extraterritorial Convention obligations to the intercepted migrants because they had not come within its authority and control. Moreno-Lax, in particular, has drawn attention to the rhetorical division asserted here by Italy (and elsewhere by other EU states)[88] between *rescue* at sea and *law enforcement* at sea.[89] Rescue is presented as an *involuntary* act resulting from compliance with a duty; as opposed to a *voluntary* assertion of jurisdiction for law-enforcement or migration control purposes. In *Hirsi,* Italy argued that the act of rescue involved neither a relevant intention to assert law-enforcement jurisdiction nor a sufficient degree of physical coercion to trigger established ECHR case law on circumstances in which an individual can come within the extra-territorial de facto 'authority and control' of a state.[90] The Court found that the *de jure* control Italy exercised aboard its warship was decisive irrespective of the minimal physical control actually exercised over individuals. This, and later cases, appear to demonstrate a trend towards reducing the threshold of control required for Convention rights to be engaged.[91]

Nonetheless, it may be premature to conclude that *Hirsi* spells the end of 'extra-territorial migration governance' as it is presently practiced.[92] Such a view likely underestimates the determination and legal ingenuity of states. Discussion of off-shore containment and processing of refugee flows in Africa has already surfaced,[93] and there are clear parallels to certain aspects of the Australian offshore 'Pacific solution' to irregular migration by sea.[94]

Hirsi calls for one other observation. The finding that collective expulsions can occur beyond the frontier of a state is obviously principled, but it emphasizes the increasingly de-territorialized nature of state power and authority. In migrant interdiction operations at sea:

> we find states operating ... in a physical domain where borders, as we commonly understand them, simply do not exist—at sea, on the high seas, or even in the contiguous zone or territorial waters of other states, in fact, at notional or virtual borders reconstituted on the basis of national and regional interest..... [Patrolling States] project a non-territorial conception of national interests into a common or even a contested space ... [and] the fact that migrants and those in search of refuge may be obliged to cross the seas offers new opportunities for states now to project power and influence.[95]

[88] Moreno-Lax, 'Asylum in the Mediterranean' (n 76).

[89] V Moreno-Lax, '*Hirsi Jamaa and Others v Italy* or the Strasbourg Court versus Extraterritorial Migration Control?' (2012) 12 *Human Rights Law Review* 574, 579–582.

[90] ibid, 580–81. [91] ibid, 582.

[92] ibid; see, eg, *Jaloud v The Netherlands* App No 47708/08 (ECHR 20 November 2014) finding control over persons passing through a Dutch military checkpoint despite the Netherlands not being an occupying power.

[93] H Sherwood, H Smith, L Davies, and H Grant, 'Europe Faces "Colossal Humanitarian Catastrophe" of Refugees Dying at Sea', *The Guardian*, 2 June 2014 <http://www.theguardian.com/world/2014/jun/02/europe-refugee-crisis-un-africa-processing-centres> accessed 20 December 2016.

[94] Leslie et al, 'Operation Sovereign Borders' (n 72).

[95] Goodwin-Gill, 'The Right to Seek Asylum' (n 23) 447.

Not directly addressed in *Hirsi* was the Italian practice of direct cooperation with Libya under the Gaddafi regime over the 2004–2009 period (at least),[96] which involved joint patrolling in Libyan waters. Such questions of joint responsibility for operations of such a type were addressed in section 4.5.2 above.

4.5.4 The Frontex regulation 2014 and responses to the Mediterranean migrant crisis

Whether a more rights-sensitive approach will be taken in response to the present maritime migration crisis in the Mediterranean remains to be seen. One early encouraging sign came in the form of the Frontex regulation of 2014.[97] This applies to all Frontex-coordinated maritime border surveillance operations and applies a broad understanding of the *non-refoulement* principle (under both refugee and human rights law) to all such operations.[98] It includes detailed search and rescue and disembarkation obligations for participating law-enforcement vessels of member states.[99] In particular, it stresses that the duty of rescue must be discharged 'in accordance with international law and respect for fundamental rights'.[100] The regulation is clearly to be welcomed, particularly in its express acknowledgement of the content of applicable law and the need for clear methods and processes to give effect to a duty of rescue.

However, the Frontex regulation has not been the principal mechanism invoked in response to the present surge in Mediterranean migrant smuggling. Instead, in 2015, operation 'EUNAVFOR MED' was established by Decision of the European Council. The mission of EUNAVFOR MED is:

> disruption of the business model of human smuggling and trafficking networks in the Southern Central Mediterranean ..., achieved by undertaking systematic efforts to identify, capture and dispose of vessels and assets used or suspected of being used by smugglers or traffickers, in accordance with applicable international law, including UNCLOS and any UN Security Council Resolution.[101]

Encouragingly, the preamble refers to 'prevent[ing] human tragedies', 'prevent[ing] more people from dying at sea', and notes that the operation will be conducted in accordance with the Refugee Convention and respect for the principle of *non-refoulement* under human rights law.[102] It further notes the 'obligation to assist persons in distress at sea and to deliver survivors to a place of safety' and states that EUNAVFOR MED vessels 'will be ready and equipped to perform' rescue duties.[103]

[96] Moreno-Lax, '*Hirsi Jamaa and Others v Italy*' (n 89) 575–76; Guilfoyle, *Shipping Interdiction* (n 2) 214.

[97] Regulation No 656/2014 of the European Parliament and of the Council establishing rules for the surveillance of the external sea borders in the context of operational cooperation coordinated by the European Agency for the Management of Operational Cooperation at the External Borders of the Member States of the European Union [2014] OJ 189/93.

[98] ibid, arts 1 and 4. [99] ibid, arts 9 and 10. [100] ibid, art 9(1).

[101] Council Decision (CFSP) 2015/778 of 18 May 2015 on a European Union military operation in the Southern Central Mediterranean (EUNAVFOR MED) [2015] OJL 122/31, art 1.

[102] ibid, recitals 1–2. [103] ibid, recital 6.

Nonetheless, the placement of these references in the preamble, their absence from the mission statement, and the lack of supporting detail all suggest that the focus is on finding legal mechanisms to destroy boats involved in migrant smuggling rather than preparation for a major rescue-at-sea operation with well-thought-through procedures for treatment of rescued persons.[104]

Indeed, a similar approach is found in UN Security Council resolution 2240, which was intended to give further legal support to counter-migration operations in the Mediterranean. The resolution certainly reminds states of their existing obligations under human rights and refugee law.[105] However, the only substantive powers created or obligations imposed under the resolution concern rights of search and seizure over vessels on the high seas suspected of involvement in smuggling migrants.[106]

4.5.5 Conclusion

The field of maritime interdiction of migrants is one driven by fear of the transnational threat posed by irregular migration. The projection of state borders (for migration purposes) out to sea, or even into the territorial waters of other states, substantially re-allocates the legal risks involved in irregular migration. Self-serving readings of a state's human rights obligations may result in the fragmentation or dispersal of responsibility for compliance with those rights (in practice, if not in doctrine). The result is to place much of the risk squarely onto the shoulders of those intercepted. Beyond national territory and ready access to judicial remedies, such persons often find themselves reduced to the precarious 'bare humanity' of those lacking a protected status.[107] Indeed, this may be the result even if a person has a well-founded claim to international protection. There are good reasons for considering at-sea 'screening' of protected status claims to be manifestly inadequate (eg, lack of time to prepare one's case or, indeed, to recover from shock or trauma) and likely to result in the *refoulement* of those requiring international protection.[108] For the involuntarily rescued migrant, as a non-citizen confronted with the power of a foreign state, there is a distinct risk of human rights existing more as a matter of theory than practice.[109]

[104] See, eg, J Lehmann, 'The Use of Force Against People Smugglers: Conflicts with Refugee Law and Human Rights Law', *EJIL:Talk!*, 22 June 2015 <http://www.ejiltalk.org/the-use-of-force-against-people-smugglers-conflicts-with-refugee-law-and-human-rights-law/> accessed 1 January 2016.

[105] UN Doc S/RES/2240 (2015), preamble, paras 12–13.

[106] ibid, paras 7–8.

[107] Kesby, *The Right to Have Rights* (n 75) 30.

[108] United Nations High Commissioner for Refugees, 'High Commissioner's Dialogue on Protection Challenges: Protection at Sea', 11 November 2014, para 18 <http://www.unhcr.org/5464c3dc9.pdf> accessed 20 December 2016.

[109] S Parekh, 'Resisting "Dull and Torpid" Assent: Returning to the Debate Over the Foundations of Human Rights' (2007) 29 *Human Rights Quarterly* 754, 776.

4.6 The Fall of Somali Piracy and Rise of Private Armed Security

The international response to Somali piracy produced a substantial literature.[110] The dynamics at work in this context are (or were) interesting. Somali pirates were themselves transnational actors; operating outside the constraints of a conventionally functional state; they were able to attack the shipping of numerous flag states, thus committing economically motivated violent crimes subject to a variety of national jurisdictions—as well as being subject to universal jurisdiction under the customary international law of piracy. The shipping industry itself is also a transnational actor. Not only does ninety per cent of international trade move by sea, but a merchant ship may be flagged in one state, owned by a corporation in another state, crewed by seafarers of varying nationality and be chartered by an entity of a different nationality again. This transnational industry, to protect itself against pirates, facilitated the rise of a third class of transnational actor—private maritime security.

While the Somali piracy boom of 2008–2013 gave rise to a variety of legally innovative responses, none of these involved any formal change to the law of the sea as codified in the LOSC. Broadly the response involved:

- multinational naval patrolling in the Indian Ocean and the creation of an Internationally Recommended Transit Corridor to improve vessel safety in the 'high risk area' off Somalia;[111]
- naval patrols or operations within the territorial sea or territory of Somalia, authorized under Security Council Resolutions;
- the growth of a complex ecology of intergovernmental cooperation and informal coordination mechanisms, most notably the Contact Group on Piracy off the Coast of Somalia;[112]
- a renewed interest in state building within Somalia and engagement with the 'Puntland' and 'Somaliland' territorial entities/regional governments within Somalia;
- a horizontal set of arrangements to facilitate piracy prosecutions where suspect pirates might: (i) be apprehended by an 'international' warship; (ii) be transferred for prosecution before a 'regional' court (typically in Kenya or the Seychelles); and repatriated to serve sentences in internationally established and monitored 'national' Somali prisons;[113]

[110] Eg, R Geiss and A Petrig, *The Legal Framework for Counter-Piracy Operations in Somalia and the Gulf of Aden* (OUP 2011); D Guilfoyle (ed), *Modern Piracy: Legal Challenges and Responses* (Edward Elgar 2013); P Koutrakos and A Skordas (eds), *The Law and Practice of Piracy at Sea: European and International Perspectives* (Hart 2014).

[111] Geiss and Petrig, *The Legal Framework for Counter-Piracy Operations* (n 110) 27–28.

[112] C Bueger, 'Responses to Contemporary Piracy: Disentangling the Organizational Field' in Guilfoyle (ed), *Modern Piracy*, (n 110) Chapter 5.

[113] D Guilfoyle, 'Somali Pirates as Agents of Change in International Law-Making and Organisation' (2012) 1 *Cambridge Journal of International and Comparative Law* 81, 94–105.

- the development of highly effective 'soft law' mechanisms in the form of 'Best Management Practices', which consisted of practical advice on 'hardening' ships against pirate attacks and which were partially enforced by the insurance industry (ie, non-compliant ships attracted higher premiums); and
- the growth of an industry in privately contracted armed security personnel (PCASP), commonly credited with greatly reducing the instance of successful Somali pirate attacks.[114]

Despite the extraordinary scale of the response, the absolute risk to shipping was, even at the height of Somali piracy, low. In 2011 only 1.5 out of every 1,000 ships transiting the region were hijacked.[115] The risks for the seafarers aboard captured vessels were, potentially, catastrophic. As at 12 October 2015, twenty-six seafarers were still being held hostage by Somali pirates (there were 656 hostages held at 31 December 2010).[116] However, such detention can last years, often on a subsistence diet and in conditions of appalling violence and mistreatment.[117]

Despite the very significant attention paid to multinational naval counter-piracy patrols, it now seems unlikely that these were principally responsible for the sharp reduction in the success rate of pirate attacks in the Indian Ocean over 2011–2013. Certainly, naval patrols, regional prosecutions, and industry measures all played a role in reducing both the number of total pirate attacks and the odds of any individual ship being taken by Somali pirates.[118] However, of these, the most effective measures taken were likely those adopted by the shipping industry itself. These included the largely passive 'target hardening' Best Management Practices noted above and the active recruitment of privately contracted armed security personnel.

The counter-piracy paradigm moved through a number of phases.[119] There was the early military phase, bolstered by Security Council Resolutions cast in the familiar language of authorizations to use force, which can be seen as states responding with public violence to the use of unlawful private violence by pirates. This fairly swiftly gave way to 'transnational' law enforcement involving horizontal coordination and cooperation between various governments to facilitate regional prosecutions. This cooperation was transnational in the sense that much of it was neither conducted in legally binding form, nor was it reciprocal. The prosecution of Somali pirates before regional courts usually occurred under non-binding memoranda of understanding, and while prosecutions received a degree of international support (usually through the UN Office on Drugs and Crime counter-piracy program) there was no formal reciprocity or quid pro-quo. The manner

[114] Acknowledgement of PCASP's role is found in: 'Report of the Secretary-General on Specialized Anti-Piracy Courts in Somalia and Other States in the Region', UN Doc S/2012/50, para 9.

[115] M Hijmans, 'Threats of the Sea' (2011) 67(11) *The World Today* 22, 24.

[116] 'Report of the Secretary-General on the Situation with Respect to Piracy and Armed Robbery at Sea Off the Coast of Somalia', UN Doc S/2015/776, para 3.

[117] ibid, paras 8–9. [118] ibid, paras 54–59.

[119] Guilfoyle 'Somali Pirates as Agents of Change' (n 113).

in which this 'system' of international cooperation functions has been described elsewhere.[120] The most interesting final phase of the evolution of the counter-piracy response has been the thawing of industry attitudes towards private armed security from something to be wholeheartedly avoided towards something to be cautiously embraced.

Indeed, there was a notable shift in the attitude of the industry from one where it was principally thought to be the job of navies to protect international shipping, to one where industry took an increasing degree of responsibility for its own safety.[121] Armed security personnel were originally seen by both the industry and the IMO as undesirable in principle, legally very complex, and likely to be impractical.[122]

The largest risk to be managed in the PCASP context has been the use of firearms. The sources of applicable hard and soft law are various:[123]

- IMO guidelines to states and shipowners;[124]
- the International Code of Conduct for Private Security Service Providers;[125]
- national firearms law (and law on self-defence) applicable aboard ships at sea as a matter of flag state law;
- the national law at ports of call dealing with foreign-registered firearms in internal waters; and
- in the event of injury or death arising occasioned aboard suspect pirate vessels from the use of firearms—the law of that vessel's flag state or potentially that of the state of nationality of a person wounded or killed.[126]

Nonetheless, rather than continuing to rely alone upon the protection of the world's navies (which obviously enjoy a power to use force in 'constabulary' operations such as counter-piracy), the shipping industry (or significant parts of it) assumed the

[120] ibid; Bueger, 'Responses to Contemporary Piracy (n 112); Geiss and Petrig, *The Legal Framework for Counter-Piracy Operations* (n 109) 6–36.

[121] Guilfoyle, 'Somali Pirates as Agents of Change' (n 113) 102–03.

[122] ibid.

[123] D Guilfoyle, 'The Use of Force Against Pirates' in M Weller (ed), *The Oxford Handbook of the Use of Force in International Law* (OUP 2015) 1066–71; J Kraska, 'International and Comparative Regulation of Private Maritime Security Companies Employed in Counter-Piracy' in Guilfoyle (ed), *Modern Piracy* (n 110), Chapter 10.

[124] IMO, 'Revised Interim Guidance to Shipowners, Ship Operators, and Shipmasters on the Use of Privately Contracted Armed Security Personnel on Board Ships in the High Risk Area', IMO Doc MSC 1/Circ 1405/Rev.21 (2012); 'Revised Interim Recommendations for Flag States Regarding the Use of Privately Contracted Armed Security Personnel on Board Ships in the High Risk Area', IMO Doc MSC 1/Circ 1406/Rev.1 (2012); 'Interim Recommendations for Port and Coastal States Regarding the Use of Privately Contracted Armed Security Personnel on Board Ships in the High Risk Area', IMO Doc MSC 1/Circ 1408/Rev.1 (2012).

[125] Montreux Document on Pertinent International Legal Obligations and Good Practices for States related to Operations of Private Military and Security Companies during Armed Conflict (17 September 2008), as annexed to IMO Doc MSC 89/INF.20 (8 March 2011).

[126] See discussion of the *Enrica Lexie* incident on the *EJIL: Talk!* blog <http://www.ejiltalk.org>; D Guilfoyle, 'Shooting Fishermen Mistaken for Pirates: Jurisdiction, Immunity and State Responsibility', 2 March 2012; H Sankar, 'Jurisdictional and Immunity Issues in the Story of *Enrica Lexie*: A Case of Shoot and Scoot Turns Around!', 25 March 2013.

complex legal risks surrounding the deployment of armed guards. Private security companies are now a significant feature of the maritime security environment. A number of governments were surprisingly willing to facilitate this development. A UK government minister conceded in 2012 to a House of Commons inquiry into Somali piracy:

> The Government recognises that armed private security companies are a fact of life. Some 25% of ships in the region have them on board. Many shipping lines have been pressing us very hard on that issue.[127]

That inquiry also noted that insurers thought armed security to be an effective form of risk mitigation, as did the head of the European Naval Force counter-piracy mission.[128] The United Kingdom thus produced interim Ministry of Transport 'guidelines', the effect of which was that ship security plans for UK flag vessels featuring armed guards for counter-piracy purposes can now be approved.[129] (Such ship security plans are a requirement of the ISPS, as discussed in section 4.4 above.) Of course, in any criminal proceedings arising from mistaken self-defence incidents or port-state illegal firearms charges, the final risks are likely to be borne by the security contractors themselves. For example, in the *Seaman Guard Ohio* incident thirty-five contractors aboard a private anti-piracy guard ship were imprisoned in India for illegally bringing weapons into Indian waters.[130]

4.7 Conclusion

Perhaps unsurprisingly, this chapter reveals a range of approaches to risk assessment and risk mitigation adopted in response to different maritime security issues. First, in response to the threat of terrorism, the approach taken appears to conform to a classic worst-case scenario and 'probability neglect' paradigm.[131] That is, expensive and intrusive security measures have been devised to mitigate the threat of maritime terrorism, despite the risks being low or unquantified. In addition, international standards in this field have provided a floor, not a ceiling, allowing even more

[127] House of Commons Foreign Affairs Committee, 'Piracy Off the Coast of Somalia', HC 1318 (5 January 2012), Evidence Annexe, Ev 42 <http://www.parliament.uk/business/committees/committees-a-z/commons-select/foreign-affairs-committee/publications/> accessed 20 December 2016.

[128] ibid, 22.

[129] ibid, 22–23; Department for Transport, Interim Guidance to UK Flagged Shipping on the Use of Armed Guards to Defend Against the Threat of Piracy in Exceptional Circumstances, version 1.3, June 2012 (updated December 2015) <https://www.gov.uk/government/uploads/system/uploads/attachment_data/file/480863/use-of-armed-guards-to-defend-against-piracy.pdf> accessed 20 December 2016.

[130] A Selvaraj, 'US Anti-Piracy Vessel MV Seaman Guard Ohio Crew Members Sentenced to Jail in Tamil Nadu', *Times of India*, 11 January 2016 <http://timesofindia.indiatimes.com/india/US-anti-piracy-vessel-MV-Seaman-Guard-Ohio-crew-members-sentenced-to-jail-in-Tamil-Nadu/articleshow/50530239.cms> accessed 12 January 2016.

[131] Sunstein, *Laws of Fear* (n 17) Chapter 3.

draconian national measures to be taken. This tends to place a disproportionate burden on seafarers, already a largely neglected human rights constituency.

Examining responses to irregular maritime migration shows a different dynamic at play. Maritime migrant smuggling is a genuine international concern. At the very least, it poses a significant risk to the lives of those smuggled. However, the response has largely been one of securitization, where migrant smugglers are construed as a threat to the integrity of the state and its borders. The difficulty with a security-led approach has been illustrated through the recent European experience. Unless migrant interdiction is construed as a rescue operation designed from the outset to be human rights compliant, the costs of securitization are likely to be borne by vulnerable migrants—including those with international protection claims.

Finally, while counter-piracy has involved the most significant multinational naval deployment of the early twenty-first century, it is not clear that military force has solved the problem. Transnational piracy, committing acts of predation upon the transnational shipping industry, has largely been countered by the industry itself—and through the rise of a third class of transnational actor, in the form of maritime private armed security. Nonetheless, the rise of maritime private armed security required a facilitative government regulatory framework. In this sense, the transnational security state is present through a form of tacit privatization of the protective functions traditionally associated with navies.

The picture formed of the transnational security state and its responses to risk is thus a mixed one. The LOSC has provided an enabling framework for the projection of power beyond national boundaries in a number of forms, whether it be visa requirements that limit the rights of seafarers, the subjection of maritime migrants to potentially arbitrary exercises of power, or the facilitation of the rise of transnational maritime private armed security. The picture is complicated by the apparent limits of naval hard power in suppressing piracy and the ability, at least in Europe, of regional human rights treaties to curtail the methods of migrant interdiction employed. Nonetheless, in the context of maritime security, the state has hardly withered or proven powerless in the face of perceived risks from transnational actors. The responses discussed here, however, show a distinct tendency to re-allocate risks to vulnerable individuals operating in liminal or transnational spaces, whether they be seafarers, migrants, or security contractors.

5

International Law and the Exploration and Use of Outer Space

Steven Freeland

5.1 A 'New' Frontier

On 4 October 1957, a small Soviet space object called Sputnik I was launched. It subsequently orbited the Earth over 1,400 times during the following three-month period. This unprecedented event heralded the dawn of the 'space age', arousing sentiments both of awe as regards its scientific significance, but also of fear and uncertainty, particularly in the United States and the 'West', given the then prevailing geopolitical atmosphere dominated by the Cold War.

As a consequence, the 'opening up' of space was viewed at the time very much from a military and strategic viewpoint. Both the United States and the Soviet Union had visions of space as another frontier in/from which they would compete. Moreover, their actual space-related capabilities were only regarded as part of the picture—not only was it important for each of them to demonstrate what they *could* do in space, but equally significant was the perception they could present to other states as to what they *might be able* to do. In essence, the development of space as a new technological 'battleground' provided a platform through which to develop strategic and military capability and reach, whilst at the same time generating uncertainty and fear among adversaries, as well as fermenting nationalistic pride and fervour amongst a state's own citizens.

Notwithstanding these sentiments—or perhaps more likely, *because* of them—the rest of the world made great efforts to ensure that the international regulatory response to these burgeoning space-related activities sought to highlight 'the common interest of all mankind in the progress of the exploration and use of outer space for peaceful purposes'.[1] The various United Nations resolutions that followed the Sputnik mission and subsequent 'firsts' in space each emphasized the common benefits of utilizing space through international cooperation. That said, it was clear

[1] Treaty on Principles Governing the Activities of States in the Exploration and Use of Outer Space, including the Moon and Other Celestial Bodies (adopted 27 January 1967, entered into force 10 October 1967) 610 UNTS 205 (OST), Preamble, para 2.

that the desire of the United States and the USSR in particular for ever-increasing technological prowess was as much motivated by military considerations as a wish to explore and use space for other (scientific) purposes, although no doubt these were also of relevance.

It was in this context that the international community had to react, as it walked a fine balancing line between the wishes of the two superpowers, on the one hand, and a general sense of uncertainty as to where exactly these military-driven activities might ultimately lead, on the other.

In fact, space technology has evolved at a breath-taking pace since the launch of Sputnik. Humankind is now engaged in a multitude of space activities, far beyond the contemplation of anyone at that time. The utilization of space technology now forms a crucial part of everyday society in all parts of the globe, encompassing many areas that are integral for the survival of communities (eg, disaster management satellite data, agricultural management, and protection of the environment), international trade and commerce (facilitation of financial transactions, satellite commercial product services, etc), science and exploration, as well as, of course, military and national security-related activities.

Our reliance on this technology is such that many aspects of the modern world would cease to function without constant and unimpeded access to space, particularly given the restructuring of most economies towards a reliance on communications networks that are dependent on satellite services such as GPS data; an imperative that will, if anything, become even greater for future generations. This dependency has been driven both by the increasing 'commercialization' of outer space and by its ongoing strategic and military significance. Indeed, space is often described as 'congested, contested, and competitive',[2] and military commanders fear that a 'day without space'[3]—where a nation's space assets would be disabled or jammed—would represent a national security and commercial catastrophe.

Yet, there remains a vast gulf between the space capabilities of the space 'powers' compared with the rest of the world. Between sixty and seventy states now have some form of direct space capability, although the scope varies significantly. This also means that up to 140 states currently have *no* independent capability to directly access space, despite their reliance on the technology for many aspects of their functioning and development. These countries are dependent on others for their space access, which thus both impacts upon their space 'security' and impedes internal opportunity for creativity, innovation, and international competitiveness. Their access to satellite data and their ability to utilize vital space technology in a crisis is therefore largely dependent on, and subject to, the strength and vagaries of their existing contractual relationships and political ties.

[2] See, eg, 'Schulte: Space is Contested, Congested, Competitive', *Space Watch* (June 2011) <http://www.spacefoundation.org/media/space-watch/schulte-space-congested-contested-competitive> accessed 30 December 2015.

[3] See, eg, S Magnuson, 'U.S. Forces Prepare for a "Day Without Space"', *National Defense* (9 February 2014) <http://www.nationaldefensemagazine.org/archive/2014/February/Pages/USForcesPreparefora%E2%80%98DayWithoutSpace%E2%80%99.aspx> accessed 30 December 2015.

The journey of Sputnik I immediately highlighted some difficult and controversial legal questions. The reality of humankind's aspirations in terms of exploration and future utilization of this largely unknown frontier—outer space—had now become more tangible. The world had to react—quickly—to the advent of this technology, which had led to an unprecedented event in an unregulated international legal environment.

The need for legal guidelines became a priority, not only to address the immediate questions as to the legal 'status' of outer space, but to provide a legitimate and acceptable framework for the regulation of those future activities that could reasonably be foreseen. At the time, of course, existing international law had almost exclusively been developed for 'terrestrial' purposes. Thus, even though these existing principles would no doubt be relevant in certain respects, they were not directly applicable to this new paradigm. Moreover, the 'non-sovereignty' aspect of outer space, discussed in more detail below, meant that existing national law would not prima facie apply, and would not be the appropriate international legal basis for regulating the conduct of humankind's activities in outer space.

New internationally binding rules were therefore required to address the peculiar characteristics and legal categorization of outer space. Without these rules, there were real risks associated with unregulated activities using technology that was largely missile-based.[4] As a response, the United Nations Committee on the Peaceful Uses of Outer Space (UNCOPUOS), the principal multilateral body involved in the development of international space law, was established by the United Nations General Assembly (UNGA) in 1958, shortly after the launch of Sputnik.[5] Discussions quickly ensued that resulted in a series of UNGA resolutions intended to clarify important principles underpinning the international legal framework, largely in an attempt to reinforce the 'freedom' to engage in space-related activities, subject only to agreed general restrictions. This chapter assesses the uncertainties arising from this existing international legal framework and their correlation to significant risks pertaining to the exploration and use of outer space.

5.2 A New International Legal Regime

The law of outer space has developed as an increasingly important element within the broader corpus of public international law. The existing body of international principles deals with many—although not all—aspects of the exploration and use

[4] See, eg, R Hollingham, 'V2: The Nazi Rocket that Launched the Space Age', *BBC News* (8 September 2014) <http://www.bbc.com/future/story/20140905-the-nazis-space-age-rocket> accessed 30 December 2015.

[5] See UNGA Res 1348 (XIII) (13 December 1958). The ad hoc Committee was subsequently converted into a permanent body in 1959: see UNGA Res 1472 (XIV) (12 December 1959). UNCOPUOS currently has eighty-three members, which, according to its website, makes it 'one of the largest Committees in the United Nations'. See United Nations Office for Outer Space Affairs, 'Members of the Committee on the Peaceful Uses of Outer Space' <http://www.unoosa.org/oosa/en/COPUOS/members.html> accessed 21 December 2016.

of outer space. These principles are primarily to be found in a number of United Nations-sponsored multilateral treaties and declarations which have also, to a certain degree, been assimilated into other international documents and national legislation.

Five main multilateral treaties have been finalized through UNCOPUOS,[6] dealing with various important issues relating to outer space, including the non-appropriation of outer space, the freedom of exploration and the use of outer space, a liability regime applicable in the case of damage caused by space objects, the safety and rescue of space objects and astronauts, notification to and registration of space objects/activities with the United Nations, the scientific investigation and exploitation of the natural resources of outer space, and the settlement of disputes arising from outer space activities.

However, when assessing the effectiveness of these instruments in resolving the uncertainties and risks associated with the rapid and, perhaps more significantly, largely unregulated evolution of space-related technology, it must be remembered that they were formulated in the Cold War era. As noted, the primary motivation underpinning the development of space-related technology at the time centred on military and national security concerns, and the two major space powers, the United States and the USSR, both understood that it was not in their interests to agree to a comprehensive regulatory framework. Rather, to protect their interests, they became crucial stakeholders in the development of the rules codified in these treaties. Indeed, one commentator at the time described the Outer Space Treaty (OST) as 'in essence a bilateral arrangement between the principal space-users'.[7] Thus, the provisions of the OST, as well as the other space treaties, reflect a deliberate political strategy that was very much a product of the technological and geopolitical climate extant at the time of their formulation.

Moreover, it was recognized that, given the rapid development of space technology, comprehensive standards for its regulation could not be specified in advance.

[6] OST (n 1); Agreement on the Rescue of Astronauts, the Return of Astronauts and the Return of Objects Launched into Outer Space (adopted 22 April 1968, entered into force 3 December 1968) 672 UNTS 119; Convention on International Liability for Damage Caused by Space Objects (adopted 29 March 1972, entered into force 1 September 1972) 961 UNTS 187 (LC); Convention on Registration of Objects Launched into Outer Space (adopted 14 January 1975, entered into force 15 September 1976) 1023 UNTS 15; Agreement Governing the Activities of States on the Moon and Other Celestial Bodies (adopted 18 December 1979, entered into force 11 July 1984) 1363 UNTS 3 (MA). Other treaties may also be applicable to outer space in certain respects: eg, Treaty Banning Nuclear Weapons Tests in the Atmosphere, in Outer Space and Under Water (adopted 5 August 1963, entered into force 10 October 1963) 480 UNTS 43; Convention on the Prohibition of Military or Any Other Hostile Use of Environmental Modification Techniques (adopted 10 December 1976, entered into force 5 October 1978) 1108 UNTS 151. This might even include some instruments concluded before the commencement of the space age. The International Convention Concerning the Use of Broadcasting in the Cause of Peace is considered to be applicable to outer space activities, particularly in relation to international broadcasting by satellites. International Convention Concerning the Use of Broadcasting in the Cause of Peace (adopted 23 September 1936, entered into force 2 April 1938) 186 LNTS 301; R Jakhu and S Freeland, 'The Sources of International Space Law', *Proceedings of the International Institute of Space Law* (Eleven International Publishing 2014) 461.

[7] JES Fawcett, *International Law and the Uses of Outer Space* (Manchester University Press 1968) 15–16.

Simply put, further uncertainties and potential risks would likely result from attempting to regulate for the 'unknown'.[8] There was relatively little capacity, or political will, to delve too far into international regulatory development relating to areas of activity, the nature and consequences of which were not readily apparent.

Nevertheless, notwithstanding such difficulties, the general rules elaborated in these treaties have thus far facilitated significant improvement in the standard of living of humanity through the use of space technology, for example through the work of Intelsat[9] in making available satellite communications services to less-developed countries, who would otherwise have been unable to independently develop appropriate infrastructure systems. The desire for further space applications to serve such purposes continues unabated. It is clear, therefore, that the prospects for the future use of outer space for the ongoing expansion of human activity offer both tremendous opportunities and challenges, and that international law will remain relevant to, but will continue to 'struggle' to adequately address, all aspects of this seemingly irreversible dynamic, primarily due to the largely 'reactive' and/or responsive nature of formal legal regulation. This therefore gives rise to an almost inevitable timing gap in relation to the regulation of areas of activity where the pace of technological advancement far outstrips the ability—both from a logistical but also conceptual level—to develop and put into place appropriate regulatory frameworks.

This is certainly the case with respect to the legal regulation of outer space and, given the lacunae in the existing space treaties, reference to the broader corpus of international law will thus remain necessary, albeit not necessarily sufficient, for the purposes of resolving specific disputes, including those relating to collisions between space objects (more commonly referred to as 'conjunctions'), the exploitation and ownership of space resources, questions of jurisdiction, and general areas of liability and state responsibility.

Indeed, as Article III of the OST makes clear, activities in the exploration and use of outer space are to be carried out 'in accordance with international law, including the Charter of the United Nations' (UNC). What is not clear, however, is whether, and indeed *how*, the peculiarities of the legal framework of outer space—primarily dependent on international rules and standards rather than 'territorial' factors—can seamlessly coalesce with the body of terrestrial international

8 As an example, in the context of possible future commercial space tourism, see Steven Freeland, 'Fly Me to the Moon: How Will International Law Cope with Commercial Space Tourism?' (2010) 11(1) *Melbourne Journal of International Law* 90. These concerns reflect parallels with the notion of 'second-order' risks developed in Ulrich Beck's vision of a 'risk society', which he regarded as being 'less tangible and more uncontrollable', and thus more difficult to assess and regulate; see U Beck, A Giddens, and S Lash, *Reflexive Modernization: Politics, Tradition and Aesthetics in the Modern Social Order* (Stanford University Press 1994).

9 Intelsat (International Telecommunications Satellite Consortium (later Organisation)) was founded as a public–private consortium in 1964 by the telecommunication agencies of eighteen countries. Within ten years its membership had grown to include agencies from eighty-six countries, and by 2001 about 150 countries were members. Its establishment was a direct consequence of the determination of the international community, as reflected in UNGA Res 1721 (20 December 1961), that global satellite communications should be made available worldwide on a non-discriminatory basis. See further Intelsat, <http://www.intelsat.com/about-us/overview/> accessed 24 December 2016.

law so as to effectively address 'new' space activities as they emerge. A 'Catch-22' risk environment emerges; on the one hand, the paucity of detailed legally binding regulation exacerbates ongoing uncertainties as to the 'rules of the road' arising from the exploration and use of outer space, as well as its commercial exploitation whilst, on the other hand, the risks associated with the unknown consequences of future space activities that will become possible due to technology advancement call for more legal regulation.

There are other instruments that expressly relate to aspects of the exploration and use of outer space. These include the space principles and other 'soft law' instruments.[10] In particular, five main sets of principles have been adopted by the UNGA to date.[11] These principles provide for the application of international law and promotion of international cooperation and understanding in space activities, the dissemination and exchange of information through transnational direct television broadcasting via satellites and remote satellite observations of Earth, and general standards regulating the safe use of nuclear power sources necessary for the exploration and use of outer space.

However, to the extent that these principles 'fill gaps' in the treaty regime, their non-binding nature compromises their effectiveness in terms of eliminating uncertainty; although it has been suggested that a number of the specific provisions contained in these documents may now represent customary international law and thus be binding on states.[12] This is important because the consensus decision-making approach adopted by UNCOPUOS has made the conclusion of further treaties relating to outer space activities extremely difficult. No additional *lex specialis* treaties have been concluded through UNCOPUOS since the 'failed' Moon Agreement (MA) in 1979.[13] As a consequence, the soft law approach, with its own inherent risks of greater 'non-compliance', is for the moment the only methodology for formulating guidelines for the regulation of new and emerging space activities.

Some of the implications of these legal issues are considered in the following sections; in particular the risk of colonization, the risk of environmental degradation, and the risk of armed conflict in space. Whilst, in broader terms at least, the first

[10] See S Freeland, 'For Better or for Worse? The Use of "Soft Law" Within the International Legal Regulation of Outer Space' (2011) XXXVI *Annals of Air and Space Law* 409.

[11] Declaration of Legal Principles Governing the Activities of States in the Exploration and Use of Outer Space, UNGA Res A/RES/18/1962 (13 December 1963) (Legal Principles Declaration); Principles Governing the Use by States of Artificial Earth Satellites for International Direct Television Broadcasting, UNGA Res A/RES/37/92 (10 December 1982); Principles Relating to Remote Sensing of the Earth from Outer Space, UNGA Res A/RES/41/65 (3 December 1986); Principles Relevant to the Use of Nuclear Power Sources in Outer Space, UNGA Res A/RES/47/68 (14 December 1992); Declaration on International Cooperation in the Exploration and Use of Outer Space for the Benefit and in the Interest of All States, Taking into Particular Account the Needs of Developing Countries, UNGA Res A/RES/51/122 (13 December 1996).

[12] See, eg, RJ Lee and S Freeland, 'The Crystallisation of General Assembly Space Declarations into Customary International Law', 46 *Proceedings of the Colloquium on the Law of Outer Space* (AIAA 2005) 122.

[13] See S Hobe, R Jakhu, S Freeland et al, 'The Moon Agreement' in S Hobe et al (eds), *Cologne Commentary on Space Law, Volume II—Rescue Agreement, Liability Convention, Registration Convention, Moon Agreement* (Heymanns 2013) 325.

of these has been addressed through the space law treaties, it is also tied in with the more recent technology geared towards 'mining' the mineral (and other) resources of celestial bodies. As for the environmental and military concerns relating to outer space—regarded by many as representing the two most pressing concerns associated with the future of humankind's activities in outer space—these are not dealt with at all comprehensively in the 'hard' space law instruments.

5.3 Addressing the Risks of Space 'Colonization'

5.3.1 One unresolved uncertainty—where does space begin?

As soon as Sputnik began its journey, the legal categorization of outer space for the purposes of international law became of utmost relevance. Although the USSR had not sought the permission of any other state to undertake the mission, there were no significant international protests asserting that its space object had infringed any other country's sovereignty as it circled the Earth. This international (in)action indicated that this new frontier for human activity was not to be regarded, from a legal perspective, as exhibiting the traditional elements of sovereignty that had already been well established under international law in respect of land, sea, and air space on Earth. Instead, it was assumed that outer space was an area beyond territorial sovereignty.

Describing the early emergence of this customary international principle in the context of outer space, Judge Manfred Lachs of the International Court of Justice (ICJ) observed, shortly after the OST had been finalized, that:

> [t]he first instruments that men sent into outer space traversed the air space of States and circled above them in outer space, yet the launching States sought no permission, nor did the other States protest. This is how the freedom of movement into outer space, and in it, came to be established and recognised as law within a remarkably short period of time.[14]

As noted, this represents a significant departure from the rules relating to air space, categorized as constituting part of the 'territory' of the underlying state,[15] which also reflects customary international law.[16] Civil and commercial aircraft only have certain limited rights to enter the air space of another state,[17] in contrast to the freedom principle relating to outer space.[18] Yet, in large part reflecting the 'you-don't-need-to- know' approach adopted by the major space powers in seeking to

[14] *North Sea Continental Shelf Cases (Federal Republic of Germany v Denmark and Federal Republic of Germany v The Netherlands)* [1969] ICJ Rep 3, Dissenting Opinion of Judge Lachs, 230.

[15] See, eg, Convention on International Civil Aviation (adopted 7 December 1944, entered into force 4 April 1947) 15 UNTS 295 (Chicago Convention), art 1.

[16] See *Case Concerning Military and Paramilitary Activities In and Against Nicaragua (Nicaragua v United States)* (Merits) [1986] ICJ Rep 14, 128.

[17] See Chicago Convention, arts 5 and 6.

[18] Any space activity involving a launch from Earth and/or a return to Earth will also involve a 'use' of air space, so that the law of air space may be relevant if, for example, the space object of one State travels through the air space of another State. See also LC, art II.

minimize restrictive rules relating to their space activities, an agreed 'demarcation' between air space and outer space has never been accepted under international law.[19] There has, over the years, been controversy as to how far air space extends above the surface of the Earth,[20] and many methodologies have been suggested to resolve this uncertainty, but none has thus far been accepted by UNCOPUOS.

Naturally, this uncertainty as to such a fundamental issue itself gives rise to potential risks, as it may serve to 'cloud' the reach of the fundamental space law principles. Given that, for example, the legal regulation of outer space is deliberately framed around a non-sovereignty approach, difficult questions may arise as to when or whether those boundaries have been crossed. As the range of activities in outer space expands further, the issue will become more important in relation not only to the broad principles of international space law, but also in relation to security issues and commercial applications.[21] There have been some more recent developments in relation to a possible 'boundary' in the context of both international (draft) instruments[22] and domestic space legislation.[23] However, it is by no means clear that these examples reflect an increasing willingness among all stakeholders to accept an agreed demarcation point at which to separate sovereign from non-sovereign areas.

5.3.2 One resolved uncertainty—or is it? Prohibiting the appropriation of space

Setting aside the demarcation question, from the point of alleviating the risk of conflict driven by territorial ambitions, the principle of non-appropriation of outer

[19] For a detailed discussion of the 'Air/Space Boundary Question', see F Lyall and PB Larsen, *Space Law: A Treatise* (Ashgate Publishing 2009) 153–73.

[20] On 3 December 1976, eight equatorial states signed the Declaration of the First Meeting of Equatorial Countries, which asserted that, in the absence of any legally determined upper limit to air space, those segments of the geostationary orbit (located approximately 36,000 kilometres directly above the equator) above their territory constituted part of their respective sovereign territories. Declaration of the First Meeting of Equatorial Countries, reprinted in (1978) 6 *Journal of Space Law* 193 ('The Bogotá Declaration').

[21] Eg, a demarcation seems desirable when it comes to the regulation of commercial sub-orbital space tourism activities, which, at least under current technological constraints, would involve paying passengers being taken to an altitude slightly in excess of 100 kilometres above the Earth: see Freeland, 'Fly Me to the Moon' (n 8).

[22] See, eg, art I(a) of the Draft Treaty on the Prevention of the Placement of Weapons in Outer Space and of the Threat or Use of Force Against Outer Space Objects (PPWT), which was sponsored by the USSR and China and supported by several other countries. This document defines outer space as 'space beyond the elevation of approximately 100 [kilometres] above [the] ocean level of the Earth'. As a further indication of the ongoing uncertainty around the issue of demarcation, it is pertinent to note that a revised version of the draft PPWT submitted by the USSR on 10 June 2014 omitted this definition. Draft Treaty on the Prevention of the Placement of Weapons in Outer Space and of the Threat or Use of Force Against Outer Space Objects, Document CD/1839, Conference on Disarmament, 29 February 2008 (PPWT).

[23] See, eg, the Australian Space Activities Act, which incorporates into the definition of a 'launch', a 'launch vehicle', a 'return', and a 'space object' for the purposes of the legislation a reference to 'the distance of 100 [kilometres] above mean sea level'. Space Activities Act 1998 (Cth) (Aust), as amended by the Space Activities Amendment Act 2002 (Cth) (Aust).

space was crucial. Whereas most rules relating to outer space have developed in response to the evolution of new forms of technological capability, the acceptance from the outset that outer space was to be regarded as a *res communis omnium*[24] suggested a 'proactive' approach to mitigating the risk of claims of colonization and appropriation of outer space resources.

By the time the OST was finalized, both the United States and the USSR had been engaged in an extensive range of space activities; yet neither had made a claim to sovereignty over any part of outer space, including celestial bodies. Already, by 1963, the terms of the non-appropriation principle had largely been settled in the Legal Principles Declaration,[25] and the inclusion of Article II in the OST was therefore uncontroversial.

It is no coincidence that the non-appropriation principle immediately follows Article I of the OST, which elaborates on the 'common interest' and 'freedom' principles, and confirms that the exploration and use of outer space is to be undertaken 'for the benefit and in the interests of all countries' and freely 'by all States without discrimination of any kind, on a basis of equality and in accordance with international law'. In general terms, the primary intent of Article II was to reinforce these important concepts by confirming that principles of territorial sovereignty do not apply to outer space. Unlike the corresponding provision in the United Nations Convention on the Law of the Sea (LOSC)[26] dealing with the high seas, Article II does not expressly limit itself to the purported actions of states; rather, the provision is drafted in more general terms, in that it seeks to prohibit specific actions that constitute a 'national appropriation'. With the obvious exception of the reference to 'by claim of sovereignty', there is no express limitation in Article II *only* to the actions of states.

However, the absence of a specific prohibition on non-sovereign claims has, over the years, given rise to debate as to its precise scope and, more particularly, the extent (if at all) that 'private property rights'[27] may exist in outer space, notwithstanding (or perhaps as a result of) the terms of Article II.[28] This is of particular contemporary relevance given the technological advances that have led to proposals by various private commercial organizations to engage in 'mining' activities on asteroids and other celestial bodies. In recent times, in the light of a lack of agreement at the international level, some states have resolved to take unilateral *national* legislative initiatives that, on the surface, appear to challenge the international principles.[29] This ad hoc national approach raises additional

[24] A Cassese, *International Law* (2nd edn, OUP 2005) 95.

[25] See Legal Principles Declaration, para 3, the terms of which were only slightly altered for the purposes of concluding art II of the OST.

[26] United Nations Convention on the Law of the Sea (adopted 10 December 1982, entered into force 16 November 1994) 1833 UNTS 3 (LOSC). But note LOSC, art 137(1).

[27] See DJ Harris, *Cases and Materials on International Law* (7th edn, Sweet & Maxwell 2010) 215.

[28] See also MA, art 11(2).

[29] See the statement by the International Institute of Space Law following the signing into law by President Obama in November 2015 of the US Commercial Space Launch Competitiveness Act. International Institute of Space Law, 'Position Paper on Space Resource Mining' (20 December 2015) <http://www.iislweb.org/docs/SpaceResourceMining.pdf> accessed 30 December 2015. See also 'Luxembourg Plans to Pioneer Asteroid Mining', *ABC News* (4 February 2016) <http://www.abc.net.au/news/2016-02-04/space-mining-plans-unveiled-by-luxembourg/7138380> accessed 16 February 2016.

significant uncertainties as to the future adherence to the non-appropriation principle in its current form, and also ratchets up the risk of similar moves by other space-faring states. Ideally, the relevant international principles will require further elaboration so as to minimize uncertainties or misinterpretations as to their precise scope of application,[30] although there is no indication that this will happen anytime soon.

Turning back to the broader perspective, the sentiments reflected in Article II are fundamental to the regulation of outer space and its exploration and use for peaceful purposes. It is for these reasons that a binding principle of non-appropriation is an essential element of international space law, to be preserved and followed in the conduct of all activities in outer space. It has helped to 'protect' outer space from the possibility of conflict driven by territorial or colonizing ambitions, thus encouraging a conflict-free use of outer space thus far. For this reason, unilateral state actions that may be seen as challenging these principles give rise to future risks of the sorts of action that Article II was designed to prevent.

5.4 Addressing Environmental Risks in Outer Space

Virtually all aspects of the exploration and use of outer space involve elements that are inherently damaging to the space environment—and often also to the environment of the Earth, particularly during the launch phase.[31] Over time, and with the exponential growth of space activities, this has given rise to many (potential) environmental problems, as well as the question of whether, and how, such concerns can and should be addressed within the corpus of international law.

The existing *lex specialis* of space law fails to provide a comprehensive framework for the protection of the environment of outer space. The UN Space Treaties were largely concluded before the 'environmental movement' relating to activities on Earth had begun to be established, let alone before the development of the main international environmental law instruments. Even then, the idea that the environment of outer space required rigorous regulation was beyond serious consideration, despite the fact that the protection of natural celestial environments was expressed as being 'among the earliest policies articulated at the dawn of the space age'.[32]

The 1972 Stockholm Declaration[33] was the first significant statement of fundamental international principles relating to the protection of the

[30] For further discussion, see Jakhu and Freeland, 'The Sources of International Space Law' (n 6) 49–63.

[31] For a discussion of the risks for the Earth environment associated with the use of toxic propellants in launches, see S Freeland and D Lawler, 'Whose Mess is It Anyway? Regulating the Environmental Consequences of Commercial Launch Activities', *Proceedings of the International Institute of Space Law* (Eleven International Publishing 2012) 318.

[32] LI Tennen, 'Evolution of the Planetary Protection Policy: Conflict of Science and Jurisprudence?' (2004) 24 *Advances in Space Research* 2354, 2354.

[33] United Nations Conference on the Human Environment, 'Declaration of the United Nations Conference on the Human Environment' (16 June 1972) UN Doc A/CONF.48/14/Rev.1 (1972 Stockholm Declaration).

environment.[34] By the time that instrument had been concluded, the most important fundamental principles of space law had already been codified in the OST and LC, respectively. Those treaties contained little by way of substantial protection of the outer space environment. The two space powers had nothing to gain by rigorous environmental obligations that might be perceived as having impeded their space ambitions.

Even though there are now many more stakeholders involved in space, a comprehensive binding regime has still not been introduced. Each stakeholder is motivated by factors that are not necessarily compatible with the 'protection' of the space environment—indeed, they may be *incompatible* with such concerns, particularly because of the enormous costs involved. Environmental issues are still not afforded a high priority in the planning, design, and implementation of most space activities, notwithstanding increasing evidence, for example, of the alarming proliferation of space debris in an era where there are plans to send increasing numbers of humans into space.[35]

To the extent that the UN Space treaties do refer to environmental protections, these continue to reflect the *Realpolitik* surrounding those instruments. Their language is the product of compromise and political pragmatism, and therefore general and even vague.

The most directly relevant provisions are Article IX of the OST, which focuses primarily on the issue of back-and-forward contamination,[36] and Article 7 of the MA, which addresses environmental concerns associated with the exploitation of the natural resources of the Moon and other celestial bodies.[37] More recently, there have been a number of soft law instruments directed inter alia towards the use of nuclear power sources in outer space[38] and space debris (see below); their 'voluntary' nature perhaps belying the very significant risks and uncertainties related to the use of outer space that they are intended to address.

Probably the most significant of these risks for future space activities is that posed by space debris. Given the increasingly complex and varied ways in which humankind is undertaking the exploration and use of outer space, it is inevitable that space activities will become increasingly hazardous, at least in 'popular' orbits. As at February 2014, the European Space Agency (ESA) estimated that there were more

[34] RJ Parsons, 'The Fight to Save the Planet: U.S. Armed Forces, "Greenkeeping", and Enforcement of the Law Pertaining to Environmental Protection During Armed Conflict' (1998) 10 *Georgetown International Environmental Law Review* 441, 455.

[35] See, eg, a NASA report on space debris and human spacecraft. NASA, 'Space Debris and Human Spacecraft' (27 September 2013) <http://www.nasa.gov/mission_pages/station/news/orbital_debris.html> accessed 16 February 2016.

[36] For a discussion of art IX of the Outer Space Treaty, see Sergio Marchisio, 'Article IX' in S Hobe et al (eds), *Cologne Commentary on Space Law, Volume I—Outer Space Treaty* (Heymanns 2009) 169.

[37] See, inter alia, MA, art 7. For an analysis of the environmental protection provisions in the MA, see Hobe et al, 'The Moon Agreement' (n 13).

[38] See Nuclear Power Source Principles; UNCOPUOS Scientific and Technical Sub-Committee and International Atomic Energy Agency (AIEA), *Safety Framework for Nuclear Power Source Applications in Outer Space* (2009) <http://www.fas.org/nuke/space/iaea-space.pdf> accessed 30 December 2015.

than 700,000 debris objects in Earth orbit that have the potential to damage or destroy operational satellites. Indeed, ESA suggests that:

> for many missions, the risk of losing a mission through the impact of space debris is considered to be the third highest risk, after the launch and deployment risks.[39]

Not only is the issue of space debris a major environmental concern, but it also clearly impacts upon human safety. For example, on 12 March 2009, the astronauts on board the International Space Station (ISS) were forced to evacuate the main station and remain in the escape vehicle for nine minutes, while a piece of debris about one centimetre in length passed by.[40] Had the debris hit and pierced the ISS, a fatal loss of air pressure could have ensued. This was not a one-off occurrence.[41]

One month earlier, an operational American commercial satellite (Iridium 33) and an inactive Russian communications satellite (Kosmos 2251) had collided approximately 790 kilometres above the Earth, resulting in their total destruction. This was the first time that two intact satellites had been involved in a conjunction, with the collision resulting in approximately 700 additional pieces of hazardous debris, each with the potential to remain in orbit for an extremely lengthy period of time.

These incidents, as well as the broader issue of the protection of the environment of outer space, raise many issues that challenge international law, including the regulation of the exponential growth of space debris and other forms of pollution (eg, nuclear radiation, discarded fuel, etc), the international responsibility and liability ramifications that arise, and the efficiency of existing satellite collision avoidance methods.

As noted, the existing international legal regime does not address such concerns in anything approaching a comprehensive manner. Whilst all space-faring states (and others) have increasingly become aware that a situation exists that has the potential to raise the threshold of risk to unacceptable levels, there has not been a corresponding willingness to either take 'ownership' of the problem or agree to strict, comprehensive, and binding international space environmental rules.

Adding to the complexity of this issue are the uncertainties associated with increased military capability in space. In 2007 and 2008 respectively, both China and the United States deliberately destroyed their own satellites in space, causing additional debris from the resultant explosions.[42] The fact that neither country felt constrained by existing space law, or by other principles of international law, further highlights the increasingly urgent need to develop more rigorous international rules

[39] See ESA, 'Space Situational Awareness—SST Segment' (11 February 2014) <http://www.esa.int/Our_Activities/Operations/Space_Situational_Awareness/Space_Surveillance_and_Tracking_-_SST_Segment> accessed 30 December 2015.

[40] See, eg, M McKee, 'Debris Threat Prompts Space Station Crew to Evacuate', *New Scientist* (12 March 2009) <http://www.newscientist.com/article/dn16755-debris-threat-prompts-space-station-crew-to-evacuate.html> accessed 30 December 2015.

[41] See The Watchers, 'Space Debris Forces ISS Astronauts to Evacuate the Station' (28 June 2011) <http://thewatchers.adorraeli.com/2011/06/28/space-debris-forces-iss-astronauts-to-evacuate-the-station/> accessed 30 December 2015.

[42] For background to these two incidents, see Steven Freeland, 'The 2008 Russia/China Proposal for a Treaty to Ban Weapons in Space: A Missed Opportunity or an Opening Gambit?' in 51 *Proceedings of the Colloquium on the Law of Outer Space* (AIAA 2009) 261.

to protect the space environment. In the case of the Chinese action, while much of the international reaction centred on the military consequences, the additional space debris—estimated to be in the thousands of pieces—caused by the destruction of the satellite at such a strategically important altitude raised significant concerns.

The regime under the LC, which imposes a fault liability regime for damage caused by one space object to another space object in outer space,[43] makes no reference to 'space debris', a term that itself is not defined under international law. Many commentators, however, suggest that space debris *is* incorporated within the circular definition of a 'space object',[44] although this may at times seem illogical and unsatisfactory and, in any event, requires identification of the 'object' and information as to its origins, which might not be possible in the circumstances.[45]

Even before these high-profile incidents, major space agencies had decided in 1993 to establish an Inter-Agency Space Debris Coordination Committee (IADC), an international governmental forum for the worldwide coordination of activities related to human-made and natural debris in space, whose primary purpose is:

> to exchange information on space debris research activities ... to facilitate opportunities for cooperation in space debris research, to review the progress of ongoing cooperative activities and to identify debris mitigation options.[46]

The IADC Space Debris Mitigation Guidelines (IADC Guidelines)[47] were formally adopted by consensus in October 2002 and served as a baseline for the development, by UNCOPUOS, of the UN Space Debris Mitigation Guidelines (UN Guidelines).[48] The UNGA endorsed the IADC Guidelines after agreeing that their terms should reflect existing practices as developed by a number of national and international organizations, and it invited member states to implement the guidelines through relevant national mechanisms.

The UN Guidelines recognize two broad categories of space debris mitigation measures:

1. those that curtail the generation of potentially harmful space debris in the near term—the curtailment of the production of mission-related space debris and the avoidance of break-ups; and

43 LC, art III.

44 Art I(d) of the LC provides as follows:

> The term 'space object' includes component parts of a space object as well as its launch vehicle and parts thereof.

45 Lyall and Larsen, *Space Law* (n 19) 304.

46 See IADC, 'IADC Document Registration List' <http://www.iadc-online.org/index.cgi?item=docs_pub> accessed 30 December 2015.

47 The current version of the IADC Guidelines is Inter-Agency Space Debris Coordination Committee, 'IADC Space Debris Mitigation Guidelines' (revision 1, September 2007) <http://orbital-debris.jsc.nasa.gov/library/IADC_Mitigation_Guidelines_Rev_1_Sep07.pdf> accessed 30 December 2015. The IADC Guidelines were endorsed in UNGA Res 62/217 (1 February 2008) UN Doc A/RES/62/217, para 26.

48 See UNGA, 'Report of the Committee on the Peaceful Uses of Outer Space' Annex, 47–50 UN Doc A/62/20 (2007).

2. those that limit their generation over the longer term/end-of-life procedures through the removal of decommissioned spacecraft and launch vehicle orbital stages from regions populated by operational spacecraft.

The seven UN Guidelines remain at a generalized level and 'encourage', on a voluntary basis, actions that would: limit debris released during normal operations; minimize the potential for break-ups during operational phases; limit the probability of accidental collision in orbit; avoid intentional destruction and other harmful activities; minimize potential for post-mission break-ups resulting from stored energy; limit the long-term presence of spacecraft and launch vehicle orbital stages in the low-Earth orbit region after the end of their mission; and limit the long-term interference of spacecraft and launch vehicle orbital stages with geosynchronous region after the end of their mission.

Whereas the IADC represents an open association of technical entities of space-faring states, UN agencies involve both space-faring states and those that are not. The motivations of the IADC members are thus far more homogeneous than those of the member states of UNCOPUOS. Importantly, the focus of IADC is technical, whereas UNCOPUOS is more politically influenced. The general guidelines were therefore 'transformed' (diluted) in their passage from the IADC to the UN system, in particular by UNCOPUOS. The UN Guidelines encompass far less technical detail than the IADC Guidelines, although they do refer to the IADC Guidelines,[49] and invite member states and international organizations to:

> refer to the latest version of the IADC space debris mitigation guidelines and other supporting documents, which can be found on the IADC website ... for more in-depth descriptions and recommendations pertaining to space debris mitigation measures.[50]

As noted, neither set of guidelines is binding under international law. Over the years there have been attempts to place the subject of space debris on the agenda of the Legal Subcommittee of UNCOPUOS, but with limited success.[51] Member states have tended to shy away from any formal legal discussion of the matter, a pattern that can also be observed with regard to other matters connected to aspects of sustainability in relation to space activities. Nevertheless, a number of space agencies that have taken some steps to implement the UN Guidelines are aware that such implementation serves their own interests in keeping relevant orbits accessible and useable.[52] However, the point at which they consider themselves ready to commit internationally to binding and legally enforceable regulation still seems a long time away.[53]

[49] As contained in UNGA, 'Inter-Agency Space Debris Coordination Committee Space Debris Mitigation Guidelines' (29 November 2002) UN Doc A/AC.105/ C.1/L.260, Annex (UN Guidelines).

[50] UN Guidelines, para 6.

[51] The item 'General exchange of information on national mechanisms relating to space debris mitigation measures' has appeared annually on the agenda of the Legal Subcommittee of UNCOPUOS since 2009.

[52] See, eg, the recently expired (14 December 2015) NASA Procedural Requirements. NASA, 'NASA Procedural Requirements' (14 May 2009) 8715.6A (NPR) <http://nodis3.gsfc.nasa.gov/npg_img/N_PR_8715_006A_/N_PR_8715_006A_.pdf> accessed 30 December 2015.

[53] Chapter P.1.7 of the NPR confirms that: 'This NPR shall not be construed as conferring upon any international body, agency, or committee the right to place upon the U.S. Government or NASA any restrictions or conditions as to its space operations unless required by separate agreement or treaty.'

Moreover, there remains a common perception that to introduce binding and comprehensive space debris mitigation measures will invariably increase the costs of space activities. Whether this reflects the true position in all cases, it represents a strong financial disincentive to the implementation of the guidelines.

Overall, therefore, although space debris and its cascading effects have been identified as one of the greatest challenges for the long-term sustainability of space activities, existing international 'regulation' can only be characterized as soft law at best. By implementing international guidelines via national or agency policies, policy makers might, however, ultimately contribute to the formation of a minimum standard of conduct, if international practice is sufficiently widespread and representative. In this context, the guidelines may take on an increasing relevance by providing appropriate international benchmarks, at least for presently foreseen risks and uncertainties. However, of course, voluntary non-binding instruments equally 'suffer' from the risk that states may more easily (as compared to binding instruments) decide not to abide by their terms.

In this regard, one might seek to draw upon the general principles of (terrestrial) international environmental law enunciated by the ICJ and 'transplant' their applicability to the exploration and use of outer space. In the *Legality of the Threat or Use of Nuclear Weapons* Case, the Court affirmed:

> the existence of the general obligation of States to ensure that activities within their jurisdiction and control respect the environment of other states *or of areas beyond national control* is now part of the corpus of international law relating to the environment.[54]

Applying this approach, states would be obliged to exercise their general right to explore and use outer space, as specified in Article I of the OST, with due regard to the protection of the global environment. Given the international responsibility regime specified in the OST,[55] it could be argued that they therefore have a continuing duty to take appropriate measures to prevent, minimize, and control environmental harm resulting from their space activities, whether carried out by governmental agencies or non-governmental entities.

It has been argued that the application of these principles equates to an obligation for states to act with due diligence, which is an obligation of conduct rather than of result. One commentator suggests that:

> [i]n effect Article IX of the [OST] requires states to exercise due diligence when conducting or authorising activities in outer space ... [this] has obvious parallels in international environmental law.[56]

Such due diligence would necessitate, first, the close monitoring of scientific knowledge, technological developments, and standards; second, a prompt transposition

[54] *Legality of the Threat or Use of Nuclear Weapons* (Advisory Opinion) [1996] ICJ Rep 226, para 29 (emphasis added).

[55] See OST, art VI.

[56] A Boyle, 'Outer Space and International Environmental Law' in S Hobe and S Freeland (eds), *In Heaven as on Earth? The Interaction of Public International Law on the Legal Regulation of Outer Space* (DLR 2013) 51, 52.

of new scientific and technological findings into policies and rules applicable to public and private undertakings; and, finally, at a minimum, adherence to any existing soft law guidelines related to the space environment.

However, whilst attempting to apply and incorporate broader international (environmental) law into the space environment is an interesting exercise, it lacks a certain relevance without more detailed consideration as to the appropriate methodology (and philosophy) for attempting to 'copy and paste' such principles into an extra-terrestrial setting. Is it, for example, appropriate to assume that a legal/regulatory framework developed in an attempt to deal with one particular regime can be utilized for another regime without any adaptation to adjust to the latter's specific circumstances? Indeed, is there a hierarchy of legal regimes that dictates that certain regulation can be treated as the (principal) starting point for a separate set of circumstances?

This is, to some degree, a problem that also applies to the legal regulation of military uses of outer space (see below). Notwithstanding that it appears that the space *lex specialis* contemplates that broader international law principles *may* apply, the starting point, at least from a military standpoint, is a different legal regime. However, it is much more difficult to describe precisely how this can be readily transferred to the unique characteristics of outer space.

In the end, therefore, we are left in a situation where the as yet undetermined limits of outer space activities, the effects of particular technologies and the risks associated with their (mis)use, and accidents in what still remains a hazardous endeavour, all point to the need for clearer and more rigorous rules in the area of environmental protection, including in particular when it comes to addressing the issue of space debris.

5.5 Addressing the Risks of 'Space Warfare'

As noted above, the terms of Article III of the OST reflected a concern that outer space might become a new arena for international conflict. Almost as soon as Sputnik was launched, the international community became concerned about the use of outer space for military purposes and the possibility that it might become a theatre of war. In December 1958 the UN emphasized the need 'to avoid the extension of present national rivalries into this new field'.[57]

By 1961 the UNGA had recommended that international law and the UNC should apply to 'outer space and celestial bodies'. This was repeated in the Legal Principles Declaration. The specific reference to the UNC was important, given its focus on the maintenance of international peace and security. It thus represented an important step intended to minimize the risk of conflict in outer space.

The sentiments underlying the UNC were further strengthened by the restrictions imposed in relation to nuclear weapons and weapons of mass destruction by

[57] UNGA Res 1348 (XIII) (13 December 1958), Preamble, para 3.

Article IV of the OST,[58] although this provision falls significantly short of a complete restriction on the placement of weapons in outer space.[59] Moreover, whilst most commentators were of the view that 'peaceful purposes' was directed against 'non-military' rather than 'non-aggressive' activities, the reality has been different. The primary motivations underpinning the development of space technology were, as noted, of a military nature, and the design and use of this technology has become ever more sophisticated. Indeed, in 1991, the Gulf War was referred to as the first 'space war'.[60]

Since then, the use of space technology to create an integrated battle platform to aid in the implementation of military strategy has gathered pace. Following the attacks of 11 September 2001, the US Administration embarked on a policy designed to enhance its domination of the space dimension of military operations. This necessitated having the ability to protect critical infrastructure and assets in outer space. Although the Obama administration has more recently emphasized cooperation in space to a far greater degree, those hawkish sentiments still represent the approach of the US military.

Ballistic missiles play an increasingly important role in any sophisticated national security structure, and the development of defensive systems 'is both a result of and additional factor driving' a global arms race.[61] In January 2001, a commission headed by former US Secretary of Defense, Donald Rumsfeld, suggested that an 'attack on elements of U.S. space systems during a crisis or conflict should not be considered an improbable act'.[62] The report warned of the possibility of a 'Space Pearl Harbor'—a surprise attack on the space assets of the US.

The European Union has since identified outer space as 'a key component for its European Defense and Security Policy'[63] and China and the USSR also regard space as a vital part of their respective military infrastructures. It is undeniable that the (vague) language of the international law instruments relating to space has not hampered the increasing utilization of satellite technology for an expanding array of military activities.

In this sense, therefore, the militarization of space is a given, notwithstanding that this flies in the face of the principles of the OST. The 'non-military *v* non-aggressive' debate has become a redundant argument and the focus of discussion as to the role that international law can play now centres on the risks and uncertainties associated with

[58] See OST, art IV.

[59] See, eg, G Gál, '"Threat or Use of Force"—Observations to Article 2 of the U.N. Charter and Article III of the Outer Space Treaty' (1989) 17(1) *Journal of Space Law* 54, 57.

[60] See, eg, D Kellner, 'From Vietnam to the Gulf: Postmodern Wars?' in M Bibby (ed), *The Vietnam War and Postmodernity* (University of Massachusetts Press 1999) 199, 217 (quoting General Merrill McPeak speaking in March 1991).

[61] R Hagen and J Scheffran, 'International Space Law and Space Security—Expectations and Criteria for a Sustainable and Peaceful Use of Outer Space' in M Benkö and K-U Schrogl (eds), *Space Law: Current Problems and Perspectives for Future Regulation* (Eleven International Publishing 2005) 273, 273.

[62] See J-M Stoullig, 'Rumsfeld Commission Warns Against "Space Pearl Harbor"', *SpaceDaily* (11 January 2001) <http://www.spacedaily.com/news/bmdo-01b.html> accessed 30 December 2015.

[63] Hagen and Scheffran, 'International Space Law and Space Security' (n 61) 281–82.

the trending 'weaponization' of space. The UNGA has passed numerous resolutions on this issue[64] in an effort to supplement the weaknesses of the international law regulations, in the hope of establishing an appropriate framework to protect humankind from what could otherwise be unimaginable scenarios.

Yet, the destruction by both China and the United States of their satellites, as noted above, highlights the dangers posed by the advent of this technology. The situation in outer space is complicated even further by the growing reliance of states on continuous and reliable access to privately operated satellites for the protection of their national security interests, giving rise to the phenomena of 'dual-use' satellites. This also makes any attempt to apply the *jus in bello* principles to a 'space war' fraught with difficulty, highlighting the overly simplistic assumptions behind Article III of the OST.

To continue to rely solely on existing international rules regulating warfare that were developed in a previous technological era—as important as they are—is akin to applying twentieth-century rules to twenty-first-century technology. In the absence of some additional protections, terrestrial international (humanitarian) law will most likely not be sufficient to adequately regulate all armed conflict-related contingencies in outer space.[65] Consequently, apart from the general rules provided by the *lex specialis* of space law, there exists considerable uncertainty as to what rules regulate (and thus serve to deter) the use of outer space technology in the conduct of a conflict.

However, there is reluctance among the major powers to address this question through the use of binding treaty instruments. Once again, a voluntary soft law approach has been preferred, utilizing the notion of 'transparency and confidence-building measures' (TCBMs). A principal TCBM in the area of space security has been the (draft) International Code of Conduct for Outer Space Activities (CoC), which was initially developed as a European initiative but has since become broader in scope.[66] Recent discussions intended to finalize agreement on the CoC have, however, failed, and the instrument is currently in 'bureaucratic limbo'.[67]

The draft CoC seeks to find a balance between a number of relevant (and sometimes competing) claims relating to activities in outer space, particularly as they relate to a country's (real and perceived) national security interests. It recognizes that:

[64] Refer to the numerous UNGA Resolutions, beginning with UNGA Res 36/97C (9 December 1981) UN Doc A/RES/36/97C and culminating most recently with UNGA Res 68/29 (5 December 2013) UN Doc A/RES/68/29, which have been directed towards the 'Prevention of an arms race in outer space', commonly referred to as 'PAROS'.

[65] S Freeland, 'Legal Regulation of the Military Use of Outer Space' (2011) 41 *Collegium—the Journal of the College of Europe* 87.

[66] The latest version of the draft CoC (as of 31 March 2014) can be found at EEAS, 'Draft International Code of Conduct for Outer Space Activities' (31 March 2014) (Draft CoC) <http://www.eeas.europa.eu/non-proliferation-and-disarmament/pdf/space_code_conduct_draft_vers_31-march-2014_en.pdf> accessed 30 December 2015.

[67] MJ Listner, 'The International Code of Conduct: Comments on Changes in the Latest Draft and Post-Mortem Thoughts' *The Space Review* (US, 26 October 2015) <http://www.thespacereview.com/article/2851/1> accessed 30 December 2015.

space debris affects the sustainable use of outer space, constitutes a hazard to outer space activities and potentially limits the effective deployment and utilization of associated outer space capabilities.[68]

These concerns interact with issues related to the military uses of space—particularly the physical (kinetic) destruction of space objects. Related to the issue of space debris is, of course, the issue of maintaining the integrity of space assets, both in terms of adherence to measures on space debris control and mitigation, and by minimizing the possibility that a state would destroy another state's satellite (and in the process almost certainly create additional space debris).

Whilst there are obvious benefits in developing greater trust between the space powers in issues relating to space security, the danger is that non-binding TCBMs such as the draft CoC—even if it might eventually be agreed—are, for all practical purposes, considered as the 'end game' on this issue, so that the formalization of binding obligations may *never* eventuate. At its core, the draft CoC provisions are merely guidelines or recommendations that do not have the force of law, unless they are to be regarded as reflecting rules of customary international law, itself a very difficult assertion to substantiate in the absence of, say, a ruling by the ICJ. This approach appears inadequate to meet the complex risks associated with the continued development of space-related weapons.

5.6 Conclusion

Humankind's exploration and use of outer space has seen the world change in ways that were once unimaginable. Our lives have been transformed by the opportunities offered by space technology. That said, we still do not fully understand 'the great prospects opening up before mankind as a result of [hu]man's entry into outer space'.[69] However, it is likely that an even greater range of space activities will evolve. This will give rise to considerable opportunities, but also considerable challenges.

In the context of this rapid technological evolution, the development of a legally binding regime to regulate outer space has been difficult. Whilst very important general foundational principles were initially agreed, and these have served humanity relatively well, they do not provide for a comprehensive framework for many space activities that have been, and will be made possible by further technological advancement.

Indeed, the generalized terms of these international law instruments, whilst providing clarification of a few overarching principles, themselves give rise to uncertainties in the context of rapidly developing technology and increasingly diverse uses of space. States have been able to develop their space activities without significant constraints. In this sense, given the legal *lacunae* that arise, such uncertainties

[68] Draft CoC, Preamble, para 7. [69] OST, Preamble, para 1.

increase the probability that even the most fundamental rules that have previously been agreed may in future not attract the same level of adherence.

Attempts have been made on an ad hoc basis to fill these gaps and deal with particular issues through the use of non-binding instruments. This approach is consistent with the geopolitics of outer space, but has meant that these inherent risks and uncertainties, both now and into the future, will still not be adequately addressed, unless the (major) space stakeholders alter their resistance to stricter 'regulation'.

In the meantime, our failure to address the risks of the past, as well as the uncertainties stemming from the existing international legal framework, point to a future in which we will not be able to properly utilize the opportunities that space may otherwise offer. This represents yet another challenge to the future of humanity.

PART III

RISK AND HUMAN PROTECTION

6

The European Court of Human Rights as Governor of Risk

Mónika Ambrus

6.1 Introduction

Ulrich Beck has argued[1] that '[m]odern society has become a risk society in the sense that it is increasingly occupied with debating, preventing and managing risks that it itself has produced'.[2] While it has been debated whether our society can only be seen as a society full of risk (a 'risk society' in its strict sense),[3] it is generally accepted that the management and governance of risk have become important factors in our everyday life. In general, the term 'risk' can be defined as the possibility of something bad happening. In other words, in addition to a negative event, it also incorporates a probability element. It is precisely this 'probability' (not only in the statistical sense, but also in terms of estimation and imagination) that provides the possibility to adopt measures that might prevent a harm occurring, thereby enabling the governance of risk. Law and legal institutions can thus embrace and, indeed, have embraced such measures.

In law, risk is usually associated with natural or man-made catastrophes, such as tsunamis, floods, or oil platform explosions. These issues are often discussed in international environmental law, increasingly in the context of climate change. In addition, there is a growing literature on and interest in risk to health within international trade law relating, for example, to food safety measures. Considerations of risk governance are also present in other fields of law, such as international human rights law, where the concept of risk is generally understudied. As a contribution to filling this gap, this chapter aims to explore the

[1] U Beck, *Risk Society: Towards a New Modernity* (Sage 1992) (first published in German as *Risikogesellschaft: Auf dem Weg*, Surbkamp Verlag 1986). Beck's theory has been criticized from various perspectives, including his rather radical language as to the effect of one specific phenomenon on the whole of society. See, inter alia, P O'Malley, 'Uncertain Governance and Resilient Subjects in the Risk Society' (2013) 3 *Onati Socio-Legal Series* 180, 183.

[2] U Beck, 'Living in the World Risk Society' (2006) 35 *Economy and Society* 329, 332.

[3] See, inter alia, C Aradau and R van Munster, 'Governing Terrorism Through Risk: Taking Precautions, (un)Knowing the Future' 13 (2007) *European Journal of International Relations* 89.

manner in which risk is, has been, and is being governed in international human rights law, in particular by the European Court of Human Rights (ECtHR or the Court), the guardian of the rights enshrined in the European Convention on Human Rights (ECHR).

As its starting point, the chapter relies on the Foucauldian concept of 'governmentality', according to which decisions reached by the ECtHR (as with other international (quasi-)judicial bodies) can be regarded and analysed as a mode of governance. According to Foucault, governmentality is defined as:

> [t]he ensemble formed by the institutions, procedures, analyses and reflections, the calculations and tactics that allow the exercise of this very specific albeit complex form of power, which has as its target *population*, as its principal form of knowledge *political economy*, and as its essential technical means *apparatuses of security*.[4]

As Aalberts notes, government(ality), refers not only 'to political structures and/or legitimately constituted forms of political subjection per se, but more generally to acting upon the possibilities of action of people'.[5] In this respect, the specific definitional elements of the Foucauldian concept of governmentality can be directly related to the ECtHR. The Court's target is a certain population (the 'people'), whose well-being it specifically aims to secure from a human rights perspective.[6] Both the Court's knowledge and its means thus have a significant impact on the behaviour of those governed.[7] Finally, the Court also has its own apparatuses of security, broadly understood, including, for example, techniques of interpretation, balancing of interests, and remedies. In other words, the Court has a special form of knowledge and power through which it constrains behaviour and thus constructs subjectivities.

Increasingly, the Court has included risk-related considerations in its 'form of knowledge' and its 'techniques of governance', thereby resulting in a certain adjustment of its governmentality. For example, the Court has declared as admissible complaints relating to events the occurrence of which was, to a certain extent, uncertain, and has decided in favour of the applicant. In relying on the invocation of specific 'rationalities and technologies' to govern risk, the Court is essentially using a 'risk dispositief'.[8] As pointed out by Aradau and Van Munster, '[a] dispositief of risk

[4] M Foucault, 'Governmentality' in G Burchell et al (eds), *The Foucault Effect. Studies in Governmentality* (University of Chicago Press 1991) 102 (emphases added).

[5] TE Aalberts, 'Patterns of Global Governmentality and Sovereignty' in S Guzzini and IB Neumann (eds) *The Diffusion of Power in Global Governance: International Political Economy Meets Foucault* (Palgrave Macmillan 2012) 240. She is referring to M Foucault, 'The Subject and Power' (1982) 2 *Critical Inquiry* 777, 789.

[6] As Aradau and Van Munster explain '[g]overnmental rationalities and technologies affect behavior and "construct" forms of ordered agency and subjectivity in the population to be governed as part of the social problem identified'. Aradau and van Munster, 'Governing Terrorism Through Risk' (n 3) 97.

[7] Foucault defines political economy as follows: 'the correct manner of managing individuals, goods and wealth within the family (which a good father is expected to do in relation to his wife, children and servants) and of making the family fortunes prosper'. Foucault, 'Governmentality' (n 4) 92.

[8] Aradau and van Munster, 'Governing Terrorism Through Risk' (n 3) 97.

creates a specific relation to the future, which requires the monitoring of the future, the attempt to calculate what the future can offer and the necessity to control and minimize its potentially harmful effects'.[9] A risk dispositief thus constitutes a special form of governmentality.

Against this background, this chapter analyses the Court's 'risk dispositief'[10] and explores the ways in which the Court governs risk. In this regard, two specific questions are raised. First, what are the specific features of governing uncertain future events that are adopted by the Court? This includes the identification of the forms of risk that the Court incorporates in its mode of governance and the manner in which it allocates responsibility for these risks. Second, how does the Court's risk dispositief create new subjectivities and redefine relationships? In other words, what community is being constituted by the Court's risk governmentality? The Foucauldian concept of governmentality provides the theoretical framework for exploring the Court's risk dispositief, and provides a tool for analysing the Court's techniques of risk governmentality. However, the ultimate purpose of this enquiry is to ascertain how the Court addresses risk-related complaints and how it conceptualizes risk in different contexts. In doing so, this chapter serves to provide a prima facie overview of risk governance in human rights law which may, in turn, serve as a basis for a comparison with other fields of international law, such as international environmental law and international trade law. It also provides insights into the capabilities and possibilities of (international) judicial bodies in general when they enter the world of risk governance.

In pursuing this analysis, the discussion focuses on the following rights under the ECHR: the right to life (Article 2); the prohibition of torture (Article 3); the rights to respect for and protection of certain democratic values as enshrined in Articles 10 and 11 (right to freedom of expression, freedom of assembly, and association); and the protection of the environment under Articles 6 and 8. In order to concentrate on the governance of 'normal risk' no consideration is given to situations relating to states of emergency. In other words, rather than looking at the extraordinary, the governance of 'normal risk' is scrutinized.

Reflecting the questions asked above, section 6.2 examines the features of risk governance while section 6.3 examines its impact on creating subjectivities. In each section, after a brief conceptualization, the relevant case law of the Court is analysed. Section 6.4 concludes with some reflections on the Court's risk dispositief and governmentality in a more abstract manner. While it is admitted that the discussion here is limited, it is hoped that it provides a representative analytical sample for further contemplation.

[9] ibid, 97–98. (emphasis added).

[10] 'Dispositief' in the Foucauldian sense refers to 'discourses, institutions, architectural forms, regulatory decisions, laws, administrative measures, scientific statements, philosophical, moral and philanthropic propositions'. M Foucault, 'The Confessions of the Flesh', in C Gordon (ed), *Power/Knowledge. Selected Interviews and Other Writings 1972–1977* (Pantheon Books 1980) 194.

6.2 The Court's Risk Dispositief

The different forms risk can take, as well as governance reactions to these risks, have given rise to various conceptualizations of risk both within and outside the realm of law and legal studies. Before examining the relevant case law of the Court, it is useful to provide a brief description of these various conceptualizations of the features of risk governance.

6.2.1 General features of risk governance

When it comes to the notions of risk and risk governance, four main features, or elements, can be identified and distinguished: the concept of risk; categories of risks; principles used for governing risk; and factors influencing how risk is to be governed.

With respect to the concept of risk, while risk is often allied with uncertainty,[11] conceptually risk, *stricto sensu*, means that there is knowledge about the probability of the occurrence of the harm as well as about the outcome.[12] Based on this understanding, a scale of knowledge as to probability and outcome can be elaborated, involving certainty, risk *stricto sensu*, uncertainty, and ignorance. *Certainty* means that the outcome is known and it is certain that the event will take place. In this respect, certainty is not actually associated with risk. *Uncertainty* means that there is knowledge about the outcome, but the probability of the occurrence of harm is not known. *Ignorance* is used to describe a phenomenon in relation to which there is knowledge neither about the outcome nor about the probability. In general, 'risk' (in its broad meaning) is often understood as involving not only risk *stricto sensu*, but also uncertainty and ignorance.

In addition to this multifaceted conceptualization of risk, different categorizations of risk can be divined from the literature, two of which, in particular, deserve explicit mention: *natural v man-made risk* and *public v private risk*. While the first distinction may require little explanation, the second is rather more problematic in that it is both less clear and it overlaps with the first distinction. According to Gillette and Krier,

> [p]ublic risks have been defined as man-made 'threats to human health or safety that are centrally or mass-produced, broadly distributed, and largely outside the individual risk bearer's direct understanding and control.' 'Private risks', in contrast, are either of natural origin, or, if man-made, produced in relatively discrete units, with local impacts more or less subject to personal control.[13]

[11] For a somewhat different, although implicit, conceptualization, see Beck, 'Living in the World Risk Society' (n 2) 333–34.

[12] A Arcuri, 'Governing the Risks of Ultra-Hazardous Activities. Challenges for Contemporary Legal Systems' (PhD thesis 2005) 23–24. She refers to FH Knight, *Risk, Uncertainty, and Profit* (Houghton Mifflin Company 1921) 216–17.

[13] CP Gillette and JE Krier, 'Risk, Courts, and Agencies' (1990) 138 *University of Pennsylvania Law Review* 1027, 1028–29 (footnote omitted).

The examples par excellence of public risks are nuclear power plants, while for private risks the examples most often invoked are those of diseases or cars.

With respect to the principles governing risk, two main principles have been envisaged in law, namely the principles of *precaution* and *prevention*. The main distinction between these two principles relates to the (non-)existence of scientific (un)certainty. The precautionary principle relies on the idea that scientific uncertainty should not be used as a reason to postpone necessary protective measures. The principle of prevention requires action only when there is certainty as to the harm (and/or the probability of its occurrence).[14] In other words, when the evidence as to the existence of risk is great, a state's obligation will be one of prevention rather than precaution (although as scientific certainty can never be fully achieved, the obligation of precaution will not be wholly dispensed with).

In terms of the factors influencing the governance of risk, while the literature has identified numerous factors as relevant to the assessment of risk—both in terms of experts' assessment and lay-perceptions[15]—three main factors can be identified as recurring. The first factor is often referred to as the 'dread factor', primarily because it focuses on the nature of the harm to be expected, whether and to what extent the harm/risk can be controlled/managed, and whether there is a choice element included. The second factor can be described as the 'visibility factor'; that is, whether and to what extent the risk and the nature of the harm are well known among the public and experts and whether it is an old or new type of risk. The third factor, which can be defined as the 'extent factor', essentially incorporates the most often considered aspect of risk, which is the number of people who might be affected by the harm caused.[16]

6.2.2 Features of the Court's risk governance

These features of risk governance can be seen as manifested in the case law of the Court as it relates to specific public values.

6.2.2.1 Risk to life

Article 2 of the ECHR protects the life of individuals. The obligation of states in this regard includes both negative and positive obligations, in particular the positive obligation to act when there is a risk to life. Such risks can originate primarily from two sources: other individuals or catastrophes/disasters, be they natural or man-made. In both cases the Court has clarified that states are required to take measures to protect life.

[14] A Trouwborst, 'Prevention, Precaution, Logic, and Law: The Relationship between the Precautionary Principle and the Preventative Principle' (2009) 2 *Erasmus Law Review* 105.

[15] P Slovic, B Fischhoff, and S. Lichtenstein, 'Facts and Fears: Understanding Perceived Risk', in RC Schwing and WA Albers (eds), *Societal Risk Assessment: How Safe is Safe Enough?* (Plenum Press 1980) 194; Arcuri, 'Governing the Risks of Ultra-Hazardous Activities' (n 12) 28–29.

[16] For further elaboration, see Arcuri, 'Governing the Risks of Ultra-Hazardous Activities' (n 12) 30.

With respect to risks arising from other individuals, risk to life can often originate from within the family or from a harasser, thereby requiring more from the state than merely adopting appropriate legislation. In the *Osman* case,[17] for example, which has been used as an important reference point in later cases, the Court was concerned with the question of whether the authorities should have taken measures to protect the life of Ali and Ahmet Osman from Paget-Lewis, a school teacher, who had a 'disturbing attachment to'[18] Ahmet Osman and harassed the Osman family in different ways. The Court held that:

> it must be established ... that the authorities knew or ought to have known at the time of the existence of a *real and immediate risk* to the life of an identified individual or individuals from the criminal acts of a third party and that they failed to take measures within the scope of their powers which, judged reasonably, might have been expected to avoid that risk.[19]

Thus, in the Court's view, authorities will be expected to take the necessary protective measures when the risk to life is 'real and immediate'. In addition, in determining the extent of the obligation to take the necessary measures, the Court also noted that given the difficulties involved in policing modern societies, the unpredictability of human conduct and the operational choices which must be made in terms of priorities and resources, such an obligation must be interpreted in a way which does not impose an impossible or disproportionate burden on the authorities.[20]

In the *Osman* case, consistent with its normal practice, the Court placed considerable emphasis on the extent to which the public authorities knew, or ought to have known of the risk to life. This approach could be translated as the examination of the knowledge of the probability of the occurrence of the harm and the harm itself. Put differently, the Court appears to make an implicit distinction between risk and uncertainty, the former requiring action from the state, while requiring action in the latter case would impose an unreasonable burden on the state. Accordingly, when the risk concerns a man-made and private risk, the Court relies on the concept of risk *stricto sensu*, and thus applies the principle of prevention rather than precaution.

In assessing the level of knowledge of the authorities in the *Osman* case, the following aspects of the perpetrator's conduct were considered by the Court: the nature of the previous harassing incidents (which were not life-threatening)[21] and his personality (he was not considered to constitute 'danger to the safety of young people in his charge').[22] All in all, the Court found that:

> the applicants have failed to point to any decisive stage in the sequence of the events leading up to the tragic shooting when it could be said that the police knew or ought to have known that the lives of the Osman family were at real and immediate risk from Paget-Lewis.[23]

[17] See, inter alia, *Van Colle v The United Kingdom* App No 7678/09 (ECHR, 13 November 2012).
[18] *Osman v The United Kingdom* App No 87/1997/871/1083 (ECHR, 28 October 1998) para 117.
[19] ibid, para 116 (emphasis added). [20] ibid. [21] ibid, para 119.
[22] ibid, para 118. [23] ibid, para 121.

Based on this assessment, it seems that the factors considered by the Court are the 'dread factor' and the 'visibility factor', with a great emphasis on the latter one.

Catastrophes and/or disasters can also result in risk to life and can therefore also give rise to the responsibility of a state for failing to adopt appropriate measures for the protection of human lives. Such cases are usually concerned with environmental pollution-related risks, arising from, for example, dangerous activities carried out by companies, or natural disasters such as floods or earthquakes.[24] In the Court's case-law there seems to be a distinction as to the extent of state obligations between man-made and natural disasters, the latter implying a somewhat broader margin of appreciation for the states.[25]

With regard to dangerous activities, ie man-made risk, whether public or private, the same approach is adopted as that with regard to risk originating from individuals. For example, in the *Öneryildiz* case the Court repeated the 'knew-or-ought-to-have-known' requirement in combination with the existence of 'a real and imminent risk' to the lives of people, implying that the governing principle is prevention rather than precaution.[26] This case concerned the danger stemming from a rubbish tip located near an inhabited area, which resulted in an accident. The Court explained that:

> the Turkish authorities at several levels *knew or ought to have known* that there was a *real and immediate risk to a number of persons* living near the Umraniye municipal rubbish tip. They consequently had a positive obligation under Article 2 of the Convention to take such preventive operational measures as were necessary and sufficient to protect those individuals ..., especially as they themselves had set up the site and authorised its operation, which gave rise to the risk in question.[27]

As far as the factors are concerned, as highlighted in the above quote, positive obligations are imposed on states due to the *harmfulness* of the dangerous activities (dread factor), the *foreseeability* of the risks to life (visibility factor), and the *number* of individuals potentially affected (extent factor).[28]

Although the margin of appreciation is broader when the risk concerns natural disaster, states still have some obligations in this respect as well. As the Court indicated in the *Budayeva* case, which concerned a mudslide in 2000 in Tyrnauz, Turkey, which killed at least eight people and left a further nineteen people missing,

> [i]n the sphere of emergency relief, where the State is directly involved in the protection of human lives through the mitigation of natural hazards, these considerations should apply in so far as the circumstances of a particular case point to the *imminence* of a natural hazard that had been *clearly identifiable*, and especially where it concerned a *recurring calamity* affecting a distinct area developed for human habitation or use.[29]

[24] Of course, the distinction between dangerous activities and natural disasters is not always clear-cut; nevertheless, for the sake of a conceptual discussion it provides a useful tool.

[25] See, eg, *Budayeva and Others v Russia* App Nos 15339/02, 21166/02, 20058/02, and 15343/02 (ECHR, 20 March 2008) para 135. See also Council of Europe, *Manual on Human Rights and the Environment* (2nd edn, Council of Europe Publishing 2012) 39.

[26] *Öneryildiz v Turkey* App No 48939/99 (ECHR 30 November 2004) paras 90, 93, 100. See also Council of Europe, ibid, 39.

[27] *Öneryildiz v Turkey*, ibid, para 101.

[28] Council of Europe, *Manual on Human Rights and the Environment* 36 (n 25).

[29] *Budayeva and Others v Russia* (n 25) para 137. See also Council of Europe, *Manual on Human Rights and the Environment* (n 25) 39.

Thus, the Court required a high level of certainty as to the hazard that will occur in order to establish state responsibility. Given the high level of certainty required by the Court, clearly the principle being applied by the Court was that of prevention rather than precaution.

Moreover, in *Budayeva*, which concerned natural disasters as opposed to man-made risk, the Court also considered the other factors mentioned above in assessing whether or not the state should be held responsible. In general, the Court pointed to 'the imminence of a natural hazard'[30] (visibility factor), 'whether it concerned a recurring calamity'[31] (visibility factor), the 'origin of the threat',[32] and 'the extent to which one or the other risk is susceptible to mitigation'[33] (dread factor). *In concreto*, the Court first looked very carefully at the foreseeability of the mudslide. It pointed out that the town 'is situated in an area prone to mudslides' and that it could be 'reasonably assumed that a mudslide was likely'.[34] Second, it assessed whether the authorities could have known that the scale of the mudslide would be larger than usual. Based on the warnings submitted by various agencies, the Court concluded that the authorities 'were aware that any mudslide, regardless of its scale, was capable of causing devastating consequences'.[35] All in all, the Court came to the conclusion that:

> there was no justification for the authorities' omissions in implementation of the land-planning and emergency relief policies in the hazardous area of Tyrnauz regarding the foreseeable exposure of residents, including all applicants, to mortal risk.[36]

In addition, the Court also observed that the mudslide 'killed eight people' and 'threatened the lives of an uncertain number of other residents of Tyrnauz'.[37] Accordingly, the Court clearly relied on the dread and the visibility factors, as well as—although to a much lesser degree—the extent factor.

6.2.2.2 Risk of ill-treatment

Cases involving the risk of ill-treatment generally concern refugees and asylum seekers. More concretely, receiving states have an obligation not to send refugees and asylum seekers back to their country in situations where they may be at risk of ill-treatment. In this context, the Court has developed a steady line of jurisprudence concerning risk assessment. The elements mentioned in these cases are: there is a substantial ground for the existence of real risk; the risk has to be real (not speculative); the consequences have to be foreseeable; and the risk can be related to both the individual at stake and the group to which he/she belongs. This last aspect renders the risk both private and public. In addition, as the Court indicated, for example, in the *Saadi* case:

> the existence of domestic laws and accession to international treaties guaranteeing respect for fundamental rights in principle are not in themselves sufficient to ensure adequate

[30] *Budayeva and Others v Russia* (n 25) para 137. [31] ibid. [32] ibid.
[33] ibid. [34] ibid, para 147. [35] ibid, para 149. [36] ibid, para 158.
[37] ibid, para 161.

protection against the risk of ill-treatment where, as in the present case, reliable sources have reported practices resorted to or tolerated by the authorities which are manifestly contrary to the principles of the Convention.[38]

This observation of the Court essentially gives rise to two aspects of risk assessment. First, the applicant has to prove that there are substantial grounds for believing in the existence of a real risk. This requires a high level of knowledge about both the probabilities and the outcome and can thus be qualified as risk *stricto sensu*. Second, as soon as the applicant has established that there are substantial grounds to believe that a real risk exists, the state cannot merely rely on the existing legislation to prove the lack of such risk. Put differently, not only is a high standard of proof required for the existence of a risk, but the state must also meet a high standard of proof if it wants to rebut the argument in favour of the existence of the risk. This two-step procedure essentially results in risk being equated with the guarantees provided by the state of origin.[39] This conception of man-made risk brings the state obligation closer to the principle of prevention than precaution.

As far as the factors are concerned, in the *Saadi* and similar cases, the Court relies on two factors, namely the dread and the visibility factors, to define whether the state can be held responsible for violating the prohibition of ill-treatment. In these types of cases, the extent factor does not have much importance given that the Court usually has to assess the risk regarding one specific individual. Obviously, in cases where the assessment concerns the effect on a group, the extent factor also becomes relevant. The Court emphasizes that the risk has to be real, i.e. that 'substantial grounds have been shown that there is a real risk that the applicant would be subjected to treatment contrary to Article 3 of the Convention if he were to be deported to Tunisia'.[40] A 'real risk' seems to include both the visibility and the dread factors; indeed, the Court explained that it 'must examine the foreseeable consequences of sending the applicant to the receiving country'[41] (visibility factor) and that 'ill-treatment must attain a minimum level of severity'[42] (dread factor).

6.2.2.3 Risk to democratic values

The cases involving risk to democratic values address the risk in terms of justification and not as interference. In other words, in these cases it is the state that has to prove that there was a risk to democratic values which required the limitation of the specific right at stake. For example, in the *Refah Partisi* case the Court explained that in order to establish whether such risk existed, it was necessary to assess 'whether there was plausible evidence that risk to democracy, supposing it had been proved to exist, was sufficiently *imminent*' and 'whether the acts and

[38] *Saadi v Italy* App No 37201/06 (ECHR, 28 February 2008) para 147.

[39] Some states have also relied on diplomatic assurances, which '[i]n practice, however, the Court has never found … reliable enough whenever a risk of torture or ill-treatment had been found'. G Gentili, 'European Court of Human Rights: An Absolute Ban on Deportation of Foreign Citizens to Countries where Torture or Ill-Treatment is a Genuine Risk' (2010) 8 *I-CON* 311, 320.

[40] *Saadi v Italy* (n 38) para 146. [41] ibid, para 130. [42] ibid, para 134.

speeches imputable to the political party formed a whole which gave a clear picture of a model of society conceived and advocated by the party which was *incompatible with the concept of a "democratic society"*.[43] In the *Vona* case the Court further specified these requirements, explaining that 'when any danger to democracy is being assessed, regard must be had to the actual influence of such organisations'.[44] In the Court's view, the above-mentioned 'imminent' requirement can also be neglected so that 'the State is entitled to act preventively' where 'it is established that such a movement has started to take concrete steps in public life to implement a policy incompatible with the standards of the Convention and democracy'.[45] Thus, in effect, the concrete measures adopted by such an organization establish the immanency of the risk. Immanency can also be interpreted as including that the risk is real; in essence, once real, the risk is imminent. Accordingly, the threshold for establishing the existence of risk for interference with the freedom of assembly is similar to that invoked in cases involving Articles 2 and 3 of the ECHR, even though it is expressed in somewhat different terms. In other words, the knowledge required for this type of risk, in terms of both the probability and the outcome, is again rather high. Accordingly, the Court is applying the concept of risk *stricto sensu* with regard to this man-made public risk and the principle of prevention rather than precaution.

In cases relating to democratic values, which, as indicated above, are addressed under the proportionality analysis, the dread and the visibility factors play a rather important role, while the extent factor is implicit in the concept of democracy and democratic values. In the *Refah Partisi* case, and several times since then, the Court has explained that a state is entitled to intervene as soon as 'the danger of that policy for democracy is sufficiently established and imminent'.[46] This requirement can be translated as incorporating the dread and the visibility factors; danger for democracy, as explained by the Court, can be regarded as the former factor, while its imminent nature as well as the 'sufficient' establishment of the danger itself can be taken as the latter factor. More concretely, in the Court's view, given:

> that Refah's policies were dangerous for the rights and freedoms guaranteed by the Convention, the real chances that Refah would implement its programme after gaining power made that danger more tangible and more immediate.[47]

The Court also assessed the main grounds for the dissolution of the party by the Constitutional Court, thereby invoking, yet again, the dread factor.[48]

> In a rather similar manner, in the *Vona* case, which repeated the main findings from *Refah Partisi*, the Court added that 'when any danger to democracy is being assessed, regard must

[43] *Refah Partisi (The Welfare Party) and Others v Turkey* App Nos 41340/98, 41342/98, 41343/98, and 41344/98 (ECHR, 13 February 2003) para 104 (emphasis added).

[44] *Vona v Hungary* App No 35943/10 (ECHR, 9 July 2013) para 56.

[45] ibid, para 57.

[46] *Refah Partisi (The Welfare Party) and Others v Turkey* (n 43) para 102.

[47] ibid, para 110.

[48] ibid, paras 116–31.

be had to the actual influence of such organisations'.[49] This can be translated as a reference to the dread factor and, implicitly, to the extent factor. The Court then went on to combine the dread factor with the visibility factor, highlighting that the State is entitled to take preventive measures to protect democracy vis-à-vis such non-party entities as well if a *sufficiently imminent* prejudice to the rights of others *undermines the fundamental values* upon which a democratic society rests and functions. One of such values is the cohabitation of members of society without racial segregation without which a democratic society is inconceivable.[50]

6.2.2.4 *Risks to environment under Article 8*

In addition to the right to life, risks to the environment may also affect other human rights within the Convention's system including, for example, the right to health and physical integrity, as well as the right to home. Cases involving these issues are generally considered the environmental cases under the Convention, and, to a certain extent, they have also been addressed in terms of risk and risk assessment.[51] Importantly, in these cases the Court has also addressed the procedural aspects of the right, and has elaborated on the procedural obligations incumbent on the state when environmental risks are at stake. Indeed, the Court has been rather clear about requiring the state to provide access to information as to the danger posed as a procedural aspect of the specific right. Moreover, the Court has also relied on Article 6 of the ECHR concerning 'serious, specific and imminent environmental risk' when 'the danger reaches a degree of probability which makes the outcome of the proceedings directly decisive for the rights of those individuals concerned'.[52] In addition, a distinction has been made between man-made and natural disasters leading to risk to health, physical integrity, or home. Such a distinction has been made, for example, in cases relating to noise disturbance, pollution stemming from a gold ore extraction plant, or other industrial pollution by state owned or private companies.

In the *Dubetska* case, which concerned long term exposure to pollution generated by two state-owned industrial facilities, the Court explained that 'an arguable claim under Article 8 may arise where an environmental hazard attains a *level of severity* resulting in significant impairment of the applicant's ability to enjoy his home, private or family life'.[53] The Court took several factors into account in establishing whether the required level of severity had been reached, 'such as the intensity and duration of the nuisance and its physical or mental effects on the individual's health or quality of life'.[54] The Court also considered whether the risk was new or old, and whether the state knew and/or should have known about the existence of

[49] *Vona v Hungary* (n 43) para 56.

[50] ibid, para 57 (emphases added).

[51] See, inter alia, C Hilton, 'Risk and the European Convention on Human Rights: Towards a New Approach' (2008–2009) 11 *The Cambridge Yearbook of European Studies* 353.

[52] Council of Europe, *Manual on Human Rights and the Environment* (n 25) 24.

[53] *Dubetska and Others v Ukraine* App No 30499/03 (ECHR, 10 February 2011) para 105 (emphasis added).

[54] ibid.

the risk.[55] Interestingly, this language is rather similar to the Court's narrative in cases involving Article 2 of the ECHR.

In the *Tatar* case, which concerned a gold ore extraction plant where sodium cyanide was used to extract gold, the Court also concluded on the basis of environmental impact assessments that 'a *serious and substantial threat* to the applicants' well-being existed'.[56] Here the Court explicitly emphasized the precautionary principle, which created obligations for the states. Whether the Court considered that the 'serious and substantial threat' amounted to proper knowledge about probabilities and outcome or whether it included some uncertainty is somewhat unclear from the judgment. If the latter, then the reference to the precautionary principle was correct. If the former, then the Court should have referred to the principle of prevention.

The applicability of the precautionary principle was again assessed in the *Luginbühl* case, where the issue was whether a complaint concerning the impact of a mobile phone antenna on health could be regarded as admissible. The Court indicated that it would require 'at least *some scientific validity* of the claim that a certain activity is dangerous to the environment and/or health'.[57] In doing so, the Court implicitly applied the precautionary principle.

The distinction as to the approach towards risk between dangerous activities and natural disasters was also addressed, albeit implicitly, in the *Taskin* case.[58] That case involved the risk of negative impact on the applicant's health caused by a specific mining technique used by a gold mine in Turkey. In the Court's view, as soon as the environment is heavily polluted, the likelihood of a negative effect on an individual's well-being could easily be accepted. This is already the case with regard to natural disasters. 'However, in case of "dangerous activities" the Court requires a "sufficiently close link" to be established'[59] with the right at stake, meaning that it comes close to the 'serious and substantial threat' standard. Accordingly, it seems that with regard to natural disasters, the Court seems to be willing to work with the concept of uncertainty, while in case of dangerous activities it requires the existence of risk *stricto sensu*.

With regard to the factors that the Court takes into account in environmental cases, the *Dubetska* case is instructive. Here the Court again took all three factors into account in establishing whether the required level of severity had been reached. First, the dread factor can clearly be identified in the Court's reference to 'the intensity and duration of the nuisance and its physical or mental effects on the individual's health or quality of life',[60] and its observation that '[n]otwithstanding the effort, for more than twelve years the State authorities have not been able to put in place an effective solution for the applicants' personal situation, which throughout

[55] ibid, para 108.

[56] *Tatar v Romania* App No 67021/01 (ECHR, 27 January 2009) para 107. See also Council of Europe, *Manual on Human Rights and the Environment* (n 25) 50 (emphasis added).

[57] Council of Europe, *Manual on Human Rights and the Environment* (n 25) 50 (emphasis added); *Luginbühl v Switzerland* App No 42756/02 (ECHR, decision, 17 January 2006).

[58] *Taskin and Others v Turkey* App No 46117/99 (ECHR, 10 November 2004).

[59] Council of Europe, *Manual on Human Rights and the Environment* (n 25) 51; *Taskin and Others v Turkey*, ibid, para 113.

[60] *Dubetska and Others v Ukraine* (n 53) para 105.

this period has remained virtually the same'.[61] Second, the Court also considered whether the risk was new or old, and whether the state knew and/or should have known about the existence of the risk; that is, whether and to what extent the risk was 'visible'.[62] Finally, the Court also considered the extent factor—although in a somewhat different manner than usual—when it examined whether a proper balance had been reached. The Court acknowledged that the state had a rather complex task to fulfil with regard to addressing the environmental pollution caused by the mines, which had been 'piling up waste for over fifty years'.[63] Nevertheless, the number of individuals affected was rather limited in this case, given that 'these industrial facilities were located in a rural area and the applicants belonged to a very small group of people ... who lived nearby and were most seriously affected by pollution'.[64] Given the limited number of individuals affected, the Court found that the state should have been able to remedy their situation.

In conclusion, as the above exploration and analysis, summarized in Tables 6.1 and 6.2 indicates, the Court's techniques of governmentality have been extended to include various risk-related aspects, whereby it relies on specific 'rationalities and technologies' to govern risk.[65] Put differently, one might conclude that the Court's power now extends to controlling and monitoring the future.

Table 6.1 Overview of the features of the Court's risk dispositief relating to the specific public values

	Scale of knowledge	Man-made vs natural Public v private	Prevention v precaution
Risk to life	Risk	Man-made—private and public Natural—public	Prevention
Risk of ill-treatment	Risk	Man-made—private	Prevention
Risk to democratic values	Risk	Man-made—public	Prevention
Risk to environment	Risk Uncertainty?	Man-made—public Natural—public	Prevention

Table 6.2 Overview of the factors influencing risk governance relating to the specific public values

	Dread factor	Visibility factor	Extent factor
Risk to life			
—man-made/private	X	X	–
—man-made/public	X	X	X
—natural/public	X	X	X
Risk of ill-treatment	X	X	Only in certain cases
Risk to democratic values	X	X	Implicit
Risk to environment	X	X	X

[61] ibid, para 147. [62] ibid, para 108. [63] ibid, para 155.
[64] ibid, para 155.
[65] Aradau and van Munster, 'Governing Terrorism Through Risk' (n 3) 97.

6.3 Subjectivities of Risk Governance

In addition to the features of the Court's risk dispositief, another important aspect of the Court's risk governance concerns the subjectivities of risk governance. The question here relates to who are the relevant agencies in the governance of risk that are created or envisaged by the Court. In other words, what is the nature of this 'risk community'? After a brief explanation of the theoretical underpinnings of this point, the case-law of the Court is placed under scrutiny from this perspective.

6.3.1 Risk community

The Court's risk dispositief has created various relations at the domestic level, many of which are relevant to proceedings before the Court. The theoretical underpinnings of this 'risk community' are derived from Foucault's formulation of 'governmentality', in which a governing body—in the present case, the Court—'ha[s] to act upon these relations … and these ha[ve] to be understood and administered using a whole range of strategies and tactics to secure the well-being of each and of all'.[66] In some scholarly work the concepts of governmentality and risk have been combined to create a focus on the manner in which 'risk as a framework of government' 'creates new subjectivities and redefines relationships'.[67] From the perspective of the Court, the question can thus be posed: what subjectivities have been created, and how have certain relationships become relevant for the Court?

6.3.2 Subjectivities created by the Court

In cases relating to the right to life—in addition to individuals as victims—individuals as well as legal entities (eg, corporations)[68] have become relevant as potential sources of risk. In the *Osman* case, for example, a school teacher was regarded as a potential risk to one of his students. In order to assess whether there was, in fact, a risk to life, the Court relied on the reports prepared by a psychiatrist at the domestic level.[69] In cases relating to public risk, be it man-made or natural disasters, the Court has also relied on expert reports prepared at the domestic level.[70]

[66] N Rose, P O'Malley, and M Valverde, 'Governmentality' (2006) 2 *Annual Review of Law Social Science* 83, 87.

[67] P O'Malley, 'Governmentality and Risk', in JO Zinn (ed), *Social Theories of Uncertainty and Risk: An Introduction* (Blackwell Publishing 2008) 63.

[68] See, eg, *Taskin and Others v Turkey* (n 58).

[69] 'The applicants are especially critical of Dr Ferguson's psychiatric assessment of Paget-Lewis. However, that assessment was made on the basis of three separate interviews with Paget-Lewis and if it appeared to a professional psychiatrist that he did not at the time display any signs of mental illness or a propensity to violence it would be unreasonable to have expected the police to have construed the actions of Paget-Lewis as they were reported to them by the school as those of a mentally disturbed and highly dangerous individual.' *Osman v The United Kingdom* (n 18) para 118.

[70] In the *Öneryildiz* case, the Court took into account expert report commissioned by the Third Division of the Üsküdar District Court, the report prepared by the committee of experts appointed by the Üsküdar public prosecutor, and scientific opinions by the chief inspector appointed by the Ministry of the Interior. *Öneryildiz v Turkey* (n 26) paras 98 and 99. Relating to the *Budayeva* case, the Court noted

When the case concerns a risk of ill-treatment, the Court primarily relies on risk assessment, although it does not use this specific term, carried out by non-governmental organizations (NGOs) or certain government sources.[71] In the *Saadi* case, for example, the Court noted that it 'has attached importance to the information contained in recent reports from independent human rights protection associations ... or governmental sources'.[72] More specifically, 'the Court has had regard ... to the reports of Amnesty International and Human Rights Watch on Tunisia ..., which describe a disturbing situation. The conclusions of those reports are corroborated by the report of the US Department of State.'[73]

In relation to risk to democratic values, the Court attributes significant expertise to itself, such as the assessment of whether there is a risk to democratic values, assessment of the effect of political parties on public opinion, or the assessment of legal-political history. For example, in *Refah Partisi,* the Court noted that it 'must not lose sight of the fact that in the past political movements based on religious fundamentalism have been able to seize political power in certain States and have had the opportunity to set up the model of society which they had in mind'.[74] Similarly, in the *Vona* case, the Court reached the conclusion that:

> [i]n view of historical experience ... the reliance of an association on paramilitary demonstrations which express racial division and implicitly call for race-based action must have an intimidating effect on members of a racial minority, especially when they are in their homes as a captive audience.[75]

It is instructive that in these cases no separate experts or expertise were relied upon.

Finally, in cases of risk to the environment, one would expect a rather important role to be afforded to experts and environmental risk assessment. However, to date such an approach has not dominated the Court's case law, at least not with regard to cases involving risk in the absence of actual harm. Nevertheless, in the *Dubetska* case the Court found it important to 'examine whether the authorities conducted sufficient studies to evaluate the risks of a potentially hazardous activity'.[76] In a similar manner, the Court clearly explained that:

> in a case involving State decisions affecting environmental issues there are two aspects to the inquiry which it may carry out. Firstly, the Court may assess the substantive merits of the national authorities' decision to ensure that it is compatible with Article 8. Secondly, it may scrutinize the decision-making process to ensure that due weight has been accorded to the interests of the individual ...[77]

Often, environmental impact assessment is considered in relation to the procedural aspects of a case. In addition, in these cases industrial polluters are also

that relating to 'the mudslide of August 2000 the authorities of the KBR received a number of warnings that should have made them aware of the increasing risks'. *Budayeva and Others v Russia* (n 25) para 148.

[71] 'Traditionally, the Court has relied on reports drafted by independent international human rights organizations or government sources to assess the risk of ill-treatment.' G Gentili, 'European Court of Human Rights' (n 39) 316.

[72] *Saadi v Italy* (n 38) para 131.

[73] ibid, para 143.

[74] *Refah Partisi (The Welfare Party) and Others v Turkey* (n 43) para 124.

[75] *Vona v Hungary* (n 44) para 66.

[76] *Dubetska and Others v Ukraine* (n 53) para 143.

[77] *Taskin and Others v Turkey*, (n 58) para 115.

seen as potential perpetrators, thus constituting a new subjectivity within this context.[78]

As far as states are concerned, the above analysis reveals that the Court has extended the (positive) obligations on states through its risk dispositief, thereby having an impact on the sovereignty of states. Even though the public values vary, the concept of risk that the Court has incorporated into its technique of governance has been rather similar. The Court has been careful not to impose obligations upon states with regard to future harms in situations of uncertainty where the probability of the future harm is not known. Accordingly, state sovereignty is reconfigured only with regard to harms which, in the Court's assessment, constitute a 'real risk'. Put differently, although state sovereignty has not remained untouched by risk to certain public values under the human rights regime, it has only 'lightly' been affected by the extension of obligations relating to 'risk'. Sovereignty has thus been reloaded in a slightly amended manner.[79]

Undoubtedly, the more subjectivities being created in the Court's risk dispositief, the less room there is for the state to act freely—irrespective of the particular role of the specific agencies. In other words, any new subjectivities involved impose additional responsibility upon the state. This reconfiguration of state sovereignty can be observed in the increasing extent of positive state obligations imposed by virtue of the involvement of new agencies, the requirement that states rebut evidence provided by certain agencies, and the expectation on states that they act in accordance with certain opinions such as those expressed in scientific/expert reports. Nevertheless, from this perspective, too, state sovereignty is only 'lightly' reconfigured.

6.4 Conclusion

Although the wording of the ECHR does not necessarily imply that risk to the rights enshrined in the Convention will be protected, the Court has interpreted some of the provisions as including this dimension, thereby making the Court a relevant actor in risk governance. With respect to risk, using a language resembling that of Foucault, Beck has argued that risk 'is a socially constructed phenomenon, in which some people have a greater capacity to define risks than others'.[80] If translated into the context of the Convention's system, it could be argued that while risk is simultaneously being constructed by the member states of the Council of Europe and their population, by certain entities involved in the protection of human rights, as well as by private companies active within the territory of the member states of the Council of Europe, the Court has been given a rather important role in defining

[78] See, eg, *Dubetska and Others v Ukraine* (n 53).

[79] Traditional IR scholars would discuss sovereignty in terms of limitation imposed by the Court. However, and interesting to note, the Court, by imposing more positive obligations upon states, essentially 'increases' the power the sovereigns have over their population.

[80] U Beck, 'Living in the World Risk Society' (n 2) 333.

what actually constitutes risk. Indeed, the prominence of the Court's role in this risk definition and risk governance is evident in its role as the arbiter of which risk-related complaints will be regarded as admissible and, thus, which states can ultimately be held responsible. By establishing a rather high threshold as to the probability of the occurrence of the risk, the Court limits the scope of claims that will be admissible, leaving individuals helpless with regard to certain future scenarios that have been anticipated in one way or another. However, a limited form of risk has been included and, thus, has modified the 'traditional understanding of risk as an individual responsibility'.[81] Nevertheless, it must be remembered that the Court's role in this regard is influenced by the subsidiarity principle and by state sovereignty. This demonstrates the manner in which governmentality at the international or global level and state sovereignty mutually influence each other.

This point can also be reversed, and the question asked whether, and to what extent, risk has acquired a prominent place in the governmentality of the Court. Although the Court has not always been explicit in this regard, this chapter has disclosed some of the rationalities and technologies through which the Court governs risk, and which thus form part of its risk dispositief. It has been demonstrated that, within the means available to it, the Court does try to calculate the future and to minimize its negative impacts. Interestingly, looking at the case law through the lens of risk assessment, the analysis has revealed that even though various public values might be affected by a risk scenario, the Court carries out a rather similar (and implicit) assessment. While the Court has attempted to distinguish between certain forms of risk, such as natural and man-made, the difference is almost invisible in the actual interpretation and application of the particular provisions.

All in all, the future of the Court's risk dispositief is quite straightforward; states will be held responsible for clear-cut risks, but not for potential harms which include uncertainty. This approach may have important consequences for the subjectivities of risk governance, such as individuals who consider themselves to be potentially affected in the future by certain decisions made by their government which involve significant uncertainty such as, for example, decisions concerning measures for mitigating the effects of climate change.

[81] Aradau and van Munster, 'Governing Terrorism Through Risk' (n 3) 99.

7

Imagining Future People in Biomedical Law

From Technological Utopias to Legal Dystopias within the Regulation of Human Genetic Modification Technologies

Britta van Beers

7.1 Introduction: The Rise of Utopian Technologies

Emerging technologies such as medical biotechnology, artificial intelligence, and cognitive sciences, have elicited wild speculation about, and vivid imageries of, the future of mankind, even beyond the realm of fantasy novels and science-fiction movies. Apparently, the fact that human beings are becoming the object of far-reaching technological interventions and inventions is to many a development of such an unprecedented nature that new images and vocabularies are invoked to describe both the hopes and the fears that these technologies engender. Charged expressions such as 'taking evolution into our own hands', 'playing God', and 'the Promethean drive to mastery', are a commonplace in these discussions.

Among scientists, prophetic statements about humanity's future can also be heard. A recent example is Stephen Hawking's much discussed proclamation that 'the development of full artificial intelligence could spell the end of the human race'. Even if existing forms of artificial intelligence enable the heavily paralysed theoretical physicist to communicate, he is concerned that in the future a more evolved type of artificial intelligence 'would take off on its own, and re-design itself at an ever increasing rate'. Hawking fears that 'humans, who are limited by slow biological evolution, couldn't compete, and would be superseded'.[1]

Where Hawking's warnings go back to a bleak and dystopian imagination of the future, other scientists' speculations on artificial intelligence are overtly utopian. For example, computer scientist Raymond Kurzweil predicts that a coming artificial 'intelligence explosion' will allow humans to transcend their biological natures, overcoming the limitations and fragilities of their bodies and brains.[2] Kurzweil is

[1] R Cellan-Jones, 'Stephen Hawking Warns Artificial Intelligence Could End Mankind', *BBC News*, 2 December 2014 <http://www.bbc.com/news/technology-30290540> accessed 18 April 2015.

[2] R Kurzweil, *The Singularity is Near: When Humans Transcend Biology* (Penguin 2006).

Imagining Future People in Biomedical Law: From Technological Utopias to Legal Dystopias within the Regulation of Human Genetic Modification Technologies Britta van Beers.

not alone in his techno-optimism. Other, equally 'transhumanist' scientists believe, for example, that a combination of artificial intelligence, regenerative medicine,[3] and cryogenic preservation[4] will allow them to attain immortality within their current life times. As French philosopher of science Dominique Lecourt aptly states, these hopes of human transcendence through technological means border on religious faith; the transhumanist project can be described as a form of *techno-theology*.[5]

In a way, it should not surprise anyone that even scientists are caught fantasizing out loud. The classic view of scientific practice, according to which scientists reveal and analyse the 'cold' facts of nature, is no longer tenable—if it ever was—as scientists are openly *engineering* nature within these new, technological contexts. Indeed, Kurzweil's dreams and prophesies illustrate how emerging technologies not only give rise to utopian narratives, but are often based themselves on utopian motives. They are, in essence, 'utopian technologies',[6] to use a phrase coined by philosopher of science Hans Jonas, who explains these technologies' utopian nature as follows:

> By the kind and size of its snowballing effects, technological power propels us into goals of a type that was formerly the preserve of Utopias.... The one thing we can really know of them is their extremism as such—that they concern the total condition of nature on our globe and the very kind of creatures that shall, or shall not, populate it.[7]

Moreover, since contemporary scientific practice heavily depends on financial investments from third parties, investors' personal imaginations of the future are also increasingly influencing technological developments. Recent statements by well-known billionaire Silicon Valley entrepreneurs Elon Musk and Peter Thiel offer striking illustrations of that tendency. Musk's quest to make space travel routine and affordable for everyone goes back to his dream to make humans 'a multiplanetary species'. The science-fiction novel *Foundation* by Isaac Asimov serves as his main source of inspiration.[8] Thiel, in his turn, invests large sums of money into the construction of artificial islands where people can live according to libertarian ideas. Ayn Rand's capitalistic utopia *Atlas Shrugged* serves as the guiding light to his project.[9]

[3] Eg, A de Grey, a well-known scientist in the field of regenerative medicine, believes that the first persons to become 150 years or older have already been born. See, K Kelland, 'Who Wants to Live Forever? Scientist Sees Aging Cured', *Reuters*, 4 July 2011 <http://www.reuters.com/article/2011/07/04/us-ageing-cure-idUSTRE7632ID20110704> accessed 19 April 2015.

[4] Eg, several prominent members of the Oxford Future of Humanity Institute will have their heads frozen after death in the hope that someday they can be brought back to life. See J Leake, 'Freeze a Jolly Good Fellow: Three Oxford Dons are Paying to be Cryonically Preserved', *Sunday Times*, 9 June 2013 <http://www.thesundaytimes.co.uk/sto/news/uk_news/Education/article1271389.ece> accessed 19 April 2015.

[5] D Lecourt, *Humain, Posthumain. La Technique et la Vie* (Presses Universitaires de France 2003) 12.

[6] H Jonas, *The Imperative of Responsibility: In Search of an Ethics for the Technological Age* (University of Chicago Press 1985) 21–22, 42.

[7] ibid, 21.

[8] R Carroll, 'Elon Musk's Mission to Mars', *The Guardian*, 17 July 2013 <http://www.theguardian.com/technology/2013/jul/17/elon-musk-mission-mars-spacex> accessed 9 May 2015.

[9] 'Floating Cities: PayPal Billionaire Plans to Build a Whole New Libertarian Colony Off the Coast of San Francisco', *Daily Mail*, 25 August 2011 <http://www.dailymail.co.uk/news/article-2024761/Atlas-Shrugged-Silicon-Valley-billionaire-reveals-plan-launch-floating-start-country-coast-San-Francisco.html#ixzz3ZdeRPWgF> accessed 9 May 2015.

Some of these technologies are now also targeting human nature itself as an object of change. These so-called human enhancement technologies, which aim to improve human evolution or to redirect the human condition, open up the possibility of turning certain visions of the human, or the post- or trans-human, into reality. Especially within the field of assisted reproductive technologies (ARTs), the once science-fiction scenarios of genetically designed human beings are on the verge of becoming a reality.

Tellingly, in a period of less than two decades, many of the technologies to select and engineer children before birth, which were depicted, albeit in a negative way, in the 1997 science-fiction movie *Gattaca,* have become, or are about to become, available. Pre-implantation genetic diagnosis, for example, has facilitated genetic selection of embryos since the 1990s; in 2012, prenatal whole genome sequencing was used to map an embryo's entire genome for the first time;[10] and in 2015 it was announced that a new technology, known as 'human gene-editing', will soon make it possible to modify the embryo's genetic constitution.[11] The technology of human gene-editing will be further explained below, as it will be used as a recurring example to illustrate the main arguments of this chapter.

As these rapid developments in the field of assisted reproduction make abundantly clear, technological projects of human *autopoiesis* necessitate reflection on the question of what makes humans human in the first place. In the words of the German philosopher Jürgen Habermas, 'whether these speculations are manifestations of a feverish imagination or serious prediction, an expression of displaced eschatological needs or a new variety of science-fiction science', they are all 'examples of an instrumentalisation of human nature initiating a change in the ethical self-understanding of the species'.[12]

Interestingly, to regulate these utopian technologies, a legal field has emerged which equally relies on future scenarios, fictions, imaginations, and symbolizations of the human. However, as will become clear, the legal imaginations of the future in this field tend to be more dystopian in nature.

In this chapter, I explore and analyse the ways in which imaginings of the future of mankind, and mankind itself, have found their way into international legal regulation of biomedical technologies. As will be shown, the use of different types of legal fictions to represent the human is one of the primary ways within international biomedical law, also called *biolaw*, to deal with the uncertainties caused by these emerging technologies. Moreover, as the texts of several international conventions and declarations in biomedical law indicate, one of the main aims of international biolaw is to protect no less than the future interests of humankind.

The increasing recognition of the importance of imagination for both the development and international regulation of biomedical technologies can be illustrated by a 2015 international summit on biotechnology: *Biotechnology*

[10] HC Fan, W Gu, J Wang et al, 'Non-Invasive Prenatal Measurement of the Fetal Genome' (2012) 487 *Nature* 320.

[11] For more on this, see section 7.2.1.

[12] J Habermas, *The Future of Human Nature* (Polity Press 2003) 42.

and the Ethical Imagination: A Global Summit (BEINGS 2015). This meeting was organized in the spirit of the famous 1975 Asilomar Conference, which brought together biomedical experts to develop guidelines in reaction to the then recently established moratorium on DNA recombinant technologies. What makes BEINGS 2015 of interest for this chapter is that all speakers and participants were explicitly invited to 'reimagine the aspirations of biotechnology'[13] in order to contribute to the development of international guidelines. For that purpose, prominent biomedical scientists were brought together with policy makers, corporate partners, and scholars from varying backgrounds, ranging from literature to religion. Tellingly, one of the keynote speakers was Margaret Atwood, novelist of critically acclaimed dystopian novels on biomedical technology, such as *Oryx and Crake*.[14]

This chapter discusses the importance of imagination for legal and ethical frameworks in the field of the biosciences. It builds on German–American phenomenological philosopher Hans Jonas's reflections on the emergence of technological risks for humanity, as developed in his influential work, *The Imperative of Responsibility*.[15] The chapter's main argument is that Jonas's thoughts can explain three important characteristics of international biolaw: its reliance on dystopian rather than utopian scenarios (section 7.2); the metaphysical nature of the view of humanity on which international biolaw relies to protect against future risks and uncertainties (section 7.3); and finally, the use of imagination and fiction in this legal field (section 7.4). Throughout this chapter, these points will be illustrated by recent debates on the international ban on human germline genetic engineering. This prohibition, which is at the heart of international biolaw, is currently being questioned, as recent scientific breakthroughs in the field of gene-editing are about to turn human genetic engineering into a reality.

7.2 Human Genetic Modification: Between Technological Utopia and Legal Dystopia

7.2.1 The rise of human genetic modification technologies

As the technology of human germline modification is currently making the transition from science fiction to actual science, and is generating much debate on its risks and dangers, it offers the perfect case to examine how possible futures and future people are imagined within biomedical regulation. Human germline modification involves making changes to the human genome that are passed on to future generations. Although human genetic engineering was not technologically possible until recently, it has been prohibited in international law documents since the 1990s. A prime example is Article 13 of the Council of Europe's Convention

[13] See the summit's site <http://www.beings2015.org/about.html> accessed 11 June 2015.

[14] M Atwood, *Oryx and Crake* (McClelland and Stewart 2003).

[15] Jonas, *The Imperative of Responsibility* (n 6).

of Human Rights and Biomedicine,[16] which states that 'an intervention seeking to modify the human genome may only be undertaken for preventive, diagnostic or therapeutic purposes and only if its aim is not to introduce any modification in the genome of any descendants'. In 1997, when the Convention came into force, this provision was based on mere speculation. In early 2015, however, the significance of Article 13 was revitalized when two technologies in the field of human genetic germline modification made international headlines: mitochondrial replacement and human gene-editing.

In February 2015, the United Kingdom became the first state worldwide to legalize mitochondrial replacement.[17] The aim of this technology is to prevent the transmission of mitochondrial diseases to children-to-be. It involves enucleating an egg cell of a third party, and filling it with the nucleus of an egg cell from the prospective mother. This special egg cell is subsequently fertilized with the sperm of the prospective father. The resulting embryo is popularly known as a 'three parent embryo', as the child will be genetically related to two women and one man. Moreover, the technology could be said to constitute a form of germline genetic modification as described in Article 13, because the genetic alterations will be passed on to future generations. Nevertheless, as the intervention affects only mitochondrial DNA, and the nucleus remains unaffected, this technology establishes only minor heritable changes to the germline. Advocates of this technology therefore state that it is far-fetched to speak of designer babies in this context.[18]

This seems much less the case for the second biogenetic technology, which has been the subject of vigorous debates since the beginning of 2015. Several leading scientific journals[19] announced in March 2015 that a remarkably simple and cheap genome engineering method, called CRISPR-Cas9, was close to being successfully applied to human genomes. This 'gene-editing' technology allows scientists to 'cut and paste' DNA with extreme precision. According to the authors of said scientific articles, human gene-editing marks no less than 'the advent of a new era in biology and genetics'[20] as it brings the possibility of 'engineering the perfect baby'[21] within reach. Nevertheless, it is beyond doubt that this technology aims to realize interventions with the human genome that are prohibited by, for instance, Article 13.

[16] Convention for the Protection of Human Rights and Dignity of the Human Being with Regard to the Application of Biology and Medicine: Convention on Human Rights and Biomedicine (Convention on Human Rights and Biomedicine) (adopted 4 April 1997, entered into force 1 February 1999) CETS 164.

[17] H Devlin, 'Britain's House of Lords Approves Conception of Three-Person Babies', *The Guardian*, 24 February 2015 <http://www.theguardian.com/politics/2015/feb/24/uk-house-of-lords-approves-conception-of-three-person-babies> accessed 20 March 2015.

[18] ibid. Also see, eg, ethicist John Harris's viewpoint as voiced in S Connor, 'Scientist Who Pioneered "Three-Parent" IVF Embryo Technique Now Wants to Offer It to Older Women Trying for a Baby', *The Independent*, 8 February 2015 <http://www.independent.co.uk/news/science/threeparent-embryos-an-ivf-revolution-or-a-slippery-slope-to-designer-babies-10031477.html> accessed 14 May 2015.

[19] A Regalado, 'Engineering the Perfect Baby', *MIT Technology Review*, 5 March 2015 <http://www.technologyreview.com/featuredstory/535661/engineering-the-perfect-baby/> accessed 10 May 2015; and E Lanphier, F Urnov, S Ehlen Haecker et al, 'Don't Edit the Human Germline' (2015) 519 *Nature* 410; D Baltimore, P Berg, M Botchan et al, 'A Prudent Path Forward for Genomic Engineering and Germline Gene Modification', (2015) 348 (6230) *Science* 36.

[20] Baltimore et al, ibid, 38.

[21] Regalado, 'Engineering the Perfect Baby' (n 19).

The question is how this legal ban will affect current scientific developments, and, vice versa, how these technologies will affect the legal status of Article 13. The aforementioned articles suggest that for now, a majority within the scientific community is in favour of a moratorium on human gene-editing. However, this could change since, as will be discussed below, many of the current objections are not absolute in nature. In addition, one can doubt how effective legal bans on human genetic engineering will prove to be. International legal documents, such as the Convention on Human Rights and Biomedicine, have not been ratified in many countries. Moreover, even if they have been, the question is how they can be enforced. Indeed, shortly after the international discussion on a possible moratorium had begun, a group of Chinese scientists announced that they had already applied CRISPR-Cas9 to human embryos to modify an aberrant gene that causes beta-thalassaemia, albeit with mixed results.[22] Finally, because the legal ban on human genetic engineering is one of the central provisions in international biolaw, the rise of human genetic modification raises the larger question of what the projected risks are against which biolaw aims to protect, and why the biolegal framework features quite a pessimistic outlook on the possible outcomes of biomedical developments. Section 7.2.2 focuses on these last questions.

7.2.2 Biolaw's dystopian approaches to utopian technologies

Biomedical technologies enable interventions with the human body and human life on a biogenetic level. From the perspective of the biosciences, human life is perceived as a set of building blocks which can be regrouped, remodelled, rebuilt, recombined, and replicated at will. As such, biomedical interventions may have far-reaching effects on a collective level, both positive and negative. Indeed, according to the human rights conventions and declarations that have been developed since the 1990s to regulate biomedical developments, these technologies ultimately affect the interests of humanity, both in the present and the future. The preamble of the Convention on Human Rights and Biomedicine (Council of Europe) describes these interests as follows:

> Conscious that the misuse of biology and medicine may lead to acts endangering human dignity;
> Affirming that progress in biology and medicine should be used for the benefit of present and future generations;
> Stressing the need for international co-operation so that all humanity may enjoy the benefits of biology and medicine.

Even if these sentences also stress the huge possible benefits of biomedical science, in general, international biolaw seems to focus more on its potential harms and dangers. It could be said, somewhat paradoxically, that within the legal regulation of these 'utopian

[22] I Sample, 'Scientists Genetically Modify Human Embryos in Controversial World First', *The Guardian*, 23 April 2015 <http://www.theguardian.com/science/2015/apr/23/scientists-genetically-modify-human-embryos-in-controversial-world-first> accessed 10 May 2015.

technologies', dystopian scenarios tend to prevail. Accordingly, the legal framework of biomedical regulation is characterized by prohibitions on and restrictions of the use and development of biomedical technologies. The most important international conventions and declarations in this field prohibit, in addition to human germline genetic modification, eugenic practices, in particular those aiming at the selection of persons,[23] using ARTs to select a future child's sex,[24] the creation of human embryos for research purposes,[25] the use of the human body and its parts for financial gain,[26] and creating genetically identical human beings.[27]

All these prohibitions involve speculation on several levels. As some of these technologies, such as human cloning, have not been developed yet, and as the actual effects of these technologies are therefore as yet unknown, these prohibitions necessarily involve the regulation of potential, future situations. Moreover, these provisions aim to protect the interests of possible future legal subjects. Some technologies, such as ARTs, look to the creation of future persons; others establish genetic changes which can be passed down to future generations. Finally, to express the possible harms involved, relatively vague expressions are used, such as respect for human life and human dignity. In all these cases it remains unclear what the views of these future people on these technologies will be, or how their fates will be exactly affected. Techno-optimists view these uncertainties as a major weakness of current international regulation of biomedical developments. At the aforementioned global summit, BEINGS 2015, for instance, a recurring complaint was that vague fears and highly speculative harms are now thwarting biomedical progress, thereby standing in the way of saving millions of lives. Moreover, the cautious and even dystopian tenet within ethical and legal approaches to biomedical technologies was heavily criticized. As one of the summit's participants voiced his disdain: 'we need to resist bowing at the altar of amorphous existential risks without identifiable harms'.[28]

These criticisms have been largely left unanswered in legal discourse. One of the central arguments in this chapter is that the anti-utopian approach advocated by Jonas in *The Imperative of Responsibility* can fill this gap. His view of emerging technologies and their accompanying uncertainties can explain the cautious approach to biomedical technologies that is generally employed in international law.

[23] EU Charter of Fundamental Rights (adopted 18 December 2000, entered into force 1 December 2009), OJEC C 364, art 3(2)(b).

[24] Convention on Human Rights and Biomedicine, art 14.

[25] Convention on Human Rights and Biomedicine, art 18(2).

[26] Convention on Human Rights and Biomedicine, art 21; EU Charter of Fundamental Rights (n 23), art 3(2)(c).

[27] Additional Protocol to the Convention for the Protection of Human Rights and Dignity of the Human Being with Regard to the Application of Biology and Medicine, on the Prohibition of Cloning Human Beings (adopted 12 January 1998, entered into force 1 March 2001) CETS No 168, art 1; EU Charter of Fundamental Rights (n 23), art 3(2)(d); Universal Declaration on the Human Genome and Human Rights (adopted 11 November 1997, the United Nations Educational, Scientific and Cultural Organization (UNESCO) Res 29 C/17, endorsed by UN General Assembly Declaration, United Nations General Assembley (UNGA) Res 53/152, 9 December 1998), art 11.

[28] M Darnovsky, 'Tired Tropes and New Twists in the Debate about Human Germline Modification', *Biopolitical Times*, 28 May 2015 <http://www.biopoliticaltimes.org/article.php?id=8618> accessed 3 December 2015.

According to Jonas, emerging technologies are of such an unprecedented, utopian scale, and will have such far-reaching effects for the future of mankind, that they necessitate a new ethical paradigm. The new type of ethics which he advocates does not limit itself to establishing the rights and duties towards contemporary members of the legal community, but also takes into account responsibilities towards future generations. Within his *Fernethik*, 'the indefinite future, rather than the contemporary context of the action, constitutes the relevant horizon of responsibility'.[29] As a starting point to this future-oriented type of ethics, Jonas formulates his famous revision of Kant's categorical imperative to express the responsibilities to future people: 'Act so that the effects of your action are compatible with the permanence of genuine human life.'[30]

Nevertheless, it is clear that predictions of the long-range effects of our technological actions are characterized by a high level of uncertainty. Jonas describes our current predicament as follows:

> Living now constantly in the shadow of unwanted, built-in, automatic utopianism, we are constantly confronted with issues whose positive choice requires supreme wisdom—an impossible situation for man in general, because he does not possess that wisdom, and in particular for contemporary man, because he denies the very existence of its object, namely, objective value and truth. We need wisdom most when we believe in it least.[31]

As a result, a certain degree of imagination and speculation is inevitable in legal and ethical frameworks that are developed to regulate technological interventions. For Jonas, this state of affairs does not pose an insurmountable obstacle. On the contrary, it forms the starting point for his ethic of the future. In this vein, as will be discussed in a later section, Jonas uses imagination as the cornerstone of his methodological approach. Moreover, for him uncertainty has important normative implications, which he expresses through the formulation of a new ethical principle. This principle commands ethical and legal decision-making 'to give in matters of a certain magnitude—those with apocalyptic potential—greater weight to the prognosis of doom than to that of bliss'.[32] For his proposed precautionary and overtly anti-utopian approach, Jonas offers three reasons.[33] First, by taking evolution in our own hands, we are compressing the slow and gradual process of natural evolution, with its small 'mistakes' along the way, into a much more fast-paced and ambitious process of reform of human nature, with accordingly much larger, even catastrophic risks. As a result, the stakes involved in technological interferences with human evolution will be much higher and its potential effects more radical than is the case with natural evolution. Second, Jonas observes that technological developments often gather an internal dynamic and momentum of their own, escaping from explicit moral deliberation. Third, he argues that precaution is in place because ultimately nothing less than human nature is at stake.

[29] Jonas, *The Imperative of Responsibility* (n 6) 9. [30] ibid, 11. [31] ibid, 21.
[32] ibid, 34. [33] ibid, 31–33.

7.3 Imagining the Dangers of Human Genetic Modification within Biolaw

Jonas's anti-utopian approach is able to explain the dominance of dystopian scenarios within biolaw. Moreover, his proposal to give priority to negative prognoses over positive ones corresponds with the precautionary approaches which can be recognized within international biolaw. However, an important question remains unanswered: what is the exact nature of the risks involved in regulation of contested biomedical developments?

In order to answer this question, this section focuses on the rationale behind the ban on altering the human germline, as expressed in Article 13. Three possible scenarios that may have influenced Article 13 will be sketched and explored: the scenarios of classic risk governance, existential risk, and dangers to human dignity. Which reading offers the most convincing explanation of the ban on human genetic germline modification in light of the Explanatory Report to the Convention?[34] Answering this question will allow, more generally, a better understanding of the special nature of risk within biolegal discourse.

A first possible reading of the ban is that the application of this technology to the human genome is still unsafe and poses serious health risks for those involved. As the scientists who are calling for a moratorium point out, 'the precise effects of genetic modification to an embryo may be impossible to know until after birth' and 'potential problems may not surface for years'.[35] Their main recommendations are more research and better education of the public by experts 'about this new era of human biology'.[36]

The clinical risks of the technology of human gene-editing, in its current stage of development, certainly warrant a classic system of risk governance based on the precautionary approach. After all, although the precautionary principle is most famously applied in the field of environmental law, it is also widely accepted to apply to public health interests.[37] Additionally, some of the concerns about interventions with the human genome resemble concerns which can be recognized in environmental law. To a certain extent, genetically modified organisms (GMOs), for instance, raise concerns similar to those raised by genetically modified human embryos. Similarly, protection of biodiversity could be understood to include protection of diversity in the human gene pool.

However, it seems that a traditional risk approach falls short within public deliberation on this issue on several levels. A risk approach seems to turn the issue

[34] *Explanatory Report to the Convention on Human Rights and Biomedicine*, DIR/JUR (97)5 <http://www.coe.int/en/web/conventions/full-list/-/conventions/treaty/164> accessed 18 February 2017.

[35] Lanphier et al, 'Don't Edit the Human Germline' (n 19) 411.

[36] Baltimore et al, 'A Prudent Path' (n 19) 38.

[37] As the European Commission notes in its communication on the principle, 'The precautionary principle is not defined in the Treaty, which prescribes it only once—to protect the environment. But in practice, its scope is much wider, and specifically where preliminary objective scientific evaluation indicates that there are reasonable grounds for concern that the potentially dangerous effects on the environment, human, animal or plant health may be inconsistent with the high level of protection

of human gene-editing into merely a safety issue. From that perspective, all that is needed is a scientific assessment of the clinical risks involved in human gene-editing. These should then be weighed against the possible clinical benefits. The public debate would then merely have to focus on finding a balance between these scientific perspectives. However, such an approach ignores key aspects of the issue of human gene modification. As a group of scholars, including prominent science and technologies scholar Sheila Jasanoff, eloquently describes the deficit of a classic risk approach to human genome engineering as a reaction to the aforementioned call for a moratorium on human gene-editing:

> the problem is not simply a lack of technical knowledge. The answer to how we should act does not lie in the technological details of CRISPR. It is our responsibility to decide, as parents and citizens, whether our current genetic preferences should be edited, for all time, into our children and our children's children. A moratorium without provisions for ongoing public deliberation narrows our understanding of risks and bypasses democracy.... Even in technologically advanced societies, we tend to defer to expert judgments about which risks are reasonable to worry about, and which are not. This is a democratic deficit. *It inhibits our capacity to participate thoughtfully in imagining the futures we want and governing technological change accordingly* [emphasis added].[38]

In other words, a classic risk approach to human gene-editing obfuscates the essentially political and moral nature of this issue. Indeed, even if gene-editing would be safe for clinical application in humans, this still would not take away many of the most serious concerns that people have about this technology. In fact, the comments in the Explanatory Report to the Convention of Human Rights and Biomedicine on Article 13 hardly mention patient safety. The concerns seem of a larger scale than can be grasped from a clinical risk perspective. As the Explanatory Report states:

> The progress of science, in particular in knowledge of the human genome and its application, has raised very positive perspectives, but also questions and even great fears. Whilst developments in this field may lead to great benefit for humanity, misuse of these developments may endanger not only the individual but the species itself.[39]

In other words, human germline genetic engineering not only poses risks to public health, but also to the continued existence of the entire human species. Similarly, within biolegal scholarly literature, concerns about the future of the human species have been expressed within the context of human genetic engineering. For instance, health law scholar George Annas warns that lifting the ban on this technology may open the door to genetic genocide.[40] By this he means that 'inheritable

chosen for the Community', Commission of the European Communities, 'Communication on the Precautionary Principle', *COM* (2000)1 (2 February 2000) 3.

[38] S Jasanoff, JB Hurlbut, and K Saha, 'Human Genetic Engineering Demands More Than a Moratorium', *The Guardian* (7 April 2015) <http://www.theguardian.com/science/political-science/2015/apr/07/human-genetic-engineering-demands-more-than-a-moratorium> accessed 11 May 2015.

[39] *Explanatory Report to the Convention on Human Rights and Biomedicine* (n 34) para 89.

[40] See, eg, G Annas, 'Crimes Against the Human Species (Type II Crimes Against Humanity Explained)' in BC van Beers et al (eds), *Humanity Across International Law and Biolaw* (CUP 2015) 129.

genetic alteration carries the prospect of developing a new species of humans that could turn into either destroyers or victims of the human species'.[41] Additionally, in order to protect 'the endangered human', Annas, together with scholars Isasi and Andrews, proposes a *Convention on the Preservation of the Species*. As they write, their project can be described as conservative in that they seek to conserve the human species.[42] Their 'bioconservatism', as the school of thought which unites all sorts of different criticisms of biomedical technologies is called,[43] can therefore be understood quite literally as aimed at biogenetic conservation. Their concerns seem to echo Hawking's aforementioned fear that new forms of artificial intelligence might spell the end of the human race.

The type of risk that surfaces in both Hawking's and Annas's thoughts could be described as existential risk. Nick Bostrom, prominent transhumanist scholar and director of the Oxford Future of Humanity Institute, offers the following definition: 'an existential risk is one that threatens the premature extinction of Earth-originating intelligent life or the permanent and drastic destruction of its potential for desirable future development'.[44] More than a traditional risk perspective, this approach is able to grasp the large scale of the stakes involved in human genetic engineering. As the preambles to the most important conventions and declarations in this legal field emphasize, it is indeed ultimately mankind, the human species, humanity or however one wishes to designate the human collective, that is involved in the biomedical project. Similarly, Habermas describes the ethics that should guide us within the regulation of human genetic engineering as an 'ethics of the species' (*Gattungsethik*).[45]

Nevertheless, even if texts of international biolaw seem to originate in a fear that our humanity is at risk, the existential risk approach is not able to get to the core of the ban on human germline modifications. The main problem is that an existential risk approach seems to reduce the ban on human germline modification to a special measure of wildlife conservation, with the difference being that it is now humans who are protected as endangered species. Yet, a closer look at Article 13 reveals that it is not the fear of human extinction, decimation, or other grave material risks for the human species which serves as guiding thought, but rather a fear of the destruction of humanity in less tangible ways. As is written in the subsequent words of the Explanatory Report to Article 13: 'The ultimate fear is of intentional modification of the human genome so as to produce individuals or entire groups endowed with particular characteristics and required qualities.'[46] In other words, regardless of the safety issues involved in germline modification, and

[41] GJ Annas, LB Andrews, and RM Isasi, 'Protecting the Endangered Human: Toward an International Treaty Prohibiting Cloning and Inheritable Alterations' (2002) 28 *American Journal of Law & Medicine* 151.

[42] ibid.

[43] In debates on biomedical issues, it is common to distinguish bioconservatives from transhumanists. See, eg, N Bostrom, 'In Defense of Posthuman Dignity' (2005) 19 *Bioethics* 202.

[44] N Bostrom, 'Existential Risk Prevention as Global Priority' (2013) 4(1) *Global Policy* 15.

[45] Habermas, *The Future of Human Nature* (n 12) 71.

[46] *Explanatory Report to the Convention on Human Rights and Biomedicine* (n 34) para 89.

the question whether this technology would put the prolonged existence of the human species at risk, it is undesirable to produce human individuals or groups according to a certain design or to satisfy a list of desired characteristics. Even if the remaining comments on Article 13 do not offer further explanation of these vague words, it is clear that, according to this Article, the main problem resides in the fact that human genetic modification opens up the possibility of one person designing the other.

It is perhaps not a coincidence that the Explanatory Report does not offer more guidance. The harm involved in the resulting 'self-instrumentalisation of the species'[47] is hard to put into words. It goes beyond the harm principle, and beyond a violation of rights. As French biolegal scholar Labrusse-Riou states: 'The problem is that nobody suffers in this issue. What suffers is society, the frame of reference, culture, which is probably graver.'[48] Indeed, as many philosophers writing on these issues point out, whether they are in favour of the use of these technologies or not, the prospect of one person designing the other calls into question no less than the foundational distinctions of any rights-based system of governance:[49] the distinction between persons and things,[50] between chance and choice,[51] and between the given and the made.[52] In legal philosopher Ronald Dworkin's words:

> The overall structure of our moral and ethical experience ... depends, crucially on a fundamental distinction between what we are responsible for doing or deciding, individually or collectively, and what is given to us, as a background against which we act or decide, but which we are powerless to change.... We dread the prospect of people designing other people because that possibility in itself shifts ... the chance/choice boundary that structures our values as a whole, and such a shift threatens, not to offend any of our present values, derivative or detached, but, on the contrary, to make a great part of these suddenly obsolete.[53]

[47] Habermas, *The Future of Human Nature* (n 12) 66.

[48] Labrusse-Riou made these remarks as a member of the French national ethical committee CCNE. See M Marcuzzi, 'La revendication des corps' in E Dockès and G Lhuilier (eds), *Le corps et ses représentations* (Litec 2001) 31.

[49] In Fukuyama's words, 'What is it that we want to protect from any future advances in biotechnology? The answer is, we want to protect the full range of our complex, evolved natures against attempts at self-modification. We do not want to disrupt either the unity or the continuity of human nature, and thereby the human rights that are based on it.' F Fukuyama, *Our Posthuman Future: Consequences of the Biotechnology Revolution* (Farrar, Straus en Giroux 2002) 172.

[50] In Habermas's words: '[...] advances of genetic engineering tend to blur the deeply rooted categorical distinctions between the subjective and the objective, the grown and the made. What is at stake, therefore, with the instrumentalization of prepersonal life is the ethical self-understanding of the species, which is crucial for whether or not we may go on to see ourselves as committed to moral judgment and action.' Habermas, *The Future of Human Nature* (n 12) 71.

[51] R Dworkin, 'Playing God: Genes, Clones, and Luck' in R Dworkin, *Sovereign Virtue. The Theory and Practice of Equality* (Harvard University Press 2000) 443–44.

[52] In Sandel's words, 'To appreciate children as gifts is to accept them as they come, not as objects of our design, or products of our will, or instruments of our ambition.' M Sandel, *The Case Against Perfection: Ethics in the Age of Genetic Engineering* (Harvard University Press 2007) 45.

[53] Dworkin 'Playing God' (n 51) 443–44.

Correspondingly, the feared harm does not seem to be of a physical nature, as in public health concerns or fears for 'genetic genocide'. Instead, what is feared could be described as a 'metaphysical destruction', in the words of international law scholar Delmas-Marty.[54] As Jonas also points out, such metaphysical or symbolic 'risks' do not lend themselves to risk calculation, as they can hardly be measured and weighed.[55]

In a similar vein, if human genetic modification is believed to touch upon human nature, it is not so much human nature in the biological or genetic sense of the word. In a way, it makes no sense to want to conserve the human genome as it is. As Article 3 of UNESCO'S Universal Declaration on the Human Genome and Human Rights[56] aptly states: 'The human genome, which by its nature evolves, is subject to mutations.' Rather, the reason why humanity may be affected by human genetic engineering is that it seems to undermine our 'normative self-understanding', in Habermas's words.[57] By this he means the image of the person on which legal and ethical systems of thought are based: the view of the person as an end in himself, endowed with an intrinsic and absolute value, who is to be distinguished from things, animals, instruments, and commodities.

The common expression for this normative view of humanity, also in legal discourse, is, of course, human dignity. Until recently, one could regard human dignity's normative view of mankind as 'merely' the founding fiction of human rights discourse, and therefore consider its meaning hardly legally relevant outside the context of the preambles to international human rights declarations and conventions. However, within the context of international biolaw, human dignity's image of humanity has been reinvented as a legal guideline for the technological remaking of human nature. It has become part of a normative anthropology that has been developed to guide the technological remaking of the human species.

As such, human dignity has been elevated to being the central principle within legal regulation of biomedical developments, both on a national and an international level. As the Explanatory Report to the Convention on Human Rights and Biomedicine states, 'The concept of human dignity, which is also highlighted, constitutes the essential value to be upheld. It is at the basis of most of the values emphasised in the Convention.'[58] Nevertheless, the meaning of human dignity remains shrouded in controversy, also on a legal level. One of the main problems is that the normative image of humanity, as implied by human dignity, is surrounded by fictions and speculations which are not grounded in empirical reality, let alone biogenetic reality.

[54] M Delmas-Marty, 'Certitude et Incertitudes du Droit' in H Atlan et al (eds), *Le Clonage Humain* (Le Seuil 1999) 92.

[55] Jonas, *The Imperative of Responsibility* (n 6) 33–34.

[56] Universal Declaration on the Human Genome and Human Rights (n 27).

[57] Habermas, *The Future of Human Nature* (n 12) 72.

[58] *Explanatory Report to the Convention of Human Rights and Biomedicine* (n 34) para 9.

7.4 From Science Fiction to the Legal Fiction of Human Dignity

As discussed in section 7.3, the uncertainties involved in biomedical technologies necessitate a legal approach which exceeds the level of protection offered by traditional modes of risk governance. It could be said that through this special legal approach, a new level of speculation is introduced. Biomedical regulation does not only rely on 'what-if' scenarios and prognoses of possible effects, but also operationalizes a fictional, normative account of mankind: the subject of human dignity. As Article 1 of the Universal Declaration of Human Rights[59] describes that subject, 'All human beings are born free and equal in dignity and rights. They are endowed with reason and conscience and should act towards one another in a spirit of brotherhood.' Interestingly, the dystopian scenarios of biolaw are thus mobilized to protect a rather utopian view of man.

The idealized and at the same time inherently contradictory nature of that view of mankind is not a secret. In fact, it is clear, as the Declaration's preamble also states, that this image of humanity was invoked in post-war human rights discourse as a reaction to the historical fact that 'disregard and contempt for human rights have resulted in barbarous acts which have outraged the conscience of mankind'. Nevertheless, the fictional character of human rights and their implicit view of man is attacked every now and again, whether it is by calling human rights discourse 'nonsense upon stilts'[60] or by comparing the belief in human rights with the belief in witches and unicorns.[61]

Since the rebirth of human dignity within the context of international biolaw, the critique of the fictional character seems to have revived. From that perspective, within the context of biolaw, Schmitt's notorious adage 'whoever says humanity, seeks to deceive' has gained new significance. More generally, the biosciences seem to have caused new tensions between normative and empirical views of the human. On the one hand, in response to biomedical developments, legal scholars reaffirm their belief in human rights as 'a revolt against the laws of nature, a refusal to stay confined within the limits of the biological conception of man'.[62] On the other hand, from the perspective of the biosciences, the belief in *liberté, égalité, fraternité*, which could be regarded as an important founding 'myth' of human rights, seems to lose much of its credibility.

This latter tenet becomes clear upon closer inspection of the motto's three components in the light of biomedical developments. All human beings are born free

[59] Adopted 10 December 1948, UN General Assembly Resolution 217A(III), GAOR, 3rd Sess, Part I, Resns, 71.

[60] J Bentham, *Anarchical Fallacies; Being an Examination of the Declaration of Rights Issued During the French Revolution* (1792), line 198 <http://oll.libertyfund.org/titles/bentham-the-works-of-jeremy-bentham-vol-2/simple#lf0872-02_label_001> accessed 17 May 2015.

[61] A MacIntyre, *After Virtue: A Study in Moral Theory* (Gerald Duckworth 1981) 67.

[62] Delmas-Marty, 'Certitude et Incertitudes' (n 54) 107 (author's translation).

in human rights discourse, yet in biological reality many chances in life appear to depend on genetic predispositions. All human beings are born equal, yet knowledge of our genomes is bringing new inequalities to light. Finally, when it comes to brotherhood, the question is to what extent current systems of solidarity will be undermined now that the life sciences are lifting the 'veil of ignorance' which covered our genetic fates until recently. Human genome-editing will cause even more friction between biomedical and dignity-based views of humanity. In this vein, UNESCO's International Bioethics Committee expresses the following fear in a statement on human genome-editing:

> The goal of enhancing individuals and the human species by engineering the genes related to some characteristics and traits ... impinges upon the principle of respect for human dignity in several ways. It weakens the idea that the differences among human beings, regardless of the measure of their endowment, are exactly what the recognition of their equality presupposes and therefore protects. It introduces the risk of new forms of discrimination and stigmatization for those who cannot afford such enhancement or simply do not want to resort to it.[63]

Consequently, an increasingly popular line of attack on human dignity is to depict it as a harmful fiction, not grounded in reality. A recent piece, tellingly entitled 'The Stupidity of Dignity', written by well-known Harvard psychologist Steven Pinker, can serve as an example of this tendency to debunk the fiction of human dignity on empirical grounds. According to Pinker, the concept of human dignity has gained too much importance in public debates on biomedical issues. In his view, dignity is nothing more than a phenomenon of human perception: '[j]ust as the smell of baking bread triggers a desire to eat it, and the sight of a baby's face triggers a desire to protect it, the appearance of dignity triggers a desire to esteem and respect the dignified person'.[64] Pinker contrasts his view of dignity with the prevailing interpretation of human dignity underpinning biomedical laws. One of his prime allegations is that such readings of human dignity are out of touch with reality:

> Ever since the cloning of Dolly the sheep a decade ago, the panic sown by conservative bioethicists, amplified by a sensationalist press, has turned the public discussion of bioethics into a miasma of scientific illiteracy. *Brave New World*, a work of fiction, is treated as inerrant prophesy. Cloning is confused with resurrecting the dead or mass-producing babies. Longevity becomes 'immortality', improvement becomes 'perfection', the screening for disease genes becomes 'designer babies' or even 'reshaping the species'. The reality is that biomedical research is a Sisyphean struggle to eke small increments in health from a staggeringly complex, entropy-beset human body.... In every age, prophets foresee dystopias that never materialize, while failing to anticipate the real revolutions.[65]

[63] UNESCO International Bioethics Committee, *Report of the IBC on Updating Its Reflection on the Human Genome and Human Rights* (Paris 2015) <http://unesdoc.unesco.org/images/0023/002332/233258E.pdf> accessed 3 December 2015.

[64] S Pinker, 'The Stupidity of Dignity: Conservative Bioethics' Latest, Most Dangerous Ploy', *The New Republic*, 28 May 2008 <https://newrepublic.com/article/64674/the-stupidity-dignity> accessed 14 May 2015.

[65] ibid.

In other words, Pinker reduces the humanizing legal fiction of human dignity to the type of fiction involved in science fiction. According to him, only evidence-based arguments, which demonstrate clear and identifiable harms of certain technologies, can serve as a reason to restrict biomedical research. Any other considerations, such as the question what kind of future we want for the human species, seems of no importance. This raises the question of what Pinker's view is on ethics. In an opinion on CRISPR, Pinker offers a clear answer to this question:

> The primary moral goal for today's bioethics can be summarized in a single sentence. *Get out of the way.* A truly ethical bioethics should not bog down research in red tape, moratoria, or threats of prosecution based on nebulous but sweeping principles such as 'dignity,' 'sacredness,' or 'social justice'. Nor should it thwart research that has likely benefits now or in the near future by sowing panic about speculative harms in the distant future.[66]

Although Pinker's approach is based on a rather caricatured and reductionist view of human dignity, his polemic against the role of human dignity in bioethics and biolaw does raise a valid question: how can the reliance on imagination and doom scenarios within the context of biolaw be justified? Indeed, biolegal discourse seems to be replete with fictions, speculations, and allusions to dystopian scenarios of the future. Moreover, there does seem to be a special connection between human dignity and imagination, even if most people will agree, unlike Pinker, that human dignity is more than mere science fiction. The question then becomes what the role of imagination and the fiction of human dignity should be in coming to a legal understanding of the possible dangers involved in biomedical developments.

To come to a better understanding of the role of imagination within regulation of emerging technologies in general, and the role of human dignity's *homme rêvé*[67] more specifically, Jonas's reflection offers several clues. To unfold the role of imagination for the development of moral and legal frameworks to guide emerging technologies, Jonas uses the concept of 'the heuristics of fear'. According to the heuristics of fear, 'moral philosophy must consult our fears prior to our wishes to learn what we really cherish'.[68] In other words, an imagination of the risks and dangers of future developments is heuristically needed to uncover, identify, and explicate the principles at stake. Ultimately, this negative approach can, in Jonas's view, also lead to a better understanding of the meaning of human dignity in these issues. In Jonas's words:

> Just as we should not know about the sanctity of life if we did not know about killing ...; and just as we should not know the value of truth without being aware of lies, nor of freedom without the lack of it, and so forth—so also in our search after an ethics of responsibility for distant contingencies, it is an anticipated *distortion* of man that helps us to detect that in the

[66] S Pinker, 'The Moral Imperative for Bioethics', *The Boston Globe*, 1 August 2015 <https://www.bostonglobe.com/opinion/2015/07/31/the-moral-imperative-for-bioethics/JmEkoyzlTAu9oQV76JrK9N/story.html> accessed 2 December 2015.

[67] Delmas-Marty, 'Certitude et Incertitudes' (n 54) 107; DWJM Pessers, *Menselijke Waardigheid en het Persoonsbegrip in het Recht* (Lemma 2005).

[68] Jonas, *The Imperative of Responsibility* (n 6) 27.

normative conception of man which is to be preserved from it. And we need the *threat* to the image of man—and rather specific kinds of threat—to assure ourselves of his true image by the very recoil from these threats.[69]

Jonas's reliance on negative scenarios, which also surfaces in this quote, has already been discussed in the previous sections. What seems more interesting, at this point, is which new role for law and morality is implied by his heuristics of fear. In general, two different interpretations are possible.

A first interpretation of Jonas's heuristics of fear emphasizes the aspect of fear as a guideline for decision-making. Within this line of thinking, there is a truth to the primitive feelings and basic intuitions raised by biomedical developments. Indeed, Jonas himself writes that 'the revulsion of feeling which acts ahead of knowledge'[70] can help us apprehend the values at stake.

In a similar vein, a certain strand in bioethical thought stresses the wisdom hiding in feelings of repugnance. Probably the best known effort to bring this line of thought to fruition comes from Leon Kass, one of the central targets of Pinker's rant against theoconservative ('theocon') bioethics. Kass himself explains the wisdom of repugnance in an article with the same title:

Revulsion is not an argument; and some of yesterday's repugnances are today calmly accepted—though, one must add, not always for the better. In crucial cases, however, repugnance is the emotional expression of deep wisdom, beyond reason's power fully to articulate it.[71]

A more moderate version of Kass's wisdom of repugnance can be recognized in Michael Sandel's essay *The Case Against Perfection*. Although the feelings of 'moral vertigo' and 'unease' which are raised by biomedical developments can hardly be expressed in terms of conventional arguments such as autonomy, fairness, and individual rights, this fact is, according to Sandel, only a sign that contemporary 'science is moving faster than moral understanding'.[72] Similarly, Habermas argues that the 'revulsion' many of us feel at being confronted with 'the chimaera that bear witness to a violation of the species boundaries that we had naively assumed to be inalterable', or the 'disgust' we experience when thinking about the creation of embryos for industrial purposes, is an indication of the fact that biomedical technologies ultimately 'affect the very concept we have of ourselves as cultural members of the species of "humanity"'.[73]

Kass's proposal to use feelings of revulsion and repugnance as signposts for normative deliberation has been heavily criticized.[74] Indeed, to rely on unreflected intuitions, gut feelings, and primitive emotions within the regulation of these issues brings with it a major risk of unfounded, prejudiced, and irrational conservatism.

[69] ibid, 26–27. [70] ibid, 27.

[71] LR Kass, 'The Wisdom of Repugnance', (1997) 216(22) *New Republic* (2 June 1997) 17–26, 22.

[72] Sandel, *The Case Against Perfection* (n 52) 9.

[73] Habermas, *The Future of Human Nature* (n 12) 39–40.

[74] See, eg, J Harris, 'Clones, Genes and Human Rights' in J Burley (ed), *The Genetic Revolution and Human Rights. The Oxford Amnesty Lectures 1998* (OUP 1999) 82–83; MC Nussbaum, *Hiding from Humanity. Disgust, Shame, and the Law* (Princeton University Press 2004) 81–82.

Correspondingly, human dignity within this approach quickly devaluates into either a 'theocon' slogan used to cover up the absence of sound arguments, as Pinker writes, or into a knock-down argument against which no counter-evidence is possible.

Nevertheless, the less radical approach of Sandel and Habermas to the role of intuitions and emotions in bioethical decision-making still leaves the door open to a second, more constructive interpretation of Jonas's heuristics of fear. Within this interpretation, the important role of imagination and symbolization for legal and ethical decision-making on biomedical developments is emphasized. According to this reading of Jonas's heuristics of fear, lawyers and ethicists must first visualize and imagine the possible long-range effects of anticipated technological developments, to be able to develop a proper normative framework. As Jonas describes this new type of anticipatory ethical and legal reflection:

> What is here contemplated, therefore, is a casuistry of the imagination which, unlike the customary casuistries of law and morality that serve the trying out of principles already known assists in the tracking and discovering of principles still unknown. The serious side of science fiction lies precisely in its performing such well-informed thought experiments, whose vivid imaginary results may assume the heuristic function here proposed. (See, eg, A Huxley's *Brave New World*).[75]

Whereas Pinker refers to omnipresent allusions to *Brave New World* as an example of the naïve and unrealistic worldview of many contemporary biolawyers and bioethicists, Jonas regards the use of imagination in legal-ethical contexts and the reliance on dystopian scenarios as indispensable for the development of new normative frameworks. In a way, it is only logical that as a reaction to the utopian scale of current technological developments, and the techno-theological beliefs and aspirations of the scientists involved, a legal discourse has come into being which equally relies on imaginations and fictions. From that perspective, biolaw's dystopian scenarios on the possible dangers of emerging technologies counterbalance the utopian scenarios in which emerging technologies ultimately root.

Moreover, in answer to Pinker's critique, it can be stressed that Jonas's 'casuistry of the imagination' is intended to be mobilized at a preliminary stage of decision-making; that is, during the construction of a normative framework for further deliberation. It only serves as a heuristic device to detect the principles and interests worth protecting. This means that when it comes to application of these newly found principles to specific situations, mere imagination cannot suffice. As Jonas puts it, in that stage of decision-making, the uncertainty of 'long-term projections becomes a grievous weakness'.[76] Instead, from then on, more realistic prognoses of the future need to take over. Nevertheless, the basic uncertainty of future consequences remains. At this point in his line of reasoning, Jonas unfolds his precautionary rule that in political deliberation on technological developments the bad prognosis should prevail over the good one.

[75] Jonas, *The Imperative of Responsibility* (n 6) 30.
[76] ibid.

Jonas's case for the use of imagination in legal and ethical approaches to technological developments is able to offer new perspectives on the role of biolaw and its central principle—human dignity—in the regulation of biomedical developments.[77] First, his approach throws light on the deficit of traditional concepts of risk, as exemplified by risk assessment discourse. It could be said that scientists such as Pinker, who argue for 'evidence-based' regulation, in which solely tangible risks offer enough weight for legal bans and restrictions, make use of a very 'narrow imagination of risk'.[78] Such a narrow conception of risk, often accompanied by a certain disdain for notions such as human dignity, seems to go back to what could be called a scientistic tendency within debates on emerging technologies; the thought that it should be ultimately up to scientists to decide what counts as risk, and thus as a sufficient ground for more restrictive approaches. The scientistic bias can lead to a conceptual impoverishment of democratic deliberation, disengaging the public from moral and political reflection on the question of which goals emerging technologies should serve. As Hurlbutt writes in an article on the governance of human genome-editing: '[i]t is our technologies that should be subject to democratically articulated imaginations of the future we want, not the opposite.... Imagining what is right and appropriate for our world—and what threatens its moral foundations—is a task for democracy, not for science.'[79] The importance of the principle of human dignity for public, democratic deliberation on this issue can be explained against this background. The legal concept of human dignity can be regarded as an essential tool for citizens in democratic societies to imagine the future that they want for humanity, and to use that moral imagination as a guideline for biomedical regulation.

Moreover, contrary to what Pinker seems to believe, the use of imagination in bioethical and biolegal deliberation can also be used in more nuanced ways than merely posing blanket legal bans. For example, more implicit images of the human can be discerned within legal frameworks which offer practical rules for the creation, transfer, and conservation of technological hybrids of human origin in contemporary bioeconomies, such as human immortalized cell lines, human embryonic stem cells, or frozen human egg cells. Within legal discourse, these human semi-objects are not treated as normal objects of property law that can be sold or used for industrial purposes, but instead symbolized as objects with a special status.[80]

[77] In this chapter, I focus on the importance of imagination for biolegal decision-making. For reflection on the importance of imagination for ethical decision-making on emerging technologies, see M Coeckelberg, *Human Being @ Risk: Enhancement, Technology and the Evaluation of Vulnerability Transformations* (Springer 2013) 103–06.

[78] S Jasanoff, JB Hurlbutt, and K Saha, 'CRISPR Democracy: Gene Editing and the Need for Inclusive Deliberation' (2015) 32 *Issues in Science and Technology* <http://issues.org/32-1/crispr-democracy-gene-editing-and-the-need-for-inclusive-deliberation/> accessed 2 December 2015.

[79] JB Hurlbutt, 'Limits of Responsibility: Genome Editing, Asilomar, and the Politics of Deliberation' (2015) 5 *Hastings Center Report* 12.

[80] See, eg, D Dickenson, *Property in the Body: Feminist Perspectives* (CUP 2007); M Quigley, 'Property in Human Biomaterials—Separating Persons and Things?' (2012) 32 *Oxford Journal of Legal Studies* 659; J Wall, 'The Legal Status of Body Parts: A Framework' (2011) 31 *Oxford Journal of Legal Studies* 783; R Rao, 'Genes and Spleens: Property, Contract, or Privacy Rights in the Human Body?' (2007) 35 *J L Med Ethics* 371.

Additionally, Jonas's appeal to legal and ethical imagination finds resonance with the fact that also, on a deeper level, 'law is part of a distinctive manner of imagining the real', to use the words of anthropologist Clifford Geertz.[81] Interestingly, this function of law in symbolizing, imagining, and representing the world around us gains special significance within the context of biolaw. After all, biomedical technologies are blurring, as mentioned, the distinctions between foundational categories, such as subject and object, life and death, and animal and human. As existing vocabularies seem to be falling short of making sense of biomedical developments, legal discourse is stepping in to contribute to the creation of an *imaginaire social* to symbolize these new biomedical hybrids. Without doubt, other systems of meaning profoundly affect the legal process of symbolization, such as medical, religious, and economic perspectives. However, when the symbolic orders of these systems collide, as is mostly the case in bioethical matters, law has to mediate between these competing systems of value and meaning. Under these circumstances of symbolic uncertainty, the law, with its intricate systems of multiple and inter-related terms, qualifications, constructions, and categories, can become of vital importance to the overall cultural-symbolic process to come to terms with technological hybrids.[82]

The same could be argued in relation to the new status questions raised by human genetic engineering. What should we make of the 'three parent babies' of mitochondrial replacement? Should women who donate their egg cells for this procedure be recognized as a second legal mother? And in the likely case that the law answers this question in the negative, should her genetic ties with the child, even if they are quite minimal, be reflected in other ways in family law? Even if these questions seem almost impossible to answer, the law will nevertheless have to come up with solutions.

What about the designer babies of human gene-editing? The confounding complexity of the questions which are raised by human genetic engineering can be illustrated by the emergence of wrongful life claims from children who are born out of new technological settings. In the future, the law will without a doubt also be faced with wrongful life claims from children in case of mistakes which are made during the process of human gene-editing, or in case these children would rather have been born with a different genetic profile. Can they sue their makers or designers for these 'defects'? Can they claim the right to be born with a different genetic profile, or even in a different body? And if so, what does that mean for law's concept of the person? While coming to an answer to these immensely difficult questions, judges will inevitably have to draw up new lines between person and thing, artifice and nature, and chance and choice.

[81] C Geertz, 'Local Knowledge. Fact and Law in Comparative Perspective' in C Geertz, *Local Knowledge. Further Essays in Interpretive Anthropology* (Basic Books 1983) 184.

[82] Elsewhere, I have analysed law's special role in the general process of cultural-symbolic representation of biomedical hybrid objects more elaborately. See BC van Beers, 'From Winged Lions to Frozen Embryos, Neomorts and Human-Animal Cybrids: The Functions of Law in the Symbolic Mediation of Biomedical Hybrids' in B van Klink et al (eds), *Symbolic Legislation and Developments in Biomedical Law* (Springer 2016).

Additionally, the symbolic perspective on technological interventions is also able to make sense of the feelings of moral vertigo and the emotions of revulsion, to which Sandel, Habermas, and Jonas refer when they discuss the impact of technological developments on existing normative frameworks. These feelings and emotions could be regarded as an indication of the radical ways in which emerging technologies question existing cultural-symbolic categories. However, as mere indications of the radical impact of technological interventions, these feelings and emotions cannot replace legal and ethical arguments, as already argued.

One can wonder whether law is up to this task of imagining future biomedical realities and countering the symbolic uncertainties caused by biomedical hybrids. However, the fact is that law is already called upon to answer the semi-metaphysical questions raised by technological developments, even if law is perhaps not the most likely or best equipped candidate to do so. Decisions from European courts on the meaning of human dignity for technological regulation can serve as illustrations.[83] These decisions attest to the fact that even if the risks involved in biomedical developments are rather of a metaphysical than a physical nature, this does not preclude the possibility of a gradual process of legal symbolization, in which existing foundational categories can be reconstructed and reconsidered along the way. It could be said that in this process, law makers and judges are unfolding, what Bruno Latour has called, an *experimental metaphysics*.[84] Applied to law, the perspective of experimental metaphysics can be taken to mean that the categorical distinctions between human and animal, alive and dead, and person and thing, which are each being uprooted by biomedical technologies, can be renegotiated in international biolaw through a continuous, case-by-case, and therefore experimental approach, in which different symbolizations and representations of the human gradually take shape.

7.5 Conclusion

Imagining the future; that is what scientists are currently doing by creating new futures and even new modes of human existence. If that is the case, lawyers cannot but join them in this effort of the imagination if societies want to offer some direction for these essentially political and ethical questions. Drawing from Jonas's normative framework for utopian technologies, this chapter has argued that legal imagination is primarily involved on two levels.

First, as the long-term consequences of biomedical technologies, such as human genetic engineering, are unknown yet potentially catastrophic for human evolution or human existence, law makers are called upon to give priority to the negative over

83 See, eg, on IVF and gamete donation: *Evans v United Kingdom* [GC] No 6339/05 (Grand Chamber, 10 April 2007); *SH v Austria* No 57813/00 [GC] (Grand Chamber, 3 November 2011); on organ donation: *Elberte v Latvia* No 61243/08 (Fourth Section, 13 January 2015); and on the use of embryos for industrial or commercial purposes: Case C-34/10 *Brüstle v Greenpeace eV* [2011] ECR I-09821.

84 B Latour, *Politiques de la Nature. Comment Faire Entrer les Sciences en Démocratie* (La Découverte 2004) 97.

the positive prognosis. This strategy is clearly visible in precautionary regulatory approaches. From that perspective, there is a legitimate place for dystopian ways of thinking and imagining in biolegal discourse.

Second, human genetic engineering and other human enhancement technologies bring about uncertainties and risks also on a more conceptual level. Much of the controversy surrounding these emerging technologies is due to the fact that categorical distinctions, such as between person and thing, and chance and choice, are blurred in radical ways. As a consequence, the emergence of biomedical technologies also entails what could be called metaphysical risks and symbolic uncertainties. How should we come to an understanding of three-parent embryos, gene-edited children, or human–animal cybrids? Indeed, all of these biomedical 'hybrids' seem to surpass existing foundational categories. Interestingly, the law is becoming of increasing importance in the social-cultural process of imagining and evaluating possible new creations. Also in this sense, law's imaginative powers are increasingly mobilized to regulate and represent the new realities which may be called into existence by emerging technologies.

PART IV

RISK AND THE ENVIRONMENT

8

Prevention in International Environmental Law and the Anticipation of Risk(s): A Multifaceted Norm

Leslie-Anne Duvic-Paoli

8.1 Introduction

The rationale of international environmental law is anticipatory; it aims to ensure that our planet remains a viable place to live. Put in a simplified way, it aims to preserve the 'future' of the Earth and its inhabitants. At the heart of this anticipatory perspective is the principle of prevention, which imposes an obligation on states to exercise due care in the face of risks of environmental damage with the view to avoiding or mitigating the occurrence of harm.

The principle of prevention, which forms the cornerstone of international environmental law, was articulated in its modern form in Principle 21 of the 1972 Stockholm Declaration on the Human Environment (Stockholm Declaration), which reads:

> States have, in accordance with the Charter of the United Nations and the principles of international law, the sovereign right to exploit their own resources pursuant to their own environmental policies, and the responsibility to ensure that activities within their jurisdiction or control do not cause damage to the environment of other States or of areas beyond the limits of national jurisdiction.[1]

This formulation was found to be an expression of customary international law by the International Court of Justice (ICJ) in its 1996 Advisory Opinion on the *Legality of the Threat or Use of Nuclear Weapons*.[2] However, although the obligation to prevent future harm is well accepted, and its anticipatory approach is acknowledged, the fact that prevention can contribute to building a better future in the

[1] United Nations Conference on the Human Environment, 'Declaration of the United Nations Conference on the Human Environment' (16 June 1972) UN Doc A/CONF.48/14/Rev 1 (Stockholm Declaration), Principle 21.

[2] *Legality of the Threat or Use of Nuclear Weapons* (Nuclear Weapons Advisory Opinion) [1996] ICJ Rep 226, para 29.

long term is often disregarded. For example, the outcome document of the Rio+20 Summit, entitled 'The Future We Want',[3] is all about imagining the future, but it does not once mention the prevention principle and thereby ignores the main obligation that allows for a legal framing of the future. As a general matter, prevention is often envisaged as a short-term solution to limit a particular risk at a specific time, and not as an obligation the performance of which contributes to the future viability of our planet. Yet the specificity of prevention lies in the fact that it has moved from the reactive perspective which underpins the classical regime of state responsibility for wrongful acts to require the taking of action to preserve the integrity of the planet. Instead of concentrating on the occurrence of harm and its reparation, prevention focuses on risks and their anticipation.

The objective of this chapter is to examine the manner in which prevention operates as a multifaceted norm, providing a broad legal framework that is able to respond to a multiplicity of risks, and to discuss what this tells us about the way international environmental law conceptualizes the future.[4] Section 8.2 discusses the manner in which prevention has been construed as a legal response to curb environmental risks. The rest of the chapter presents prevention as a multifaceted norm which operates at multiple levels in order to ensure that multiple types of risks are covered under its umbrella. To that end, it analyses prevention from three different angles. Section 8.3 identifies its material scope by detailing the different categories of risks which are covered by prevention under treaty law. Section 8.4 looks at the temporal scope of prevention and highlights the multiple conceptions of the future found in the principle. Finally, section 8.5 identifies the potential beneficiaries of the preventive rationale and explains how it aims to shape the future of different audiences. The chapter concludes with some comments on the future of the principle of prevention by presenting some of the challenges brought about by its multifaceted nature.

8.2 Prevention as a Response to Environmental Risks

The following brief historical perspective on the emergence of prevention illustrates how prevention has emerged as a legal response to curb the risks of environmental degradation created by industrial development and has become, in its customary form, an obligation which embraces an integrative approach to risk and harm.

[3] UNGA Res 66/288 (27 July 2012) UN Doc A/RES/66/288.

[4] While this author recognizes the complex normative depth of prevention, the objective of the chapter is not to engage in a discussion on the nature of the norm; as a result, the piece uses rather loosely the term of 'principle' when referring to the norm which translates the preventive rationale in the international legal framework. For a presentation of the different functions performed by prevention in international environmental law, see L-A Duvic-Paoli and JE Viñuales, 'Principle 2: Prevention' in JE Viñuales (ed), *The Rio Declaration on Environment and Development: A Commentary* (OUP 2015) 107, 120.

8.2.1 The emergence of prevention in the context of environmental degradation

The emergence of the obligation of prevention has moved the focus of international law from the concept of responsibility for reparation for the consequences of human activities on the environment to the concept of responsibility centred on the future of the planet. Traditionally, international law dealt with natural resources only from a reactive perspective; looking to the past by sanctioning illegal behaviour. Indeed, the prohibition against causing transboundary harm (also known as the 'no-harm rule'), articulated in the famous *Trail Smelter* Case,[5] was primarily concerned with providing a framework for reparations after the commission of an internationally wrongful act. Today, however, the obligation of prevention, while closely linked to the no-harm rule, has moved beyond that retrospective rule, looking, instead, to the future and aiming to anticipate risks before they occur. As a result, the obligation of prevention requires states to be proactive in their avoidance of environmental harm. In sum, the regulation of risks, with prevention at its core, has completely changed the manner in which international law looks at natural resources and the environment.

The articulation of the principle of prevention in Principle 21 of the Stockholm Declaration coincided with the realization that activities potentially harmful to the environment were multiplying.[6] As a result, it became evident that an anticipatory legal framework was necessary to ensure that the risks of environmental degradation were limited. The dangers of industrial development had become clearly visible after World War II, when several ecological catastrophes, the first of their kind, struck industrialized countries in the 1950s and 1960s. Images of the first oil spill in Europe, the *Torrey Canyon* disaster in 1967, contributed to the realization that the environment is fragile and that its exploitation can have disastrous consequences for human life.[7] The multiplication of catastrophic oil spills, partly explained by the steady increase in global consumption of oil, shocked public opinion. The advent of nuclear capability at the end of World War II also played an essential role in raising environmental consciousness.[8] As the danger of a nuclear holocaust lessened in the 1960s, concerns about the effects of routine or accidental radiation during energy production and nuclear testing multiplied.[9]

[5] *Trail Smelter* (*United States v Canada*) (Arbitration Tribunal) (1941) 3 RIAA 1905, 1965.

[6] Pursuant to para 1 of the Preamble of the Stockholm Declaration, 'In the long and tortuous evolution of the human race on this planet a stage has been reached when, through the rapid acceleration of science and technology, man has acquired the power to transform his environment in countless ways and on an unprecedented scale.' See also UNGA Res 2398 (XXIII) (3 December 1968), which convened the Stockholm Conference, recognizing the 'grave dangers' of 'modern scientific and technological developments'. UNGA Res 2398 (XXIII) (3 December 1968), Preamble, paras 1–2.

[7] J-P Quéneudec, 'L'incidence de l'affaire du Torrey Canyon sur le droit de la mer' (1968) 14 *Annuaire français de droit international* 701, 703.

[8] J Grinevald, *La Biosphère de l'anthropocène : climat et pétrole, la double menace. Repères transdisciplinaires (1824–2007)* (Georg 2007) 99.

[9] For a more detailed analysis of the factors which contributed to the holding of the Stockholm Conference, see, inter alia, L Caldwell, *International Environmental Policy: From the Twentieth to the Twenty-First Century* (3rd ed, Duke University Press 1996) 48–63.

In addition to concerns over the multiplication of potentially harmful activities, apprehension over the consequences of the degradation of the environment began to grow. The problem of air pollution, vividly highlighted by the deaths of fish in Scandinavian lakes and the destruction of forests caused by acid rain, achieved prominent notoriety, as did the infamous and, to many, fatal, London smogs, caused by air pollution emanating from the burning of coal mixing with special weather conditions.[10] Direct experience of these deteriorating environmental conditions raised public awareness considerably and played a significant role in spurring government action.[11]

The risks of industrial development, which became evident from the 1960s, justified the adoption of a legal framework based on anticipation aimed at avoiding the occurrence of the ecological catastrophes that were so concerning to public opinion. The Stockholm Declaration, envisaged as a document of basic principles which would stimulate governmental action and public participation in relation to the protection of the environment, was adopted in this context, with Principle 21 enshrining the preventive rationale.[12]

8.2.2 Prevention and the anticipation of risks of environmental harm

Despite having emerged as a response to the multiplication of risks of environmental degradation, it is important to note that the principle of prevention is only concerned with risks of environmental harm which meet certain criteria, and does not simply address any type of risk.[13] The International Law Commission (ILC) Articles on the Prevention of Transboundary Harm from Hazardous Activities (Prevention Articles),[14] which aim to codify the obligation of prevention in its customary form, provide guidance as to the circumstances in which the customary duty of prevention applies. The Prevention Articles deal with the legal framework applicable to activities not prohibited by international law which involve a risk of causing significant transboundary harm through their physical consequences.[15] They rely on a complex likelihood/impact matrix, which reveals that it is the combination of risk and harm which establishes the particular circumstances in which the obligation of prevention is deemed applicable.

[10] For an explanation of the acid rain phenomenon, see W Coppoc, 'The Environment: No Respecter of National Boundaries' (1978) 43 *Albany Law Review* 520, 521–24. For an analysis of the London smogs, see, eg, M Bell, D Devra, and T Fletcher, 'A Retrospective Assessment of Mortality from the London Smog Episode of 1952: The Role of Influenza and Pollution' (2004) 112 *Environmental Health Perspectives* 6.

[11] Eg, the holding of the first 'Earth Day' in the United States in 1970 gathered 20 million people. 'Mood is Joyful as City Gives its Support; Millions Join Earth Day Observance Across the Nation', *New York Times* (by Jack Manning) 23 April 1970.

[12] UNGA, 'Report of the Preparatory Committee for the United Nations Conference on the Human Environment, First session' UN Doc A/CONF.48/PC/6 (1970) 19, para 35.

[13] ILC, 'Draft Articles on Prevention of Transboundary Harm from Hazardous Activities (with Commentaries)' (2001) UN Doc A/56/10 (ILC Prevention Articles), art 2(a) and Commentary to art 2(3).

[14] ILC Prevention Articles.

[15] ILC Prevention Articles, art 1.

The Prevention Articles apply to activities with a 'risk of causing significant transboundary harm'. This is further defined as activities which present a high probability of causing significant transboundary harm or a low probability of causing disastrous transboundary harm.[16] In other words, the significance of the risk is assessed on the basis of two elements: (i) the probability that the risk will materialize; and (ii) the magnitude of harm which may be caused. The first element, concentrating on known consequences, is a definitional element of prevention which distinguishes it from precaution, which is applicable when harm is unforeseeable due to scientific uncertainty.[17] The second element makes prevention applicable only in circumstances when harm is foreseen to be 'significant',[18] which is understood as meaning more than 'detectable' but not necessarily serious or substantial.[19] Following this matrix, if the likelihood and the impact of the activity are expected to be low, the risk is deemed acceptable; on the contrary, if the likelihood and the impact are expected to be high, the planned activity should not go ahead. The obligation to take preventive measures to avoid or manage risks applies in cases of middle-ground scenarios, when there is a high likelihood of low impact, or a low likelihood of high impact.

The likelihood/impact matrix found in the ILC Prevention Articles may seem to leave uncertain the issue of whether the preventive obligation is concerned with harm or with the risk of harm. As the two are closely related, disentangling them is indeed a challenge. Admittedly, the ultimate objective of prevention is to avoid the occurrence of harm—as presented in the title of the ILC Articles on the 'prevention of transboundary *harm* from hazardous activities'. However, the fulfilment of the obligation of prevention, as an obligation of due diligence, is solely assessed on the basis of whether the state has taken sufficient action against the *risk* presented by an activity, and not on the basis of whether damage has occurred.[20] Two main reasons justify this latter approach: (i) harmful activities are often carried out by private actors rather than by the state itself; and (ii) the outcome of preventive measures being often unpredictable, harm can occur despite best efforts to avoid it. It is therefore the manner in which a state has dealt with risk—and not with harm per se—which defines the lawfulness or unlawfulness of an activity. In sum, although the preventive rationale finds its legitimation in the avoidance of harm, the obligation of prevention in practice does not go so far as to prohibit the occurrence of harm per se, but rather concentrates on how states anticipate risks.

The principle of prevention operates as a fundamental rationale for the evolution of new responses capable of adapting to new and emerging risks. As an umbrella obligation, the customary obligation of prevention ensures the absence

[16] ILC Prevention Articles, art 2(a).

[17] AA Cançado Trindade, 'Principle 15: Precaution' in JE Viñuales (ed), *The Rio Declaration on Environment and Development: A Commentary* (OUP 2015) 403, 421–23.

[18] It should, however, be noted that under treaty law, the threshold of harm can vary depending on the nature of the activity and the damage that is foreseen, ranging from a zero tolerance threshold to different thresholds of gravity, reflective of different perceptions of the acceptability of certain risks in light of social benefits provided by an economic activity.

[19] ILC Prevention Articles, Commentaries to art 2(4).

[20] ILC Prevention Articles, Commentaries to art 3(7).

of any lacunae; all risks are covered, including those that are not subject to a tailored preventive obligation expressed in a treaty. The fact remains, however, that in the absence of a particular treaty articulation of the content of the obligation in specific situations, its application is problematic as it provides only limited guidance as to how states should act in the face of risks. Forests, for example, remain vulnerable to the risks of deforestation in the absence of any international legal framework dealing with those risks in a comprehensive manner.[21] Clearly, some environmental risks are neglected by international law, either because of a lack of political consensus around the necessity to regulate, or because of a lack of scientific knowledge regarding their adverse impacts. In sum, the imagined future is the result of a subjective construction of the risks that states acknowledge and those that they ignore.

8.3 The Objects of Prevention

This section concentrates on how the risks that states decide to acknowledge are construed in treaty law. Although there is a general understanding that the preventive rationale under international environmental law aims to curb environmental risks,[22] this would be an over-simplification. Indeed, despite the fact that prevention emerged as a legal response to multiplying environmental risks, the object of prevention—in other words, its material scope—is not limited to risks to the environment. For instance, the ILC Prevention Articles do not refer to the obligation to prevent environmental damage per se but, rather, seek to avoid the 'physical consequences' of transboundary risks[23] that might harm 'persons, property or the environment'.[24] The broad material scope of prevention can be partly explained by the fact that a consensual definition of what constitutes the 'environment'—which can be defined as vaguely as the place 'where we all live'[25]—is lacking. As a result, what qualifies as risks to the environment remains broad, and often includes other, more tangible, risks. Consequently, the rationale for, and the content of, the obligation of prevention is expressed in international environmental treaties in a variety of ways, depending on the type of harm sought to be avoided. This section identifies five main categories of risks which fall under the scope of the preventive rationale under treaty law: risks to the sovereignty of another state; risks of pollution; risks to resource exploitation; risks to human health; and risks to ecosystems.

21 Forests fall primarily under the scope of non-legally binding instruments, including the 'Non Legally Binding Instrument on All Types of Forests', UNGA Res 62/98 (17 December 2007) UN Doc A/RES/62/98.

22 See, eg, G Hafner and I Buffard, 'Obligations of Prevention and the Precautionary Principle' in J Crawford, A Pellet, S Olleson (eds), *The Law of International Responsibility* (OUP 2010) 521–34, 525.

23 ILC Prevention Articles, art 1.

24 ILC Prevention Articles, art 2(b).

25 RD Munro and J Lammers (eds), *Environmental Protection and Sustainable Development: Legal Principles and Recommendations Adopted by the Experts Group on Environmental Law of the World Commission on Environmental and Development* (Graham & Trotman 1987) xi.

8.3.1 Risks to the sovereignty of another state

At its roots, the principle of prevention does not come from any particular concern for the environment. It originated from traditional legal concepts including the *sic utere tuo ut alienum non laedas* ('Use your own property in such a manner as not to injure that of another') and abuse of rights doctrines, which define the limits of the sovereignty of a state in relation to the right of other sovereign states to be free from external interferences.[26] Admittedly, the obligation is only a basic expression of the preventive rationale because it merely seeks to prevent transboundary harm to avoid wrongfulness. Compared to other, more developed, expressions of the preventive rationale (presented below), its objective is less anticipatory and less protective of the environment per se. Nevertheless, the prohibition against causing transboundary harm remains an influential (albeit incomplete) expression of the preventive rationale, in particular given that it is one of the core components of Stockholm Principle 21. As a result, the preventive rationale finds its expression in obligations aimed at protecting the sovereignty of other states. For instance, the obligation to take measures to avoid harmful effects to the water flow and water quality of international watercourses[27] is at the heart of watercourse law, a field of law that aims to ensure that the rights and obligations of riparian states are respected when utilizing and exploiting the shared resource. Under this perspective, the preventive rationale does not aim to curb direct risks to the environment, but, rather, to limit the risks that environmental harm represents to the territorial sovereignty of states.

8.3.2 Risks to resource exploitation

The preventive rationale also finds its origins in early resource management treaties that aimed to put an end to the unrestrained exploitation of natural resources. Their objective was to protect resources in order to better exploit them.[28] This category of risk continues to fall under the scope of the preventive rationale in the form of the more contemporary obligation of 'conservation'.[29] It is not perfectly clear whether conservation includes utilization of resources.[30] However, if that is the case, then

26 A Kiss, 'Abuse of Rights', *Max Planck Encyclopedia of Public International Law* (OUP 2006); J Brunnée, 'Sic utere tuo ut alienum non laedas', *Max Planck Encyclopedia of Public International Law* (OUP 2010).

27 UNECE Convention on the Protection and Use of Transboundary Watercourses and International Lakes (adopted 17 March 1992, entered into force 6 October 1996) (1992) 31 *ILM* 1312 (UNECE Water Convention), art 2(1); UN Convention on the Law of the Non-Navigational Uses of International Watercourses (adopted 21 May 1997, entered into force 17 August 2014) (1997) 36 *ILM* 700 (New York Watercourse Convention), art 7.

28 M Bowman, P Davies, and C Redgwell, *Lyster's International Wildlife Law* (2nd edn, CUP 2010) 4–6.

29 'Conservation' can be defined as protection and preservation as well as 'the maintenance, restoration, sustainable utilization and enhancement of a natural resource or the environment'. See R Rayfuse, 'Biological Resources' in D Bodansky, J Brunnée, and E Hey (eds), *The Oxford Handbook of International Environmental Law* (OUP 2007) 362, 372.

30 Some treaties distinguish between the two—see, eg, Convention on Biological Diversity (CBD) (adopted 22 May 1992, entered into force 29 December 1993) (1992) 31 *ILM* 822 (CBD) arts 8–10 (the requirements for the conservation of biodiversity are different from those to ensure sustainable use)—while

the obligation of conservation is an expression of the rationale of prevention which is more limited than a purely environmental rationale and which is constrained by an economic interpretation of biological resources.

This approach differs from the one described above because it underscores the need to protect resources irrespective of state sovereignty; as a result, it gives more consideration to the environment as an entity operating irrespective of territorial boundaries. However, the law is not directly concerned with risks to the environment per se, but rather with risks to natural resources, understood to be at the disposal of human beings. Under this perspective, environmental risks are framed only in relation to the potential impacts they represent to resource exploitation and are taken into account only because they might endanger economic growth.

8.3.3 Risks of pollution

The two rationales presented in sections 8.3.1 and 8.3.2 largely influenced the consecration of the preventive rationale in the Stockholm Declaration. Designed as a solution to the environmental issues faced in the 1970s, the principle of prevention provided a solution for the main type of risk with which the international community was concerned: pollution. As a result, the preventive rationale found its expression in treaty law in a variety of obligations with the objective to limit pollution from a specific source (eg, vessels[31]), activity (eg, exploitation of resources in the Area[32]), or substance (eg, ozone-depleting substances[33]).

Contrary to the other types of risk presented in this section, this category does not concentrate on the consequences of the damage (to state sovereignty or resource exploitation, for instance) but rather on the source of the damage (pollution). As a result, prevention in the form of an obligation to prevent pollution is less driven by inter-state concerns and gives more consideration to the environment per se. This is exemplified by the fact that the obligation is particularly important[34] and well developed[35] in relation to the marine environment; the Law of the Sea Convention (LOSC) does not merely concentrate on prohibiting causing damage by pollution 'to other States'[36] but also, and more generally, to the 'marine environment'.[37]

others do not—see, eg, Convention on Wetlands of International Importance Especially as Waterfowl Habitat (adopted 2 February 1971, entered into force 21 December 1975) 996 UNTS 245, art 3(1).

[31] United Nations Convention on the Law of the Sea (adopted 10 December 1982, entered into force 16 November 1994) 1833 UNTS 3 (LOSC), art 211.

[32] LOSC, arts 145(a) and 209.

[33] Convention for the Protection of the Ozone Layer (adopted 22 March 1985, entered into force 22 September 1988) (1985) 26 *ILM* 1529.

[34] For instance, a specific principle (Principle 7) was devoted to the obligation to 'prevent pollution of the seas' in the Stockholm Declaration.

[35] For instance, the LOSC (Part XII, Section 5) devotes a specific section to the obligation to 'prevent, reduce and control pollution of the marine environment' and addresses six main forms of marine pollution.

[36] LOSC, art 194(2). [37] LOSC, art 194(1).

The scope of the obligation of pollution prevention necessarily depends on the definition given to pollution.[38] Pollution can generally be defined as the introduction by man of substances into the environment which results or is likely to result in deleterious effects.[39] Such a definition is wide enough to cover a large array of sources of environmental harm. As a result, and because pollution is the most evident cause of environmental degradation, some authors consider the obligation to prevent pollution as the unique expression of the principle of prevention.[40] However, although a large part of environmental risks are risks of pollution, the obligation to prevent pollution cannot be understood as providing a legal solution to every type of environmental risk.[41]

8.3.4 Risks to human health

Irrespective of the source of the harm, environmental risks are often framed in relation to their consequences on human health. The primarily anthropocentric perspective of international environmental law means that its core objective is to limit environmental risks that might endanger human livelihoods. The relationship between the obligation to prevent environmental risks and the objective to reduce risks to human health is not always spelled out in treaties. However, some treaties explicitly recognize that the preventive rationale in international environmental law has a dual objective, one relative to risks to the environment; and the other relative to risks to human health.[42] Admittedly, this dual objective can be interpreted as the expression of two separate obligations of prevention. However, the two are closely inter-related because the objective to limit environmental risks is often driven by the willingness to avoid their impacts on human health.

The difficulty in dissociating the two obligations is confirmed by the fact that the obligation to prevent environmental damage and the objective of limiting risks to human health can explicitly merge under treaty law. This convergence can find different expressions. For instance, the ASEAN Agreement on Transboundary Haze

[38] For the different definitions given to pollution, see, in particular, A Springer, 'Towards a Meaningful Concept of Pollution in International Law' (1977) 26 *International and Comparative Law Quarterly* 531.

[39] See, eg, LOSC definition of pollution, art 1(4).

[40] D Hunter, J Salzman, and D Zaelke, *International Environmental Law and Policy* (4th edn, Foundation Press; Thomson/West 2011) 507; T Koivurova, *Introduction to International Environmental Law* (Routledge 2014) 109.

[41] *Chagos Marine Protected Area (The Republic of Mauritius v The United Kingdom of Great Britain and Northern Ireland)* (Permanent Court of Arbitration), 18 March 2015, paras 320 and 538; *South China Sea Arbitration (The Republic of the Philippines v The People's Republic of China)* (Permanent Court of Arbitration), Award on the Merits, 12 July 2016, para 945.

[42] See, eg, Convention for the Protection of the Ozone Layer (adopted 22 March 1985, entered into force 22 September 1988) (1985) 26 *ILM* 1529, Preamble; Protocol on Water and Health to the 1992 Convention on the Protection and Use of Transboundary Watercourses and International Lakes (adopted 11 June 1999, entered into force 4 October 2005) 2231 UNTS 202, art 1; Convention on Persistent Organic Pollutants (adopted 22 May 2001, entered into force 17 May 2004) (2001) 40 *ILM* 532, Preamble; Minamata Convention on Mercury (adopted 10 October 2013, not yet in force), <http://www.mercuryconvention.org/> accessed 8 February 2016, Preamble.

Pollution[43] reaffirms Stockholm Principle 21 by extending its scope to the prohibition against causing harm to human health. Indeed, Article 3 provides that states have the 'responsibility to ensure that activities within their jurisdiction or control do not cause damage to the environment and harm to *human health* of other States or of areas beyond the limits of national jurisdiction'.[44] The inclusion of human health within Principle 21 shows that the obligation to protect human health has the same legal basis as the obligation to protect the environment. A similar logic is found in the Protocol on Strategic Environmental Assessment to the Convention on Environmental Impact Assessment in a Transboundary Context,[45] which aims to 'provide for a high level of protection of the environment, including health'.[46] Prevention is expressed here in the form of an ambitious objective of protection which applies to risks of environmental damage, understood as inclusive of risks to human health. The provision makes it clear that the two types of risks cannot be distinguished. Similarly, the right to a healthy environment, as found, for instance, in the Additional Protocol to the American Convention on Human Rights in the Area of Economic, Social and Cultural Rights,[47] also requires states to take preventive measures to protect the environment with the view to limiting the health impacts of environmental risks. In sum, given that the preventive rationale in international environmental law seeks to protect human life on the planet, risks to human health fall under the scope of the obligation.

8.3.5 Risks to ecosystems

More recently, international law has broadened its conceptualization of environmental risks by embracing an ecosystem-oriented approach. As a result, the preventive rationale sometimes translates into an obligation to avoid causing harm to ecosystems, which can be found in treaties relative to the protection of international watercourses,[48] oceans,[49] biodiversity,[50] fisheries,[51] and the climate.[52] This obligation to protect ecosystems embodies an approach that understands the environment as a fragile inter-dependent system and

[43] ASEAN Agreement on Transboundary Haze Pollution (adopted 10 June 2002, entered into force 25 November 2003) <http://haze.asean.org/?wpfb_dl=32/> accessed 20 December 2016.

[44] ibid, art 3.

[45] Protocol on Strategic Environmental Assessment to the Convention on Environmental Impact Assessment in a Transboundary Context (adopted 21 May 2003, entered into force 11 July 2010) UN Doc ECE/MP/EI/2003/2.

[46] ibid, art 1.

[47] Additional Protocol to the American Convention on Human Rights in the Area of Economic, Social and Cultural Rights (adopted 16 November 1988, entered into force 16 November 1999) OAS Treaty Series No 69, art 11.

[48] See, inter alia, UNECE Water Convention, arts 2(2)(d) and 3(1); New York Watercourse Convention, art 20.

[49] LOSC, arts 192 and 194(5).

[50] CBD, art 2.

[51] Agreement for the Implementation of the Provisions of the United Nations Convention on the Law of the Sea of 10 December 1982 relating to the Conservation and Management of Straddling Fish Stocks and Highly Migratory Fish Stocks (adopted 4 August 1995, entered into force 11 December 2001) 2167 UNTS 3, Preamble.

[52] United Nations Framework Convention on Climate Change (adopted 9 May 1992, entered into force 24 March 1994) 1771 UNTS 107 (UNFCCC), Preamble and art 2.

highlights the need to avoid disruptions between living and non-living components of the environment.[53] Risk is no longer conceptualized as the danger of a specific type of harm, but rather as the danger of affecting an entire, complicated, system which relies on a fragile equilibrium that should not be disrupted. Under this perspective, the preventive rationale embraces a comprehensive outlook on environmental risks which seeks to protect the environment in an integrated and holistic manner.

It should nevertheless be noted that this obligation to prevent risks to ecosystems remains difficult to implement.[54] Two main obstacles explain this. First, translating our limited scientific understanding of ecosystemic interactions into an appropriate normative standard can be challenging. Second, enforcing an obligation which operates irrespective of the Westphalian structure of the law can be problematic. As a result, it is difficult to ascertain the extent to which the approach legally constrains the behaviour of states.[55]

8.3.6 Conclusion

This brief overview of the main risks covered by the preventive rationale in international environmental law shows that the objects which fall under its scope vary significantly. It reveals an evolution in the legal approach to risks under international environmental law; although the preventive rationale tends to apply to risks which only give indirect consideration to the protection of the environment, there is a move towards recognizing environmental risks in the strict sense of the word, irrespective of other considerations.

The categorization proposed above should not cloud the fact that the five types of risks are not mutually exclusive. Indeed, the different categories may operate in parallel within one treaty regime to ensure that different types of risks are covered. For instance, although the preventive rationale is primarily expressed in relation to risks to human health in treaties relative to hazardous substances, it also takes the form of concerns over risks to the sovereignty of other states and the risk of pollution.[56] In general, contemporary environmental treaties combine both traditional and more progressive approaches to risk; a preventive obligation embodying an ecosystemic approach will usually operate as a supplement to other, older, approaches to risk. For instance, this is the case in the field of watercourse law, where the preventive rationale finds its expression in the basic obligation not to cause transboundary harm,[57] as well as in the progressive duty to

[53] The CBD defines 'ecosystems' as follows: 'a dynamic complex of plant, animal and micro-organism communities and their non-living environment interacting as a functional unit'. CBD, art 2.

[54] D Tarlock, 'Ecosystems' in D Bodansky, J Brunnée, and E Hey (eds), *The Oxford Handbook of International Environmental Law* (OUP 2007) 574–96, 576.

[55] Y Tanaka, *The International Law of the Sea* (2nd edn, CUP 2015) 251.

[56] See, eg, Convention on the Control of Transboundary Movements of Hazardous Wastes and their Disposal (adopted 22 March 1989, entered into force 24 May 1992) (1989) 28 *ILM* 657, art 4(2)(c) on risks to human health; art 4(2)(d) on transboundary impacts; and art 4(2)(a) on pollution minimization.

[57] See, eg, New York Watercourse Convention, art 7; and UNECE Water Convention, art 2(1).

protect ecosystems.[58] Given that each of the categories discussed above has its own advantages and limitations, a combination of these different risks ensures that the legal framework is designed to cover a diversity of risks which might directly or indirectly affect the environment.

8.4 The Temporalities of Prevention

Section 8.3 has shown that the anticipatory nature of the obligation of prevention requires it to be expressed in multiple forms in order to respond to different types of risk. It is now necessary to look at what this regulatory preventive framework tells us about the way international law conceptualizes the future. The term 'future' is a broad concept; in particular, it does not say anything about the temporality that is envisaged—the future can be near or far. While the anticipatory nature of international environmental law is evident, its relation to temporality is complex. It appears that prevention operates at three different temporal levels which embrace three different futures: the imminent; the emergency; and the responsive. This combination of futures highlights the complexity of environmental harm which cannot be understood as a one-off event because its impacts spread throughout different temporal dimensions.

8.4.1 Imminence

While the future with which prevention is concerned is not made explicit in international environmental law, an implicit conceptualization of the future can be extracted from the manner in which the preventive obligation is conceived. It seems that when the likelihood of occurrence of damage can be predicted, the law considers that the risk is operating in the realm of 'imminence'. This temporal application of prevention is made clear in European Directive 2004/35/CE, which defines an 'imminent' threat of damage as situations in which there is a 'sufficient likelihood that environmental damage will occur in the near future'.[59] This understanding of the term 'imminent' has also been articulated by the ICJ in the *Gabčikovo-Nagymaros* Case. While the ICJ was referring to imminence in the context of justifying a state of necessity, the Court's reasoning is equally applicable to the issue of prevention. In the Court's opinion, 'a "peril" appearing in the long-term might be held to be "imminent" as soon as it is established, at the relevant point in time, that the realization of that peril, however far off it might be, is not thereby any less certain and inevitable'.[60] In the case of prevention, the 'imminence' of the threat is linked to the probability of the threat occurring rather

[58] See, inter alia, New York Watercourse Convention, art 20 and UNECE Water Convention, arts 2(2)(d) and 3(1).

[59] Directive 2004/35/CE of the European Parliament and of the Council of 21 April 2004 on environmental liability with regard to the prevention and remedying of environmental damage, (2004) OJ L143, art 2(9).

[60] *Gabčikovo-Nagymaros Project* (*Hungary/Slovakia*) [1997] ICJ Rep 7, para 54.

than to its closeness, in terms of timing, to the present. In other words, the future is conceptualized not in relation to its temporality, per se, but rather to the likelihood of the occurrence of damage.

As a result, international law does not define a specific timeframe for its anticipatory vision; in other words, the preventive rationale can be expressed in the form of an obligation requiring short-term or long-term action in light of a threat deemed imminent. Different levels in the temporal definition of imminence are found, for example, in the Paris Agreement to the UNFCCC, which translates the preventive rationale into two distinct expressions: a short-term procedural obligation, which requires states to submit a nationally determined contribution every five years communicating their emissions reduction targets,[61] and a long-term objective, which calls on states to aim to achieve a carbon-neutral world within the second half of the twenty-first century.[62] In sum, although both short-term and long-term expressions of prevention qualify as responses to 'imminent' risks, their translation into legal norms varies greatly.

8.4.2 Emergency

Prevention is not only concerned with risk that is imminent, but may also be concerned with risk that is urgent. Risk may be urgent because the risk was not foreseeable in the long term or because measures of prevention were not undertaken or did not succeed in avoiding the occurrence of harm. Given the prevalence of disasters occurring every year (eg, in 2015 there were 371 disasters related to natural hazards and 203 related to technological hazards[63]), the applicability of the obligation to prevent these emergencies, or at least to mitigate their effects, is of fundamental importance. In this scenario, the anticipatory action required is concerned with the occurrence of environmental harm in the very near future; indeed, almost in the present.

Despite operating in a different, more immediate, temporal sphere, the obligation still remains an obligation of prevention. This was the approach taken by the ILC Prevention Articles, which include an obligation of emergency preparedness that requires states to anticipate emergencies by developing contingency plans.[64] It qualifies as an obligation of prevention because harm remains foreseeable—a necessary criteria in the application of prevention—thanks, inter alia, to early warning systems. As the ILC commentaries make clear, 'suddenness does not denote that the situation needs to be wholly unexpected'.[65] As a result, even in situations when there is very limited time to act, the preventive obligation still applies.

[61] Paris Agreement to the UNFCCC (adopted 12 December 2015, in force 4 November 2016) Doc FCCC/CP/2015/10/Add.1 (Paris Agreement), art 4(9).

[62] Paris Agreement, art 4(1).

[63] International Federation of Red Cross and Red Crescent Societies, *World Disasters Report 2016*, 236 <http://media.ifrc.org/ifrc/publications/world-disasters-report-2016//> accessed 20 December 2016.

[64] ILC Prevention Articles, art 16.

[65] ILC Prevention Articles, Commentaries to art 17, 169, para 2.

8.4.3 Response

In addition to its anticipatory nature, prevention also spreads its effects *after* the damage has occurred. When the first two stages of prevention have failed, the obligation of prevention remains relevant to avoid further harm once the harmful event has occurred. This integration of an ex post perspective within an anticipatory obligation binds the past to the future. While apparently paradoxical, the approach makes sense given that prevention is an obligation of due diligence which is more concerned with the risk than with the occurrence of the harmful event per se. As a result, the obligation of prevention remains applicable, even in cases where the harmful event has already occurred, as a mechanism for addressing environmental damage subsequent to that harmful event. In keeping with the rules on state responsibility, the obligation to prevent is a continuous one, which 'extends over the entire period during which the [harmful] event continues and remains not in conformity with that obligation'.[66]

Indeed, the obligation of prevention most often enters into play when harm has already occurred and when the aim of prevention is then to limit the scope of the harm. International tribunals have recognized that the customary obligation to prevent also encompasses an obligation to mitigate harm.[67] Similarly, treaty obligations stipulating prevention do not restrict their approach to an obligation of *ex ante* prevention, but also include related obligations of harm elimination, mitigation, and minimization. The climate regime provides a striking example in this regard; climate law rarely refers to an obligation of prevention per se but prefers the term 'mitigation'. This is explained by the fact that climate change cannot be completely prevented because changes in the climate are already occurring.[68] Thus, despite the fact that only their furtherance can be limited, the preventive rationale remains applicable. In sum, despite being an anticipatory obligation, prevention is less concerned with its temporal applicability than with the risks it aims to curb, and therefore does not operate on the basis of strict temporal boundaries.

8.5 The Addressees of Prevention

Just as the concept of 'future' is applicable to different moments of time, its definition also depends on the actor conceptualizing the future. As a result, prevention plays to different audiences for whom it aims to ensure harm avoidance. Its content

[66] ILC, 'Draft Articles on Responsibility of States for Internationally Wrongful Acts (with Commentaries)' (2001) *Yearbook of the International Law Commission* (vol II, part 2) A/56/10, 31, art 14(3).

[67] *Iron Rhine Railway* (*Belgium v Netherlands*) (Permanent Court of Arbitration) (2005) 27 RIAA 35, para 59; *Indus Waters Kishenganga Arbitration* (*Pakistan v India*) (Permanent Court of Arbitration) Final Award, 20 December 2013, para 112.

[68] Intergovernmental Panel on Climate Change (IPCC), RK Pachauri and LA Meyer (eds), 'Summary for Policymakers' in *Climate Change 2014: Synthesis Report* (CUP 2014), para 1.1: 'Warming in the climate system is unequivocal, and since the 1950s, many of the observed changes are unprecedented over decades to millennia.'

thus changes form depending on the audience. In other words, just as prevention adapts to the type of risk, it is also malleable, depending on the entity whose environmental integrity is in issue. In this respect, the obligation of prevention aims to regulate the future of three different types of entities: the state; the individual; and the planet.

8.5.1 The future of the state

First, and perhaps most obviously for a legal framework based on a Westphalian perspective, international environmental law is concerned with the future of the state. At the heart of Stockholm Principle 21 lie two competing visions of the future: one concerned with the right of the state to use its resources as it sees fit (expressed in the concept of permanent sovereignty over natural resources), and the other concerned with the protection of the environment (expressed in the prohibition against the causing of environmental harm). These two concepts are not necessarily inherently contradictory. The degradation of the environment can indeed be detrimental to the sovereignty of the state. In this respect, the ICJ recognized that the concerns expressed by Hungary for the environmental state of the Gabčikovo-Nagymaros region could be justified as an essential interest of the state, constituting a state of necessity that could preclude the wrongfulness of an otherwise unlawful act.[69] Although the Court considered that Hungary had failed to prove that there was a grave and imminent danger, which would justify the invocation of a state of necessity, it nevertheless acknowledged that environmental degradation could harm the integrity of the state.[70]

However, faced with environmental damage, not all states are equal. In particular, states are more or less vulnerable to the current degradation of our planet.[71] The most striking example of the danger represented by environmental harm to a state is the example of climate change and associated sea level rise, which threatens the survival of low-lying island states.[72] Put simply, there may not be a future for these states.[73] Problematically, these states are low emitters of greenhouse gases, yet they face the most severe consequences of the industrialization of developed states. For low-lying island states the future is thus catastrophic, while for developed industrialized states it is merely difficult and/or different. Although states may have a 'common future'[74] because they share the same planet, it does not mean that

[69] *Gabčikovo-Nagymaros Project* (n 60) para 53.

[70] *Gabčikovo-Nagymaros Project* (n 60) para 57.

[71] IPCC, 'Summary for Policymakers' (n 68) para 2.3: 'Risks are unevenly distributed and are generally greater for disadvantaged people and communities in countries at all levels of development.'

[72] IPCC, CB Field, VR Barros, DJ Dokken et al (eds), *Climate Change 2014: Impacts, Adaptation, and Vulnerability* (CUP 2014) 1618.

[73] For a legal perspective on this issue, see JG Stoutenburg, *Disappearing Island States in International Law* (Brill Nijhoff 2015). See also, E Crawford and R Rayfuse, 'Climate Change and Statehood' in R Rayfuse and S Scott (eds), *International Law in the Era of Climate Change* (Edward Elgar 2012) 243.

[74] World Commission on Environment and Development, 'Our Common Future' (4 August 1987) UN Doc A/42/427.

they all envisage the future in the same way. Rather, their 'common future' is just a negotiated political and legal construct that is necessary to coordinate actions to protect a 'common' good. In other words, the notion of 'common future' refers to a common objective to avoid environmental degradation, but does not necessarily infer that the future will actually be the same for each state.

8.5.2 The future of individuals

Second, international environmental law also focuses on the effects of environmental harm on individuals and communities, regularly linking the abstract notion of 'future' to the well-being of the population of the planet. Indeed, the anticipatory vision of international environmental law does not necessarily aim to regulate the future in general, but rather 'our' future, as highlighted by international documents making references to '*our* common future'[75] or 'the future *we* want'.[76]

This anthropocentric conceptualization of the future, which focuses on individuals, is important for the obligation of prevention. The recognition of the customary nature of the principle of prevention by the ICJ in the *Nuclear Weapons Advisory Opinion* is found in the same paragraph as the recognition that 'the environment is not an abstraction but represents the living space, the quality of life and the very health of human beings, including generations unborn'.[77] This assertion appears to infer that the preventive obligation is directly derived from the recognition that the environment should be protected for the benefit of human beings. It thereby acknowledges the anthropocentric vision of international environmental law, which values environmental protection in relation to how the state of the Earth, 'our home',[78] will affect 'our' future.

The question which arises is, therefore, who is this 'our' in the expression 'our future'? The term 'our' is understood as emphasizing the common fate which binds humanity in the face of environmental degradation. International law is not only interested in the future of the state in the face of environmental degradation, but also in the future of human beings. As a result, the obligation of prevention can be found in human rights law, in the form of the state obligation to protect individuals from deprivation of their human rights by third parties causing environmental harm.[79] This focus on the individual leaves open the possibility of considering the future of 'future generations'.

[75] ibid. [76] 'The Future We Want' (n 3).

[77] *Legality of the Threat or Use of Nuclear Weapons* (n 2) para 29.

[78] United Nations Conference on Environment and Development, 'Declaration of the United Nations Conference on Environment and Development' (3–4 June 1992) A/CONF.151/26 (Vol I) (Rio Declaration), Preamble.

[79] The jurisprudence of human rights bodies has established that states have the obligation to exercise due diligence to prevent environmental harm within a domestic context if environmental degradation affects existing human rights. See, eg, *López Ostra v Spain* App No 16798/90 (ECHR 9 December1994); *Guerra and Others v Italy* App No 116/1996/735/932 (ECHR 19 February 1998); *Öneryildiz v Turkey* App No 48939/99 (ECHR 30 November 2004); *Taskin and Others v Turkey* App No 46117/99 (ECHR 10 November 2004); The Social and Economic Rights Action Center and the Center for Economic and Social Rights/Nigeria, African Commission on Human and Peoples' Rights, Communication 155/96, October 2001.

As the ICJ *Nuclear Weapons Advisory Opinion* noted, while recognizing the customary status of the principle of prevention, the environment has an impact on human beings, 'including generations unborn'.[80] This approach has the potential to broaden the temporal scope of prevention by dictating a more long-term, inter-generational perspective to the obligation to prevent environmental harm. The 'our' in 'our future' does not only refer to a same generation but to a same species, the human species spanning multiple generations.

8.5.3 The future of the planet

Finally, international environmental law appears to be moving away from its utilitarian goal of protecting the environment for the sole objective of preserving the integrity of states and the well-being of individuals, to protecting its very object—the environment—for its intrinsic value. Admittedly, it can sometimes be difficult to assess the motivations of the law behind the rules relative to the protection of the environment and to pinpoint the measures which are being taken irrespective of any instrumental gain they might bring to humans. Indeed, international environmental law, as a product of man's conceptualization, is intrinsically governed by anthropocentric motivations; human beings protect the environment only in as much as this is needed for their well-being and livelihood.

However, there are some indications that the law is increasingly concerned with the integrity of the planet itself, irrespective of anthropocentric considerations. The ecosystem approach mentioned in section 8.3 contributes to the recognition of the planet's intrinsic value because it sees the environment as a complex mix of inter-relationships between natural entities and systems and does not rely on the territorial divisions which characterize the Westphalian system.[81] Admittedly, the ecosystem approach results from an increased recognition of the services offered by nature, and thereby of the enhanced instrumental values that these represent. However, the ecosystem approach also recognizes the 'environment' as an ensemble; obligations to protect ecosystems are therefore concerned with the future state of the planet, and not uniquely with the future of a state or an individual. It is undeniable that the environment gains from being protected via an ecosystem approach. By recognizing that harm to one species can destabilize an entire ecosystem, the ecosystem approach acknowledges the fragility of the balance upon which the planet is based.

Thus, it could be said that international environmental law is increasingly embracing a dual approach to the planet; being driven by anthropocentric motivations but also recognizing the value of the planet as such. By way of example, the conference of the parties of the CBD has recognized that ecosystems should be managed for 'their

[80] *Legality of the Threat or Use of Nuclear Weapons* (n 2) para 29.

[81] For the ecosystem approach see, inter alia, LOSC, art 192; New York Watercourse Convention, art 20; and ILC, 'Third Report of the Special Rapporteur, Mr Shinya Murase, on the Protection of the Atmosphere' (2016) UN Doc A/CN.4/692, draft guideline 3 on the obligation to protect the atmosphere.

intrinsic values and for the tangible or intangible benefits for humans'.[82] This recognition of a dual approach reveals a broader aim to the obligation of prevention as being to seek to avoid harm not only for the benefit of the state, or even for the benefit of individuals, but also for the benefit of the planet as a whole.

8.6 Conclusion

The principle of prevention is recognized as the cornerstone of international environmental law. The rationale of prevention has infiltrated international environmental law, and the content of the obligation has adapted to regulate a variety of environmental risks. Just as risk is not uniform, so, too, the legal response has been seen to be malleable. As this chapter has demonstrated, prevention is an intricate, multifaceted, norm which not only finds different expressions in the law, but also applies at different temporal phases and speaks to different audiences. The density of the principle is dictated by the complexity of the risks which it aims to curb.

This complexity means that the cartography of prevention offered in this chapter necessarily simplifies the reality. In particular, it should not give the impression that the boundaries between the different categories are clear-cut. On the contrary, it merely aims to provide clarity regarding the responses to environmental degradation developed by a complex, constantly evolving, international legal system. This calls for two final comments regarding the evolution of the principle of prevention—in other words, regarding its future.

First, the multifaceted nature of the principle raises questions as to whether some aspects are, or should be, given priority. For example, the human rights approach to environmental damage which is currently gaining in importance[83] favours an expression of the preventive rationale which focuses on the individual as its beneficiary. On the one hand, this expression does not fully conceptualize environmental risks; on the other hand, its focus on the impacts of environmental risks on human livelihoods gives a stronger incentive to act towards environmental protection. Prioritizing this expression of the preventive rationale would, therefore, have important consequences. Similarly, while the different temporalities of prevention ensure that risks spanning different temporal dimensions are covered, the principle does not necessarily encourage states to act at the earliest possible stage. Indeed, states can decide to take preventive measures at the first emergence of the risks, or at a later stage, merely with the view to counteracting their potential effects. In other words, the different temporal dimensions of prevention might share the same ultimate objective, but the environment will be affected differently depending on which temporal dimension is prioritized. In sum, these two examples show that the

[82] CBD, Fifth Conference of the Parties, Decision V/6, 'Ecosystem Approach' (2000) section B, Principle 1.

[83] See, eg, 'Report of the Independent Expert John H. Knox on the Issue of Human Rights Obligations Relating to the Enjoyment of a Safe, Clean, Healthy and Sustainable Environment' (2012) A/HRC/22/43.

principle of prevention could evolve differently depending on which of its multiple aspects are given more consideration.

Second, the study offered in this chapter has presented a legal preventive framework which ultimately aims to shape the future of different audiences. However, it should not be forgotten that this same framework is also shaped by those audiences, in particular by the governments and peoples that were urged by the Stockholm Declaration to take action.[84] This raises broader questions relating to the subjective choices of those audiences when attempting to resolve issues involving multiple conceptions of risk and differing expectations regarding how to limit those risks. The evolution of the content of the principle of prevention, and of international environmental law in general, will depend on whether, and if so in what manner, we take these differences into consideration when designing legal responses to environmental risks as conceived by all. The challenge will be to ensure that international law aims to construct a 'common future', while acknowledging the different conceptions of its future.

[84] Stockholm Declaration, Preamble, para 7.

9

Conceptions of Risk in an Institutional Context: Deep Seabed Mining and the International Seabed Authority

Aline Jaeckel and Rosemary Rayfuse

9.1 Introduction

When the Maltese Ambassador to the United Nations, Dr Arvid Pardo, made his famous speech to the General Assembly in 1967 calling for the deep seabed and its resources to be designated the 'common heritage of mankind', he was imagining a future in which untold riches would be gained from mining the deep sea floor; riches, that it was feared would be appropriated by the few developed states capable of exploiting the resources.[1] For Malta and other newly independent and emerging developing states, the risks of this future were seen not merely as financial. Militarization of the deep sea was perceived as a security threat and monopolization of exploitation of deep seabed resources by developed states was expected to have significant, even devastating, negative consequences for developing states, many of whose economies were heavily dependent on land-based mineral production.[2] The New International Economic Order, which these developing states sought to achieve as a means of bringing equity to the world economy, required the development of a new legal framework for the sharing of the riches of the deep sea based on the premise that these resources were the preserve of humankind as a whole.[3] As Payoyo puts it, 'the physical phenomenon of the deep ocean floor and its resources

[1] UNGA, 'Examination of the Question of the Reservation Exclusively for Peaceful Purposes of the Sea-Bed and the Ocean Floor, and the Subsoil Thereof, Underlying the High Seas Beyond the Limits of Present National Jurisdiction, and the Use of their Resources in the Interest of Mankind' UN Doc A/C.1/PV1515 and A/C.1/PV 1516 (1967).

[2] E Luard, *The Control of the Sea-Bed: A New International Issue* (Heinemann 1974) 49–60.

[3] See, eg, RC Ogley, 'The Law of the Sea Draft Convention and the New International Economic Order' (1981) 5 *Marine Policy* 240; FH Paollilo, 'The Future Legal Regime of Seabed Resources and the NIEO: Some Issues' in K Hossain (ed), *Legal Aspects of the New International Economic Order* (Frances Pinter 1980) 165; L Juda, 'UNCLOS III and the New International Economic Order' (1979) 7 *Ocean Development & International Law* 221; RL Friedheim, *Negotiating the New Ocean Regime* (University of South Carolina Press 1993) 220–22.

Conceptions of Risk in an Institutional Context: Deep Seabed Mining and the International Seabed Authority Aline Jaeckel and Rosemary Rayfuse.
Published 2017 by Oxford University Press.

became inter-twined with the eminently political question of who has control, or who ought to have control, over it'.[4]

The question of who would have control over the deep seabed and its resources was ultimately resolved with the adoption of the 1982 United Nations Convention on the Law of the Sea (LOSC).[5] Part XI of the LOSC declared the international seabed, known as the 'Area',[6] and its resources to be the common heritage of mankind.[7] To give effect to this concept, Part XI established a new inter-governmental organization, the International Seabed Authority (ISA), charged with organizing and controlling seabed mining activities in the Area and administering its resources on behalf of humankind as a whole.[8] Pardo's imagined future of perceived potential economic benefits and access to resources had resulted in the adoption of a wholly new form of international regime, premised on the collectivization of the benefits of seabed mining in the Area embodied in the notion of the common heritage of humankind. While some of the controversial aspects of the common heritage regime, particularly those relating to benefit sharing, were subsequently modified by the 1994 Implementing Agreement to the LOSC,[9] the collective ownership of and responsibility for the seabed resources remains vested in the international community as represented by the ISA.

Despite these legal and institutional developments, the gold rush envisaged by Ambassador Pardo has not yet materialized. Deep seabed mining has turned out to be extremely challenging—both technologically and financially.[10] Although there is growing interest from a number of commercial operators and international entities, the economic conditions for its profitability have not yet emerged. Moreover, in the decades since Ambassador Pardo's speech, our knowledge of the deep ocean, its resources, and its ecosystems has increased.[11] Our growing understanding of the complexities and importance of the deep oceans has led to an increased appreciation of the uncertainty as to the risks of deep seabed mining. Importantly, while the vision of economic benefit and the corresponding imperatives of economic risk remain, the risks associated with deep seabed mining have increasingly come to be

[4] PB Payoyo, *Cries of the Sea: World Inequality, Sustainable Development and the Common Heritage of Humanity* (Martinus Nijhoff 1997) 170.

[5] United Nations Convention on the Law of the Sea (adopted 10 December 1982, entered into force 16 November 1994) 1833 UNTS 3 (LOSC).

[6] The 'Area' is defined as 'the seabed and ocean floor and subsoil thereof, beyond the limits of national jurisdiction'. LOSC, art 1(1).

[7] LOSC, art 136.

[8] LOSC, arts 137, 156, and 157. For an overview of the history of the ISA regime, see SN Nandan, MW Lodge, and S Rosenne, *The Development of the Regime for Deep Seabed Mining* (Kluwer Law International 2002).

[9] Agreement relating to the Implementation of Part XI of the United Nations Convention on the Law of the Sea of 10 December 1982 (adopted by UNGA Res 48/263 28 July 1994, entered into force 16 November 1994) 1836 UNTS 3 (Implementing Agreement).

[10] See, eg, ISA, 'Polymetallic Nodule Mining Technology—Current Status and Challenges Ahead', Proceedings of a Workshop Held by the International Seabed Authority in Chennai, India 18–22 February 2008 (ISA 2012) <http://isa.org.jm/files/documents/EN/Pubs/Chennai.pdf> accessed 20 November 2016.

[11] See, eg, M Williams, H Mannix, K Yarincik et al, *Scientific Results to Support the Sustainable Use and Conservation of Marine Life: A Summary of the Census of Marine Life for Decision Makers* (Census of Marine Life International Secretariat 2011).

characterized as environmental.[12] The collectivization of benefits inherent in the common heritage principle has also led to the collectivization of the environmental risks, which are borne by, and the concern of, all of humanity.

As the central institution that manages and regulates seabed mining in the Area, the ISA has found itself walking the tightrope between developing and promoting the practice of deep seabed mining, on the one hand, and protecting the marine environment from the impacts of that mining, on the other. In this regard, it provides an institutional platform in which differing conceptualizations of the risks and uncertainties surrounding deep seabed mining can be transformed into a regulatory framework. This chapter examines the manner in which the environmental risks associated with deep seabed mining have been imagined and conceptualized within the ISA and the manner in which the ISA has sought to regulate in the face of uncertainty. Section 9.2 begins with a discussion of the conceptualization of the risks. Since exploitation has not yet occurred on a commercial scale, the risks of mining fall to be imagined by extrapolation from other activities such as prospecting, exploration activities, and scientific research. Section 9.3 then explores the way in which the ISA attempts to resolve conflicting imageries of the environmental risks and uncertainties associated with deep seabed mining through an incremental approach to regulation and management. In doing so, it is hoped to reveal something about the extent to which the existence of an institutional platform, the ISA, affects how the imagined future of perceived economic riches is balanced against the present and ongoing requirement to protect a marine environment about which relatively little is still known.

9.2 Conceptualizing the Risks of Deep Seabed Mining

Traditionally considered out of sight and out of mind, as demand for resources and technological capacity has grown, both our knowledge of and our footprint on the oceans has grown as well. Once considered an empty expanse, we now know that deep ocean habitats are multiple and diverse and contain perhaps the largest reservoir of biodiversity left on Earth.[13] Over the past two to three decades, scientists have begun to understand that deep sea biogenic habitats show high vulnerability to extractive human activities, due to slow growth rates and the extreme longevity of their constituent species.[14] Thus, where once no environmental risk

[12] ISA, *Decision of the Council of the International Seabed Authority Relating to an Environmental Management Plan for the Clarion-Clipperton Zone*, ISBA/17/C/19 (21 July 2011); J Halfar and RM Fujita, 'Danger of Deep-Sea Mining' (2007) 316 *Science* 987; CL van Dover, 'Mining Seafloor Massive Sulphides and Biodiversity: What Is at Risk?' (2010) 68 *ICES Journal of Marine Science* 341.

[13] E Ramirez-Llodra, A Brandt, R Danovaro et al, 'Deep, Diverse and Definitely Different: Unique Attributes of the World's Largest Ecosystem' (2010) 7 *Biogeosciences* 2851, 2852; see also B Ebbe, DSM Billett, A Brandt et al, 'Diversity of Abyssal Marine Life' in AD McIntyre (ed), *Life in the World's Oceans: Diversity, Distribution, and Abundance* (Wiley-Blackwell 2010) 139.

[14] H Thiel and A Koslow (eds), 'Managing Risks to Biodiversity and the Environment on the High Sea, Including Tools Such as Marine Protected Areas: Scientific Requirements and Legal Aspects', Proceedings of the Expert Workshop held at the International Academy for Nature Conservation, Isle of Vilm, Germany, 27 February–4 March 2001 <http://www.bfn.de/fileadmin/MDB/documents/proceed1.pdf> accessed 20 November 2016.

was contemplated, environmental risks associated with deep seabed mining are increasingly being identified. The identification of these real and potential risks has given rise to competing conceptualizations of their importance, ranging along a continuum from negligible to great, or, in some cases, even catastrophic.

9.2.1 The environmental risks of seabed mining

In terms of their identification, the environmental risks involved in mining seabed minerals depend in part on the habitat associated with the minerals. Polymetallic nodules, for example, lie on the seafloor, often partially buried in soft sediments. Formed around a core, their concentric layers of iron and manganese hydroxides have accumulated over millions of years from metals dissolved in seawater.[15] Mining of nodules may involve removal and destruction of sediments, living organisms, and hard substratum which provides the habitat for a range of species, as well as the creation of near-bottom and mid-water sediment plumes,[16] all of which may lead to alterations in seabed and water column communities and food-web interactions.[17]

Polymetallic sulphide deposits occur around hydrothermal vents which, apart from the mineral resources they provide,[18] also offer a unique habitat for chemosynthetic ecosystems. These life forms are powered by chemical energy instead of sunlight and their discovery has been described as one of 'the greatest scientific discoveries of the 20th century'.[19] These ecosystems offer insights 'ranging from Earth processes ... to an understanding of the various ways life can exist in the absence of sunlight and oxygen, ... to defining the lowest branches of the "Tree of Life" and possibly the origin of life itself on Earth and on other planets'.[20] Mining polymetallic sulphides will likely result inter alia in the loss of habitat for chemosynthetic ecosystems, extinction of endemic or rare taxa, decreased diversity at all levels, and decreased seafloor primary production.[21]

Similarly, ferromanganese crusts, which form through very slow precipitation of dissolved metals in seawater, accumulate on the volcanic rock of seamounts and underwater

[15] UN Division for Ocean Affairs and the Law of the Sea (UNDOALOS), 'Marine Mineral Resources: Scientific Advances and Economic Perspectives' (2004) 59.

[16] See generally Ramirez-Llodra, 'Deep, Diverse and Definitely Different' (n 13); H Thiel, 'Evaluation of the Environmental Consequences of Polymetallic Nodule Mining Based on the Results of the TUSCH Research Association' (2001) 48 *Deep Sea Research II* 3433; UNGA, 'Report of the Secretary-General (Addendum)' (18 August 2004) UN Doc A59/62/Add 1, paras 227–29.

[17] PA Jumars, 'Limits in Predicting and Detecting Benthic Community Responses to Manganese Nodule Mining' (1981) 3 *Marine Mining* 213; BS Ingole, S Pavithran, and ZA Ansari, 'Restoration of Deep-Sea Macrofauna after Simulated Benthic Disturbance in the Central Indian Basin' (2005) 23(4) *Marine Georesources & Geotechnology* 267; T Radziejewska, *Meiobenthos in the Sub-Equatorial Pacific Abyss. A Proxy in Anthropogenic Impact Evaluation* (Springer 2014).

[18] UNDOALOS, 'Marine Mineral Resources' (n 15), 48–51.

[19] CL van Dover, CR Smith, J Ardron et al, *Environmental Management of Deep-Sea Chemosynthetic Ecosystems: Justification of and Considerations for a Spatially-Based Approach* (ISA Technical Study No 9 2011) 2; MC Baker, EZ Ramirez-Llodra, PA Tyler et al, 'Biogeography, Ecology, and Vulnerability of Chemosynthetic Ecosystems in the Deep Sea' in A McIntyre (ed), *Life in the World's Oceans: Diversity, Distribution, and Abundance* (Wiley-Blackwell 2010).

[20] van Dover et al, *Environmental Management of Deep-Sea Chemosynthetic Ecosystems* (n 19) 2.

[21] van Dover, 'Mining Seafloor Massive Sulphides' (n 12).

volcanic mountain ranges at depths which also provide habitat for cold water corals.[22] Extracting these crusts requires separating them from the underlying rock substrate which will destroy fauna on the crusts themselves[23] and destroy habitat. Importantly, there is a high potential for species extinctions owing to the suspected endemic nature of seamount biota[24] and the centuries-long time frames required for their recovery.[25]

Additional environmental risks from seabed mining include pollution caused by lifting the minerals to vessels, disposing of tailings from the separation of the minerals from slurry, and transporting the minerals for further processing.[26] Plumes in surface water from discharges may also 'interfere with primary productivity by increasing nutrient levels and decreasing light penetration into the ocean'.[27] In addition, lifting cold water from the deep oceans can alter local sea surface temperature and release carbon dioxide into the atmosphere.[28] Each of these risks is aggravated by the potential for the pollution to be transferred more broadly throughout the water column due to the fluid nature of the medium.[29]

Moreover, the risks involved are cumulative. As van Dover puts it, '[o]f particular concern is the impact of cumulative mining events in a region, with potential for species extinctions and unanticipated changes in ecosystem structure and function if the extractive activities aren't appropriately managed'.[30] In addition, the risks of seabed mining must be considered in the context of other human-induced impacts, such as vessel-source pollution, deep sea fishing, or climate change, leading to cumulative effects which are difficult to quantify or monitor.[31] Addressing such cumulative risks is challenging. While some uncertainties can be reduced over time, studying biodiversity and deep ocean ecosystems involves ontological uncertainties which go beyond strictly scientific uncertainties.[32] Moreover, the cumulative

[22] UNDOALOS, 'Marine Mineral Resources' (n 15) 62–64, 69; JR Hein, 'Cobalt-Rich Ferromanganese Crusts: Global Distribution, Composition, Origin and Research Activities' in *Polymetallic Massive Sulphides and Cobalt-Rich Ferromanganese Crusts: Status and Prospects* (ISA Technical Study No 2 2002) 36–89.

[23] AG Glover and CR Smith, 'The Deep-Sea Floor Ecosystem: Current Status and Prospects of Anthropogenic Change by the Year 2025' (2003) 30 *Environmental Conservation* 219, 231.

[24] JA Koslow, K Gowlett-Holmes, JK Lowry et al, 'Seamount Benthic Macrofauna off Southern Tasmania: Community Structure and Impacts of Trawling' (2001) 213 *Marine Ecology Progress Series* 111.

[25] J Murray Roberts, AJ Wheeler, and A Freiwald, 'Reefs of the Deep: The Biology and Geology of Cold-Water Coral Ecosystems' (2006) 312 *Science* 543.

[26] See generally, CL Morgan, NA Odunton, and AT Jones, 'Synthesis of Environmental Impacts of Deep Seabed Mining' (1999) 17 *Marine Georesources & Geotechnology* 307.

[27] ISA, *Recommendations for the Guidance of Contractors for the Assessment of the Possible Environmental Impacts Arising from Exploration for Marine Minerals in the Area*, ISBA/19/LTC/8 (1 March 2013) para 25.

[28] ibid.

[29] P Herring, *The Biology of the Deep Ocean* (OUP 2001) 254.

[30] CL van Dover, 'Impacts of Anthropogenic Disturbances at Deep-Sea Hydrothermal Vent Ecosystems: A Review' (2014) 102 *Marine Environmental Research* 59, 69; See also CL van Dover, 'Tighten Regulations on Deep-Sea Mining' (2011) 470 *Nature* 31, 33.

[31] KJ Mengerink, CL van Dover, J Ardon et al, 'A Call for Deep-Ocean Stewardship' (2014) 344 *Science* 696; Ramirez-Llodra et al, 'Deep, Diverse and Definitely Different' (n 13).

[32] WE Walker, P Harremoës, J Rotmans et al, 'Defining Uncertainty: A Conceptual Basis for Uncertainty Management in Model-Based Decision Support' (2003) 4 *Integrated Assessment* 5, 13–14; R Cooney, 'A Long and Winding Road? Precaution from Principle to Practice in Biodiversity Conservation' in R Fisher et al (eds), *Implementing the Precautionary Principle: Perspectives And Prospects* (Edward Elgar 2006) 229.

nature of the effects of seabed mining contributes to the complexity of the potential impacts, which in turn adds to the persistence of uncertainties.[33] For example, even if knowledge of the ecology of a particular mine site might advance to the point where the local impact can be predicted with some confidence, uncertainties may remain regarding the geographical distribution and temporal extent of the harm as well as the cumulative effects.

In short, economic and technological hurdles aside, seabed mining poses a number of risks and uncertainties relating to the potential destruction of a vast array of unusual and rarely studied ecosystems and species from benthic disturbances, habitat destruction, sediment plumes and toxic effects on the water column from leakage or discharge of slurry and tailings.[34] These uncertainties give rise to competing conceptualizations of the risks involved.

9.2.2 Conceptualizations of the risks

Despite concerns as to the environmental risks posed by seabed mining, since the 1960s a number of private and government-owned entities have invested in developing the technologies needed to explore, and eventually exploit, seabed minerals. Although many technological hurdles still exist, an increasing range of sophisticated prospecting and exploration technologies have been developed to enable acquisition of data and information about mineral occurrence and composition and the environment of the deposits in order to establish the commercial viability of eventual exploitation.[35]

Proponents of seabed mining conceptualize the risks as minimal or, in any event, well worth taking. They highlight the potential of seabed mining to provide a less invasive and more environmentally friendly process to mine minerals than terrestrial mining.[36] This conceptualization of mining as beneficial rests on the assumption that seabed mining will provide an alternative, rather than an addition, to land-based mining and that it is necessary to provide metals needed for the 'Green Economy'. In short, for proponents, the risks of mining are either negligible, less likely to occur, or, if they do occur, less damaging to humanity than the risk of economic loss or waste. In other words, the risks associated with inaction—of not mining—outweigh any risks of action.

These positive conceptualizations of the potential benefits of seabed mining stand in stark contrast, however, to its conceptualization as potentially environmentally harmful; although, perhaps unsurprisingly, there is considerable disparity even among the various negative conceptualizations. For example,

[33] R Cooney, *The Precautionary Principle in Biodiversity Conservation and Natural Resource Management: An Issue Paper for Policy-Makers, Researchers and Practitioners* (IUCN 2004) 27.

[34] See, eg, van Dover, 'Mining Seafloor Massive Sulphides' (n 12); International Council for the Exploration of the Sea (ICES), 'Report of the ICES/NAFO Joint Working Group on Deep-Water Ecology', 16–20 February 2015, ICES CM 2015/ACOM: 27, 44–45.

[35] ISA, 'Polymetallic Nodule Mining Technology' (n 10).

[36] See, eg, presentation given by M Johnston, CEO of Nautilus Minerals at the Conference on 'Global Challenges and Freedom of Navigation' held in Seoul, Korea, 1–3 May 2013 <http://www.virginia.edu/colp/pdf/Seoul-NautilusMinerals.pdf> accessed 21 November 2016.

scientists[37] and the ISA[38] mainly warn of *serious or severe* risks of seabed mining. The reports published by non-governmental organizations (NGOs) range from pointing out the serious and cumulative risks to the substantial uncertainties, as well as the social risks,[39] while some media reports paint a picture of potentially *catastrophic* risks.[40]

Each of these conceptualizations reflects a different appreciation of, and concern for, the known and the unknown. For example, it is known that mining the deep oceans will involve major interference with the marine environment. However, this interference will affect largely unknown ecosystems in, as yet, equally unknown, or at least partly uncertain, ways. The realization of just how little is known about the deep oceans, their flora and fauna, and the level of resilience of deep ocean ecosystems significantly fuels the notion of serious risk. This is compounded by the knowledge that minerals will not recover within human lifetimes, that vast areas of seafloor could be affected, and by the potential for pollution and harmful effects to be transported beyond the mine site. It is precisely this inability to know what might be damaged or destroyed, by what process, and in what manner, that causes apprehension.[41]

At the extreme, these risks may even be conceptualized as catastrophic, particularly in relation to the potential harm to biodiversity. Both marine ecosystems and biodiversity in general are fundamental for human existence.[42] Yet it is recognized that we are nearing a number of potential tipping points that would catastrophically reduce the capacity of ecosystems to provide the essential ecosystem services on which humans depend.[43] The risks of seabed mining must be conceptualized not just through the frame of pollution but also through the frame of biodiversity loss where the risk of wiping out entire species and ecosystems is compounded by endemism. Thus, seabed mining can lead to not only serious but also irreversible harm, resulting in forgone opportunities to increase scientific understanding of marine ecosystems and Earth–system processes, as well as foregone economic opportunities from bioprospecting activities.[44] The harm may even be catastrophic

[37] See, eg, Halfar and Fujita, 'Danger of Deep-Sea Mining' (n 12); Glover and Smith, 'The Deep-Sea Floor Ecosystem' (n 23); Ramirez-Llodra et al, 'Deep, Diverse and Definitely Different' (n 13); H Thiel, 'Anthropogenic Impacts on the Deep Sea' in PA Tyler (ed), *Ecosystems of the Deep Oceans* (Elsevier Science B.V. 2003) 450.

[38] ISA, *Recommendations for the Guidance of Contractors, 2013* (n 27) para 9.

[39] See, eg, A Craw, 'Deep Seabed Mining: An Urgent Wake-Up Call to Protect Our Oceans' (Greenpeace 2013) 4, 12; H Rosenbaum, 'Out of Our Depth—Mining the Ocean Floor in Papua New Guinea' (Deep Sea Mining Campaign 2011).

[40] See, eg, S Goldenberg, 'Marine Mining: Underwater Gold Rush Sparks Fears of Ocean Catastrophe', *The Guardian*, 2 March 2014 <http://www.theguardian.com/environment/2014/mar/02/underwater-gold-rush-marine-mining-fears-ocean-threat> accessed 21 November 2016; D Shukman, 'UK Seabed Resources Joins Deep-Ocean Mineral-Mining Rush', BBC, 14 March 2013 <http://www.bbc.com/news/science-environment-21774447> accessed 21 November 2016.

[41] See European Commission, *EU Stakeholder Consultation on Seabed Mining—Summary of Responses*, (2015) 119 final (9 June 2015) <http://ec.europa.eu/dgs/maritimeaffairs_fisheries/consultations/seabed-mining/doc/swd-2015-119_en.pdf> accessed 21 November 2016.

[42] Williams et al, *Scientific Results* (n 11).

[43] Secretariat of the Convention on Biological Diversity, *Global Biodiversity Outlook 3* (2010), foreword by Ban Ki-Moon 5.

[44] There is no agreed definition of bioprospecting, but it broadly involves the study of marine genetic resources, in particular of their processes and properties, and the commercialization of this

should it involve a loss of biodiversity or other ecosystem services critical for 'maintaining life sustaining systems of the biosphere'.[45] It is in the context of these competing conceptualizations of harm that the ISA has been developing normative answers to the questions these risks and uncertainties raise.

9.3 Regulating in the Face of Uncertainty—The Institutional Response of the ISA

It is fair to say that protection of the marine environment was not the driving force behind the development of the international seabed mining regime. Rather, the focus was on establishing a regime to regulate access to seabed minerals and the sharing of benefits from their exploitation. Nevertheless, the negotiators of the LOSC were prescient enough to recognize that uncontrolled seabed mining could have adverse effects on the marine environment,[46] an environment about which little was known at the time. In what might be referred to as an instance of 'institutionalised precaution',[47] the ISA was established not only to regulate future mining in the Area but also to take measures necessary to ensure effective protection of the marine environment, including its biodiversity and ecological balance, from the harmful effects of that seabed mining.[48] In short, the ISA was tasked with regulating an uncertain future in the present.

Two aspects of the ISA regime are particularly interesting in the context of responding to the conceptualizations of environmental risk and uncertainties surrounding deep seabed mining: (i) the incremental approach to regulating environmental uncertainty in the ISA regime; and (ii) the incorporation of scientific advice and public opinion into the ISA's procedural and institutional structures. These are examined here as a means of illustrating the manner in which the presence of a competent international organization can, through the design and application of essentially procedural mechanisms, contribute to the regulation of risk and uncertainty.

9.3.1 Incremental approach to regulating environmental uncertainty

An important feature of the ISA regime is what can be described as its incremental, or evolutionary, approach to regulating in the face of environmental (and commercial) uncertainty. As noted above, the importance of addressing potential

information, eg in the biotechnology industry. See D Leary, M Vierros, G Hamon et al, 'Marine Genetic Resources: A Review of Scientific and Commercial Interest' (2009) 33 *Marine Policy* 183, 184.

[45] Convention on Biological Diversity (adopted 5 June 1992, entered into force 29 December 1993) 1760 UNTS 79, Preamble, para 2.

[46] R Rayfuse, 'Precaution and the Protection of Marine Biodiversity in Areas Beyond National Jurisdiction' (2012) 27(4) *The International Journal of Marine and Coastal Law* 773.

[47] ibid, 778. [48] LOSC, art 145.

environmental harm caused by seabed mining was recognized from the very start.[49] Thus, while mandating the ISA to manage the exploration and exploitation of minerals in the Area, the ISA was simultaneously charged with ensuring the protection and preservation of the marine environment. However, given the rudimentary state of knowledge about the deep oceans when the LOSC was being negotiated, the Convention left the detailed environmental standards and protective measures to be developed incrementally and over time by the ISA. To that end, the ISA was granted regulatory powers to adopt rules, regulations, and procedures, including for 'the prevention, reduction and control of pollution and other hazards to the marine environment', as well as for 'the protection and conservation of the natural resources of the Area and the prevention of damage to the flora and fauna of the marine environment' from seabed mining.[50] The ISA was further required to take 'necessary measures ... to ensure effective protection for the marine environment from harmful effects which may arise' from exploration for or exploitation of minerals in the Area.[51] These powers were complemented by the ISA's mandate to promote and encourage the conduct of marine scientific research in the Area,[52] with 'particular emphasis on research related to the environmental impact of activities in the Area'.[53] In this way, it was envisaged that the ISA's environmental standards would develop and evolve over time in order to respond flexibly to advances in scientific knowledge.

It is worth noting that the ISA regime is unique in that a central institution to organize, control, and regulate seabed mining activities was established well before commercial mining has become a reality.[54] In this sense, while precaution is nowhere specifically mentioned in the LOSC, the establishment of the ISA could, in itself, broadly be interpreted as a precautionary, or at least, visionary, moment.[55] Indeed, as the advent of commercial mining has been postponed, primarily due to economic factors, the ISA has enjoyed the relative luxury of being able to focus on scientific research and incrementally develop the regulatory framework for seabed mining in light of advances not only in science and technology but also in law, including the development of the precautionary principle. At the institutional level this is being done through the development of the ISA's 'Mining Code', the title of which refers to the entirety of the rules, regulations, and procedures adopted by the ISA to regulate prospecting, exploration, and exploitation of seabed minerals in the Area.

The first steps in the development of the Mining Code were the adoption of three sets of regulations for prospecting and exploration for polymetallic nodules,

[49] G Le Gurun, 'Environmental Impact Assessment and the International Seabed Authority' in T Koivurova and CJ Bastmeijer (eds) *Theory and Practice of Transboundary Environmental Impact Assessment* (Brill 2007) 225–26.

[50] LOSC, art 145; see also arts 137(2), 160(2(f)(ii), 162(2)(o)(ii), 209, and annex III, art 17(1)(b)(xii).

[51] LOSC, art 145 [52] LOSC, art 143.

[53] Implementing Agreement, annex, section 1(5).

[54] See also Le Gurun, 'Environmental Impact Assessment' (n 49) 262.

[55] R Rayfuse, 'Precaution and the Protection of Marine Biodiversity' (n 46).

polymetallic sulphides, and cobalt-rich ferromanganese crusts in 2000,[56] 2010,[57] and 2012,[58] respectively (collectively referred to as the 'Exploration Regulations'). Adoption of these regulations has enabled the ISA to approve over twenty-five applications for contracts to explore minerals at sites across the world's oceans.[59] The Exploration Regulations establish broad environmental requirements, which oblige contractors, for example, to collect environmental data, to establish baselines of the environmental conditions present in their contract area, and to monitor the effects of those exploration activities deemed to have the potential to cause serious harm.[60] These requirements are further specified through Recommendations issued by the ISA's Legal and Technical Commission, which have themselves been revised in light of increased scientific knowledge to provide greater specificity as to the detailed observations and measurements that are to be made while performing certain activities and recommended data collection, reporting, and archiving protocols.[61] This approach is intended to help address the problematic lack of knowledge and data about the environmental conditions at future mine sites.[62] However, as will be readily apparent, its success is dependent on contractor compliance and the existence of systems to ensure comparability of data, both of which have been lacking in the past.[63]

The incremental approach to the evolution of the ISA's environmental mandate is also evident in the developing stringency of the Exploration Regulations, particularly with regard to the application of the precautionary approach. When the Nodules Regulations were adopted in 2000, they required the ISA and sponsoring states to

[56] *Regulations on Prospecting and Exploration for Polymetallic Nodules in the Area* (ISBA/6/A/18, 13 July 2000, as amended by ISBA/19/C/17 (22 July 2013), ISBA/19/A/12 (25 July 2013), and ISBA/20/A/9 (24 July 2014) (Nodules Regulations).

[57] *Regulations on Prospecting and Exploration for Polymetallic Sulphides in the Area* (ISBA/16/A/12/Rev.1, 15 November 2010, as amended by ISBA/19/A/12, 25 July 2013, and ISBA/20/A/10, 24 July 2014) (Sulphides Regulations).

[58] *Regulations on Prospecting and Exploration for Cobalt-Rich Ferromanganese Crusts in the Area* (ISBA/18/A/11, 27 July 2012, as amended by ISBA/19/A/12, 25 July 2013) (Crusts Regulations).

[59] See <https://www.isa.org.jm/deep-seabed-minerals-contractors> accessed 21 November 2016.

[60] Nodules Regulations, regs 5(2), 18(b), 31(6), 32, annex VI sections 5.2–5.4, 10.2(a); Crusts Regulations, regs 5(2), 20(1)(b), 33(6), 34, annex IV sections 5.2–5.4, 10.2(a); Sulphides Regulations, regs 5(2), 20(1)(b), 33(6), 34, annex IV sections 5.2–5.4, 10.2(a). See also LOSC, art 165(2)(h); Implementing Agreement, annex, section 1(7); ISA *Recommendations for the Guidance of Contractors, 2013* (n 27) paras 11, 19–21, 23, 24.

[61] ISA, *Recommendations for the Guidance of the Contractors for the Assessment of the Possible Environmental Impacts Arising from Exploration for Polymetallic Nodules in the Area, Issued by the Legal and Technical Commission*, ISBA/7/LTC/1/Rev 1** (13 February 2002); ISA, *Recommendations for the Guidance of Contractors for the Assessment of the Possible Environmental Impacts Arising from Exploration for Polymetallic Nodules in the Area*, ISBA/16/LTC/7 (2 November 2010); ISA, *Recommendations for the Guidance of Contractors, 2013* (n 27).

[62] MW Lodge, 'Environmental Regulation of Deep Seabed Mining' in A Kirchner (ed), *International Marine Environmental Law: Institutions, Implementation and Innovations* (Kluwer Law International 2003) 57.

[63] ISA, *Summary Report of the Chair of the Legal and Technical Commission on the Work of the Commission During the Twentieth Session of the International Seabed Authority*, ISBA/20/C/20 (16 July 2014), annex I, para 12; Seascape Consultants Ltd, 'Review of Implementation of the Environmental Management Plan for the Clarion-Clipperton Zone—Report to the International Seabed Authority' (20 May 2014) <http://isa.org.jm/files/documents/EN/20Sess/LTC/CCZ-EMPRev.pdf> page 10, para 3.3.1 accessed 21 November 2016.

apply a precautionary approach but did not extend the same obligation to contractors.[64] This position was changed in the 2010 Sulphides Regulations, the standard clauses of which require the application of a precautionary approach by both sponsoring states and by contractors.[65] Moreover, in its 2011 Advisory Opinion on the *Responsibilities and Obligations of States Sponsoring Persons and Entities with Respect to Activities in the Area*,[66] the Seabed Disputes Chamber of the International Tribunal for the Law of the Sea considered that the obligation to apply a precautionary approach was not only applicable to sponsoring states and the ISA in respect of activities in the Area but was also an integral part of the general obligation of due diligence of sponsoring states, applicable even beyond the scope of the Regulations.[67] Thus, while the contractual obligation on sponsored contractors to apply a precautionary approach had been omitted from the Nodules Regulations adopted in 2000, this did not relieve a sponsoring state of its own obligation to ensure the application of a precautionary approach by the contractors it sponsored. In the event, the Nodules Regulations and standard contractual clauses were amended in 2013 to incorporate the specific requirement for contractors to apply a precautionary approach.[68]

The challenge now for the ISA, and the next step in its incremental progress, lies in drafting regulations to govern the commercial exploitation (as opposed to mere prospecting and exploration) of seabed mineral resources. The ISA has commenced work on the new 'Exploitation Regulations' which, by virtue of the ISA's mandate, will have to balance seabed mining with the protection of the marine environment from serious harm. However, the monumentality of this task is revealed in the 2011 statement of the ISA Secretary General that, '[t]he current level of understanding of deep-sea ecology is not yet sufficient to allow conclusive risk assessment of the effects of large-scale commercial mining'.[69] What is needed are scientifically rigorous environmental baselines against which impacts on the marine environment can be assessed. This in turn requires the development of effective management plans to ensure the acquisition of such data and effective regulation of the activities.

In 2012, the ISA adopted its first environmental management plan for the Clarion-Clipperton Zone in the Eastern Central Pacific Ocean,[70] an area considered to be a prime location for commercially viable deposits of polymetallic nodules.[71] The vision of the future articulated by the ISA is 'of a sustainably exploited

[64] *Regulations on Prospecting and Exploration for Polymetallic Nodules in the Area*, ISBA/6/A/18 (13 July 2000), reg 31, annex 4 section 5.1.

[65] Sulphide Regulations, annex 4 section 5.1.

[66] *Responsibilities and Obligations of States Sponsoring Persons and Entities with Respect to Activities in the Area* (Advisory Opinion) (Seabed Disputes Chamber, Case No 17, 1 February 2011).

[67] ibid, para 131.

[68] Nodules Regulations, regs 2(2), 5(1), 31(2) and (5), annex IV section 5.1.

[69] ISA, *Report of the Secretary-General of the International Seabed Authority under Article 166, Paragraph 4, of the United Nations Convention on the Law of the Sea*, ISBA/12/A/2 (13 June 2011) para 68. See also Halfar and Fujita, 'Danger of Deep-Sea Mining' (n 12).

[70] ISA, *Environmental Management Plan for the Clarion-Clipperton Zone*, ISBA/17/LTC/7 (13 July 2011) (EMP-CCZ).

[71] MW Lodge, 'Some Legal and Policy Considerations Relating to the Establishment of a Representative Network of Protected Areas in the Clarion-Clipperton Zone' (2011) 26 *The International Journal of Marine and Coastal Law* 463.

Clarion-Clipperton Zone that preserves representative and unique marine habitats and species' in which the ISA 'facilitate[s] mining while minimizing as far as practically possible the impact of seabed mining activities, and preserving and conserving marine biodiversity and ecosystem structure and function in the Clarion-Clipperton Zone'.[72] To these ends the plan, which is based on the guiding principles of the common heritage of mankind, the precautionary approach, protection, and preservation of the marine environment, prior environmental impact assessment, conservation and sustainable use of biodiversity, and transparency,[73] adopts what it calls 'a holistic approach to the environmental management of the [Zone] in its entirety'.[74] The operational and management objectives relating to the conduct, collation, and exchange of environmental baseline and impact data provided by contractors and others are based on current understandings of best-practice management of damaging human activities in the marine environment.[75]

Importantly, the plan specifically incorporates the requirements of flexibility and adaptive management in the face of identification of future, or resolution of current, uncertainties. For example, the plan provides for the designation of a representative network of nine areas of particular environmental interest closed to exploration and exploitation of minerals. These areas have been selected to capture the full range of ecosystems, habitats, communities, and species of different biogeographic regions in the Zone. While recognizing the 'representative approach' as the most suitable at present, the plan also recognizes the likely need for modification of location and size of such areas as more information becomes available about mining activities and their impact, as well as biological data.[76] Similarly, the plan requires the application of 'best available environmental practices and techniques',[77] which itself implies an ever evolving obligation. This is further articulated in the ISA's vision of what constitutes a 'holistic approach' which, according to the plan includes, 'where appropriate, consideration of cumulative impacts, incorporating environmental risk assessments of new and developing technologies, while giving due consideration to relevant global initiatives and new legislation'.[78]

Leaving aside the many challenges as to the effective implementation of this plan, what remains to be seen is whether the ISA can develop a standardized approach to the adoption of environmental management plans throughout the Area.[79] More importantly, even if the ISA is able to establish environmental baselines throughout the Area, the success of its mining regime will depend on the way in which environmental harm is defined. In this respect, the integration of scientific advice and public opinion into the ISA's work play an important role.

[72] EMP-CCZ, paras 32–33. [73] ibid, para 13. [74] ibid, para 34.
[75] ibid, para 21. [76] ibid, paras 25–29. [77] ibid, para 38.
[78] ibid, para 34.
[79] AL Jaeckel, *The International Seabed Authority and the Precautionary Principle—Balancing Deep Seabed Mineral Mining and Marine Environmental* (Brill 2017), Chapter 6.3.1.

9.3.2 Incorporating scientific advice and public opinion

The second important aspect of the ISA regime in terms of its ability to respond to the risks of deep seabed mining by conceptualizing the future in the present relates to the generation of new knowledge through research and the consideration of public opinion. A significant feature of the ISA's mandate is its obligation to promote and encourage the conduct of marine scientific research in the Area, with 'particular emphasis on research related to the environmental impact of activities in the Area'.[80] This research is critical to our understanding of what may or may not constitute a serious environmental impact as well as the uncertainties at play, and it provides the essential basis on which to design and implement long-term management, including risk-management, options. Equally critical is the need to ensure, through the input of public opinion into the review and decision-making processes, the acceptance by the international community of any proposed impacts.

Although the ability of the ISA to conduct its own marine scientific research is limited by a lack of financial and human resources,[81] from its earliest days the ISA has collaborated on external research projects and has commissioned and convened scientific and technical studies and workshops aimed at: generating knowledge and understanding of the deep sea environment and its resource potential; developing standardized recording and reporting formats; and establishing environmental baselines and environmental management options. Early work included a workshop on the prospects for international collaboration in marine environmental research,[82] which led to the initiation of a project (the 'Kaplan Project'), examining faunal diversity in the Clarion-Clipperton Zone. Before the project, which was conducted between 2002 and 2007, knowledge about the species residing in the Zone was very limited. While constrained by relatively small sample sizes, the project resulted in substantial advances in scientific understanding of the biodiversity in the Clarion-Clipperton Zone. Importantly, this work contributed to knowledge regarding the biological factors involved in the formation of polymetallic nodules and demonstrated, in particular, that instead of the Zone being one continuous habitat, biodiversity varies substantially in different geographical locations. These findings enabled the researchers to suggest the establishment of no-mining areas as an option to best manage biodiversity and to identify a number of criteria for designing such areas to ensure protection of the different faunal species across the region.[83] Other project work focused on the development of a geological model of the Clarion-Clipperton Zone for the purposes of improving assessment of resource distribution in the absence of comprehensive sampling data from much of the

[80] Implementing Agreement, annex section 1(5); LOSC, art 143.

[81] Jaeckel, *The International Seabed Authority and the Precautionary Principle* (n 79), Chapter 6.2.

[82] ISA, 'Prospects for International Collaboration in Marine Environmental Research to Enhance Understanding of the Deep Sea Environment' in Proceedings of the International Seabed Authority's workshop held in Kingston, Jamaica, 2002 (ISA 2006) <http://www.isa.org.jm/files/documents/EN/Pubs/2002-Collab.pdf> accessed 21 November 2016.

[83] CR Smith, G Paterson, J Lambshead et al, *Biodiversity, Species Ranges, and Gene Flow in the Abyssal Pacific Nodule Province: Predicting and Managing the Impacts of Deep Seabed Mining* (ISA Technical Study No 3 2008).

region.[84] It was the scientific findings generated by these projects which led directly to the identification of the future management options and research and data collection needs, which were ultimately incorporated into the environmental management plan for the Zone.

Similar workshops have also been convened, aimed at improving our knowledge and understanding of resource availability and deep ocean ecosystems, establishing specific environmental baselines, and examining the potential environmental effects of mining for polymetallic sulphides and crusts.[85] These workshops have informed the development of the Exploration Regulations and have contributed to identifying what are currently accepted as best environmental practices. In particular, an ISA commissioned study on the management of chemosynthetic ecosystems associated with sulphide deposits identified design principles, management options, and best environmental practices in respect of these recently discovered and critically important ecosystems.[86]

The ISA has also collaborated with the Census of Marine Life, to assess the patterns of community composition and faunal diversity on seamounts, to examine gaps in the scientific knowledge, and to collate information on the impact of seabed mining activities on seamount biodiversity and the biogeography of seamount species.[87] Current collaborations include those with the European Union-funded MIDAS project (Managing Impacts of Deep-seA reSource exploitation), which is investigating the environmental impacts of extracting mineral and energy resources from the deep seabed, and the JPI Oceans initiative (Joint Programming Initiative Healthy and Productive Seas and Oceans), investigating the ecological aspects of deep sea mining.

What these activities demonstrate is the institutional process through which the ISA is able to identify substantial uncertainties, imagine and conceptualize the future of seabed mining and its potential impacts on the marine environment in light of those uncertainties, and then move to adopt tangible, but flexible management options based on the determination of what constitutes best environmental practices. Moreover, these workshops and commissioned studies provide fora for the participation of the wider scientific and legal community in the work of the ISA. The new understandings gained of deep ocean processes and marine biodiversity and their resilience are all the more important against the background of the

84 ISA, *A Geological Model of Polymetallic Nodule Deposits in the Clarion Clipperton Fracture Zone* (ISA Technical Study No 6 2010).

85 Eg, ISA, *Polymetallic Sulphides and Cobalt-Rich Ferromanganese Crusts Deposits: Establishment of Environmental Baseline and an Associated Monitoring Programme During Exploration*, Proceedings of the International Seabed Authority's Workshop held in Kingston, Jamaica (ISA, 2004); ISA, *Polymetallic Sulphides and Cobalt-Rich Ferromanganese Crusts Deposits: Establishment of Environmental Baseline and an Associated Monitoring Programme During Exploration*, Proceedings of the International Seabed Authority's Workshop held in Kingston, Jamaica (ISA, 2004).

86 CL van Dover, CR Smith, J Ardron, S Arnaud, Y Beaudoin, J Bezaury, G Boland, et al, *Environmental Management of Deep-Sea Chemosynthetic Ecosystems: Justification of and Considerations for a Spatially-Based Approach* (ISA Technical Study No 9 2011).

87 MR Clark, *Fauna of Cobalt-Rich Ferromanganese Crust Seamounts* (ISA Technical Study No 8 2010) 3.

need to address global environmental challenges, such as declining ocean health and climate change.

Nevertheless, despite its successes in generating new knowledge, while scientific research is crucial to understanding and addressing the risks posed by deep seabed mining, the scope of scientific advice is ultimately limited, particularly in the case of complex ecosystems and pioneering activities. In this respect, both transparency and the consideration of public opinion are important in determining what levels of risk and harm may be deemed acceptable. Unfortunately, while the need for scientific advice is reflected in the ISA's institutional structure, no specific mechanisms currently exist to incorporate public opinion or to ensure transparent decision-making processes sufficient to enable the public to understand why and how decisions are reached. To fill this void the ISA has developed an ad hoc measure to obtain the views from all stakeholders, including states, private industry, academia, and NGOs, on the development of the future Exploitation Regulations,[88] bringing us full circle, once again, to the importance of its incremental approach to its mandate. While this approach invites criticism because it can result in postponement of decisions over protective measures, it does allow the ISA to proceed while simultaneously retaining some control over the future of seabed mining and leaving space for consideration of the values that the international community as a whole places on the potential gains and harms of seabed mining.

9.4 Conclusion

During the first United Nations Conference on the Law of the Sea in the 1950s, it was not yet thought necessary to develop a specific legal regime for the Area and it was assumed that seabed minerals would be subject to free and non-exclusive access together with the resources of the water column of the high seas.[89] Had this position persisted, the regulation of seabed mining would most likely have taken a different path; one involving appropriation by the few most able to exploit. Instead, the LOSC declared the Area and its mineral resources to be the common heritage of humankind and established an institution charged with the future management of seabed mining activities and the protection of the marine environment from the harmful effects of those activities. Being a future activity with the potential to cause serious environmental harm, the seabed mining regime offers an insightful case-study on the conceptualization of future risks and the extent to which the existence of an institutional platform can influence and affect approaches to their regulation and management.

As the previous discussion has highlighted, the ISA's incremental approach to the development of the regulatory framework for deep seabed mining allows it to

[88] ISA, 'Developing a Regulatory Framework for Mineral Exploitation in the Area', ISBA/Cons/2016/1 (July 2016) <https://www.isa.org.jm/files/documents/EN/Regs/DraftExpl/Draft_ExplReg_SCT.pdf> accessed 21 November 2016.

[89] AV Lowe, 'The International Seabed: A Legacy of Mistrust' (1981) 5 *Marine Policy* 205.

respond to advances in science and technology, as well as changing legal realities. While not possessed of a magic crystal ball, this evolutionary approach, together with its express mandate to commission and carry out marine scientific research, allows the ISA to imagine and continually re-imagine a vision of the future management of an environmentally risky activity as informed by constantly developing best scientific evidence. While the performance of the ISA in addressing the as yet future risks of deep seabed mining is by no means perfect, this 'institutionalized precaution' does provide a unique platform in which the risks and uncertainties associated with that mining can be conceptualized, discussed and, ultimately, regulated.

10

Imagining Unimaginable Climate Futures in International Climate Change Law

Jacqueline Peel

10.1 Introduction

In the climate change law course I teach at Melbourne Law School, I often begin classes with a guest presentation from Professor David Karoly, a leading Australian climate scientist. Professor Karoly explains to my students that climate change does not signal the end of the world; after all, our planet, Earth, has weathered many climatic changes over the millennia.[1] Rather, climate change is a threat to the world as we (humans) know it. In a climate-changed future, he says, we can expect soaring temperatures, melting polar ice caps, rising seas, and more weather extremes.[2] Accompanying these environmental changes are likely increases in the spread of disease, displacement of peoples, water shortages, threats to food security, and a greater potential for conflict.[3] In my students' faces—even as they digest the scientific information about climate change impacts—the consternation is clear. How do you begin to imagine a world that humans have never experienced and perhaps may not survive? What tools are available to manage and regulate the risks and uncertainties associated with such an unimaginable future?

This chapter examines these questions from the perspective of international law. International law has been a vital component of the regulatory response to climate change given the global scope of the greenhouse gas-emitting human activities that give rise to the problem, and the need for coordinated, cooperative efforts to

[1] W Dansgaard, SJ Johnsen, HB Clausen et al, 'Evidence for General Instability of Past Climate from a 250 kyr Ice-Core Record' (1993) 364 *Nature* 218; National Research Council (NRC), *Surface Temperature Reconstructions for the Last 2,000 Years* (National Academy Press 2006). Indeed, the present period of climatic stability may be the exception rather than the norm.

[2] See Intergovernmental Panel on Climate Change (IPCC), 'Summary for Policymakers', in TF Stocker et al (eds), *Climate Change 2013: The Physical Science Basis. Contribution of Working Group I to the Fifth Assessment Report of the Intergovernmental Panel on Climate Change* (CUP 2013).

[3] IPCC, 'Summary for Policymakers', in CB Field et al (eds), *Climate Change 2014: Impacts, Adaptation, and Vulnerability. Contribution of Working Group II to the Fifth Assessment Report of the Intergovernmental Panel on Climate Change* (CUP 2014).

address climate change risks.[4] While there are now many areas of international law concerned with aspects of climate change,[5] this chapter focuses on the treaties and institutions of the dedicated international climate change regime. These include the IPCC that prepares periodic scientific assessments of the risks and likely consequences of climate change,[6] and three treaty instruments: the 1992 United Nations Framework Convention on Climate Change (UNFCCC),[7] its 1997 Kyoto Protocol,[8] and the recently concluded 2015 Paris Agreement.[9] It is these laws and institutions that have primary responsibility for the international regulatory response to climate change risk.

Section 10.2 describes how climate futures have been imagined in the international climate change regime, and the evolution of those imaginings over time. From an early stage, climate risk constructs favoured in the regime have been shaped by scientific views and expert knowledge that has cast climate change as a problem of emissions reduction (or *climate change mitigation*).[10] Using tools such as scenario analysis, the scientific community has achieved an impressive level of consensus around the existence and mechanisms of climate change, and necessary mitigation measures to prevent dangerous levels of global warming. However, a widening gap between scientific articulations of potentially catastrophic climate risks and emissions reductions implemented or pledged by states to address those risks,[11] has directed attention to alternative climate futures. These futures centre on managing unavoidable climate change impacts and reducing human vulnerabilities (*climate change adaptation*),[12] and addressing climate-change-induced economic and non-economic harms that exceed the capacity of adaptation measures (*loss and damage*).[13]

[4] P Sands and J Peel, *Principles of International Environmental Law* (CUP 2012) 274–99.

[5] For an excellent discussion of the international legal response to climate change beyond the climate change regime, see R Rayfuse and S Scott (eds), *International Law in the Era of Climate Change* (Edward Elgar 2012).

[6] IPCC, 'Organization' <https://www.ipcc.ch/organization.shtml> accessed 10 September 2015.

[7] United Nations Framework Convention on Climate Change (adopted 9 May 1992, entered into force 21 March 1994) 1771 UNTS 107 (UNFCCC).

[8] Kyoto Protocol to the United Nations Framework Convention on Climate Change (adopted 11 December 1997, entered into force 16 February 2005) 2303 UNTS A-30822 (Kyoto Protocol).

[9] Paris Agreement, Paris (France), 13 December 2015, in force 4 November 2016 (in UNFCCC, Report of the Conference of the Parties on its Twenty-First Session, Addendum, UN Doc FCCC/CP/2015/10/Add.1, 29 January 2016) (Paris Agreement).

[10] According to the IPCC, climate change mitigation is an anthropogenic intervention to reduce the sources or enhance the sinks of greenhouse gases: IPCC, RT Watson, DL Albritton, D Barker et al (eds), *Climate Change 2001: Synthesis Report. A Contribution of Working Groups I, II, III to the Third Assessment Report of the Intergovernmental Panel on Climate Change* (CUP 2001).

[11] See United Nations Environment Programme (UNEP), *The Emissions Gap Report 2014* (UNEP 2014).

[12] The IPCC defines climate change adaptation as adjustment in natural or human systems in response to actual or expected climatic stimuli or their effects, which moderates harm or exploits beneficial opportunities. IPCC, *Climate Change 2001: Synthesis Report* (n 10).

[13] 'Loss and damage' does not have an agreed meaning in the literature, though it is often used to refer to unavoidable impacts, i.e. those that cannot be avoided through mitigation and adaptation efforts. See S Huq, E Roberts, and A Fenton, 'Loss and Damage' (2013) 3 *Nature Climate Change* 947.

Section 10.3 then explores how these evolving imaginings of climate risk futures have shaped the development of the legal instruments that make up the international climate change regime. It traces the shift from an almost exclusive focus on mitigation in the early stages of the regime—exemplified by the Kyoto Protocol's approach of setting targets and timetables for emissions reduction by developed countries—to a broader consideration of both the causes and effects of climate change, as well as their equity dimensions. The Paris Agreement epitomizes this transition. With its bottom-up structure and holistic focus on mitigation, adaptation, and loss and damage, it is a markedly different international instrument from its Kyoto Protocol predecessor. The Paris Agreement cements the international climate regime's evolution over its more than twenty-year history from a complicated system of risk assessment, reduction, and avoidance to one that pays much greater attention to the consequences of those risks, especially for the states and communities that will be most vulnerable to the adverse effects of climate change.

Even though the Paris Agreement recognizes climate change risk as a matter of adaptation and loss and damage, alongside mitigation, it remains hopeful in its outlook for the future. Indeed, one of the signature achievements of the Paris Agreement is an ambitious long-term goal of holding the increase in the global average temperature to 'well below' 2°C above pre-industrial levels and 'pursuing efforts to limit the temperature increase to 1.5°C above pre-industrial levels, recognizing that this would significantly reduce the risks and impacts of climate change'.[14] Nonetheless, with countries' current pledged mitigation actions putting the world on track for warming well above 2°C by the end of the twenty-first century,[15] darker imaginings of our climate future persist, as section 10.4 discusses. Catastrophic climate risk scenarios include the potential for unmanageable climate change with rising seas that subsume low-lying lands and small-island countries, forcing the displacement of millions of people, and extreme weather-related disasters that overwhelm disaster management systems and resources. Attempts to avoid climate catastrophe through the deployment of geoengineering technologies, such as solar radiation management (SRM), may bring their own risks.[16] While the international climate change regime already has some of the tools necessary to mobilize expert knowledge and regulatory responses around such unimaginable futures, and to manage the uncertainties they raise, effective action to address catastrophic risks is likely to require closer integration with other areas of international law, including in the fields of security, human rights, and disaster response.

[14] Paris Agreement, art 2.1(a).

[15] See UNFCCC Secretariat, 'Synthesis Report on the Aggregate Effect of the Intended Nationally Determined Contributions' (30 October 2015) FCCC/CP/2015/7. This report estimates a rise of 2.7°C. See also Climate Action Tracker, 'Effect of Current Pledges and Policies on Global Temperature' <http://climateactiontracker.org/global.html#footnote1> accessed 10 September 2015.

[16] Geo-engineering embraces a wide range of activities, from carbon dioxide removal (CDR) approaches such as increased tree planting or, more controversially, ocean iron fertilization, to large-scale SRM techniques that involve science-fiction-like scenarios of giant mirrors in space reflecting the sun's rays away from Earth. See C Redgwell, 'Geoengineering the Climate: Technological Solutions to Mitigation—Failure or Continuing Carbon Addiction' (2011) *Carbon and Climate Law Review* 178.

10.2 Imagining Climate Futures

Climate change presents us with the prospect of 'unimaginable' futures, or rather futures that we can only envision through imagination given that we have no historical yardstick of human experience to go by. Efforts to imagine a climate-changed future have been attempted by artists, writers, and filmmakers. For example, environmentalist Bill McKibben, writing in 1989, imagined the future with climate change as 'the end of nature'; a world where everything, including formerly natural processes, has become 'a subset of human activity'.[17] Through uncontrolled greenhouse gas (GHG) emissions, he wrote, 'We have built a greenhouse, *a human creation*, where once there bloomed a sweet and wild garden.'[18] More recently, the Museum of London's *London Futures* show featured work by digital artists Robert Graves and Didier Madoc-Jones exploring how the city might look in 2100 after climate change had taken its toll.[19] The images—including those of a flooded Thames turning London into Venice, Buckingham Palace surrounded by slums and climate refugees, and Piccadilly Circus underwater and studded with wind power turbines—were designed to provoke debate and help people 'connect' with climate change.[20]

Imagining our potential climate future is not just an art form; it has also become an important field of scientific research and analysis. Scientific envisioning of possible climate futures is undertaken using climate change scenarios. These alternative 'storylines' are derived by combining scientific data with a series of assumptions about future economic, social, technological, and environmental conditions.[21] Scenarios 'describe plausible trajectories of different aspects of the future that are constructed to investigate the potential consequences of anthropogenic climate change'.[22] In working with scenarios, the scientists' goal is 'not to predict the future but to better understand uncertainties and alternative futures, in order to consider how robust different decisions or options may be under a wide range of possible futures.'[23]

Climate change scenarios have formed a key element of the periodic climate change risk assessments undertaken by the IPCC.[24] The IPCC, established in

[17] W McKibben, *The End of Nature* (Random House 1989) 78. [18] ibid.

[19] A selection of the images featured in the exhibition can be seen on the artists' webpage, R Graves and D Madoc-Jones, 'Postcards from the Future' <http://www.postcardsfromthefuture.co.uk> accessed 10 September 2015.

[20] A Vaughan, 'Images of London after Climate Change "are Lazy", Say Refugee Groups' *The Guardian* (27 October 2010) <http://www.theguardian.com/environment/2010/oct/27/future-london-climate-images> accessed 10 September 2015.

[21] IPCC, 'Summary for Policy Makers', in *Special Report on Emissions Scenarios* (IPCC 2000) 3.

[22] IPCC, 'Scenario Process for AR5', Data Distribution Centre <http://sedac.ipcc-data.org/ddc/ar5_scenario_process/index.html> accessed 10 September 2015.

[23] ibid.

[24] The IPCC has used emissions and climate scenarios as a central component of its work. For past assessments, the IPCC convened authors and modellers, provided terms of reference, and approved the scenarios through an intergovernmental process. Previous IPCC scenarios include the 1990 IPCC Scenario A (SA90) used in the First Assessment Report, the 1992 IPCC Scenarios (IS92) used in the

1988 by the World Meteorological Organization and the UNEP, is tasked with assessing:

on a comprehensive, objective, open and transparent basis the scientific, technical and socio-economic information relevant to understanding the scientific basis of risk of human-induced climate change, its potential impacts and options for adaptation and mitigation.[25]

The institution does not conduct its own scientific research; rather, it undertakes peer review of existing research to produce periodic reports. These reports are distilled into summaries for policy makers, with governments approving the conclusions drawn from the scientific material on a line-by-line basis.[26] Since 1988, the IPCC has released assessment reports in 1990, 1995, 2001, 2007, and 2014.[27]

Scenarios employed by the IPCC in its reports have been based on different projected emissions trajectories. Hence, the focus of these scenarios is on future GHG emissions, measures taken to reduce emissions levels, and climate change mitigation. For example, in its 2014 report, the IPCC examined climate futures associated with four alternative 'representative concentration pathways' (RCPs). These ranged from the most optimistic scenario, RCP 2.6—a stringent mitigation scenario—to RCP 8.5—a high emissions scenario.[28] In the IPCC's report, the climate consequences of different emissions trajectories, together with associated uncertainty ranges, were represented in 'objective' scientific terms using graphs[29] tracking potential global average temperature increases, sea level rise, and other climate variables.[30]

The IPCC's approach to climate risk assessment—regarded as the 'gold standard' in the field[31]—has generated, over time, a high degree of scientific consensus around the reality and causes of climate change, as well as the utility of scenario tools for predicting and evaluating the risks associated with different emissions trajectories. In its 2014 report, the IPCC concluded that '[w]arming of the climate system is unequivocal' and cited anthropogenic emissions and drivers as 'extremely likely [95–100% confidence] to have been the dominant cause of the observed

Second Assessment Report, and the Special Report on Emissions Scenarios used in the Third and Fourth Assessment Reports. For the Fifth Assessment Report (AR5), the IPCC relied on scenarios developed in the scientific research community, limiting its role to catalysing and assessing scenarios.

[25] *Principles Governing IPCC Work*, as amended (Vienna, 1 October 1988) <https://www.ipcc.ch/pdf/ipcc-principles/ipcc-principles.pdf> accessed 10 September 2015 (Principles Governing IPCC Work).

[26] IPCC, 'Procedures for the Preparation, Review, Acceptance, Adoption, Approval and Publication of IPCC Reports' in *Principles Governing IPCC Work* (n 25) Appendix A.

[27] Copies of the IPCC's assessment reports can be accessed on the IPCC webpage. IPCC, Reports <https://www.ipcc.ch/publications_and_data/publications_and_data_reports.shtml> accessed 10 September 2015.

[28] IPCC, RK Pachauri and LA Meyer (eds), 'Summary for Policymakers', in *Climate Change 2014: Synthesis Report. Contribution of Working Groups I, II and III to the Fifth Assessment Report of the Intergovernmental Panel on Climate Change* (IPCC 2014) 8.

[29] For a discussion of technical scientific tools and representations such as graphs, and the extent to which they allow for social construction of scientific facts, see the seminal work by B Latour and S Woolgar, *Laboratory Life: The Social Construction of Scientific Facts* (2nd edn, Princeton University Press 1986).

[30] IPCC, 'Summary for Policymakers', in *Climate Change 2014: Synthesis Report. Contribution of Working Groups I, II and III* (n 28) Figure SPM6 for the period 2006–2100 11.

[31] Nature Editorial, 'Wanted: An IPCC for Biodiversity' (2010) 465 *Nature* 525.

warming since the mid-20th century'.[32] Developments in climate science have also allowed scientists to quantify maximum 'safe' levels of anthropogenic warming and the associated 'carbon budget' necessary to stay below that threshold. The general scientific consensus—summarized by the IPCC in its 2007 report—is that a 2°C increase above pre-industrial levels represents the upper limit of acceptable warming,[33] with many scientists calling for much lower levels of warming (e.g. no more than 1°C above 2000 levels) in order to safeguard low-lying areas and to prevent extensive species loss.[34] To have a likely chance of staying below these temperature thresholds, climate scientists have estimated that total carbon emissions should not exceed 1,000 billion tonnes.[35] With more than sixty-five per cent of the available carbon budget already used since the industrial revolution,[36] emissions will need to be drastically checked over the next two decades in order to hold the temperature increase below 2°C in the twenty-first century.[37]

Despite the increasing clarity of scientific climate risk assessments, a substantial gap exists between emissions levels necessary to keep to 2°C or below, and the levels likely to be brought about by emissions reduction measures implemented or pledged by states. This gap was emphasized by the UNFCCC parties when adopting the Paris Agreement. The adopting decision of the UNFCCC Conference of the Parties (COP) noted 'with concern' that estimated aggregate GHG emissions levels in 2025 and 2030 resulting from parties' tabled emissions reduction pledges 'do not fall within least cost 2°C scenarios' and hence 'much greater emissions reduction efforts will be required'.[38] The persistent 'emissions gap' as it has been dubbed in successive reports produced by the UNEP,[39] has necessitated a re-focusing of scientific imaginings of climate futures in later IPCC reports.

This shift was first signalled in the 2007 IPCC report, which noted that continuing high levels of emissions that would sustain increased temperatures over a longer period meant some impact from climate change would be unavoidable. The 2007 report consequently devoted substantial consideration to climate change impacts, human vulnerabilities, and adaptation measures, in addition to mitigation scenarios.[40] This change was further pronounced in the IPCC's 2014 report issued in the lead-up to the Paris negotiations. A central message of this report was that postponing ambitious mitigation action would increase the chances of crossing adaptation limits

[32] IPCC, Summary for Policymakers', in *Climate Change 2014: Synthesis Report. Contribution of Working Groups I, II and III* (n 28) 2 and 4.

[33] H-H Rogner and D Zhou (eds), 'Introduction' in B Metz et al (eds), *Climate Change 2007: Mitigation. Contribution of Working Group III to the Fourth Assessment Report of the Intergovernmental Panel on Climate Change* (CUP 2007) 99–100.

[34] See, eg, JE Hansen, JM Sato, R Ruedy et al, 'Global Temperature Change' (2006) 103(39) *Proceedings of the National Academy of Sciences* 14288.

[35] See M Meinshausen, N Meinshausen, W Hare et al, 'Greenhouse-Gas Emission Targets for Limiting Global Warming to 2°C' (2009) 458 *Nature* 1158.

[36] World Resources Institute, 'Infographic: The Global Carbon Budget' <htpp://www.wri.org/sites/default/files/WR113-IPCCinfographic-FINAL_web.png> accessed 10 September 2015.

[37] IPCC, Summary for Policymakers', in *Climate Change 2014: Synthesis Report. Contributions of Working Groups I, II and III* (n 28).

[38] UNFCCC, Conference of the Parties, 'Adoption of the Paris Agreement (n 9) para 17.

[39] For the latest such UNEP report, see UNEP, *The Emissions Gap Report 2014* (n 11).

[40] IPCC, *Climate Change 2007: Synthesis Report* (CUP 2007), particularly Chapter 4.

and could lead to irreversible loss and damage to ecosystems and societies, particularly in poor countries.[41] The report included a chapter on 'emergent risks', including risks associated with human migration and displacement, conflict and insecurity.[42] The IPCC also surprised many by canvassing—for the first time in its reports—the possibility of geo-engineering and its associated risks. While finding that geo-engineering could provide 'potential climate change abatement benefits', it also warned that such techniques could pose 'widespread risks to society and ecosystems'.[43]

10.3 Evolving Climate Futures in International Climate Law

The scientific representations of climate change futures used in successive IPCC reports have been influential in shaping the constructs of climate risk adopted in the legal instruments of the international climate change regime. Like the IPCC reports, the early climate treaties framed climate change primarily as a problem of emissions reduction and mitigation. The foundational UNFCCC treaty thus has as its 'ultimate objective' the 'stabilization of greenhouse gas concentrations in the atmosphere at a level that would prevent dangerous anthropogenic interference with the climate system'.[44] While the Convention does not define 'dangerous anthropogenic interference', states have looked to scientific assessments to help inform this judgement. In the Cancun Agreements reached at the UNFCCC COP in 2010,[45] parties endorsed limiting temperature rises below 2°C above pre-industrial levels as the regime's 'long-term goal', while also calling for a review of this goal 'on the basis of the best available scientific knowledge' to determine whether it should be strengthened to 1.5°C (the level pushed for by small island states as the maximum temperature rise that could be tolerated while also ensuring the survival of their countries).[46]

The UNFCCC's central objective is supplemented by guiding principles and a series of commitments by parties largely addressed to domestic mitigation actions. Among the guiding principles agreed to by the UNFCCC parties was a call for 'precautionary measures to anticipate, prevent or minimise the causes of climate

[41] K van der Geest and K Warner, 'What the IPCC 5th Assessment Report Has to Say About Loss and Damage' UNU–EHS Working Paper No 6 (United Nations University Institute of Environment and Human Security 2015).

[42] IPCC, 'Summary for Policymakers', in CB Field et al (eds), *Climate Change 2014: Impacts, Adaptation, and Vulnerability* (n 3) Chapter 19.

[43] ibid, 1043. The IPCC was more cautious in its 2007 report, concluding that geo-engineering options 'remain largely speculative and unproven, and with the risk of unknown side-effects': IPCC, 'Summary for Policymakers' in B Metz et al (eds), *Climate Change 2007: Mitigation of Climate Change* (CUP 2007) 15.

[44] UNFCCC, art 2.

[45] The 'Cancun Agreements' are made up of two reports, one adopted by the COP and the other by the Meeting of the Parties to the Kyoto Protocol reflecting the different negotiation tracks under the UNFCCC and Kyoto Protocol. See UNFCCC, *Report of the Conference of the Parties on Its Sixteenth Session, Held in Cancun from 29 November to 10 December 2010*, FCCC/CP/2010/7/Add 1, 15 March 2011 and UNFCCC, *Report of the Conference of the Parties Serving as the Meeting of the Parties to the Kyoto Protocol on Its Sixth Session, Held in Cancun from 29 November to 10 December 2010*, FCCC/KP/CMP/2010/12/Add 1, 15 March 2011.

[46] Decision 1/CP.16, 'The Cancun Agreements: Outcome of the Work of the Ad Hoc Working Group on Long-Term Cooperative Action Under the Convention' in UNFCCC, *Report of the Conference of the Parties on its Sixteenth Session*, ibid, para 4.

change and mitigate its adverse effects' (the precautionary principle).[47] As the science of climate change has strengthened over the past two decades and uncertainties regarding likely impacts have decreased, the international climate change regime has arguably shifted from a precautionary to a more preventative footing focused on avoiding known risks.[48] Another central principle of the UNFCCC is the principle of 'common but differentiated responsibilities and respective capabilities' (CBDRRC) expressed as the notion that:

> The Parties should protect the climate system for the benefit of present and future generations of humankind, on the basis of equity and in accordance with their common but differentiated responsibilities and respective capabilities. Accordingly, the developed country Parties should take the lead in combating climate change and the adverse effects thereof.[49]

This principle drove the burden-sharing arrangements for mitigation adopted under the UNFCCC and subsequently the Kyoto Protocol, putting the primary responsibility for taking measures to 'combat' climate change on developed countries who—in 1992—were the principal GHG emitters.[50]

As these principles indicate, the main focus of the UNFCCC is risk prevention and avoidance, something that is also evident in the sections of the treaty dealing with parties' commitments. For instance, a tortuously worded provision in Article 4 of the UNFCCC requires each developed country party to:

> adopt national policies and take corresponding measures on the mitigation of climate change by limiting its anthropogenic emissions of greenhouse gases and protecting and enhancing its greenhouse gas sinks and reservoirs.[51]

This was intended to 'demonstrate that developed countries are taking the lead in modifying longer-term trends in anthropogenic emissions consistent with the objective of the Convention'.[52]

Even more so than the UNFCCC, the 1997 Kyoto Protocol concentrates on climate change mitigation measures for emissions reduction. The treaty established 'quantified emission limitation and reduction commitments' for developed country parties to be achieved over the 'first commitment period' running from 2008 to 2012.[53] These provisions aimed at a modest five per cent reduction in developed country emissions compared with 1990 levels.[54] In 2012, parties agreed to an extension of this approach for a 'second commitment period' covering the years from 2013 to 2020.[55] The treaty amendment necessary to extend the Protocol in

[47] UNFCCC, art 3(3).

[48] International Law Association, *The Legal Principles Relating to Climate Change*, Washington Conference 2014 21–22.

[49] UNFCCC, art 3(1).

[50] L Rajamani, 'The Principle of Common but Differentiated Responsibility and the Balance of Commitments Under the Climate Regime' (2000) 9(2) *Review of European Community and International Environmental Law* 120.

[51] UNFCCC, art 4(2)(a). [52] ibid. [53] Kyoto Protocol, art 3.1. [54] ibid.

[55] Doha Amendment to the Kyoto Protocol (adopted 8 December 2012, not yet in force) C.N.718.2012.TREATIES-XXVII.7.c (Doha Amendment).

this way has not yet entered into force,[56] although at the Paris Conference, Kyoto Protocol parties that had not already done so were urged to ratify and implement the amendment.[57] During the second commitment period, participating developed country parties will pursue new individual emissions reduction targets with the aim of achieving a collective emissions reduction of eighteen per cent below 1990 levels by 2020.[58] These emissions cuts represent only a fraction of the reductions called for by scientists in order to keep warming below 2°C.[59]

The risk avoidance orientation of the early climate treaties reflected a choice by climate scientists and governments to focus initial international cooperative efforts on mitigation rather than adaptation.[60] In part, this represented an understanding that the institution of robust and rapid mitigation measures would obviate the need for extensive adaptation. However, during the early treaty negotiations, adaptation was often treated as a 'taboo' topic, regarded 'with the same distaste that the religious right reserves for sex education in schools. That is, both constitute ethical compromises that in any case will only encourage dangerous experimentation with the undesired behaviour.'[61] Leading players in the early climate negotiations expressed the view that international climate law should adopt a mitigation-oriented framing of climate change rather than an adaptation-based one. For example, Vice President Al Gore, writing in his book, *Earth in the Balance*, published shortly before the conclusion of the UNFCCC, dismissed adaptation as 'a kind of laziness, an arrogant faith in our ability to react in time to save our skin'.[62]

The consequences of this choice to favour mitigation in the UNFCCC and the Kyoto Protocol is evident in the virtual sidelining of alternative climate futures associated with adaptation or loss and damage. The UNFCCC obliquely references adaptation in its objective, calling for emissions stabilization to:

> be achieved within a time frame sufficient to allow ecosystems to adapt naturally to climate change, to ensure that food production is not threatened and to enable economic development to proceed in a sustainable manner.[63]

Adaptation is conceived of narrowly as the marginal impacts on communities and environments of climate change caused by anthropogenic GHG emissions. This framing in turn has limited the scope of adaptation measures and funding assistance provided for under the early climate change treaties. For example, the UNFCCC placed a requirement on developed country parties to assist developing countries particularly vulnerable to the effects of climate change but only 'in meeting costs of adaptation *to those adverse effects*'.[64] The Kyoto Protocol, for its part, contains minimal

[56] Seventy-five countries (including the twenty-seven member states of the European Union) have so far approved the Doha Amendment, which requires 144 ratifications to enter into force.

[57] UNFCCC, Conference of the Parties, 'Adoption of the Paris Agreement' (n 9) para 106(a).

[58] Doha Amendment, art 3 *bis*.

[59] For instance, the 40–70% below 2010 levels by 2050 called for by the IPCC in its 2007 report.

[60] R Pielke Jr, G Prins, and S Rayner, 'Climate Change 2007: Lifting the Taboo on Adaptation' (2007) 445 *Nature* 597.

[61] M Thompson and S Rayner, 'Cultural Discourses' in S Rayner and EL Malone (eds), *Human Choice and Climate Change Vol. 1: The Societal Framework* (Battelle Press 1998) 265.

[62] A Gore, *Earth in the Balance: Ecology and the Human Spirit* (Houghton Mifflin Co 1992) 240.

[63] UNFCCC, art 2. [64] ibid, art 4.4 (emphasis added).

mention of adaptation beyond providing for the establishment of the Adaptation Fund to assist with developing countries' adaptation costs. Even here, the source of funds for adaptation comes from a mitigation mechanism: emissions reducing projects undertaken pursuant to the Clean Development Mechanism by developed countries in developing countries.[65]

Neither the UNFCCC nor the Kyoto Protocol contemplates a climate future of unmanageable climate change associated with extensive loss and damage in vulnerable or other countries. Histories of the negotiations suggest that this was not because negotiating states were unaware of the potential for significant climate change harms, but rather because of the desire to prioritize risk prevention and avoidance as the primary objective of the regime.[66] As a result, neither treaty contains provisions on responsibility for climate damage. Conversely, a number of small island states, foreseeing this future, appended declarations to their ratifications of the UNFCCC preserving rights under international law 'concerning state responsibility for the adverse effects of climate change'.[67]

The narrow framing of adaptation, and the exclusion of loss and damage, in the early climate treaties contrasts with broader understandings of the climate change problem that have emerged in other international fora, particularly in the lead-up to and aftermath of the IPCC's 2007 report. Fora focused on sustainable development (such as the Rio+20 meeting[68] and the 2015 UN Sustainable Development Summit)[69] and disaster risk reduction (such as the Third UN World Conference on Disaster Risk Reduction),[70] have progressively taken the view that climate change represents another stressor that can exacerbate the effects of existing problems or disaster events.[71] The Sendai Framework for Disaster Risk Reduction 2015–2030, concluded in March 2015, recognizes climate change as one of several 'disaster risk drivers'.[72] It calls for disaster risk reduction through enhanced efforts to build community resilience that will address not just the specific impacts of climate change, but also contribute more broadly to goals of sustainable development and poverty eradication. This effort is conceived of as one requiring coordination and coherence

[65] Kyoto Protocol, art 12. For further information on the Adaptation Fund, including institutional structures established for its operation, see UNFCC, 'Adaptation Fund' <htpp://unfccc.int/cooperation_and_support/financial_mechanism/adaptation_fund/items/3659.php> accessed 10 September 2015.

[66] R Verheyen, *Climate Change Damage and International Law* (Brill 2005).

[67] See text of the declarations submitted upon signature or ratification of the Convention by Fiji, Kiribati, Nauru, and Papua New Guinea. UNFCCC, 'Declarations by Parties' <http://unfccc.int/essential_background/convention/items/5410.php> accessed 10 September 2015. The Convention does not permit reservations (UNFCCC, art 24) and the legal effect of these declarations has not yet been tested.

[68] The Rio+20 meeting was held in 2012 on the twentieth anniversary of the original Rio Earth Summit (the United Nations Conference on Environment and Development) held in 1992.

[69] The latter Summit agreed new sustainable development goals (SDGs) for the period 2015–2030. See UNGA Res 69/L.85 (12 August 2015), 'Draft Outcome Document of the United Nations Summit for the Adoption of the Post-2015 Development Agenda', UN Doc A/69/L.85.

[70] See further <http://www.wcdrr.org/> accessed 21 November 2016.

[71] See, eg, UNGA Res 66/288 (11 September 2012) 'The Future We Want', UN Doc A/RES/66/288 (outcome document from the Rio+20 Summit).

[72] Third UN World Conference, 'Sendai Framework for Disaster Risk Reduction 2015–2030' (18 March 2015) A. CONF.224/CRP.1 (Sendai Framework).

across different institutions and treaty mandates, including the UNFCCC, in order to 'contribute to building resilience and achieving the global goal to eradicate poverty'.[73] Likewise the SDGs, finalized by the United Nations in September 2015 as part of the global 2030 Agenda for Sustainable Development, include a specific goal to 'take urgent action to combat climate change and its impacts'.[74]

Following the IPCC's 2007 report, a shift within the international climate regime itself towards the management of climate risk and associated impacts on communities was evident, spurred on by recognition of the growing emissions gap and fading hopes for climate change mitigation. The Bali UNFCCC COP in 2007, which developed a 'road map' for future negotiations that eventually led to the Paris Agreement, featured a substantial focus on adaptation measures and capacity building.[75] Attention to adaptation continued to strengthen in subsequent negotiation rounds. For example, the Copenhagen COP in 2009—infamous for nations' failure to agree on targets for post-2012 emissions cuts[76]—nonetheless saw consensus reached on the need for developed countries to 'provide adequate, predictable and sustainable financial resources, technology and capacity-building to support the implementation of adaptation action in developing countries'.[77] At Copenhagen developed countries also pledged to provide 'new and additional' funding approaching US$30 billion for the period 2010–2012 and committed to a goal of mobilizing jointly US$100 billion per year by 2020 to address the needs of developing countries.[78]

In 2010, the concept of loss and damage that had received limited endorsement in the international climate change regime to that point was officially sanctioned, with the COP initiating consideration of approaches for dealing with loss and damage.[79] This was followed by agreement at the UNFCCC COP held in Warsaw in 2013 to set up a new international mechanism 'to address loss and damage associated with impacts of climate change, including extreme events and slow onset events, in developing countries that are particularly vulnerable to the adverse effects of climate change'.[80] The Warsaw Loss and Damage Mechanism was tasked with

[73] Sendai Framework, paras 11 and 13.

[74] UNGA Res 70/1 (25 September 2015), 'Transforming Our World: The 2030 Agenda for Sustainable Development', UN Doc A/RES/70/1, Sustainable Development Goal 13.

[75] UNFCCC, Conference of the Parties, Decision 1/CP.13 (14 March 2008), 'Bali Action Plan', *Report of the Conference of the Parties on its Thirteenth Sessions Held in Bali from 3 to 15 December 2007*, FCCC/CP/2007/6/Add 1, para 1(c) (Bali Action Plan).

[76] D Bodansky, 'The Copenhagen Climate Conference: A Postmortem' (2010) 104 *American Journal of International Law* 230.

[77] These declarations were made as part of the so-called Copenhagen Accord, para 3. The Accord was not formally adopted by the COP due to a lack of consensus support. Rather, parties 'took note' of it by way of Decision 2/CP.15 (18 December 2009), 'Copenhagen Accord'. UNFCCC, Conference of the Parties, *Report of the Conference of the Parties on its Fifteenth Session, Held in Copenhagen from 7 to 19 December 2009, Addendum, Part Two: Action Taken by the Conference of the Parties at its Fifteenth Session*, FCCC/CP/2009/11/Add 1 (Copenhagen Accord).

[78] ibid, para 8. [79] Huq et al, 'Loss and Damage' (n 13) 947.

[80] 'Warsaw International Mechanism for Loss and Damage Associated with Climate Change Impacts' Decision 2/CP. 19 (31 January 2014). UNFCCC, Conference of the Parties, *Report of the Conference of the Parties on Its Nineteenth Session, Held in Warsaw from 11 to 23 November 2013, Addendum, Part Two: Action Taken by the Conference of the Parties at its Nineteenth Session*, FCCC/CP/2013/10/Add 1.

functions relating to the coordination of efforts, knowledge development, technical guidance, and facilitating support for actions to address loss and damage.[81]

The Paris Agreement, concluded by UNFCCC parties in December 2015 and in force from 4 November 2016, consolidates these trends and signals a new holistic focus for the international climate regime on both the causes and the consequences of climate risk. Unlike the Kyoto Protocol, which was concerned almost entirely with setting internationally enshrined emissions reduction targets for developed country parties, the Paris Agreement takes a more flexible, comprehensive, bottom-up approach to climate action.[82] Its central requirement is for parties—both developed and developing countries—to 'prepare, communicate and maintain successive nationally determined contributions' (NDCs) to the global response to climate change.[83] Provisions of the Paris Agreement regarding NDCs continue to have a strong concentration on emissions reduction measures, especially for developed countries. However, they may also include an 'adaptation communication' that deals with a country's adaptation priorities, implementation and support needs, plans, and actions.[84]

In addition, the Paris Agreement provides for a periodic global 'stocktake' of countries' proposed actions that must consider 'mitigation, adaptation and the means of implementation and support'.[85] This stocktake is designed 'to assess the collective progress towards achieving the purpose of [the] Agreement and its long-term goals'. These goals not only include the long-term temperature goal of staying 'well below' 2°C and pursuing efforts to limit global average temperature rise to 1.5°C, but also that of '[i]ncreasing the ability to adapt to the adverse impacts of climate change and foster climate resilience and low GHG emissions development, in a manner that does not threaten food production'.[86] The clear implication is that mitigation and adaptation now stand on an equal footing in the international climate change regime.[87] Moreover, adaptation is no longer so strongly segregated from mitigation, nor climate action from broader agendas dealing with development and disaster risk reduction. The Paris Agreement recognizes both the potential for mitigation/adaptation linkages[88] and the linkages between climate change and issues of sustainable development, poverty eradication, food security, and human rights.[89]

Consistent with this new recognition of adaptation in the international climate regime is the Paris Agreement's articulation of a 'global goal on adaptation' designed to enhance adaptive capacity, strengthen resilience, and reduce vulnerability to climate change, 'with a view to contributing to sustainable development and ensuring an adequate adaptation response' in the context of the Agreement's long-term temperature goal.[90] The parties also acknowledged adaptation as 'a key component of the long-term global response to climate change' that is necessary 'to protect people, livelihoods and ecosystems', with a special focus on the 'urgent and immediate' needs of vulnerable developing country parties.[91] While adaptation financing was

[81] ibid, para 5.

[82] M Doelle, 'The Paris Agreement: Historic Breakthrough or High Stakes Experiment?' (2016) 6(1) *Climate Law* 1 <http://papers.ssrn.com/sol3/papers.cfm?abstract_id=2708148> accessed 21 November 2016.

[83] Paris Agreement, art 4(2).

[84] ibid, arts 7(10) and (11).

[85] ibid, art 14.1.

[86] ibid, art 2.

[87] See also ibid, art 3.

[88] ibid, art 4.7.

[89] ibid, Preamble.

[90] ibid, art 7.1.

[91] ibid, art 7.2.

only dealt with in general terms in the Agreement (and, indeed, progressed little beyond the $100 billion annual commitment made at the Copenhagen COP) the Paris Agreement's provisions indicate the regime's shift to embrace the management of the consequences of climate risk, alongside risk prevention and risk avoidance.

The Paris Agreement provides less clarity with respect to futures imagining unmanageable climate change impacts, such as significant loss and damage to vulnerable communities, massive displacement of people as a result of climate change, or the risks associated with the failure or termination of potential geo-engineering measures. As discussed further in section 10.4, the Agreement offers only glimpses into such catastrophic climate futures, preferring to maintain attention on possibilities for mitigation and adaptation. The most extensive treatment is reserved for loss and damage, which makes its first appearance in an international climate treaty in Article 8 of the Paris Agreement.[92] This provision, however, is limited to enhancing 'understanding, action and support, including through the Warsaw International Mechanism, as appropriate'.[93] While this will direct welcome attention to preventative and mitigation measures such as early warning systems, emergency preparedness, risk insurance facilities, and comparative risk assessment and management processes, it does not (for the present) extend to the provision of compensation by major emitting countries to those most harmed by climate change. The COP decision adopting the Paris Agreement explicitly provides that Article 8 of the Paris Agreement 'does not involve or provide a basis for any liability or compensation'.[94]

Overall, the Paris Agreement recognizes, more fully than the early climate treaties, alternative climate futures and the risks that they pose, particularly for the most vulnerable developing countries and communities. This has resulted in greater treatment of issues of adaptation and loss and damage, as well as of the implementation and support mechanisms (financing, technology transfer, and capacity building) that will be necessary to facilitate developing country participation, including by the least developed countries and small island developing states.[95] In return, developing countries are expected to shoulder a greater share of the emissions reduction burden through adopting NDCs that include mitigation actions. The principle of CBDRRC remains in the Agreement but as a basis for flexible tailoring of climate action and support measures in light of national circumstances, rather than as a 'firewall' between the mitigation obligations of developed and developing country parties.[96] As one least developed countries (LDC) negotiator commented at the conclusion of the 2015 negotiations, what was achieved in Paris was 'yellow-bus diplomacy ... Maybe the G20 are sitting on the seats, but the rest of us are there,

[92] For analysis of the history and future of loss and damage in the international climate regime, see William CG Burns, 'Loss and Damage and the 21st Conference of the Parties to the United Nations Framework Convention on Climate Change', Forum for Climate Engineering Assessment (2 January 2016) <http://papers.ssrn.om/so13/papers.cfm?abstract_id=2710086> accessed 21 November 2016.

[93] Paris Agreement, art 8.3.

[94] Adoption of the Paris Agreement, para 52.

[95] See particularly Paris Agreement, arts 9–11.

[96] For analysis of the 'careful balance between ambition and differentiation' struck in the Paris Agreement, see L Rajamani, 'Ambition and Differentiation in the 2015 Paris Agreement: Interpretative Possibilities and Underlying Politics' (2016) 65(2) *International and Comparative Law Quarterly* 493.

holding on to the sides and the back.'[97] Moreover, implicit in this approach, as the negotiator noted, is an important acknowledgement by developed countries that '[i]f we save the vulnerable, the rest of the world will be saved, too'.[98]

More broadly, the turn to adaptation and greater consideration of loss and damage issues in the international climate regime may also assist in building public support for climate change regulation; support that is ultimately necessary to drive strengthened mitigation measures. A growing body of social science research on climate risk perception suggests that people are more readily able to relate, and more responsive, to framings of climate change that focus on building community resilience in the face of disaster threats.[99] Drawing on cultural cognition theory, Rob Verchick argues that the local orientation of adaptation (and loss and damage) measures makes it easier to engage with citizens in terms of their closely held values.[100] As such, adaptation efforts, in his view, are 'the cognitive gateway' for addressing climate change. This approach also resonates with calls for climate change to be viewed, not just as an emissions reduction issue, but also as an aspect of broader sustainable development and human rights challenges. As former Maldives President, Mohamed Nasheed, has poignantly put it, '[g]lobal warming should be seen not as an environmental crisis but as a human rights issue that risks the lives, livelihoods and homes of millions of people'.[101]

10.4 Darker Imaginings—Catastrophic Climate Risk Scenarios

The Paris Agreement has been hailed as a 'historic' achievement with potential to put the world on the pathway to a sustainable climate future.[102] However, amidst the euphoria over conclusion of the agreement after many years of stalemated negotiations, more cautious and critical assessments are emerging. Leading climate scientist, James Hansen—the 'father of climate change awareness'—labelled the agreement 'a fraud' with 'no action, just promises' and warned that '[a]s long as fossil fuels appear to be the cheapest fuels out there, they will be continued to be burned'.[103] Even those, like author and activist Bill McKibben, who sees the Paris

[97] A Little, 'What the Paris Agreement Means for Vulnerable Nations' *The New Yorker* (15 December 2015) <http://www.newyorker.com/news/news-desk/what_the_paris_climate_agreement_means_for_vulnerable_nations> accessed 10 January 2016 (quoting Olai Uludong, Palau's ambassador to the European Union).

[98] ibid.

[99] HM Osofsky and J Peel, 'Energy Partisanship' (2016) 65 *Emory LJ* 695 <htpp://papers.ssrn.com/sol3/papers.cfm?abstract_id=252391> accessed 10 January 2016.

[100] RM Verchick. 'Culture, Cognition, and Climate' (2015) *U ILL L Rev* (2016) 969 <http://works.bepress.com/robert_verchick/58> accessed 10 January 2016.

[101] See Know Climate Change <http://know.climateofconcern.org/index.php?option=com_content&task=article&id=187> accessed 10 September 2015.

[102] J Worland, 'World Approves Historic "Paris Agreement" to Address Climate Change' *Time* (Paris, 12 December 2015) <http://time.com/4146830/cop-21-paris-agreement-climate/> accessed 10 January 2016.

[103] O Millman, 'James Hansen, Father of Climate Change Awareness, Calls Paris Talks "a Fraud"' *The Guardian* (12 December 2015) <http://www.theguardian.com/environment/2015/dec/12/james-hansen-climate-change-paris-talks-fraud> accessed 10 January 2016.

Agreement as providing a 'new tool' for climate action and energy transition, note 'we'll try to keep hoping that it adds up fast enough to matter [though] [t]hat's a little hard, as the hottest year ever measured draws to a close'.[104] The risk that national mitigation actions will not 'add up fast enough' to keep below 2°C remains a significant one given the lack of sufficient ambition in present pre-2020 actions and existing pledges for 2025 and 2030. To bridge this gap, the Paris Agreement offers processes of review, transparency, and stocktaking,[105] but whether this will be sufficient to motivate states and other actors to take the stronger measures needed to address climate change in a timely fashion is unknown. Darker climate futures therefore remain on the horizon, albeit not well articulated as yet in international climate change law.

While the international climate change regime remains largely positive and forward looking in its view of climate risk, it, nevertheless, has some of the necessary tools in place to envision and respond to catastrophic climate risk. The UNFCCC's objective of avoiding dangerous anthropogenic interference with the climate system—now supplemented by the Paris Agreement's long-term temperature goal—has driven scientific assessments considering what the climate would look like without mitigation and adaptation. For instance, the IPCC's 2014 report predicted that without additional efforts to reduce emissions beyond those in place today, global mean surface temperature increases by the end of the century could range from 3.7°C to 7.8°C.[106] In conjunction, seas would rise by up to a metre or more, flooding small islands and low-lying areas throughout the world. Life as we know it would not be sustainable in a world with 4°C plus of warming.[107] Or as IMF Managing Director Christine Lagarde has said, '[u]nless we take action on climate change, future generations will be roasted, toasted, fried and grilled'.[108]

How international climate change law would respond to a climate catastrophe of this kind is only vaguely outlined in the existing international instruments; a by-product of the predominant focus on mitigation in the early climate treaties. However, the Paris Agreement provides some indications of the likely future evolution of the regime if deep emissions cuts and adequate adaptation measures fail to materialize.

The clearest response to futures associated with catastrophic climate risk is the new provision on loss and damage, outlined in section 10.3. Both Article 8 of the Paris Agreement and the Warsaw Loss and Damage Mechanism that it incorporates are designed to address economic and non-economic harms associated with the impacts of climate change in vulnerable developing countries, whether

[104] W McKibben, 'Falling Short on Climate in Paris' *New York Times* (13 December 2015) <http://www.nytimes.com/2015/12/14/opinion/falling-short-on-climate-in-paris.html?r=0> accessed 10 January 2016.

[105] Paris Agreement, arts 13 and 14.

[106] IPCC, 'Summary for Policymakers', in *Climate Change 2014: Synthesis Report. Contribution of Working Groups I, II and III* (n 28) 20.

[107] World Bank, *Turn Down the Heat: Why a 4°C Warmer World Must Be Avoided* (World Bank 2012).

[108] Quoted in D Runnalls, '"Roasted, Toasted, Fried and Grilled": Climate Change Talk from an Unlikely Source' *The Globe and Mail* (1 February 2013) <http://www.theglobeandmail.com/globe-debate/roasted-toasted-fried-and-grilled-climate-change-talk-from-an-unlikely-source/article8077946/> accessed 10 September 2015.

arising from extreme events (eg, hurricanes) or 'slow onset events' (eg, sea level rise). Nonetheless, the exclusion of liability and compensation may limit the effectiveness of the loss and damage provisions, unless parties in future COPs agree to direct funding towards assisting countries' response to, and rebuilding after, climate disaster. Present indications are that such funding would need to be substantial.[109] Article 8 of the Paris Agreement also leaves open the window for further strengthening of the Warsaw Mechanism in the future.[110]

Other catastrophic risk scenarios, and responses to them, are hinted at, but not elaborated, in the Paris Agreement. For instance, the substantial leeway given to parties in formulating their NDCs would not seem to preclude the deployment of geo-engineering techniques, including the more controversial approaches of SRM, in addition to, or possibly in place of, emissions reductions. Significantly, developed country parties are subject only to a soft obligation to 'continue taking the lead by undertaking economy-wide absolute emissions reduction targets' and developing countries are merely 'encouraged to move over time' to such targets.[111] This places no binding requirement on countries to reduce their absolute GHG emissions. The resulting gap is likely to encourage further discussion and advocacy for geo-engineering options, which some argue are the only 'ethical' approach in the face of faltering mitigation efforts.[112] As a practical matter, others argue that the ambitious 1.5°C goal set by the Paris Agreement is likely out of reach without the deployment of geo-engineering techniques.[113]

Whether geo-engineering, especially SRM measures, should be endorsed as a potential mitigation mechanism to avert catastrophic climate impacts remains extremely controversial and could itself 'entail numerous uncertainties, side effects, risks and shortcomings'.[114] As the IPCC noted in its 2014 report, if SRM were instituted and then terminated, this would carry its own risks of catastrophe due to

[109] The IPCC's 2014 report reported global estimates of between US$70 and $100 billion per year between 2010 and 2050 but noted low confidence in these estimates. UNEP's *Adaptation Finance Gap Update* report released in the lead-up to the Paris Conference found that these costs significantly underestimate the resources that will need to be deployed for adaptation by a factor of 3 to 5. See UNEP, *The Adaptation Finance Gap Update* (2015) <http://web.unep.org/sites/default/files/gapreport/UNEP_Adaptation_Finance_Gap_Update.pdf> accessed 10 January 2016.

[110] Paris Agreement, art 8(2).

[111] ibid, art 4(4). The soft language in this article was the result of a last-minute intervention by the US government concerned that mandatory language would require Senate approval of the Paris Agreement and jeopardize US implementation. See John Vidal, 'How a "Typo" Nearly Derailed the Paris Climate Deal', *The Guardian* (16 December 2015) <http://www.theguardian.com/environment/blog/2015/dec/16/how-a-typo-nearly-derailed-the-paris-climate-deal> accessed 21 November 2016.

[112] For discussion of the social and ethical implications of climate engineering, see A Corner and N Pidgeon, 'Geoengineering the Climate: The Social and Ethical Implications' (2010) 52 *Environment: Science and Policy for Sustainable Development* 24.

[113] D Farber, 'Does the Paris Agreement Open the Door to Geo-Engineering?', *Legal Planet Blog* (14 December 2015) <http://legal-planet.org/2015/12/14/does-the-paris-agreement-open-the-door-to-geoengineering> accessed 21 November 2016; see also J Shepherd, 'What Does the Paris Agreement Mean for Geo-Engineering?', *The Royal Society* (17 February 2016) <http://blogs.royalsociety.org/in-verba/2016/02/17/what-does-the-paris-agreement-mean-for-geoengineering/> accessed 21 November 2016.

[114] IPCC, 'Summary for Policymakers', in *Climate Change 2014: Synthesis Report. Contribution of Working Groups I, II and III* (n 28) 25–26.

a rapid rise in surface temperatures impacting ecosystems susceptible to rapid rates of change.[115] The Paris Agreement provides little indication of how international climate change law might approach risks of climate catastrophe in this case, other than through an oblique preambular reference to parties' recognition that they 'may be affected not only by climate change, but also by the impacts of the measures taken in response to it'.[116]

The Paris Agreement's consideration of scenarios of massive climate-induced displacement of peoples, as well as the human rights violations and security risks that might entail, is also limited. On human rights, the preamble to the Agreement includes an acknowledgment that:

> Parties should, when taking action to address climate change, respect, promote and consider their respective obligations on human rights, the right to health, the rights of indigenous people, local communities, migrants, children, persons with disabilities and people in vulnerable situations and the right to development, as well as gender equality, empowerment of women and intergenerational equity.[117]

This reference formalizes a growing international recognition of human rights–climate change linkages,[118] and may open the door, in the future development of the international climate change regime, to strengthening human rights safeguards for vulnerable groups.

Climate-related population displacement raises another series of potentially catastrophic climate risk scenarios. For small island states and low-lying areas, for example, sea level rise as a result of polar ice cap melt and ocean expansion may result in the total displacement of populations from these areas. Long before the eventual drowning of island states in the sea, life in these countries is likely to become unsustainable as a result of the intrusion of salt water into freshwater reserves, severe storms, and ocean surge that take an increasing toll on local communities.[119] In other parts of the world, climate change will take the form of extended drought and famine.[120] Impacts are expected to build and compound as climate change increases, exacerbating other development and security threats. Particular concerns in this regard relate to water shortage, food security, and how such risks, coupled with climate-related displacement of peoples from their homelands, might merge into threats to peace and security.[121]

Again, little guidance for responding to these possible futures is afforded by the Paris documents, with the only reference being in the COP decision adopting the Agreement. This provides, in the section on loss and damage, for the establishment

[115] ibid, 26. [116] Paris Agreement, preambular recital 7.

[117] ibid, preambular recital 11.

[118] JH Knox, 'Human Rights Principles and Climate Change' in C Carlarne et al (eds), *Oxford Handbook of International Climate Change Law* (OUP 2015).

[119] UNEP, *Emerging Issues for Small Island Developing States. Results of the UNEP Foresight Process* (UNEP 2014) 41–47.

[120] IPCC, 'Summary for Policymakers', in *Climate Change 2014: Impacts, Adaptation, and Vulnerability* (n 3).

[121] ibid. See also J McAdam and B Saul, 'An Insecure Climate for Human Security? Climate-Induced Displacement and International Law' in A Edwards and C Ferstman (eds), *Human Security and Non-Citizens: Law, Policy and International Affairs* (CUP 2010).

of a task force to work with existing bodies and expert groups under and outside the UNFCCC 'to develop recommendations for integrated approaches to avert, minimize and address displacement related to the adverse impacts of climate change'.[122] This could provide a platform for integration of expertise from the climate field with that from the areas of human rights, migration, and security to articulate ways of dealing with large-scale population displacement in the face of climate change.

Although the Paris Agreement (and even more so the lengthy COP decision adopting it) point the way to the development of more integrated approaches that will be required to respond to multifaceted catastrophic risk scenarios like climate displacement, the fragmented nature of the international legal system continues to pose significant challenges. An effective response to climate displacement and human security risks, for instance, would require the coordination of several separate international regimes, including treaties on human rights, migration, and international peace and security. Likewise, managing the effects and unintended consequences of geo-engineering would necessitate interaction of the climate regime with those dealing with outer space, marine pollution, and biodiversity, among others.[123] While there have been proposals for new treaties to deal with the specific catastrophic consequences climate change portends for areas like human rights and displacement of peoples,[124] the appetite for new treaty making in this area seems minimal. Far more likely is that responses will be developed through greater integration between the relevant international legal regimes.

This work was already underway before the Paris Agreement as non-climate-focused bodies considered how climate change might affect their mandates and environmental institutions sought to factor questions of (climate) disaster risk reduction and management into their treaty instruments.[125] Such activities are likely to receive a further boost from the Paris outcome, especially the provisions of the COP decision concerning institutional coordination, and sharing learning to enhance adaptation and loss and damage responses. Coordination and coherent policy making of this kind will be vital to the capacity of international law to mount effective responses to the catastrophic risks climate change may create.

10.5 Conclusion

Over the past three decades, international climate law has developed a sophisticated regime of processes and measures for imagining and seeking to regulate the risks of climate change. The focus of the early climate treaties on mitigation has given way in recent years to a more balanced attention to both mitigation and adaptation; a

[122] Adoption of the Paris Agreement, para 50.

[123] Rayfuse and Scott, *International Law in the Era of Climate Change* (n 5).

[124] D Hogkinson, 'We Need a Treaty to Help People Displaced by Climate Change', *The Conversation* (12 September 2012) <https://theconversation.com/we-need-a-treaty-to-help-people-displaced-by-climate-change-9150> accessed 10 September 2015.

[125] See, eg, activities on disaster risk reduction and management being coordinated under the auspices of UNEP. UNEP, 'Disaster Risk Management' <http://www.unep.org/disastersandconflicts/Introduction/DisasterRiskReduction/tabid/104159/Default.aspx> accessed 10 September 2015.

trend cemented by the Paris Agreement. With the widening of the gap between needed and actual or planned emissions reductions, scientific constructs of climate risk, with their focus on emissions levels and mitigation actions, have also had to evolve to accommodate alternative visions of climate change; ones that focus on the consequences of weather-related disasters, the harm visited on communities, and ways to build greater resilience that will also address broader challenges of sustainable development and poverty alleviation. The prospect of insufficient mitigation action producing runaway climate change also has seen emphasis on darker futures such as those associated with potentially risky geo-engineering solutions, massive population displacement, and deteriorating security conditions.

Presently, it seems that the international climate regime is at a turning point. Most scientific assessments are that with stringent mitigation action we could significantly reduce the risks from climate change, although it is impossible to avoid damage entirely. In this minimal impact scenario, global emissions would need to peak as early as 2020 and substantially decline thereafter.[126] The Paris Agreement acknowledges this (although in less specific language) through its collective aim for parties to reach global peaking of emissions 'as soon as possible' and achieve net zero carbon emissions 'in the second half of this century'.[127] A recent report of the International Energy Agency (IEA) showing global emissions levelling off in 2014 for the first time offers some cause for hope.[128] Even so, the window for taking effective mitigation action is fast narrowing.

Our future now is one where we are locked into some level of climate change and will have to deal with the impacts on communities, countries, and environments. In doing so, it is likely that some countries and communities will suffer disproportionately more than others. The consequences of climate change will also be inter-generational, with some climate impacts initiated by current emissions levels continuing to be felt for centuries to come. In the future, the climate regime will need to focus even greater attention on questions of financing and assistance to vulnerable countries, mechanisms for addressing loss and damage, and ways that these activities can be integrated with the work of development, security, and disaster risk reduction institutions.

As UK climate scientist, Kevin Anderson, has written, the only thing that is certain about our climate future is that it will be 'different' from what has gone before.[129] Moreover, as Bill McKibben remarks in his latest book *Eaarth*, '[t]his is not some mere passing change, this is the Earth shifting'. Whether human societies and our regulatory systems, including those at the international level, can also shift, and in time, remains to be seen.[130]

[126] IPCC, 'Summary for Policymakers', in *Climate Change 2014: Synthesis Report. Contribution of Working Groups I, II and III* (n 28).

[127] Paris Agreement, art 4.1.

[128] International Energy Agency, 'Global Energy-Related Emissions of Carbon Dioxide Stalled in 2014' (13 March 2015) <http://www.iea.org/newsroomandevents/news/2015/march/global-energy-related-emissions-of-carbon-dioxide-stalled-in-2014.html> accessed 10 September 2015.

[129] K Anderson, 'To Meet International Commitments on "Avoiding Dangerous Climate Change", Wealthy Nations Must Reduce Emissions by Over 10% Each Year' *Swedish Daily* (7 November 2012) <http://kevinanderson.info/blog/wp-content/uploads/2012/11/Opinion-Piece-by-Anderson-for-SvD-Swedish-Daily-Newspaper_Nov-2012.pdf> accessed 10 September 2015.

[130] W McKibben, *Eaarth: Making Life on a Tough New Planet* (Times Books 2010), 4.

11

Catastrophic Climate Change, Precaution, and the Risk/Risk Dilemma

Floor M Fleurke

11.1 Introduction

This chapter explores the dilemma of risk/risk trade-offs in the face of potentially catastrophic climate change, and examines the contours of a precautionary regulatory response to such impasses.

The prominence of risk/risk trade-offs on the regulatory agenda is increasing, and there is every reason to believe that this will continue to be the case in the future. The reason for this is the growing awareness that many of humankind's most daunting problems (relating to the climate, biodiversity, environmental quality, energy, pandemics, refugees, etc) are situated in wider complex global ecological, social, and economic systems. Those systems are 'complex' in the specific sense that changes in a particular element of any such system will reverberate across the totality of all systems, often in unpredictable ways. For regulators, the dilemma is that whilst the seriousness of a given problem may call for immediate and targeted intervention, the ensuing uncertain impacts on other elements of inter-connected systems may be equally deleterious, necessitating a gradual, considered, and holistic approach.

Climate change is a prime example of such a risk/risk dilemma. Global warming and its consequences show no signs of slowing down, and no substantial progress has been achieved at the international political level. The Paris Agreement[1] has recently been hailed as a turning point in global environmental governance, but it is wise to remain cautious about its immediate environmental impact for as long as the crucial issue of implementation is disputed. The Agreement provides a framework for the future ongoing commitment to cutting greenhouse gas (GHG) emissions, although many earlier ambitions were deleted or watered down considerably. Moreover, the Agreement's commitments with regard to GHG emission mitigation are not well defined; states are merely obliged to make voluntary

[1] UNFCCC Conference of the Parties (COP-24), Decision 1/CP-21, Adoption of the Paris Agreement (12 December 2015) UNFCCC/CP/2015/L.9/Rev 1, Annex (UNFCCC).

pledges—so-called nationally determined contributions (NDCs)—every five years. Monitoring mechanisms are established to oversee implementation of the NDCs and, according to Article 14 of the Agreement, global stocktaking will first be undertaken in 2023 'to assess the collective progress towards achieving the purpose of this Agreement and its long-term goals'. However, no 'hard' enforcement chapter is included; Article 15 of the Paris Agreement merely foresees a committee of experts that will facilitate compliance 'in a manner that is ... non-adversarial and non-punitive'. All things considered, it is therefore fair to wonder how effective the NDCs will be, given that—with the exception of pledges by some individual national authorities and the European Union—the international community as a whole is still not prepared to adopt a strong emissions reduction target. The international community's refusal to commit itself to binding enforceable emission cuts is curiously at odds with earlier widely expressed political sentiment that the Paris Summit represented humankind's best chance to save the planet, and that there is 'no planet B'.[2] At least as alarming, its acquiescence to near-certain regulatory failure is also impossible to square with the scientific community's devastating apocalyptic assessment of the seriousness of the climate challenge. A recent paper reports that the near-term effects of climate change could be much more catastrophic at a global average temperature rise of only 2°C than even previously expected.[3]

It is against this gloomy background of continued regulatory impotence regardless of possible impending ecological catastrophe that more radical regulatory approaches—such as climate engineering (CE), biotechnology, and synthetic biology—are increasingly being considered. Biotechnology, for example, can be put to use to combat the effects of climate change. Genetic modification of crops identified as useful biofuels can increase fuel availability and efficiency, and may reduce reliance on fossil fuels. This technology could also present a solution to the negative impacts of irrigation related to changes (both in terms of quantity and quality) in soil and water quality, for instance, by engineering drought-resistant plants.

However, the deployment of technologies as a regulatory modality intended to directly and immediately alter the chemical composition of the atmosphere or the reflectiveness of planet Earth (so-called climate engineering) invariably carries risks itself. It is true that there exist a great variety of CE techniques, each with different risk profiles, some of them ostensibly relatively benign. Yet, all those techniques possess one crucial common characteristic that sets them apart from traditional regulatory approaches, which is that instead of targeting the behaviour of regulatees for the sake of effecting a gradual slowing down of climate change, they directly intervene in the climate to realize immediate and, depending on the technique used, dramatic results. It is not difficult to see that direct interventions in

[2] See, eg, The White House, 'Remarks by President Obama at the First Session of COP21' <https://www.whitehouse.gov/the-press-office/2015/11/30/remarks-president-obama-first-session-cop21> accessed 10 January 2016.

[3] J Hansen, M Sato, P Hearty et al, 'Ice Melt, Sea Level Rise and Superstorms' (2016) 16 *Atmospheric Chemistry and Physics* 3761.

complex ecological systems offer even more fertile ground for sudden unwelcome spill-overs and surprises than gradual policies targeting behavioural change.

Although the previous observation is of paramount importance for the risk debate, the differences between these existing and future techniques, in terms of cost, risk, and scale,[4] remain significant and need to be briefly addressed. Technologies designed to remove atmospheric GHGs have long been part of the climate change discourse but have remained mostly in the shadows with respect to international climate politics, negotiations, and policies. This appears ready to change as the capabilities, costs, and risks of various negative emissions technologies become less uncertain. Bio-energy carbon capture and storage (BECCS) is the most considered negative emission technology. The idea is to remove the carbon from biomass either before or after combustion and pipe it underground so that the invisible gas can be contained in rock formations without leaking.

More controversial are technologies to cool the Earth itself. Broadly, such CE techniques are divided into two categories: carbon dioxide removal (CDR) and solar radiation management (SRM).[5] CDR aims to collect and sequester GHGs from the atmosphere. Examples include capturing carbon dioxide from ambient air, fertilizing oceans to increase biological uptake, and enhanced mineral weathering. CDR addresses the threat of climate change relatively close to its source, but is expensive and slow.[6] SRM techniques aim to increase the earth's reflectiveness, thereby counteracting the warming up of the planet. Injecting aerosols into the upper atmosphere, spraying seawater to increase cloud brightness, and injecting microbubbles into the ocean are all examples of SRM. These techniques may, however, result in a different composition of the atmosphere.

Nevertheless, contrary to CDR techniques, SRM proposals hold the promise of being fast and cheap.[7] However, proposals to develop the means to intervene intentionally and on a massive scale in global physical, chemical, and biological systems in order to counterbalance climate change are highly controversial. Like climate change itself, such initiatives pose uncertain risks to the ecosystem and to human health. SRM, in particular, may have significant and unpredictable negative environmental impacts. Global climate and precipitation patterns could change (affecting agricultural practices, for instance), and incoming light would be more diffuse, altering plant productivity and ecosystems.[8]

[4] The Royal Society, *Geoengineering the Climate: Science, Governance and Uncertainty* (2009) 17–18.

[5] The term 'geoengineering' is more current; however, the term 'climate engineering' is more accurate and avoids confusion with geoengineering in the context of civil engineering.

[6] MK McNutt, W Abdalati, K Caldeira et al, *Climate Intervention: Carbon Dioxide Removal and Reliable Sequestration* (National Academies Press 2015); MK McNutt, W Abdalati, K Caldeira et al, *Climate Intervention: Reflecting Sunlight to Cool Earth* (National Academies Press 2015).

[7] See, eg, J Grolle, 'Cheap But Imperfect: Can Geoengineering Slow Climate Change?', *Spiegel Online* (20 November 2013) <http://www.spiegel.de/international/world/scientist-david-keith-on-slowing-global-warming-with-geoengineering-a-934359.html> accessed 10 January 2016.

[8] Intergovernmental Panel on Climate Change (IPCC), 'Summary for Policymakers' in RK Pachauri and LA Meyer (eds), *Climate Change 2014: Synthesis Report* (IPCC 2015); KN Scott, 'International Law in the Anthropocene: Responding to the Geoengineering Challenge' (2013) 34 *Michigan Journal of International Law* 309.

These examples serve to illustrate that, with the rise of technology-driven regulatory options, in the future, regulators will increasingly be confronted with complex risk/risk trade-off situations in their quest to address potentially catastrophic climate change effectively. In essence, the risk of inaction or ineffective action must be weighed against the risk of resorting to increasingly tempting, and arguably effective, (technological) responses to mitigate or adapt to the effects of climate change. It is most unlikely that any single principle (legal, scientific, political, or ethical) can offer solid, let alone incontestable guidance, as to how to make such hard choices. Indeed, although this problem has been identified in risk regulation literature (often as part of a wider argument against the use of the precautionary principle), little attention has been attributed to the complexities of risk/risk trade-offs in the climate change context. Importantly, the role of the precautionary principle—a core principle of EU environmental policy and risk regulation—in the risk/risk arena remains to be largely clarified.[9]

Precaution is a tool to deal with uncertain risks without dictating outcomes. Although it is commonly associated with a negative regulatory tilt (banning or constraining certain risky products, activities, substances, or technologies), it can also serve to warrant and, according to some, mandate the use of, for example, a new technology or substance in order to reduce risks.[10] The impact of precaution when technologies are deployed directly to alter the atmosphere (to slow down or reverse climate change) or the living environment (to design in capabilities to withstand the effects of climate change) is hence, a priori, neutral; it may both incentivize and discourage the deployment of any given technology. Consequently, the question arises whether precaution is intrinsically incapable of playing a constructive role in dealing with risk/risk trade-offs that characterize regulatory challenges that inevitably arise in dealing with potential ecological catastrophes such as climate change, or whether it can also serve a useful purpose in those (futuristic) settings.

11.2 Risk/Risk Trade-Offs and Alternative Climate Solutions

In order to comprehend the role of the precautionary principle in risk/risk trade-offs, it is necessary to understand the risks posed by climate change and potential responses to it. Since the Industrial Revolution, atmospheric concentrations of GHG emissions

[9] See, however, JD Graham and JB Wiener, *Risk vs Risk Tradeoffs in Protecting Health and the Environment* (Harvard University Press 1997). This book provided the first systematic effort to explore the problem of 'risk/risk trade-offs' in risk regulation in the United States. On precaution applied in a climate change context, see R Rayfuse, 'Precaution and Climate Change: What Role for the Precautionary Principle in Addressing Global Warming' in A Proelss (ed), *Protecting the Environment for Future Generations—Principles and Actors in International Environmental Law* (Erich Schmidt Verlag 2017); H Grassel and B Metz, 'Climate Change: Science and the Precautionary Principle' in European Environment Agency, *Late Lessons from Early Warnings: Science, Precaution, Innovation*, Report No 1/2013, Chapter 14.

[10] See, eg, A Trouwborst, *Precautionary Rights and Duties* (Brill 2006). Trouwborst concludes that precaution can be a source of duties for states to act, although he does not enter into the debate what this could imply in a specific context; JL Reynolds and FM Fleurke, 'Climate Engineering Research: A Precautionary Response to Climate Change?' (2013) 2 *Carbon and Climate Law Review* 101, 106.

have risen at an unprecedented rate, and emissions continue to grow. Both temperature and precipitation figures are increasing. There is now extensive evidence confirming that anthropogenic global climate change is occurring[11] and that climate change is accelerating. Because climate change effects manifest themselves later than the emissions that cause them, there remains substantial uncertainty about their future impacts. Thus, although the precise ramifications of climate change are impossible to predict, some effects are already observable and certain future impacts are no longer controversial. For example, for species that are already threatened with unprecedented rates of extinction, climate change forms an exacerbating factor.[12] The economic annual cost of climate change is estimated at between one per cent and twenty per cent of global economic activity.[13] Food production and water resources are increasingly disrupted, and sea levels are rising, causing low-lying coastal areas to become inundated. Infectious diseases, such as malaria,[14] extreme weather events, and climate migration are likely to occur on a massive scale, hitting especially the poorest populations in the Global South. Yet, the precise scale of these future impacts on humans and their distribution at a global, regional, or local level remain fundamentally uncertain.[15]

Despite the Paris Agreement, international attempts to keep global warming at a level below 2°C relative to pre-industrial times lack robustness, whilst the financing of adaptation measures appears equally inadequate.[16] Models that extrapolate current trends predict that global warming could reach 4°C by 2100, which is widely believed would result in catastrophic impacts across the globe.[17] Because climate change shows no sign of slowing down and ecological catastrophe is, thus, increasingly feared, the prospect of resorting to controversial new regulatory options that may radically improve on the performance of the current regulatory regime is becoming both more attractive and more compelling.[18]

[11] See IPCC, *Climate Change 2013: The Physical Science Basis* (7 June 2013), TS 2.1. It discusses advancements in scientists' understanding of climate change and its own position.

[12] IPCC, 'Summary for Policymakers', *Climate Change 2014* (n 8) 6–16.

[13] N Stern, *The Economics of Climate Change: The Stern Review* (CUP 2006). See also RSJ Tol, 'The Economic Effects of Climate Change' (2009) 23 *Journal of Economic Perspectives* 29.

[14] According to a recent World Bank report, a warming of 2–3°C will put an additional 150 million people at risk for malaria. See The World Bank, *Shockwaves, Managing the Impact of Climate Change on Poverty* (Washington 2015). In response, research is now focusing on genetically modified malaria mosquitoes. See VM Ganz, N Jasinskiene, O Tatarenkova et al, 'Highly Efficient Cas9-Mediated Gene Drive for Population Modification of the Malaria Vector Mosquito *Anopheles stephensi*' (2015) *112 Proceedings of the National Academy of Sciences* E6736–E6743. See also, in particular, the Science and Technology Select Committee, *Genetically Modified Insects* (HL 2015-16, 68-I).

[15] IPCC, 'Summary for Policymakers', *Climate Change 2014* (n 8) 2; AE Camacho, 'Adapting Governance to Climate Change: Managing Uncertainty Through a Learning Infrastructure' (2009) 59 *Emory Law Journal* 1, 10.

[16] CB Field, VR Barros, DJ Dokken et al, *Climate Change 2014 Impacts, Adaptation, and Vulnerability Part A: Global and Sectoral Aspects* (CUP 2014); International Energy Agency, *World Energy Outlook 2015* (International Energy Agency 2015).

[17] RA Betts, M Collins, DL Hemming et al, 'When Could Global Warming Reach 4°C? (2011) 369 *Philosophical Transactions of the Royal Society A: Mathematical, Physical and Engineering Sciences* 67.

[18] H Somsen, 'When Regulators Mean Business: Regulation in the Shadow of Environmental Armageddon' (2011) 40 *Rechtsfilosofie en Rechtstheorie* 47–57. Webster dictionary defines catastrophe as 'a momentous tragic usually sudden event marked by effects ranging from extreme misfortune to utter overthrow or ruin'.

Faced with regulatory ineffectiveness, regulatory scholarship has suggested avenues to expand the regulatory toolbox beyond traditional command-and-control regulation.[19] This has resulted in the development of self-regulatory and market instruments, such as the European Emissions Trading System, that complement and sometimes replace more traditional instruments. Most recently, and in response to increasingly irrefutable evidence of possible ecological catastrophe in the absence of effective action, Somsen has advocated a renaissance of environmental law in which technologies become the regulatory modality of choice. He argues that regulators who have effectiveness as their primary concern must consider travelling down that final avenue; the use of environmental technologies that secure realization of public environmental policy goals, by designing out any room for non-compliance. As Somsen puts it, '[a]s scientific certainty increasingly exposes the bankruptcy of the status quo, rational regulators will give the benefit of the doubt to new technologies promising great ecological gains'.[20] Although Somsen's argument is an intricate one, in his vision technologies should be considered: (i) to put in place Panoptic global surveillance; (ii) to 'dictate' human behaviour in environmentally sustainable ways; and (iii) to intentionally re-engineer the living and non-living environment in ways that serve human and ecological imperatives.[21]

More recent technological interventions, of which CE techniques would be an example, often promise substantial environmental gains.[22] However, they are often also accompanied by uncertain risks which, depending on the technological intervention considered, may themselves be of potentially catastrophic proportions, even at the field-testing phase. To date, CE options, of which, in particular, SRM could be risky, remain untested and could, according to the IPCC, produce numerous uncertain risks and side effects of significant magnitude.[23]

A risk/risk trade-off, meaning a change in the portfolio of risks that occur when a countervailing risk is generated (knowingly or inadvertently) by an intervention to reduce the target risk, is thus inevitable.[24] When one type of adverse risk is replaced by another adverse risk in the same target population we speak of 'risk substitution'.[25] The dilemma for regulators is that they must choose between a rock and a hard place, at least in all those cases where risks must be addressed as a matter of urgency regardless of the fact that responses result in uncertain risks.[26] The climate problem is increasingly perceived as constituting precisely such a challenge; the urgency of the problem is hardly in dispute and calls for an immediate and decisive

[19] N Gunningham, P Grabosky, and D Sinclair, *Smart Regulation* (Clarendon Press 1998).

[20] Somsen, 'When Regulators Mean Business' (n 18).

[21] See H Somsen, 'From Improvement Towards Enhancement: A Regenesis of Environmental Law at the Dawn of the Anthropocene', *SSRN* (December 2015) <http://papers.ssrn.com/sol3/papers.cfm?abstract_id=2705450> accessed 10 January 2016.

[22] DW Keith, 'Why Capture CO_2 from the Atmosphere?' (2009) 325 *Science* 1654; DW Keith, *A Case for Climate Engineering* (MIT Press 2013).

[23] IPCC, 'Summary for Policymakers', *Climate Change 2014* (n 8) 25; K Caldeira and KL Ricke, Prudence on Solar Climate Engineering (2013) 3(100) *Nature* 941.

[24] Graham and Wiener, *Risk vs. Risk Tradeoffs* (n 9), 23.

[25] ibid. [26] RA Posner, *Catastrophe: Risk and Response* (OUP 2004).

response. As argued above, if effectiveness becomes of primary importance, that response more likely than not will be technology-driven, notwithstanding its associated uncertain risks. Acclaimed climatologist Jason Box recently expressed this sentiment in no uncertain terms:

> we need an aggressive atmospheric decarbonisation program. We have been too long on a trajectory pointed at an unmanageable climate calamity; runaway climate heating.[27]

To be sure, the task at hand is particularly complex, especially where both the potential benefits and the potential risks remain uncertain as a result of scientific uncertainty or scientific ignorance, and where the scale of both the problem and the response is global. This conjures up a distinctly unsettling picture in which, whatever course of action we decide to pursue in our fight against anthropogenic climate change, there appears no 'right' option or, more disturbing still, even a 'best' option.

Climate change thereby is a classic example of a 'wicked problem' which, by definition, cannot be 'solved', in the sense that it is possible to find solutions that have no serious negative implications.[28] As Grint puts it: 'we cannot solve wicked problems because we cannot know what to do'.[29] This is not merely, or even primarily, because we are dealing with scientific uncertainty, ambiguity, or ignorance (where, as will be discussed below, precaution can provide useful procedural guidance), but because such problems also concern complex adaptive systems (complexity), that are in part socially constructed (ie, what is a 'normal' summer/winter?) and because regulatory modalities themselves also offer fertile ground for contestation. In short, wicked problems score high on two axes: the first is of a scientific nature and consists of uncertainty/complexity; the second is normative and is represented by value conflicts/controversial response strategies.[30]

This is not to say, however, that the precautionary principle has no valuable role to play in risk/risk trade-off situations or wicked problems. On the contrary, precaution is a principle that serves to engage scientific uncertainty, precisely by allowing alternative sources of rationality to come to play a role in risk management, and is hence of particular relevance in breaking the risk/risk deadlock. The following sections address precisely how the precautionary principle plays that role.

[27] See, eg, 'Climatologist Says Arctic Carbon Release Could Mean "We're Fucked"', *IFLScience!* (4 August 2014) <http://www.iflscience.com/environment/climatologist-arctic-carbon-release-could-mean-%E2%80%9Cwere-fucked%E2%80%9D> accessed 10 January 2016.

[28] See, eg, RJ Lazarus, 'Super Wicked Problems and Climate Change: Restraining the Present to Liberate the Future' (2009) 94(5) *Cornell Law Review* 101.

[29] K Grint, 'Wicked Problems and Clumsy Solutions: The Role of Leadership' in S Brook and K Grint (eds), *The New Public Leadership Challenge* (Palgrave Macmillan 2010) 170.

[30] RF Durant and JS Legge, '"Wicked Problems", Public Policy, and Administrative Theory: Lessons from the GM Food Regulatory Arena' (2006) 38 *Administration and Society* 309–334. SS Batie and DB Schweickhardt, 'Societal Concerns as Wicked Problems: The Case of Trade Liberalization', *Policy Responses to Societal Concerns in Food and Agriculture. Proceedings of an OECD Workshop* (2–3 November, Paris); BJ Head and J Alford, 'Wicked Problems: Implications for Public Policy and Management' (2015) 47 *Administration & Society* 711–39.

11.3 Precaution

The precautionary principle was born out of unease about the functioning of the law. The principle is not an articulation of a pillar of the legal system, but rather must be seen as an adjustment to the existing legal system.[31] Law—with its primary function to contribute to societal stability, certainty, and predictability—was incapable of engaging with cases of imminent risks or threats for which the scientific bases remain uncertain.[32] Risk, in this regard, is a function of the probability of an adverse environmental or public health effect and the severity of that effect consequential to a hazard. Risk is mostly understood as a chance of exposure to a specified danger as an unfortunate consequence of engaging in an activity or action. At the political level, the concept of risk—or better, the demand for safety—has become a predominant paradigm for current debates and policy. Beck has elaborated this idea in his seminal *Risk Society*, in which he claims that the conflict of contemporary times does not, as in industrial society, concern the distribution of societal 'goods', but relates to the distribution of the 'bads' produced by modern risks.[33] De Sadeleer articulates three differences between post-industrialized environmental risks and earlier types of risks. First, post-industrial risks are often global and concern an accumulation of ecological impacts. Second, post-industrialized risks may give rise to damage outside the realm of commerce. Third, such risks are permeated with scientific uncertainty or even ignorance, making it difficult to assess their impact on the environment and human health.[34]

Risk assessment itself is a tricky business. In fact, the dichotomy between risks (probability x effect = calculated harm) and uncertain risks (unknown probability or unknown effect) is neither particularly absolute nor profound. Harremoës et al, for example, have shown that certainty about risks ultimately can only become really apparent after harm is identified.[35] Van Asselt et al therefore find the distinction between risk and uncertainty confusing, even damaging, and prefer the term 'uncertain risk'. The notion of uncertain risks indicates a particular kind of situation that matters to decision-making, in which there are suspicions of hazard, although scientific or historical evidence is lacking.[36] They have noted that uncertain hazards such as waste disposal or effects of climate change are still talked about in terms of risk by experts, politicians, and the public.[37]

[31] FM Fleurke, *Unpacking Precaution: A Study on the Application of the Precautionary Principle in Europe* (Edward Elgar forthcoming); Reynolds and Fleurke, 'Climate Engineering Research' (n 10) 101.

[32] N de Sadeleer, *Environmental Principles. From Political Slogans to Legal Rules* (OUP 2002), 3.

[33] U Beck, *Risk Society: Towards a New Modernity* (Sage 1992).

[34] De Sadeleer, *Environmental Principles* (n 32).

[35] P Harremoës, D Gee, M MacGarvin et al, *The Precautionary Principle in the 20th Century: Late Lessons from Early Warnings* (Earthscan 2002). In the collection, fourteen case studies on different risks were conducted. The studies included risks from benzene, radiation, chemical contamination of lakes, and hormones as growth promoters. Originally published as: European Environment Agency, *Late Lessons from Early Warnings: The Precautionary Principle 1996–2000*, Report No 22 (EEA 2002). See also H Grassl and B Metz, 'Climate Change: Science and the Precautionary Principle' in European Environment Agency, *Late Lessons from Early Warnings: Science, Precaution, Innovation*, Report No 1/2013 (EEA 2013) 337.

[36] Grassl and Metz, ibid, 363.

[37] M van Asselt, E Vos, and B Rooijackers, 'Science, Knowledge and Uncertainty in EU Risk Regulation' in M Everson and E Vos (eds), *Uncertain Risks Regulated* (Routledge-Cavendish 2009).

Uncertain risks are problematic because they imply that science cannot deliver a sufficiently solid basis for regulatory action. Scientific uncertainty characterizes a situation in which possible outcomes are known, but the likelihood of those outcomes remains uncertain.[38] Scientific uncertainty is to be distinguished from scientific ignorance, which involves situations in which both the outcome and the likelihood of occurrence are uncertain. Scientific uncertainty may result from, for example, the variable chosen, the measurements made, the samples drawn, the models used, the causal relationship employed, the novelty of the technology or activity. Scientific uncertainty may also arise from a controversy about existing data, or the lack of relevant data.[39] Uncertainty may relate to both quantitative and qualitative elements of the analysis.[40] In fact, scientific certainty might never be achieved in a number of areas, including climate change. Given these difficulties, the precautionary principle has developed as a tool to address the disconnection between law and contemporary technological modernity.[41]

The rise of the precautionary principle has provoked an intense debate between its proponents and opponents, both within and outside academia.[42] Yet at its core precaution is a common-sense principle; look before you leap. The need for precaution is therefore not controversial, although the precise reach of the principle undeniably is. Nevertheless, the importance of the precautionary principle is to bring environmental and public health interests to the fore, without determining any prioritization of those issues.[43] It is thus obvious that the precautionary principle should offer more than just soft guidance if it is to engage effectively with uncertain risks. It is precisely the concrete impact of precaution in any given concrete case that lies at the heart of the controversy.[44]

Although numerous articulations of the precautionary principle exist, Principle 15 of the Rio Declaration is often regarded as offering its most generally accepted formulation:

> In order to protect the environment, the precautionary approach shall be widely used by States according to their capabilities. Where there are threats of serious or irreversible damage, lack of full scientific certainty shall not be used as a reason for postponing cost-effective measures to prevent environmental degradation.[45]

Conceived in this way, the precautionary principle may be perceived to be a regulatory principle, in the sense that it lowers barriers for taking regulatory action. It triggers the

[38] See F Knight, *Risk, Uncertainty and Profit* (Houghton Mifflin 1921).

[39] European Commission, Communication COM (2000)1, 14.

[40] R von Schomberg, 'The Precautionary Principle and Its Normative Challenges' in E Fisher et al (eds), *Implementing the Precautionary Principle: Perspectives and Prospects* (Edward Elgar 2006) 19–42.

[41] A Arcuri, 'Reconstructing Precaution, Deconstructing Misconceptions' (2007) 3 *Ethics and International Affairs* 359–379.

[42] See for an excellent overview of this debate, ibid.

[43] In international law, the adoption of precaution in the Rio Declaration and its incorporation in the Convention on Biological Diversity and the UN Convention on Climate Change signalled its widespread acceptance as a soft law norm. The principle will normally be embedded in a concrete regulatory context and not operate in a vacuum.

[44] See, eg, GE Marchant and KL Mossman, *Arbitrary and Capricious. The Precautionary Principle in the European Courts* (International Policy Press 2005) 8.

[45] United Nations Conference on Environment and Development, 'Declaration of the United Nations Conference on Environment and Development' (3–4 June 1992) A/CONF.151/26 (Vol I) (Rio Declaration), Principle 15.

competence to act which, were it not for precaution, would remain dormant. Thus, where full scientific certainty about risk would normally be necessary to prevent or restrict certain activities, precaution operates to lower this threshold so that regulatory action can be taken to the extent that such action is proportional relative to its broadly understood costs. To be sure, application of the precautionary principle may seriously hamper industrial activities (for instance, the creation of genetically modified products), give rise to financial burdens, and affect international trade.

Moreover, not only is the threshold of proof lowered as a result of precaution, the burden of proof is also often apportioned to the actor (private or public) proposing the activity giving rise to the potential risk.[46] This constitutes a fundamental departure from traditional liberal principles that seek to ensure that public intervention is permitted only to avert proven risk of harm.[47]

This enabling function of precaution is operationalized through one or more of the constitutive elements of the precautionary principle:[48] 'serious or irreversible harm' should be recognized; scientific uncertainty should be acknowledged; responsibilities of regulatees to prove safety are differently apportioned; public participation and deliberation is to be stimulated; alternative options are to be considered; the principle of proportionality should be respected; and environmental performance should be monitored to ensure the provisional nature of measures. It is through the totality of these combined and individual elements that precaution impacts multiple domains of environmental and human health law.

The first constitutive element, the qualitative threshold of 'serious or irreversible harm' is of fundamental importance, with the definition of what is considered 'serious' or 'irreversible' being further specified in environmental treaties or legislation decided at the political level. Indeed, treaties or secondary legislation will always contain some *qualitative* benchmark for determining what, in different contexts, should be understood as 'serious or irreversible', and which is then usually *quantitatively* operationalized in the form of various types of standards. The precautionary principle implies that scientific uncertainty does not rule out regulatory action to safeguard such qualitative standards.

In the context of climate change, Article 3(3) of the United Nations Framework Convention for Climate Change (UNFCCC)[49] acknowledges precaution as follows:

> The Parties should take precautionary measures to anticipate, prevent or minimize the causes of climate change and mitigate its adverse effects. Where there are threats of serious

[46] An example of this shift is REACH, a Regulation of the European Union, adopted to improve the protection of human health and the environment from the risks that can be posed by chemicals. REACH places the burden of proof on companies. To comply with the regulation, companies must identify and manage the risks linked to the substances they manufacture and market in the European Union. They have to demonstrate to ECHA how the substance can be safely used.

[47] De Sadeleer, *Environmental Principles* (n 32).

[48] Fleurke, *Unpacking Precaution*(n 31) 34 et seq; Ch Vlek, 'A Precautionary-Principles Approach Towards Uncertain Risks: Review and Decision-Theoretic Elaboration' (2002) 2 *Erasmus Law Review* 71–118; FM Fleurke, 'Future Prospects for Climate Engineering Within the EU Legal Order' (2016) 1 *European Journal of Risk Regulation* 60–74.

[49] United Nations Framework Convention on Climate Change (adopted 9 May 1992, entered into force 21 March 1994) 1771 UNTS 107, art 3.3.

or irreversible damage, lack of full scientific certainty should not be used as a reason for postponing such measures taking into account that policies and measures to deal with climate change should be cost-effective so as to ensure global benefits at the lowest possible cost....

Hence, the qualitative standard to take precautionary measures in the context of climate change is to 'prevent or minimize the causes of climate change and mitigate its adverse effects'. Deployment of environmental technologies to combat climate change could therefore fall under the scope of the UNFCCC if they effectively mitigate adverse effects, are cost effective, and ensure global benefits. In addition, Article 3(3) UNFCCC calls for precautionary measures to be cost-effective. Certainly, technologies (eg, CE technologies) can be considered as 'measures'. In addition, CE, when compared to the alternative of emission reduction, could possibly be cost effective, as acknowledged even by its adversaries.[50]

The question whether technological interventions to reverse climate change will be of 'global benefit' or instead further burden the Global South is more difficult to answer. However, it would surely be odd if we were to insist on global uniformity of benefits of climate action when the adverse effects of inaction or ineffective action are distributed highly unevenly, hitting the Global South disproportionally severely.

Finally, the UNFCCC calls for the development and diffusion of technology and research 'related to the climate system and intended to further the understanding and to reduce or eliminate the remaining uncertainties regarding the causes, effects, magnitude and timing of climate change and the economic and social consequences of various response strategies'.[51] Although it is not specified which technologies and what research are called for, it may be taken as at a minimum not excluding CE research (as opposed to deployment) and the proliferation of the results of such research.

The results of the Paris Agreement are relevant in this regard. At its heart is the commitment to keep the increase in global average temperature to below 2°C, and ideally even to 1.5°C. Considering the 'long tail' problem of climate change, this goal seems to be achievable only through the deployment of negative emission technologies that remove carbon dioxide from the atmosphere.[52] Many of these technologies give rise to classic risk/risk trade-off problems, as they are untested and are potentially risky when implemented on a large scale.

Interestingly, Article 4 of the Paris Agreement seems to endorse deployment of negative emission technologies by stating that 'in order to achieve the long-term temperature goal set out in Article 2 of the Paris Agreement, Parties aim to reach global peaking of greenhouse gas (GHG) emissions as soon as possible, recognizing that peaking will take longer for developing country Parties'. These rapid reductions

[50] See, eg, 'Cheap But Imperfect' (n 7).

[51] UNFCC, arts 4.1(g) and (h).

[52] CDR technologies such as carbon capture and storage or ocean fertilization. On the problem of long time lag of climate change, see E Biber, 'The Sting of the Long Tail: Climate Change, Backlash and the Problem of Delayed Harm' UC Berkeley Public Law Research Paper No 1292529 (1 November 2008) <http://ssrn.com/abstract=1292529> accessed 10 January 2016; JL Reynolds, 'The Regulation of Climate Engineering' (2011) 3 *Law, Innovation and Technology* 113–36.

should be undertaken in accordance with best available science, 'so as to achieve a balance between anthropogenic emissions by sources and removals by sinks of greenhouse gases in the second half of this century'. Article 5 of the Paris Agreement furthermore asserts that 'Parties should take action to conserve and enhance, as appropriate, sinks and reservoirs of greenhouse gases.' As such, decarbonization programs that contribute to keeping global average temperature increases under control are also compatible with the Paris Agreement.

11.4 Precaution and Risk/Risk Trade-Offs

In the context of climate change, precaution may simultaneously direct towards the use and the prohibition of climate technologies, including CE and biotechnology, since both climate change and its responses are surrounded by uncertain risks for the environment and human health.

For this reason, critics have claimed that precautionary regulation is incoherent and creates potential for risk/risk trade-offs, where one type of risk will increase as a result of attempts to manage others.[53] For example, banning a new chemical on account of its potential adverse effects may perpetuate more serious toxicity effects caused by the substitute old chemical.[54] Sunstein explains:

> There is an obvious difficulty with the precautionary principle: both regulation and non-regulation will often give rise to risks; if so, the principle would seem to be paralyzing, forbidding stringent regulation, inaction, and everything in between. Consider, for example, the case of genetic engineering in food. The precautionary principle might seem to call for stringent regulation of genetic engineering, on the theory that this technology contains at least some risk of causing ecological harm. But such regulation would also create risks of adverse effects, simply because genetic engineering holds out a prospect of producing ecological and health benefits. The precautionary principle would seem both to require and forbid stringent regulation of genetic engineering. The same can be said for many activities and processes, such as nuclear power and non-therapeutic cloning, simply because risks are on all sides of the situation.[55]

Often, new products and activities are regarded as more dangerous than existing ones. In debates over the use of new environmental technologies, precaution is often invoked. Research has demonstrated a bias in risk perception when thinking about new technologies. In this respect, Somsen argues that the presumption of maintaining the status quo is without empirical foundation, as 'we have as little

[53] DA Farber, 'Probabilities Behaving Badly: Complexity Theory and Environmental Uncertainty' (2003) 37 *UC Davis Law Review* 145, 169.

[54] FM Fleurke and H Somsen, 'Precautionary Regulation of Chemical Risk: How REACH Confronts the Regulatory Challenges of Scale, Uncertainty, Complexity and Innovation' (2011) 48(2) *Common Market Law Review* 357–93.

[55] CR Sunstein, 'Probability Neglect: Emotions, Worst Cases, and Law' (2002) 112 *Yale Law Journal* 61, 93. For a reply to Sunstein, see GN Mandel and J Thuo Gathii, 'Cost-Benefit Analyis versus the Precautionary Principle: Beyond Cass Sunstein's Laws of Fear' (2006) *The University of Illinois Law Review* 1036.

notion of how dangerous a future without change will be, as we understand risks of introducing new technologies'.[56] Farber finds that if the effects of regulation are also uncertain and present unforeseen risks to health and environment, then the precautionary principle seems to turn against itself, suggesting that we should not proceed with environmental regulation until we can pin down the effects of the precautionary action.[57] Hartzell-Nichols takes this a step further, and argues in the context of CE that if new, uncertain, potentially catastrophic risks are deliberately created, then CE techniques should be banned.[58] However, without a comparative assessment this approach is a recipe for paralysis.

It is striking that almost no definition of the precautionary principle pays attention to the problem of risk/risk trade-offs. Legislation or policy that implements the precautionary principle in a specific context ideally should include a provision to take risk/risk trade-offs into account, for example, in the form of a substitution clause that directs regulators to undertake comparisons.[59] This implies that once decision-makers have established that the precautionary principle is applicable, they have to decide what measures to adopt in accordance with the procedural aspects of precaution. For this, they must identify a wide range of options and examine available evidence about exposures, uncertainties, and costs associated with each alternative to address risks.[60] Identifying these options and comparing them with the technology in use amounts to what Ashford has termed technology options analysis (TOA).[61] In TOA, decision-makers must consider the ends and means of a policy proposal, and assess how the end can be achieved in a manner most consistent with sustainability, taking into account the principle of proportionality, and conducting a broad cost–benefit analysis. What is particularly interesting about TOA is that, unlike traditional technological risk assessment, it does not require quantification of all variables. Instead, a comparative assessment is conducted for different technologies to enquire if any one particular technology scores better on environmental or public health effects. In this way, risk assessment can be used to analyse trade-offs. Ashford claims that this type of assessment is 'less likely to be sensitive to initial assumptions than, for example, cost–benefit analysis, and would enable industry and government to identify more creative cost-effective solutions'.[62] If a superior

[56] Somsen, 'When Regulators Mean Business' (n 18) 223; P Slovic, 'Perception of Risk' (1987) 236 *Science*, 280 et seq.; P Slovic and EU Weber, 'Perception of Risk Posed by Extreme Events' in J Applegate et al (eds) *Regulation of Toxic Substances and Hazardous Waste* (2nd edn, Foundation Press 2011) <http://ssrn.com/abstract=2293086> accessed 22 November 2016.

[57] D Farber, *Eco Pragmatism—Making Sensible Environmental Decisions in an Uncertain World* (The University of Chicago Press Books 1999) 168.

[58] L Hartzell-Nichols, 'Precaution and Solar Radiation Management' (2012) 15 *Ethics, Policy and Environment* 158, 166.

[59] Reynolds and Fleurke, 'Climate Engineering Research' (n 10) 110.

[60] JA Tickner, 'Precautionary Assessment: A Framework for Integrating Science, Uncertainty and Preventive Public Policy' in JA Tickner (ed), *Precaution: Environmental Science and Preventive Public Policy* (Island Press 2003) 269.

[61] NA Ashford, 'Implementing the Precautionary Principle: Incorporating Science, Technology, Fairness and Accountability in Environmental, Health and Safety Decisions' (2005) 5 *International Journal of Risk Assessment and Management* 112, 118; A Ely, P van Zwanenberg, and A Stirling, 'Broadening Out and Opening Up Technology Assessment: Approaches to Enhance International Development, Co-ordination and Democratisation' (2014) 43 *Research Policy* 505.

[62] Ashford, ibid.

technology is identified, industry has an incentive to adopt that technology out of economic self-interest, or even merely in order to avoid liability. In brief, precaution becomes a process that seeks to identify early and innovative alternatives to conventional regulatory solutions.

Concretely, this means that risks of climate change and risks of CE need to be compared with regard to their relative scientific uncertainties, complexities, and scales.[63] It does not mean that a response that attempts to minimize uncertain risks should be rejected merely because it brings new, different, uncertain risks into play. Precaution can play a constructive and procedural mediating role in this kind of weighing exercise, where it is difficult to balance potential benefits and risks because of scientific uncertainty.[64]

Accordingly, precaution not only serves a regulatory function; it also has an important organizing procedural function to deal with uncertain risks, without dictating outcomes. Although precaution is generally associated with banning certain products, activities, or technologies, in reality precautionary action takes numerous forms, and sets parameters for incremental deployment of new technologies while safeguarding an opt-out in case there are early signs of adverse risks that are deemed unacceptable.[65]

Moreover, the elements enumerated above, such as proportionality and deliberation, should be sufficient to prevent arbitrary use of precaution. In this way, Tickner claims, precaution in its broadest, most progressive construction is a means of stimulating innovation and social sustainability. Its aim is to foster democratic engagement, so that society may identify the safest alternative to meet its needs.[66]

11.5 Precaution and Catastrophic Climate Change

Posner has exposed 'the contribution technology can make to averting both natural and man-made catastrophes, including the man-made catastrophes that technology itself enables or exacerbates'.[67] Regarding CE, Bodansky has envisioned that precaution will 'be invoked frequently and loudly at the international level' and possibly will contribute to an international prohibition of climate engineering'.[68] As mentioned above, there is now scientific consensus on the certainty of grave risks of anthropogenic climate change; the IPCC reports indicate threats of catastrophe, whereas current climate policies have shown to be effective in significantly reducing these risks. Although new technologies are being developed that promise gains, these carry their own substantial potential risks, which remain highly uncertain in terms of nature and scale. In these situations, it has been

[63] Posner, *Catastrophe* (n 26); CR Sunstein, *Worst-Case Scenarios* (Harvard University Press 2007); Reynolds and Fleurke, 'Climate Engineering Research' (n 10).

[64] Fleurke, *Unpacking Precaution* (n 31); and Reynolds and Fleurke, ibid.

[65] Consider calls to develop safer and greener chemicals to substitute more harmful substances.

[66] Tickner, 'Precautionary Assessment' (n 60) 156.

[67] Posner, *Catastrophe* (n 26).

[68] D Bodansky, 'May We Engineer the Climate?' (1996) 33 *Climatic Change* 309, 312.

argued that the use of precaution is two-fold. First, as explained above, precaution as a regulatory principle allows regulators to use competences to act under uncertain circumstances. Concretely, precaution in the context of the UNFCCC allows parties to consider alternative solutions such as new environmental technologies as precautionary cost-effective measures, for the purposes of tackling the uncertain effects of climate change.[69] Second, since these technologies are accompanied by uncertain risks themselves, it gives rise to 'double' precaution; the deployment of such technologies should be preceded by a separate precautionary assessment.[70] Here the organizing function of precaution steps in. Specifically, this means that the elements noted above that constitute precaution become part of the risk assessment. Of particular importance are the principle of serious and irreversible harm, and the requirements to acknowledge uncertainties and ignorance, to apportion responsibilities to establish safety, to consider alternative options, and to ensure ongoing monitoring. As a result of applying precaution in such complex situations, a strategy that seeks to reduce risks does not necessarily have to be abandoned solely because it brings new potential risks to the fore.

This debate is not merely theoretical, even though CE initiatives are still in an early phase of their development. Precaution has already been invoked on two occasions relating to the regulation of potential risks to marine environments from CE initiatives.[71] The Conference of Parties to the Convention on Biological Diversity cited 'the precautionary approach' in a non-binding statement against CE activities.[72] In this case, a moratorium on all scientific research in coastal areas except for small-scale scientific research was adopted, although no assessment was conducted of the procedural elements stated above. This example of asserting a strong form of precaution has led van den Deale to observe that the precautionary principle has become politicized, and has served to suppress innovation for reasons that have little to do with risk.[73] A much more nuanced precautionary approach was taken by the Contracting Parties of the London Convention on the Prevention of Marine Pollution by Dumping

[69] On alternative climate solutions, see O Geden, 'Modifying the 2°C Target Climate Policy Objectives in the Contested Terrain of Scientific Policy Advice, Political Preferences, and Rising Emissions' (2013) SWP Research Paper 2013/RP05 1; A Jordan, T Rayner, H Schroeder et al, 'Going Beyond Two Degrees? The Risks and Opportunities of Alternative Options' (2013) 13(6) *Climate Policy* 751.

[70] See also E Tedsen and G Homann, 'Implementing the Precautionary Principle for Climate Engineering' (2013) 2 *Carbon and Climate Law Review* 90.

[71] See Rayfuse, 'Precaution and Climate Change' (n 9) 15–17.

[72] Conference of the Parties to the Convention on Biological Diversity, Report of the Tenth Meeting of the Conference of Parties to the Convention on Biological Diversity, Biodiversity and Climate Change, (20 January 2011) UNEP/CBD/COP/10/27. See also, eg, ETC Group, 'The ABCs of Ensuring Precaution on Geoengineering: A Briefing for Delegates to Cbd Cop11' (5 October 2012) <http://www.etcgroup.org/content/abcs-ensuring-precaution-geoengineering> accessed 10 January 2016.

[73] See W van den Daele, 'Legal Framework and Political Strategy in Dealing with the Risks of New Technology: The Two Faces of the Precautionary Principle' in H Somsen, *The Regulatory Challenge of Biotechnology: Human Genetics, Food and Patents* (Edward Elgar 2007) 120.

of Wastes and Other Matter and its London Protocol.[74] As a response to a private company that intended to conduct field experiments, the contracting parties started to develop a non-binding regulatory framework for ocean fertilization in 2008.[75] The parties decided that ocean fertilization indeed falls within the scope of the London Convention and London Protocol and that ocean fertilization activities other than legitimate scientific research should not be allowed.[76] Interestingly, in a 2010 decision, a precautionary Assessment Framework was established.[77] According to this framework an environmental risk assessment needs to be conducted of exposure effects, risk characterization, and risk management.[78] It is explicitly stated that the risk management decision on the proposal should be based on a precautionary approach.[79] In addition, the researching party is to notify potentially affected countries, and is under an obligation to monitor and report the results of the impacts of the field experiment to the Secretariat, and information from these reports can provide the basis for informing and improving future decision-making.[80] In 2013, the Parties to the London Protocol approved an amendment to the London Protocol prohibiting all marine geoengineering activities listed in an accompanying annex, except for legitimate scientific research activities which require a permit issued by national authorities in accordance with the now mandatory Assessment Framework.[81] This Assessment Framework also calls for a detailed description of the proposed

[74] Convention on the Prevention of Marine Pollution by Dumping of Wastes and Other Matter (adopted 13 November 1972, entered into force 30 August 1975) 1046 UNTS 120, art I (London Convention). This article provides the terms of the London Convention, requiring states to prevent pollution of the sea caused by dumping. See also Protocol to the Convention on the Prevention of Marine Pollution by Dumping of Wastes and Other Matter (adopted 7 November 1996, entered into force 24 March 2006), 2006 ATS 11, art 3.4.

[75] International Maritime Organization (IMO), Report of the Thirty-First Meeting of the Scientific Group of the London Convention and the Second Meeting of the Scientific Group of the London Protocol (7 July 2007) Doc LC/SG 31/16; IMO, Report of the Thirtieth Consultative Meeting and the Third Meeting of Contracting Parties, Resolution LC–LP.1 (2008) on the Regulation of Ocean Fertilization (9 December 2008) Doc LC 10/16, Annex 6, Preamble 3.

[76] IMO, Report of the Thirtieth Consultative Meeting, ibid, 8.

[77] IMO, Report of the Thirty-Second Consultative Meeting and the Fifth Meeting of Contracting Parties, Assessment Framework for Scientific Research Involving Ocean Fertilization § 1 (14 October 2012) Doc LC 32/13/Annex 6.

[78] ibid, para 3. [79] ibid, paras 1.3, 2.6, and 4.3.

[80] ibid, paras 5.1–5.2.

[81] International Maritime Organisation, Report of the Thirty-Fifth Consultative Meeting and the Eighth Meeting of Contracting Parties, Resolution LP.4(8) on the Amendment to the London Protocol to Regulate the Placement of Matter for Ocean Fertilization and Other Marine Geoengineering Activities (adopted on 18 October 2013) (21 October 2013) Doc LC 35/15, Annex 4. This resolution adopted an amendment to the London Protocol to regulate marine geoengineering. Marine geoengineering is defined here as a deliberate intervention in the marine environment to manipulate natural processes, including to counteract anthropogenic climate change and/or its impacts, and that has the potential to result in deleterious effects, especially where those effects may be widespread, long lasting, or severe. This includes SRM affecting the sea. For background information, see R Rayfuse and R Warner, 'Climate Change Mitigation Activities in the Ocean: Regulatory Frameworks and Implications', in C Schofield and R Warner, *Climate Change and the Oceans: Gauging the Legal and Policy Currents in the Asia Pacific Region* (Edward Elgar 2012) 234; J Reynolds, 'Climate Engineering Field Research: The Favorable Setting of International Environmental Law' (2014) 5(2) *Washington and Lee Journal of Energy, Climate, and the Environment* 417, 459 et seq.

activity, notification of potentially affected countries and relevant regional intergovernmental agreements and arrangements, and a consultation plan.[82] Expert advice and scientific peer review is to be sought in the assessment process and made public within a specified timeframe. The assessment should also include its expected effects on the site, the proposed risk management and monitoring means, the financial resources available, the availability of other methods, the environmental impact, and the expected benefits. As has been pointed out by Rayfuse, this Assessment Framework shows a clear operationalization of precaution when regulating new activities where considerable uncertainty exists as to the potential environmental effects of that activity.[83]

As a procedural and organizing tool, precaution is indeed a rational and normatively defensible instrument to engage uncertain risk. In such settings of scientific uncertainty, precaution is rational because it allows the competing sources of rationality that come to claim authority to play roles in risk analyses. Precaution is also normatively defensible because it empowers lay citizens to pronounce on the political prioritization of different types of risk, as scientific assessment cannot provide the basis for decision-making.

Ultimately, however, if we recognize climate change as a wicked problem, it becomes immediately obvious that the precautionary principle cannot possibly be thought of as a suitable tool to engage all these challenges simultaneously, since there are multiple (political) issues at stake that go beyond a classic risk/risk trade-off dilemma.[84] The precautionary principle has nothing to say about what ultimately constitutes a desirable climate or about a fair sharing of abatement costs. Nor can anybody or anything else provide such final guidance.

It is therefore of utmost importance to disentangle the challenges of scientific uncertainty, complexity, value conflicts, and controversies about regulatory responses themselves.[85] It is these four elements, each of which invite at times overlapping but still qualitatively distinct approaches, that make up the climate change challenge. Even if, for the sake of argument, we were to reduce climate change to a challenge relating to scientific uncertainty, and presuming we opted for a precautionary approach to the problem, we would still have to deal with insolvable normative questions (eg, about distribution and responsibility) that arise when we turn our attention to the appropriate regulatory response. Somsen's proposals to intentionally re-engineer the climate in ways that serve human and ecological imperatives are not controversial because he is adamant that firm regulatory action should

[82] As it currently stands, ocean fertilization is the only marine geoengineering activity listed in the Annex for which a permit is required when it concerns legitimate scientific research.

[83] Rayfuse, 'Precaution and Climate Change' (n 9) 17.

[84] See, eg, JB Horton and J Reynolds, 'The International Politics of Climate Engineering: A Review and Prospectus for International Relations' (2016) 18(3) *International Studies Review* 438–61; RO Keohane, 'The Global Politics of Climate Change: Challenge for Political Science' (2013) 48 *Political Science and Politics* 19; Scott, 'International Law in the Anthropocene' (n 8).

[85] R Cairns and A Stirling, '"Maintaining Planetary Systems" or "Concentrating Global Power"? High Stakes in Contending Framings of Climate Geoengineering' (2014) *Global Environmental Change* 28.

be taken to address climate change.[86] Rather, they invite controversy because he suggests resort to a technological regulatory modality that could strip any room for the exercise of human agency. In the context of CE, this can be exemplified by the so-called termination problem. It is assumed that once SRM methods are being deployed it will become highly problematic to terminate (for whatever valid political reason) since surface temperatures would subsequently rise very rapidly again; technology will in that case dictate policy as well as human agency.[87]

The same can be said about complexity, which demands a regulatory response that does justice to inter-relationships between elements that make up the complex adaptive system that constitutes our environment, including the climate. On the surface, that challenge seems not so much normative as organizational. Hence, what we appear to be looking for is an organizational architecture that is communicative, and that is sensitive to and can instantaneously respond to any changes in any element of the system that will have deleterious effects for the system as a whole or other vital elements of the system.[88] In reality, even if scientific uncertainty and controversies about regulatory modalities are left out of the equation, we will have to face tough questions, for example, about the required degree of democratic accountability of those entrusted with those responses.

Finally, there is no escaping the reality that climate change governance raises distributive questions of a mind-boggling magnitude in terms of both time (present versus future generations) and space (who should shoulder which load of global climate responsibilities). Needless to say, precaution, science, or cost–benefit approaches cannot begin to answer such distributive political questions.

11.6 Conclusion

Probably the most intimidating environmental challenge that we face is constituted by the effects of climate change on the continuing well-being of the human race. We therefore must downgrade our ambitions from 'solving the climate change problem' (which is an impossibility) to 'dealing with the climate problem as best we can'. Precaution is an indispensable tool in the pursuit of that ambition, and productively engages scientific uncertainty and complexity, and even serves to acknowledge the problem of value conflicts in the sphere of what otherwise would be conceived of as 'pure science'. Few principles can claim such wide-ranging productive application. That fact notwithstanding, ultimately the international legal order will have to find ways to steer human history through contestable values, both regarding climate goals themselves and as regarding chosen regulatory approaches to attain those goals. It is true that no amount of theorizing about precaution,

[86] See H Somsen, 'Towards a Law of the Mammoth? Climate Engineering in Contemporary EU Environmental Law' (2016) 1 *European Journal of Risk Regulation* 109 et seq.

[87] IPCC, 'Summary for Policymakers', *Climate Change 2014* (n 8) 26.

[88] See, eg, A Duit and V Galaz, 'Governance and Complexity—Emerging Issues for Governance' (2008) 21 *Governance* 311.

global environmental governance, or regulatory modalities can avoid the fact that this involves choices from an endless range of alternatives, which will leave behind winners and losers. What we can and should endeavour to do, however, is to steer clear of preventable failure. If this can be accomplished it would constitute a monumental leap forward for humankind. That, in turn, calls for a division of labour between disciplines and actors at all levels of global society who must simultaneously learn to work in concert, to value each other's insights, and to combine them into a reflexive climate response that at any moment in time represents our best effort. The precautionary principle can play a limited but vital role in organizing such a response. As Rayfuse has observed, the challenge is not so much in determining whether or not precaution is applicable, but rather in determining how it should be operationalized.[89]

For future climate technologies—such as CE—that are proposed as a response to the effects of climate change, this concretely implies that in a risk/risk trade-off setting: (i) such technologies should be considered and assessed according to their comparative risks, benefits, and uncertainties, even if they harbour potential catastrophic risks themselves; and (ii) that once resort is sought to such technologies, despite their potential uncertain risks, implementation should be guided by the procedural elements of precaution.

[89] Rayfuse, 'Precaution and Climate Change' (n 9) 8.

PART V

RISK AND ECONOMIC PROSPERITY

12

The Assessment of Environmental Risks and the Regulation of Process and Production Methods (PPMs) in International Trade Law

Andreas R Ziegler and David Sifonios

12.1 Introduction

International attention to environmental issues has grown substantially during the past four decades, as the considerable development of international environmental law since the 1970s demonstrates. Global environmental concerns have emerged, such as the need to mitigate climate change, to protect biodiversity and endangered species, and to achieve sustainable development. The international community has realized that it must act to address important global environmental risks.

Implementation of environmental policies requires the adoption not just of environmental law but, in some circumstances, the adoption of trade regulations. For instance, to achieve environmental objectives, states may seek to control the physical properties of products sold in their internal markets, and thus the physical impact related to the *use* of such products, such as the pollution caused by the use of a car (product standards). However, in certain cases, the main environmental impact of a product is not caused by its consumption or by its use, but rather by its *production*, such as the pollution caused by the manufacturing of a car. States may thus be willing to adopt environmental standards addressing the environmental impact caused by the 'process and production methods' (PPMs) of a particular good. When production occurs abroad, the only possibility for a state to address the environmental impact caused by production is to condition the possibility to import products into its market on the requirement that foreign producers comply with certain PPM standards. Trade restrictions based on PPMs may take the form of an import prohibition of certain products (eg, tuna caught in a manner harmful to dolphins,[1] shrimps harvested by using methods that kill sea

[1] See, eg, GATT, *United States—Restrictions on Imports of Tuna* (3 September 1991) DS21/R (unadopted) (*US—Tuna I*).

turtles,[2] or seals killed in a cruel way[3]). They can also represent a tax on imported products based on the environmental costs caused by the production of these products, such as the pollution emitted during their manufacturing process (eg, greenhouse gas (GHG) emissions).

Traditionally, PPM trade restrictions have been viewed with suspicion under international trade rules, resulting in important tensions between environmental protection and trade liberalization.[4] PPM measures may seem to be a useful or necessary tool to address the risks posed by pollution or environmental harm caused by the production of certain products. At the same time, the imposition of PPM measures increases barriers to trade, questions the right of the exporting country to choose its environmental policies, and may give rise to important compliance difficulties for certain developing countries.[5] This chapter examines the evolution of the case law relating to the legality of PPM measures and how the respective visions of the future on which the 1947 General Agreement on Tariffs and Trade (GATT) and the 1995 World Trade Organization (WTO) agreements are based have influenced the interpretation of international trade rules applicable to such measures.

12.2 The PPM Debate

A detailed discussion of the intense controversies regarding the legality of PPM measures under multilateral trade rules goes beyond the scope of this chapter.[6] In brief, as far as WTO law is concerned, the debate has focused on two main aspects. The first is whether differences in PPMs might be relevant in the examination of whether two products are 'like' in the sense of the non-discrimination obligations contained in Articles I and III of the GATT. Article I, the Most-Favoured-Nation

[2] See WTO, Panel report, *United States—Import Prohibition of Certain Shrimp and Shrimp Products* (15 May 1998) WT/DS58/R (*US—Shrimp*, Panel report); WTO, Appellate Body report, *United States—Import Prohibition of Certain Shrimp and Shrimp Products* (12 October 1998) WT/DS58/AB/R (*US—Shrimp*, Appellate Body report).

[3] See WTO, Appellate Body report, *European Communities—Measures Prohibiting the Importation and Marketing of Seal Products* (18 June 2014) WT/DS400/R, WT/DS401/R (*EC—Seal Products*).

[4] As it has been described elsewhere, the word 'protection' 'warms the hearts of environmentalists but sends chills down the spines of free traders'. See D Esty, *Greening the GATT* (Institute for International Economics 1994) 36.

[5] See, eg, the view expressed by developing countries which are part of the Group of 77 South Summit, 'Declaration of the South Summit', 12–14 April 2000, para 21. 'While recognizing the value of environmental protection, labour standards … and protection of all universally recognized human rights and fundamental freedoms, … we reject all attempts to use these issues as conditionalities for restricting market access or aid and technology flows to developing countries.'

[6] For a discussion of the PPM debate, see, eg, S Charnovitz, 'The Law of Environmental "PPMs" in the WTO: Debunking the Myth of Illegality' (1998) 27 *Yale Journal of International Law* 59; RE Hudec, 'The Product–Process Distinction in GATT/WTO Jurisprudence' in M Bronckers and R Quick (eds), *New Directions in International Economic Law: Essays in Honour of John H. Jackson* (Kluwer Law International 2000) 187 ff; R Howse and D Regan, 'The Product/Process Distinction—An Illusory Basis for Disciplining "Unilateralism" in Trade Policy' (2000) 11 *European Journal of International Law* 249; CR Conrad, *Processes and Production Methods (PPMs) in WTO: Interfacing Trade and Social Goals* (CUP 2011). See also D Sifonios, *Environmental Process and Production Methods (PPMs) in WTO Law* (PhD thesis forthcoming).

(MFN) clause, essentially provides that any advantage granted by an importing member to any imported product originating in any other member must be accorded to like imported products originating in all other members. Article III, which articulates the National Treatment obligation, provides that imported products must not be granted less favourable treatment than like domestic products. Thus, if two products can be considered as unlike on the basis of their respective PPMs, the MFN and National Treatment obligations will not apply.

The second main debate concerns the issue of whether PPM measures, which otherwise violate Articles I and III can nonetheless be justified under the general exceptions provision of Article XX of the GATT and thus be considered to comply with the GATT.[7] In this context, various arguments have been invoked to justify a prohibition of PPM measures under the GATT. On the one hand, it has been claimed that PPM measures conflict with the principle of state sovereignty. Some have argued that PPM measures are extraterritorial, since they apply to conduct occurring abroad[8] and that they constitute interference in the internal affairs of the exporting country.[9] PPM measures have been particularly strongly criticized when developed states have adopted or considered adopting PPM measures against developing countries, which do not necessarily have the same environmental priorities or the same responsibilities as developed nations in the particular environmental threat in issue.[10] This is particularly apparent in the climate change context.

On the other hand, it has also been claimed that PPM measures could represent a threat to the basic objectives of the multilateral trading system. One of the main achievements of the GATT has been the significant reduction of tariff levels applicable to manufactured goods, from an average of forty per cent in 1947, to

[7] The PPM controversy also includes debates concerning the applicability and consequences of the rules of the TBT and SPS Agreements for PPM measures. See, eg, Conrad, *Processes and Production Methods (PPMs) in WTO* (n 6) 374 ff.

[8] See TJ Schoenbaum, 'International Trade and Protection of the Environment: The Continuing Search for Reconciliation' (1997) 91 *American Journal of International Law* 268, 279 f; B Jansen and M Lugard, 'Some Considerations on Trade Barriers Erected for Non-Economic Reasons and WTO Obligations' (1999) 2 *Journal of International Environmental Law* 530, 533 ff; K Bagwell, P Mavroidis, and RW Staiger, 'It's a Question of Market Access' (2002) 96 *American Journal of International Law* 56, 76; H Horn and P Mavroidis, 'The Permissible Reach of National Environmental Policies' (2008) 42 *Journal of International Environmental Law* 1107, 1125 *et passim*. See also GATT, *United States—Restrictions on Imports of Tuna* (16 June 1994) DS29/R (unadopted) (*US—Tuna II*) para 5.17. For a contrary position, see A Nollkaemper, 'Rethinking States' Rights to Promote Extra-Territorial Environmental Values' in F Weiss et al (eds), *International Economic Law with a Human Face* (Kluwer Law International 1998) 189; Howse and Regan, 'The Product/Process Distinction' (n 6) 274 and 278; E Vranes, *Trade and the Environment* (OUP 2009) 166.

[9] A majority of commentators have concluded that in principle trade restrictions do not violate the principle of non-intervention, except in very exceptional circumstances, such as when the producing country is largely dependent on exports. See A Appleton, *Environmental Labelling Programmes* (The Graduate Institute 1997) 83; D Luff, *Le droit de l'Organisation mondiale du commerce* (Bruylant and LGDJ 2004) 158 f; BJ Condon, *Environmental Sovereignty and the WTO* (Transnational Publishers 2006) 253.

[10] See J Jackson, 'World Trade Rules and Environmental Policies: Congruence or Conflict?' (1992) 49 *Washington and Lee Law Review* 1227, 1230; F Bierman, 'The Rising Tide of Green Unilateralism in World Trade Law' (2001) 35 *Journal of World Trade* 421, 433; Esty, *Greening the GATT* (n 4) 184. See also the Group of 77 South Summit, 'Declaration of the South Summit' (n5) para 21.

around three per cent for industrialized countries after the Uruguay Round, which concluded in 1995.[11] As a result, the attention has gradually shifted to non-tariff barriers, such as domestic regulations in the field of safety, health, consumer, or environmental protection. Such regulations currently represent the principal barriers to trade and the main source of protectionism.[12] This is because foreign producers may have difficulty in meeting the standards set by the importing country and because even prima facie non-discriminatory measures can be designed so as to burden imports or products originating from a particular country more heavily, thereby resulting in de facto discrimination. PPM measures represent a form of technical barrier to trade and some fear that allowing states to require the adoption of specific environmental practices in the exporting country would be like opening a 'Pandora's box' and would represent a 'slippery slope', by which trade rules would actually allow the adoption of regulations that represent significant obstacles to trade.[13] Based on these considerations, it has been argued by some that PPM measures should be prohibited under trade rules.[14]

Yet, the prohibition of PPM measures could, in practice, result in the inability of states to address international and global environmental problems. When the source of environmental harm is located abroad, the most efficient measures are those which allow intervention at the source (first-best solutions).[15] This can only be achieved through cooperation between the different states concerned. However, as demonstrated by the international climate change negotiations, effective international cooperation to address global environmental problems has often proved to be particularly difficult to achieve. In the absence of this cooperation, trade measures are usually the only possible means by which a state may intervene (second-best solutions),[16] in particular to sanction non-compliance with international obligations or free riding by other states which refuse to participate in international efforts.[17] If such sanctions are prohibited under trade rules, the dominant strategy for states remains non-cooperation, which leads to a classical and economically suboptimal prisoner's dilemma situation. Such cooperation failure may then lead to the 'tragedy of the commons',[18] ie degradation or destruction of global ecosystems

[11] See MJ Trebilcock and R Howse, 'Trade Liberalization and Regulatory Diversity: Reconciling Competitive Markets with Competitive Politics' (1998) 6 *European Journal of Law and Economics* 5, 6; D Carreau and P Juillard, *Droit international économique* (3rd edn, Dalloz 2007) 185 f.

[12] See Carreau and Juillard, ibid, 187.

[13] See J Bhagwati, *In Defense of Globalisation* (OUP 2004) 154 f; Jackson, 'World Trade Rules and Environmental Policies' (n 10) 1241 f. See also GATT Secretariat, 'Trade and the Environment' in *International Trade 1990–1991*, Vol 1 (Geneva 1992). 'If the door were opened to use trade policies unilaterally to offset the competitiveness effects of different environmental standards, or to attempt to force other countries to adopt domestically favoured practices and policies, the trading system would start down a very slippery slope.'

[14] See eg GATT Secretariat, ibid. This document explains that PPM measures should be excluded because otherwise it 'would invite a flood of import restrictions'.

[15] See, eg, TA Pugel, *International Economics* (Irwin McGraw-Hill 2009) 272.

[16] ibid, 281.

[17] See, eg, S Barrett, *Environment and Statecraft: The Strategy of Environmental Treaty-Making* (OUP 2007) 314 *et passim*.

[18] See the famous article of G Hardin, 'The Tragedy of the Commons' (1968) 162 *Science* 1243.

or shared resources. Thus, in brief, a prohibition of PPM measures may reinforce the risks of states' cooperation failures in the field of international environmental protection and the risks of global environmental crises.

Hence, while some have objected to the legality of PPM measures under the GATT for trade and development reasons, others have opposed the prohibition of such measures under WTO law based on environmental grounds.

12.3 Competing Imageries of the Future

The debate on the legality of PPM measures can be placed within a broader context in which interests relating to environmental protection, development, and trade co-exist. The PPM debate may be viewed as one involving competing opinions as to the nature, scope, and scale of the different risks at stake and as a debate as to which interests should ultimately prevail. These different views are influenced in part by competing imageries of the future.

A first image is that of economic prosperity. Developing countries, for example, may be seen as imagining a future in which they have achieved economic development, eradicated poverty, and guaranteed their citizens' basic needs, such as education or healthcare. Developing countries may have great difficulty in complying with environmental standards adopted by developed states because of the generated additional costs, or simply because of the lack of means to verify compliance with PPM requirements. The use of a particular production method usually does not influence the physical properties of a product (so-called non-product-related PPMs). Therefore, producing countries have to establish verification mechanisms to certify compliance with the prescribed PPM standards. Developing countries tend to see the means and costs necessary to implement such certification procedures as important obstacles to trade, or at least as interference with their own social and economic preferences.[19] As a result, they often consider the adoption of PPM measures by importing countries as entailing risks for their economic development and the achievement of their vision of a prosperous future.

A similar view may be taken by those who favour free trade. As far as international trade is concerned, free traders basically imagine a world in which the absence of trade barriers enables states to maximize their comparative advantages and wealth.[20] This increased wealth should then eventually provide states with the additional means necessary to tackle environmental problems. On this view, state regulations, including for non-economic purposes, are seen as a risk or threat to the achievement of this objective, insofar as they represent forms of technical barriers to trade, which tend to jeopardize trade liberalization.

Thus, both free traders and developing countries which oppose the use of PPM measures agree on the view that priority should be given to trade and economic

[19] See Biermann, 'The Rising Tide of Green Unilateralism in World Trade Law' (n 10) 433.

[20] See, eg, J Jackson, *The World Trading System* (The MIT Press 1997) 237.

development, in order to achieve a prosperous economic future. They argue that regulations, which put the pursuit of that future at risk, such as environmental regulations, should be eliminated. Environmental problems will eventually be addressed in this economically prosperous future, with the additional means that will be at states' disposal when this future is achieved.

The contrasting image, relied on by proponents of the use of PPM measures, tends to imagine a future in which the environment has been preserved, both at the regional and global levels. Proponents of this vision recognize that failure to address global environmental problems today may eventually lead to catastrophic environmental futures. These risks may concern the international community as a whole, at least when global environmental risks are concerned (climate change, biodiversity, species extinction, overexploitation of common fish stocks, etc), although agreement on the nature, intensity, and extent of these risks or on the need and means by which to address them may not be uniform. [21] In any event, the means to achieve this 'green' future is considered to be through environmental regulation aimed, among other things, at correcting existing market failures.[22] On this view, the expansion of international trade is perceived with suspicion. First, increased production and transport may exacerbate environmental stress. Second, it is sometimes feared that international trade rules, if unconstrained, could favour environmentally unsound production practices from 'pollution havens'.[23] Environmental trade measures are thus perceived as a way to reduce these risks and to achieve a 'green' future.

Thus, depending on the particular vision of the future adhered to, perceptions of the relative importance of the environmental, trade, and development risks at stake differ. The issue of the legality of PPM measures encapsulates the conflict between those who consider that too little constraint of such measures could jeopardize the functioning of the multilateral trading system and those who consider that overly stringent focus on trade disciplines could prevent states from achieving effective international environmental protection, leading to global environmental

[21] For instance, the United States and the European Communities did not agree, in the WTO *EC—Hormone* case (WTO, Appellate Body report, *European Communities—Measures Concerning Meat and Meat Products* [*Hormones*] (13 February 1998) WT/DS26/AB/R, WT/DS48/AB/R (*EC—Hormone*)), on whether hormone-treated beef represented an externality and whether that externality had to be internalized. This dispute concerned two developed countries and mainly concerned health issues. Yet, this case is interesting insofar as it showed, as Pauwelyn has pointed out, that the fundamental issue in this dispute was whether there was a need for the government to intervene at all or whether the market could deal with the problem. J Pauwelyn, 'Recent Books on Trade and Environment: GATT Phantoms Still Haunt the WTO' (2004) 15 *European Journal of International Law* 575, 579.

[22] On the economic justification for state intervention in cases of market failures see, eg, JE Stiglitz and CE Walsh, *Economics* (4th edn, WW Norton 2006) 252.

[23] See Schoenbaum, 'International Trade and Protection of the Environment' (n 8) 288–89; AL Strauss, 'From GATTzilla to the Green Giant: Winning the Environmental Battle for the Soul of the World Trade Organization' (1998) 19 *University of Pennsylvania Journal of International Economic Law* 769, 808; M Trebilcock and R Howse, *The Regulation of International Trade* (3rd edn, Routledge 2005) 661.

degradation. Section 12.4 examines how these different visions of the future have been visible in GATT and WTO case law.

12.4 Evolutions of the GATT and WTO Case Law on PPM Measures

One of the most notable disputes relating to trade and the environment, which was examined by two GATT 1947 panels at the beginning of the 1990s, concerned a US embargo on Mexican tuna that was caught in a manner that resulted in the incidental killings of dolphins.[24] The measure adopted by the United States also provided for a secondary embargo applying to all third countries that did not prohibit imports of tuna from Mexico. This secondary embargo was challenged under the GATT by the European Communities.[25] In 1998, after the creation of the WTO, a similar dispute arose when the United States prohibited the importation of shrimp caught in a manner which harmed sea turtles. In effect, the US legislation required shrimp-producing countries that exported shrimp products to the United States to adopt regulations mandating the use of fishing methods that did not harm sea turtles. This measure was challenged before the WTO by four Asian shrimp-exporting countries.[26] These different cases all concerned measures which prescribed the use, in the exporting country, of particular PPMs (in both cases relating to fishing methods), which did not physically affect the final product, giving rise to an intense debate as to the legality of the measures.[27]

The panels in these cases examined whether the PPM measures concerned could comply with Article XX of the GATT, which sets out a list of public policy goals which may be invoked to justify a measure that infringes GATT obligations. However, environmental protection is not one of the public policy goals listed. For this reason, environmental concerns have, in general, been examined in dispute settlement practice under subparagraph (b), which applies to the protection of human, animal, or plant life or health, and subparagraph (g), which concerns the conservation of exhaustible natural resources. Since Article XX of the GATT does not explicitly refer to PPM measures, and because of the omission of reference to environmental goals in this provision, the legal regime applicable to environmental PPM measures depends in large part on how Article XX of the GATT is interpreted in the case law; and this depends on competing interpretations of the basic concepts underlying multilateral trade rules and competing visions and imageries of the future these trade rules are designed to achieve and serve.

[24] See *US—Tuna I; US—Tuna II*. [25] See *US—Tuna II*.

[26] See *US—Shrimp*, Panel report; *US—Shrimp*, Appellate Body report.

[27] See, eg, Charnovitz, 'The Law of Environmental "PPMs" in the WTO' (n 6); Hudec, 'The Product–Process Distinction in GATT/WTO Jurisprudence' (n 6); Howse and Regan, 'The Product/Process Distinction' (n 6); J Jackson, 'Comments on *Shrimp/Turtle* and the Product/Process Distinction' (2000) 11 *European Journal of International Law* 303.

12.4.1 First phase: the GATT 1947 and the *Tuna—Dolphin* cases

The reports in the *Tuna—Dolphin* cases were not adopted by the contracting parties, because of the opposition of the United States. (Under the GATT 1947, positive consensus was required for the adoption of a panel report.) These reports thus have no legal force as such.[28] However, they have had indirect influence in that they have been quoted by subsequent reports[29] and have given rise to considerable debates in academic writings.[30] In the *Tuna—Dolphin* reports, the panels expressed the view that if the GATT allowed an importing member to adopt trade measures to force other members to change their environmental policies within their own jurisdiction, the GATT could 'no longer serve as a multilateral framework for trade among contracting parties'.[31] One of the main concerns was that accepting such a rule could mean that the GATT would provide legal certainty only between members with identical internal regulations.[32] The *Shrimp—Turtle* panel was similarly concerned with conflicting requirements between several importing countries applying to the same subject for the same exporting countries, making it impossible for the states concerned to comply with all of these requirements at the same time.[33] The panel emphatically stated that allowing such measures could 'rapidly lead to the end of the WTO multilateral trading system'.[34]

In an effort to exclude the perceived risks for the multilateral trading system arising from the use of PPM measures, the panel reports in both cases suggested that the drastic solution of prohibiting PPM measures should be applied. There was no assessment of the environmental risks at stake in these cases, which seemed to be irrelevant in the view of the panels.

The prohibition of PPM measures based on the 'risks for the multilateral trading system' has been heavily criticized in academic writings which have, for example, referred to 'fabricated illogical reasons' as to why Article XX of the GATT could not be used to justify unilateral PPM measures.[35] It has been pointed out that the panels' attitude could be counterproductive and could actually threaten the multilateral trading system by triggering concerns as to the system's hostile attitude towards broader public interests.[36] Indeed, precisely such hostile reactions did occur after the release of the *Tuna—Dolphin* reports. At that time, free-trade

[28] See WTO, Appellate Body report, *Japan—Taxes on Alcoholic Beverages* (1 November 1996) WT/DS8/AB/R, WT/DS10/AB/R, WT/DS11/AB/R, 15 (*Japan—Alcohol*, Appellate Body report). The Appellate Body, however, stated that unadopted reports could provide 'useful guidance'; *Japan—Alcohol*, Appellate Body report, 16.

[29] See, eg, *US—Shrimp*, Panel report, paras 7.16, 7.36, 7.46; WTO, Panel report, *European Communities—Measures Affecting Asbestos and Asbestos-Containing Products* (5 April 2001) WT/DS135/R, paras 8.37, 8.167, 8.272; Panel Report, *United States—Measures Affecting the Cross-Border Supply of Gambling and Betting Services* (20 April 2005) WT/DS285/R, para 6.526.

[30] See, eg, Charnovitz, 'The Law of Environmental "PPMs" in the WTO' (n 6); Hudec, 'The Product–Process Distinction in GATT/WTO Jurisprudence' (n 6); Howse and Regan, 'The Product/Process Distinction' (n 6); Jackson, *The World Trading System* (n 20); Conrad, *Processes and Production Methods (PPMs) in WTO* (n 6).

[31] *US—Tuna II*, para 5.26; *US—Tuna I*, para 5.28.

[32] See *US—Tuna I*, para 5.27.

[33] See *US—Shrimp*, Panel report, para 7.45.

[34] ibid.

[35] See S Charnovitz, 'The WTO's Environmental Progress' (2007) *10 Journal of International Environmental Law* 685, 696.

[36] ibid.

critics used the expression of 'GATTzilla' to describe what was perceived as a trading system which threatened environmental protection and state sovereignty.[37] In the eyes of these critics, the GATT unduly restricted GATT members' regulatory autonomy and entailed risks of preventing governmental action to address global environmental issues.[38] Important risks of cooperation failures could ensue, leading to international inaction in the field of environmental protection, because the imports of products produced by non-cooperating states, using environmentally harmful PPMs, could not be restricted under international trade law rules. So was the argument.

12.4.2 Second phase: the WTO and the *Shrimp—Turtle* Appellate Body Report

In 1998, only a few years after the *Tuna—Dolphin* cases, and in the first years of the newly created WTO, the issue of the legality of PPM measures under multilateral trade rules was brought again before the WTO in the *Shrimp—Turtle* case. The Appellate Body adopted a different approach from that of the *Tuna—Dolphin* and *Shrimp—Turtle* panels. It held that conditioning access to a member's domestic market on whether exporting members comply with a policy unilaterally prescribed by the importing member might be a 'common aspect' of measures falling within the scope of one of subparagraphs of Article XX of the GATT.[39] Implicitly, the Appellate Body rejected the argument that a perceived 'threat' to the multilateral trading system was an element that was relevant to the interpretation of the GATT. This finding had far-reaching consequences for PPM measures, since it implied that their 'unilateral' or 'coercive' character would not, of itself, render such measures incapable of justification.

In this dispute, the United States initially lost on appeal under Article XX of the GATT, in particular because of the lack of flexibility in the methods that could be used by exporting countries to protect sea turtles during shrimp trawling, the violation of due process requirements relating to the transparency of the certification procedures, and because the United States had negotiated an international

[37] See Esty, *Greening the GATT* (n 4) 35 ff. Critics of the *Tuna—Dolphin* reports invoking state sovereignty have referred in particular to the right of states to choose the conditions upon which products may be sold on their internal market. It should be pointed out that GATT members which opposed the use of PPM measures have also invoked state sovereignty, in particular the principle of permanent sovereignty over natural resources. In their view, this principle means that importing states cannot impose on imported products PPM standards that conflict with the right of exporting countries to exploit their natural resources as they choose to. This issue is part of the wider debate about whether PPM measures are extraterritorial in a legal sense and whether the customary international law rules on prescriptive jurisdiction restrict the ability of states to adopt PPM measures. See, eg, Sifonios, *Environmental Process and Production Methods (PPMs) in WTO Law* (n 6).

Reactions to the reports in the *US—Shrimp* case were less critical. See, eg, Charnovitz, 'The WTO's Environmental Progress' (n 35) 696. He states that through its *US—Shrimp* report, among other reports, the Appellate Body 'sent a signal to the public that the era of runaway panels on environmental matters was over'.

[38] See, eg, Strauss, 'From GATTzilla to the Green Giant' (n 23) 771.

[39] *US—Shrimp*, Appellate Body report, para 121.

agreement on sea turtle protection with some of its trading partners prior to the imposition of the import ban, but not with the complainants.[40] In the view of the Appellate Body these different elements constituted 'arbitrary or unjustified discrimination' between the exporting countries concerned, in the sense of the chapeau of Article XX of the GATT. Eventually, three years after the initial case, after the United States had made similar negotiation efforts with the complaining members and had adopted a more flexible measure which allowed the use of sea turtle protection methods that were comparable in effectiveness, the Appellate Body upheld the contested measure.[41]

The *Shrimp—Turtle* Appellate Body's report thus applied a much more subtle and balanced approach to the respective risks of stringent or lax trade rules for the functioning of the multilateral trading system and the ability of states to take environmental trade measures: PPM measures are not GATT illegal per se, but the different conditions of Article XX of the GATT discipline the ability of WTO members to enact such measures.[42]

12.4.3 Subsequent evolutions of case law

The reports in the *Shrimp—Turtle* case have shown that PPM measures were not illegal per se in WTO law. However, the precise conditions under which such measures are justifiable, and the way competing interests and risks should be taken into account in the application of the relevant provisions, have often remained unclear since this dispute. Nevertheless, the case law relating to Articles III and XX of the GATT has continued to evolve. In particular, several cases have concerned the relation between international trade rules and non-economic objectives, such as health,[43] environmental protection,[44] or public morality.[45] These cases have provided certain clarifications on the legal regime applicable to PPM measures. For the limited purpose of this chapter, however, it is not necessary to explain the details of this complex case law. Rather, certain specific aspects will be highlighted in the following sections.

[40] ibid, paras 161–76.

[41] See WTO, Appellate Body report, *United States—Import Prohibition of Certain Shrimp and Shrimp Products, Recourse to Article 21.5 of the DSU by Malaysia* (22 October 2001) WT/DS58/AB/RW, (*US—Shrimp 21.5*).

[42] The Appellate Body held in its *US—Shrimp* report that the importing country must in particular show that a 'sufficient nexus' exists with the environmental situation at stake; *US—Shrimp*, para 133. It has to establish that it has conducted 'across-the-board' international negotiations in order to conclude an international environmental agreement; *US—Shrimp*, para 166. It must also ensure that its measure is flexible enough to take into account differing conditions that may occur in the importing and exporting countries; *US—Shrimp*, para 161.

[43] See WTO, Appellate Body report, *European Communities—Measures Affecting Asbestos and Asbestos-Containing Products* (5 April 2001) WT/DS135/AB/R (*EC—Asbestos*); WTO, Appellate Body report, *Brazil—Measures Affecting Imports of Retreaded Tyres* (17 December 2007) WT/DS332/AB/R (*Brazil—Tyres*).

[44] See WTO, Appellate Body report, *United States—Measures Concerning the Importation, Marketing and Sale of Tuna and Tuna Products* (13 June 2012) WT/DS381/AB/R. This case still concerned the dispute between the United States and Mexico on the legality of the 'dolphin-safe' label on tuna products. This second dispute between the two countries, after the 1991 GATT Panel report, was examined under the rules of the Agreement on Technical Barriers to Trade.

[45] See *EC—Seal Products*. The case concerned an embargo of the European Union on seals and seal products, justified on the basis of the cruelty in the way seals were killed.

12.5 The Evolution of Case Law in the Light of Imageries of the Future

When the WTO was created in 1995, the GATT 1947 was integrated into the WTO agreements without changes to its text. In other words, the evolution of the case law regarding the legality of PPM measures, described in section12.4, has not been based on any changes in the relevant provisions of the GATT. It can be argued that it is instead a change in the vision of the future underlying the multilateral trading system that explains this evolution, at least in part.

The GATT 1947 indicates in its Preamble that this agreement has the objective of developing the 'full use of the resources of the world'. At the end of the 1940s, the focus of the GATT signatories was clearly on developing international trade, not on the linkage between trade and environmental protection. The GATT was thus founded on the vision of a 'free-trade future' described in section 12.3 above. In a way, the 1991 and 1994 *Tuna—Dolphin* reports, even though they were delivered more than forty years later, still illustrated this conception in which the GATT was seen in complete isolation from other international concerns, and in which the reduction of obstacles to trade was seen as the prevailing objective of the world trading system. In such a view, there was little room for environmental interests, at least when they entailed the imposition of non-consensual trade restrictions. In order to eliminate the risks that trade measures unduly restricted trade liberalization, GATT rules were interpreted as prohibiting PPM measures, without consideration of the risks of catastrophic environmental futures entailed by such an approach.

As mentioned, when the WTO agreements were adopted in 1995, the text of the GATT 1947 was not modified. However, the Preamble of the Marrakesh Agreement establishing the WTO (WTO Agreement) introduced an important concept, by stating that one of the objectives of the multilateral trading system was to allow the 'optimal use of the world's resources in accordance with the objective of sustainable development seeking both to protect and preserve the environment and enhance the means for doing so in a manner consistent with their respective needs and concerns at different levels of economic development'.[46]

The Appellate Body held in the *Shrimp—Turtle* case that the objective of sustainable development has to be taken into account in the interpretation of WTO law. In

[46] See the Preamble of the Marrakesh Agreement:

> The *Parties* to this Agreement, *recognizing* that their relations in the field of trade and economic endeavour should be conducted with a view to raising standards of living, ensuring full employment and a large and steadily growing volume of real income and effective demand, and expanding the production of and trade in goods and services, while allowing for the optimal use of the world's resources in accordance with the objective of sustainable development, seeking both to protect and preserve the environment and to enhance the means for doing so in a manner consistent with their respective needs and concerns at different levels of economic development (...)

Marrakesh Agreement Establishing the World Trade Organization (adopted 15 April 1994, entered into force 1 January 1995) 1867 UNTS 154, Preamble (WTO Agreement).

its view, sustainable development 'must add colour, texture and shading' to its interpretation of WTO agreements.[47] Yet, the WTO agreements contain no definition of sustainable development and the Appellate Body has not provided any details as to what sustainable development actually means, nor has it explicitly explained how it could add 'colour, texture and shading' to the interpretation of these agreements. Furthermore, there is no uniform definition of sustainable development in international law or any consensus on how to give it concrete effect in individual cases,[48] which could guide the treaty interpreter as to the way the principle of sustainable development could influence in practical terms the interpretation of the GATT provisions. It is, however, generally acknowledged in the academic literature and relevant legal documents that one of the most important aspects of sustainable development is the principle of integration, which means that sustainable development should achieve the integration of environmental protection and economic development.[49] Another important element is the principle of inter-generational equity, which states that 'sustainable development is development that meets the needs of the present generation without compromising the ability of future generations to meet their own needs'.[50]

Despite the vague character of the principle of sustainable development, it could be argued that through this principle, WTO members have contemplated a very general *common vision of the future*. As the terms used in the Preamble of the WTO Agreement show, such vision may be viewed as one which seeks to reconcile the two competing imageries of the future that underlie the PPM debate. By referring to the objective to 'protect and preserve the environment and enhance the means for doing so', the WTO Agreement Preamble refers, at the same time, to a vision of a future in which the global environment has been preserved and a vision of a future in which international trade has, through economic prosperity, brought additional means to protect the environment. The term 'optimal' use of the world's resources also indicates the need to find a balance between competing risks and interests in order to develop international trade without harming the environment in the long run. In brief, the achievement of this common vision of the future, represented by sustainable development, requires that the treaty interpreter achieve some form of trade-off between competing risks (risk/risk trade-offs).

Several concrete aspects of the Appellate Body's case law may in practice be interpreted as attempts to take into consideration competing risks; ie, to achieve such risk/risk trade-offs. On the one hand, trade liberalization and the reduction of obstacles to trade remain one of the most important bases of the GATT. It could be argued that it has directly influenced the Appellate Body's interpretation of the National Treatment obligation, in particular in relation to the concept of 'like products'. The Appellate

[47] *US—Shrimp*, Appellate Body report, para 153.

[48] See P Birnie, A Boyle, and C Redgwell, *International Law and the Environment* (3rd edn, OUP 2009) 125.

[49] See United Nations Conference on Environment and Development, 'Declaration of the United Nations Conference on Environment and Development' (3–4 June 1992) A/CONF.151/26 (Vol I), principle 4 (Rio Declaration). See also Birnie et al, ibid, 116.

[50] World Commission on Environment and Development, *Our Common Future* (OUP 1987) 43.

Body has endorsed an economic definition of this concept, which focuses on the competitive relationship between products in the marketplace.[51] It has thus rejected the view that two products could be considered to be unlike simply because they have, say, different environmental impacts,[52] at least as long as such impact does not influence consumers' tastes and habits and thus the competitive relationship between the products concerned.

On the other hand, environmental interests are taken into account through the application of Article XX of the GATT. This provision was interpreted narrowly under the GATT 1947.[53] As a result, compliance with the conditions of Article XX, in particular its necessity test, were particularly difficult to achieve.[54] By contrast, several aspects of the Appellate Body report in the *Shrimp—Turtle* case show a much more balanced and flexible approach. First, as indicated above, the Appellate Body has confirmed that a PPM measure could comply with the GATT, if certain conditions are met.[55] In brief, this case has shown that environmental risks (in this case, the risk of extinction of an endangered species) can justify a restrictive trade measure, provided that the regulating member minimizes unnecessary trade impacts.

Beside this general aspect, which may be viewed as a form of integration of trade and environmental interests, a second specific example could be mentioned. In its report, the Appellate Body held that turtles were 'exhaustible natural resources' in the sense of Article XX(g) of the GATT.[56] Complainants in this case had argued that this exception had been construed by the drafters of the GATT as applying to non-living natural resources such as minerals and not to living resources. The Appellate Body applied what has been referred to as an evolutionary interpretation[57] to include non-living resources in the scope of Article XX(g) of the GATT. In its analysis, the Appellate Body explicitly referred to the objective of sustainable development mentioned in the Preamble of the WTO Agreement as one of the bases of its interpretation.[58]

Furthermore, the Appellate Body has interpreted the conditions of Article XX of the GATT in a more flexible manner than that which prevailed under the GATT

[51] See *Japan—Alcohol*, Appellate Body report, 16; *EC—Asbestos*, para 98.

[52] See the rejection of the 'aims-and-effects' definition of 'like' products (under which two products are alike if the regulatory measure distinguishing between them pursues protectionist intent and results in protectionist effects) in the *Japan—Alcohol* case. WTO, Panel report, *Japan—Taxes on Alcoholic Bevereges* (11 July 1996) WT/DS8/R, WT/DS10/R, WT/DS11/R (*Japan—Alcohol*, Panel report) paras 6.16–6.18; *Japan—Alcohol*, Appellate Body report, 16 (endorsing the economic definition of the concept of like products).

[53] See, eg, *US—Tuna I*, para 5.22.

[54] See, eg, A Appleton, 'GATT Article XX's Chapeau: A Disguised "Necessary" Test?: The WTO Appellate Body's Ruling in *United States—Standards for Reformulated and Conventional Gasoline*' (1997) 6 *Review of European Community and International Environmental Law* 131, 136.

[55] *EC—Asbestos*; *Brazil—Tyres*.

[56] See *US—Shrimp*, Appellate Body report, para 131.

[57] ibid, para 130.

[58] ibid, para 129. In this paragraph, the Appellate Body recalled that even though the words of Article XX(g) of the GATT were crafted fifty years earlier, they had to be read by the treaty interpreter in the light of contemporary concerns of the community of nations about protection and conservation of the environment. It added that the signatories of the WTO Agreement were fully aware of the importance and legitimacy of environmental protection and that the Preamble of this agreement explicitly acknowledged the objective of sustainable development.

1947 practice. For example, it has interpreted the necessity test applicable in particular in the context of subparagraph (b) as a 'weighing and balancing' test, by which the treaty interpreter takes into account the importance of the values and interests at stake, the contribution of the measure to the achievement of the goal, and its trade-restrictiveness.[59] Through this interpretation, environmental risks and trade risks may each be considered, respectively, through the first and third criteria. In the view of the Appellate Body, the more important these non-trade interests are, the easier it would be to accept them as 'necessary'.[60] This shows that an assessment of the environmental risks at issue should be carried out to enable a proper application of this 'weighing and balancing' test.

In the same vein, the Appellate Body has held that the conditions of the chapeau mean that the treaty interpreter needs to find a 'line of equilibrium' between the substantive obligations of the GATT and the general exceptions provision.[61] The substantive obligations are meant to allow the achievement of the objective of trade liberalization. At the same time, the need to find a line of equilibrium between such obligations and the general exceptions provision, which introduces non-economic concerns that may compete with the objective of trade liberalization, shows that the GATT system allows some form of balance between competing interests and risks.

These examples illustrate how the objective of sustainable development, which may be viewed as a form of common vision of the future of WTO members, has influenced in concrete terms the Appellate Body case law.

12.6 The Limits of an Evolution of Case Law Based on a Common Vision of the Future

Even though the objective of sustainable development mentioned in the WTO Agreement Preamble has influenced the Appellate Body case law, a reference to such an objective only gives the treaty interpreter a very general indication of the common vision of the future that should be achieved. The principle of sustainable development remains vague and may not provide an answer to all the specific questions that arise in the search for a risk/risk trade-off. Indeed, making a compromise between the different risks and interests at stake indirectly affects various underlying issues, such as what risks are relevant, whose risks eventually count, which risks may be given priority, and so on.

An interesting example is that of possible climate-related trade measures. Even though no such measures have been adopted to date, both the European Union and the United States have, at some point, considered the idea of imposing taxes on imported products based on the GHGs emitted during their production

[59] See, eg, WTO, Appellate Body report, *Korea—Taxes on Alcoholic Beverages* (17 February 1999) WT/DS75/AB/R, WT/DS84/AB/R, para 163; *Brazil—Tyres*, para 178.

[60] See WTO, Appellate Body report, *Korea—Measures Affecting Imports of Fresh, Chilled and Frozen Beef* (10 January 2001) WT/DS161/AB/R, WT/DS169/AB/R, para 162.

[61] See *US—Shrimp*, Appellate Body report, para 159.

processes.[62] If such measures were adopted and contested before the WTO, various competing risks would arise—for example, the risk that the absence of measures to reduce GHGs could lead to catastrophic climate changes; the risk that the prohibition of climate-related trade measures could deprive states of meaningful means to sanction states who do not cooperate in GHGs emissions reductions or do not comply with their international commitments; the risk that a generally applicable tax or import prohibition would jeopardize the functioning of the multilateral trading system and lead to an increasing number of trade disputes, retaliations, and so on; the risk that the lack of financial and technical means of developing countries to implement the required measures could mean that they could either lose access to certain markets or reduce the resources allocated to other political priorities. The question is, which risks would be relevant, and which risks should be given priority?

All these risks exist to a certain extent and could potentially be relevant in the interpretation of international trade rules. Most of them may indeed be related directly or indirectly to the achievement of sustainable development. Taking a decision about the justifiability of a PPM measure inevitably has consequences for the respective importance of the competing risks at hand and for the issue of which risk may eventually prevail. Therefore, in the absence of clear rules about the way such competing interests and risks should be considered and integrated, recommendations of the panels and the Appellate Body on these issues will inevitably tend towards policy making rather than interpretation.

Two main consequences ensue. First, *legal certainty* may sometimes be elusive, at least as long as there is no confirmed practice in relation to the concrete manner in which risks relating to environmental protection and development should be integrated into trade interests, through an interpretation of trade rules congruent with the objective of sustainable development. Second, the margin of manoeuvre concerning the possible views about the influence that sustainable development should have on the interpretation of trade rules gives rise to the issue of the *legitimacy* of the panels and the Appellate Body to make interpretations which have a policy-making dimension.

Sensitive issues about how competing risks in relation to environmental protection, trade liberalization, or development, such as those mentioned above in relation to climate-related trade measures, should ideally be addressed through international negotiations between states and rest on solutions derived from consensus. But the international community may not necessarily succeed in achieving effective international cooperation when global environmental issues are at stake. Hence, states may sometimes be willing to use unilateral measures to sanction free riding or non-compliance with international efforts to protect the environment. Where unilateral trade measures are imposed and are contested before the WTO,

[62] See, eg, J Bhagwati and PC Mavroidis, 'Is Action against US Exports for Failure to Sign the Kyoto Protocol WTO Legal?' (2007) 6 *World Trade Review* 299; J Pauwelyn, 'U.S. Federal Climate Policy and Competitiveness Concerns: The Limits and Options of International Trade Law' (2007) Working Paper, Nicolas Institute for Environmental Policy Solutions, Duke University.

it is in practice the panels and the Appellate Body which will be faced with the task of reviewing, through their examination of the relevant conditions of the GATT, whether the enactment of the contested measure takes appropriate account of the competing risks at stake.

However, under the terms of their mandate, the panels and the Appellate Body are not supposed to 'add or diminish the rights and obligations' provided in the WTO agreements.[63] In practice though, in particular when rather vague concepts such as those used in Articles III and XX of the GATT have to be applied, the panels and the Appellate Body often actually make law,[64] since their reports are automatically adopted unless there is a consensus among all WTO members not to do so.[65] There is in theory the possibility of adopting a formal interpretation of the WTO Agreements through the 'legislative' institutions of the WTO (ie, the Ministerial Conference and the General Council), but this requires a three-quarters majority of the members.[66] In other words, checks and balances between the 'judicial' and 'legislative' branches of the WTO are very difficult to use in practice. In such circumstances, the role of the panels and the Appellate Body is quite uncomfortable, since they may have no other choice, in the absence of clear rules in the relevant provisions, other than to make recommendations which tend towards law making (or policy making), without having a mandate to do so.

It might seem tempting for the panels and the Appellate Body, in such circumstances, to avoid exposing in a transparent way their opinion about which risks are relevant, whose risks count, and which risks may be given priority. When case law lacks transparency, diverging interpretations may easily be made, which means that the Appellate Body is less likely to be criticized for 'making law'. For instance, while the Appellate Body did state that the function of the conditions of the introductory clause of Article XX of the GATT is to find a 'line of equilibrium' between the substantive obligations of the GATT and the general exceptions, it did not clearly identify the nature and extent of the competing risks and interests at stake in the *Shrimp—Turtle* case; nor did it explicitly weigh these different risks in its application of the conditions of the chapeau of Article XX of the GATT.

However, it is submitted that a lack of transparency may actually reduce the legitimacy of case law. Indeed, transparency is an important aspect of legitimacy, since it allows a meaningful criticism of the case law.[67] While the GATT provisions require the search for balanced solutions, in particular through the application of the necessity test ('weighing and balancing test') or the conditions of the chapeau ('line of equilibrium'), transparency could be enhanced if clear risk assessments were conducted. These risk assessments could concern in particular environmental

[63] Understanding on Rules and Procedures Governing the Settlement of Disputes, Marrakesh Agreement Establishing the World Trade Organization, Annex 2 (DSU), art 3.2.

[64] See AT Guzman, 'Global Governance and the WTO' (2004) 45 *Harvard International Law Journal* 303, 341–42.

[65] See DSU, arts 16(4) and 17(14).

[66] See WTO Agreement, art IX(2).

[67] See, eg, R Howse, 'Adjudicative Legitimacy and Treaty Interpretation in International Trade Law: The Early Years of WTO Jurisprudence' in JHH Weiler (ed), *The EU, the WTO, and the NAFTA* (OUP 2000) 35, 51 ff.

risks and could allow the evaluation of the intensity of the environmental threat, the importance of the natural resources at stake, the scale and magnitude of pollution or degradation, and thus the urgency of intervention, and so on. As far as the risks for trade and development are concerned, the panels and the Appellate Body could focus on the trade-restrictiveness of the measure, the actual and potential effects of the measure on trade flows, the nature and importance of the trade interests at issue, the importance of the products concerned for the exporting countries concerned, and so on.

In the WTO dispute settlement bodies' analyses of the conditions of Article XX of the GATT, these risk assessments could then serve as objective bases to explain how risk/risk trade-offs are decided, for instance in the context of the examination of the conditions of the chapeau or the necessity test. There have been some evolutions in the case law which tend to go in this direction, in particular the interpretation of the necessity test as a 'weighing and balancing test'. As explained above, this test requires, inter alia, the examination of the importance of the interests and values underlying the measure, which may include the environmental risks concerned, and the analysis of the trade restrictiveness of the measure, which may involve the nature of the trade risks at hand. The necessity analysis could thus include a more detailed—or at least a more transparent—assessment of the risks at stake, which would then be useful in the appraisal of the different conditions of Article XX of the GATT, including the conditions of the introductory clause.

12.7 Conclusion

This chapter has shown that a change in the vision of the future underlying an international agreement may result in very concrete evolutions in a legal regime applicable to certain specific issues, without any modification of the actual text of the relevant provisions. In the trade context, this new vision—the achievement of sustainable development—has allowed a better consideration of environmental risks in the context of the GATT and the appraisal of trade-related environmental measures under Article XX of the GATT.

There are, however, limits to the evolution of GATT law based solely on the interpretation of the relevant provisions in the light of a new vision of the future. The vagueness of the terms used in these provisions may justify quite different interpretations, as the evolution of the case law about the concept of 'like product' or the conditions of the chapeau of Article XX of the GATT has shown. Moreover, the objective of sustainable development—which is supposed, in the view of the Appellate Body, to bring 'colour, texture and shading' to the interpretation of these provisions—represents a rather vague concept, which may only provide very general guidance to the treaty interpreter. It cannot provide much guidance as to the concrete and practical solutions needed to integrate the competing risks to the environment, trade liberalization, or the interests of developing countries. As a result, the interpretation of these vague provisions in the light of this rather imprecise objective often tends towards law making.

Yet, the mandate of the panels and the Appellate Body does not include the possibility of engaging in law making, as they must not 'add or diminish the rights and obligations' of WTO members under the WTO agreements. In such context, the WTO dispute settlement bodies are likely to seek to avoid as much as possible findings which might be perceived as law making. Thus, the contradiction which exists between the need to clarify the existing rules and the absence of mandate to create law represents a limit to the possibility to develop, through case law, clear and coherent rules about the integration of competing risks within the GATT system.

Eventually, the adoption of clear rules about the way the common vision of the future underlying the WTO system should be achieved and how competing risks should be taken into account may require international negotiation and the conclusion of an international agreement between WTO members. They could, for example, agree on more precise rules concerning the kind of environmental risks that may justify a trade-restrictive PPM measure. They could also agree, as in the Agreement on Technical Barriers to Trade, which contains several rules designed to address the specific interests of developing countries, on the manner in which the risks that PPM measures represent for the interests of developing countries should be taken into account.

In the meantime, disputes will continue to be brought before the WTO dispute settlement bodies. The ability of the panels and the Appellate Body to keep finding, on a case-by-case basis, balanced solutions and trade-offs in cases in which competing risks are at stake, will play a crucial role in giving more substance to the vision of the future that the achievement of sustainable development represents. It will also play an important role in the legitimacy of the dispute settlement system and the WTO.

13

Risk, Responsibility, and Fairness in International Investment Law

Azernoosh Bazrafkan and Alexia Herwig

13.1 Introduction

International Investment Agreements (IIAs) emerged in the 1960s as an instrument to lower political risk for foreign investors and to facilitate political risk insurance.[1] Political risks associated with investing abroad concern uncertainties with regard to the host state's exercise of its political power (ie, government intervention) and imply that the host state government and its agencies will, by act or omission, reduce the foreign investor's ability to realize an expected return on the investment.[2] Host states' measures that could damage or completely destroy the economic basis of foreign investments vary from outright expropriation to a unilateral change in the regulatory, royalty, pricing, and tax regimes. IIAs are assumed to promote foreign investment by protecting foreign investment in host (developing) countries where domestic institutions are fragile and property rights are weak.[3] IIAs are assumed to facilitate insurance and help mitigate categories of risks by providing for efficiency, certainty, and stability in host states' legal systems and by providing guarantees for foreign investors in transition economies.[4] The legal protections and remedies

[1] P Egger and M Pfaffenmayr, 'The Impact of Bilateral Investment Treaties on Foreign Direct Investment' in KP Sauvant and LE Sachs (eds), *The Effect of Treaties on Foreign Direct Investment: Bilateral Investment Treaties, Double Taxation Treaties and Investment Flows* (OUP 2009) 254. On investment-related political risk, see TW Waelde, 'Sustainable Development and the Energy Charter Treaty: Between Pseudo-Action and the Management of Environmental Investment Risk' in F Weiss et al (eds) *International Economic Law with a Human Face* (Kluwer Law International 1998) 227.

[2] JC Hoyos, 'The Role of Bilateral Investment Treaties in Mitigating Project Finance's Risks: The Case of Colombia' (2012), 7 <http://ssrn.com/abstract=2163284> accessed 12 December 2015.

[3] According to the World Bank's 1997 World Development Report, a host government's credibility, the predictability of its rules and policies, and the consistency with which they are applied, can be as important for attracting foreign investment as the content of the rules. A Perry, 'An Ideal Legal System for Attracting Foreign Direct Investment? Some Theory and Reality' (2000) 15(6) *American University International Law Review* 1627, 1631. See also, World Bank,'World Development Report 1997: The State in a Changing World' 4 (World Trade Organization (WTO) 1997).

[4] Egger and Pfaffemayr, 'The Impact of Bilateral Investment Treaties on Foreign Direct Investment' (n1) 254.

Risk, Responsibility, and Fairness in International Investment Law Azernoosh Bazrafkan and Alexia Herwig

provided to foreign investors under IIAs require host states to internalize the cost of discriminatory or otherwise unfair and inequitable treatment of investors and the expropriation of investments by creating a liability risk for the host state for the payment of damages. As the €4.7 billion damages that Vattenfall has requested Germany to pay for its decision to exit nuclear energy shows, potentially very large sums can be at stake.[5] The effect of protecting investors against political risk is that capital can be allocated more efficiently because investors only have to contend with normal business risks and factor economic aspects into their location decisions.

Early investment disputes concerned outright nationalizations of investments or lack of protection in cases of civil unrest. In the earlier treaty and arbitral practice, it was the investor who was seen to be at risk from wilful governmental interference. The image of the future portrayed by IIAs was one in which countries that agreed to refrain from such conduct could reap the economic benefits of foreign investment in return.[6] However, since the mid-1990s, due to overly strict IIA protections in favour of the investor, an alarming competing framing of risk has emerged, which shifts the risks of unmitigated physical externalities onto the host state's population. These changes have been fuelled by investment disputes which have challenged various policy areas of the host state, such as environmental legislation, tobacco packaging legislation, measures adopted during acute balance-of-payments crises, withdrawal of green energy subsidies, and other energy policies. Under this framing of risk, it is both the host state population as well as its regulatory sovereignty which seem to be at risk through IIAs.

Nowadays, adjustments to legal provisions in IIAs give greater regulatory space for host states, but a concern remains that host state governments' policy choices to protect their local population against physical risks from that investment are under-protected. To the extent that this is the case, IIAs provide adverse incentives to potential investors[7] because unmitigated risks of externalities render foreign investment inefficient. Two types of framings of risk which need to be mitigated are, hence, at play in IIAs: political risks and risks of physical externalities. Their balancing creates a third framing of risk, much of which remains unmitigated, that of business risks.

In this chapter, we demonstrate that there is no consistency in the fine-grained framing of these risks in arbitral awards. Some awards suggest that what matters in terms of giving rise to a right to compensation is a lack of appropriate balance behind

[5] The still pending *Vattenfall (II) v Germany* (International Centre for Settlement of Investment Disputes (ICSID) Case No ARB/12/12) arbitration is about the amendment of the Atomic Energy Act by German parliament to phase-out of nuclear energy by 2020, which resulted in immediate shut-down of two reactors. In an earlier dispute between Vattenfall and Germany (*Vattenfall (I) v Germany*) (ICSID Case No ARB/09/6, Award, 11 March 2011), Vattenfall challenged Germany's environmental regulations applying to a coal power plant. In the end, Germany agreed to issue the environmental permits and to loosen some safeguards against environmental impact in favour of Vattenfall.

[6] JW Salacuse and NP Sullivan, 'Do BITs Really Work?: An Evaluation of Bilateral Investment Treaties and Their Grand Bargain' (2005) 46(1) *Harvard International Law Journal* 67, 77.

[7] M Hallward-Driemeier, 'Do Bilateral Investment Treaties Attract FDI? Only a Bit ... and They Could Bite' in KP Sauvant and LE Sachs, *The Effect of Treaties on Foreign Direct Investment: Bilateral Investment Treaties, Double Taxation Treaties, and Investment Flows* (OUP 2009) 351.

the reasons for a governmental policy, while other awards and provisions suggest that governmental conduct inconsistent with market-economy principles or policy change, as such, is the problem, regardless of the reasons for it. These inconsistencies create legal risks and threaten the authority of international investment law. We argue that the appropriate accommodation of the framings of risk must be derived from the fair and equitable treatment standard, since it operates as a broad residual standard in IIAs. We show that the requirements of fairness and equity call for a distributionally just allocation of systemic risks, and that IIAs create systemic risks. This requires ensuring that IIAs yield greater *ex ante* benefits than risks for each and every concerned stakeholder. The implications of this are twofold. First, governmental regulation necessary to protect human rights can never give rise to a right to damages under a fair and equitable treatment standard. Second, frustration of investor's expectations and imperfections in *bona fide* regulations by developing countries must be tolerated insofar as emerging development is the constitutive reason why foreign investment is likely to yield higher *ex ante* benefits than risks to investors.

13.2 IIAs as a Means of Conceptualization, Management, and Allocation of Risk

13.2.1 Types of risk in international investment law

IIAs mitigate the risks associated with investing abroad through commitments by host states to guarantee foreign investment protection by treating any such investment no less favourably than that of third states (Most-Favoured-Nation, MFN) and its own nationals (National Treatment), and by requiring fair and equitable treatment (FET). Some arbitral tribunals interpret FET to include standards of good governance, such as obligations to act consistently, transparently, without arbitrariness or discrimination, proportionally, and in accordance with good faith. The very terms of these provisions suggest that they frame the risks to foreign investors as risks from arbitrary governmental action while upholding the ability of host states to regulate physical risks. However, articulations of the National and MFN treatment clause which do not contain the qualifier of investors or investments being 'in like circumstances', or exception clauses for governmental public policy regulation, raise the question whether in such types of IIA the reasons for discrimination can render it legal.

IIAs further manage risks that impair the value of the investment through a host state's promise to ensure that foreign investors can repatriate their income and capital without fear of capital controls[8] and to provide full protection and security to the physical integrity of the investment against interferences by use of force.[9] The host state further engages itself to guarantee non-interference with the foreign investor's management of its investment by prohibiting itself from imposing

[8] R Dolzer and C Schreuer, *Principles of International Investment Law* (2 edn, OUP 2012) 214.

[9] Compensation is inter alia due when the host state fails to keep its promise of not interfering with the legal and economic stability of the investment.

conditions (eg, performance requirements).[10] These provisions frame the risk to the foreign investor as one stemming from governmental interference that reduces profits, is too interventionist, and is thus not in accordance with principles for a market-based economy. In a similar vein, in order to provide foreign investment protection under IIAs and to mitigate the risks of host state interference with foreign investment, expropriation of a foreign investor's assets is only permitted if the host state meets all of the following requirements: (i) the measure must serve a public purpose; (ii) the procedure of expropriation must follow principles of due process of law; (iii) the measure must not be arbitrary or discriminatory; (iv) the measure must be accompanied by prompt (ie, without undue delay), adequate (ie, in accordance with the fair market value of the expropriated investment), and effective (ie, payment in a convertible currency) compensation. Investment arbitration has recognized that regulatory measures that impair the investment by affecting its economic value and/or the foreign owner's ability to use, manage, or control its property in a meaningful way, are also covered by these protections.[11] On the one hand, the compensation requirement attacks the moral hazard problem on the part of the host state of transferring investment from the foreign investor to a favoured local company,[12] which is consistent with framing the risk as one of arbitrary governmental action. On the other hand, the recognition of a right to compensation against regulatory measures purely based on their effects suggests that IIAs frame the risk to be mitigated as one of business risk due to governmental regulation *as such*, while downplaying any physical risk to the local population due to regulatory chilling effects of liability to foreign investors. Put differently, a purely effects-based analysis of expropriation collectivizes an individual business risk by making the host state liable for compensation.

IIAs make host state commitments credible by providing the procedural guarantee of dispute settlement through investor–state arbitration. To protect foreign investment against a host state's breaches of its contractual promises, the so-called umbrella clauses bring those obligations under the protective provisions of an IIA. Among those contractual commitments are the 'stabilization clauses' which commit host state governments to refrain from altering the regulatory framework that affects the economic viability of the foreign investment. This allocation of risk as business risks to investors—particularly when the stabilization clause is broadly defined—limits the host state's regulatory space to take measures against physical risks through the operation of umbrella clauses in IIAs.[13] In turn, broadly defined umbrella clauses carry the danger of providing the foreign investor too strong a

[10] T Ginsburg, 'International Substitutes for Domestic Institutions: Bilateral Investment Treaties and Governance' (2005) 25(1) *International Review of Law and Economics* 107, 109. See also AK Bjorklund, 'Improving the International Investment Law and Policy System' in JE Alvarez et al (eds) *The Evolving International Investment Regime: Expectations, Realities, Options* (OUP 2011) 228.

[11] *CME v Czech Republic* (UNCITRAL, Partial Award, 13 September 2001) para 604 <http://www.italaw.com/cases/281> accessed 6 June 2016.

[12] Ginsburg, 'International Substitutes for Domestic Institutions' (n 10) 112.

[13] M Hirsch, 'Between Fair and Equitable Treatment and Stabilization Clause: Stable Legal Environment and Regulatory Change in International Investment Law' (2011) 12(6) *Journal of World Investment & Trade* 783.

remedy (investor–state arbitration) for every minor contractual breach.[14] In the new generation IIAs, host states that wish to safeguard their policy space often do not incorporate an umbrella clause.[15] Similarly, some arbitral tribunals have found breaches of FET on the basis of frustration of legitimate expectations of investors created by specific governmental assurances that the regulatory framework would not change. The danger is that policy reasons for a regulatory change are ignored. Moreover, the MFN clause could be interpreted to require the host state to extend the regulatory treatment of the status quo ante to other investors as well, even if no specific representations were made to them, posing a more comprehensive threat to the ability of the host state to regulate risks of externalities.

13.2.2 Balancing investment protection and host state's right to regulate

Investment protection guarantees under IIAs offer effective means to the foreign investor to manage and limit exposure to political risk. The most frequently invoked guarantees during investor–state arbitration that minimize the exposure of foreign investors to political risks in the host country are compensation for (indirect) expropriation, the fair and equitable treatment standard, and the non-discrimination principle.[16] However, when these principles are not narrowly defined in IIAs, they form a threat to a host state's regulatory space when the interpretation of those unqualified provisions is left to the arbitrators.[17] As a consequence, some states who have feared being the respondent in investor–state arbitrations or have preferred to preserve their regulatory discretion have attempted to include interpretative provisions, general exception clauses, carve-outs,[18] and preambular language to their IIAs.[19]

One group of IIAs acknowledges the host state's right to regulate by providing exceptions through the so-called Non-Precluded Measures (NPMs) clauses. These clauses excuse liability for harms caused by a measure where the measure taken by the host state government was 'necessary' and no other measure was available to protect essential security interests. As the Argentine financial crisis disputes demonstrate, it is not easy to determine when a measure is necessary. In these disputes, Argentina relied on the NPMs clause in the 1991 US–Argentine

[14] P Muchlinski, 'The Framework of Investment Protection: The Content of BITs' in KP Sauvant and LE Sachs, *The Effect of Treaties on Foreign Direct Investment: Bilateral Investment Treaties, Double Taxation Treaties, and Investment Flows* (OUP 2009) 58–59.

[15] C Titi, *The Right to Regulate in International Investment Law* (Nomos and Hart Publishing 2014) 48–50.

[16] R Ginsburg, 'Political Risk Insurance and Bilateral Investment Treaties: Making the Connection' (2013) 14(6) *Journal of World Investment & Trade* 943, 947. See also Titi, ibid, 276.

[17] A Van Aaken, 'The International Investment Protection Regime through the Lens of Economic Theory' in M Waibel et al (eds), *The Backlash Against Investment Arbitration* (Kluwer Law International 2010) 546.

[18] Carve-outs include an exception to the MFN treatment in the dispute settlement clause, exception to taxation, and an exception to the exhaustion of local remedies.

[19] SA Spears 'Quest for Policy Space in New-Generation International Investment Agreements' (2010) 13(4) *Journal of International Economic Law* 1037, 1048.

Bilateral Investment Treaty (BIT) to justify its emergency (capital control) measures in response to the economic and financial crisis which resulted in a great loss of the value and legal security of investments mostly in the recently privatized gas sector.[20] In *CMS, Enron*, and *Sempra*, the tribunals all applied a strict approach in line with the customary international law defence of necessity. The tribunals held that the defence of necessity and, by implication, the NPMs clause, is only available if the actions taken by the state were the only way for the state to safeguard an essential interest against a grave and imminent peril.[21] This interpretation severely restricts the successful invocation by states of the defence of necessity and limits the ability of the host state to regulate in times of acute crisis. Moreover, the tribunals held that even a successful invocation of the NPMs clause would only preclude the wrongfulness but would not exclude the host state's duty to compensate the investor.[22] In contrast, the tribunals in *LG&E* and *Continental Casualty* took the opposite approach, viewing the NPMs clause as a self-judging clause and giving considerable deference to Argentina's determination that its actions were necessary to protect essential security interests and maintain public order.[23] In *Continental Casualty*, the tribunal even departed from the stricter necessity defence under customary international law and determined that the text of the NPMs clause reflects the formulation of Article XX GATT and that it is more appropriate to refer to the concept of necessity under the GATT/WTO rather than customary international law.[24]

These diverging awards, all involving Argentina's measures during the crisis, have been criticized for creating inconsistency and legal uncertainty in the interpretation of NPMs clauses.[25] Despite the introduction of a new clause into the BIT, *CMS, Enron*, and *Sempra* continue to portray the risk at stake for the investor as one of being protected from business risks. In contrast, *LG&E* and *Continental Casualty* shift the way risk is framed in these newer IIAs; while the risk from arbitrary or insufficiently market-liberal state action is still reduced, risks of physical externalities are recognized as meriting proportionate host state regulatory action, with the consequent effect that investors must bear business risks associated with the possibility of future regulation of their activities. It is thus not the existence of a political risk per se that matters, but rather whether the imposition of the risk is reasonable

[20] In Argentine cases, investors challenged Argentina's emergency measures on several grounds: an expropriation without compensation; a breach of fair and equitable treatment; a breach of the umbrella clause; a breach of free transfer of capital; and a breach of full protection and security.

[21] *CMS v Argentina* (ICSID Case No ARB/01/8, Decision on Objections to Jurisdiction, 17 July 2003) para 331; *Enron v Argentina* (ICSID Case No ARB/01/3, Award, 22 May 2007) para 313; *Sempra v Argentina* (ICSID Case No ARB/02/16, Award, 28 September 2007) para 355.

[22] *CMS v Argentina*, ibid, para 388; *Enron v Argentina*, ibid, para 260; *Sempra v Argentina*, ibid, para 303.

[23] *LG&E v Argentina* (ICSID Case No ARB/02/1, Decision on Liability, 3 October 2006) paras 239–40, 258–59; *Continental Casualty v Argentina* (ICSID Case No ARB/03/9, Award, 5 September 2008) paras 176–81.

[24] *Continental Casualty v Argentina*, ibid, para 192.

[25] P Muchlinski, 'Trends in International Investment Agreements: Balancing Investor Rights and the Right to Regulate. The Issue of National Security' in KP Sauvant (ed), *Yearbook on International Investment Law & Policy 2008–2009* (OUP 2009) 63.

in the sense that pareto-efficiency demands, because any different regulation would reduce either the welfare of the investor or of the host state population.

Another group of IIAs recognizes the right of host states to regulate in the public interest through exceptions in order to distinguish between permissible regulation and compensable regulatory expropriation.[26] These exceptions may be as general as those found in Article XX GATT and Article XIV GATS (eg, protection of public health, and the environment), albeit conditional on the fulfilment of more procedural requirements, or they may only require that the host state's measure be determined in good faith and be proportionate to the objective sought.[27]

By interpreting the obligations under IIAs too strictly, arbitration tribunals have maximized investment protection without paying much attention to the state's sovereign responsibility to take objectively necessary policy actions. These tribunals have stretched the meaning of IIA provisions to render poorly reasoned and inconsistent decisions,[28] thereby granting foreign investors special rights, in comparison with domestic investors, to be free from regulatory interference.[29] The key concern is that as a result of the fear of liability, IIAs have a chilling effect on the host state's regulatory initiatives.[30] A further concern is that strong counter-majoritarian protection of investor rights through arbitration skews democratic decision-making on questions relating to the protection of the public interest.[31] In more substantive terms, the worry is that rights to property are over-protected relative to other constitutional or human rights, or to the public interest.[32] If these concerns are not reflected in IIAs, they might be perceived as favouring foreign investors and the arbitral awards as illegitimate intrusions on sovereignty.[33] One provision of particular importance in this respect is the FET provision because it is contained in almost all IIAs and has become one of the most relied on and successful bases for claims by investors by functioning as a standard to fill the gaps left by the other standards

26 That is a different basis than a state of necessity, national security, and the public order.

27 SA Spears, 'Quest for Policy Space in New-Generation International Investment Agreements' (n 19) 1037, 1059–62.

28 SD Franck, 'The Legitimacy Crisis in Investment Treaty Arbitration: Privatizing Public International Law Through Inconsistent Decisions' (2005) 73(4) *Fordham Law Review* 1521, 1521 *passim*. See also J Haynes, 'The Evolving Nature of the Fair and Equitable Treatment (FET) Standard: Challenging Its Increasing Pervasiveness in Light of Developing Countries' Concerns—The Case for Regulatory Rebalancing' (2013) 14(1) *Journal of World Investment & Trade* 114, 121.

29 J Kleinheisterkamp, 'Investment Treaty Law and the Fear for Sovereignty: Transnational Challenges and Solutions' (2015) 78(5) *The Modern Law Review* 793, 797.

30 Haynes, 'The Evolving Nature of Fair and Equitable Treatment' (n 28) 114 and 120. This worry extends beyond developing country host economies. As Kleinheisterkamp points out, the liability imposed under IIAs would change the more limited *Francovich* liability EU member states face for violations of EU law. J Kleinheisterkamp, 'Financial Responsibility in European International Investment Policy' (2014) 63(2) *International and Comparative Law Quarterly* 449. Kleinheisterkamp argues the more limited liability of the Union was endorsed by the CJEU precisely to prevent regulatory chill. J Kleinheisterkamp, 'Who is Afraid of Investor-State Arbitration? Unpacking the Riddle of "No Greater Rights" in the TTIP' (2014) 5(4) *IISD Investment Treaty News*, 9.

31 G Van Harten, 'Investment Treaty Arbitration, Procedural Fairness, and the Rule of Law' in SW Schill (ed), *International Investment Law and Comparative Public Law* (OUP 2010) 656–57.

32 J Kleinheisterkamp, 'Investment Treaty Law' (n 29) 803 [with further references].

33 JW Yackee 'Sacrificing Sovereignty: Bilateral Investment Treaties, International Arbitration, and the Quest for Capital' (2006) *USC Center in Law, Economics and Organization*, Research Paper No C06-15, 6.

of protection.[34] The reliance on FET is claimed to have resulted in an open-ended and unbalanced approach, which unduly favours investor interests and overrides the host state's sovereign and legitimate regulation in the public interest.[35]

13.3 IIAs Themselves Create Legal Risks

13.3.1 IIAs as a source of legal risks

Arbitral tribunals have taken on an important role in fine-tuning the framings of risk based on their own assessments of whose risks matter. In addition to framing foreign investment-related risks, IIAs have their own distinct category of legal risks arising from conflicting interpretations which compromise the legal certainty and predictability of international investment rules.[36] This uncertainty affects the extent of political risk for investors as well as the threat of the effect of liability of governments regulating physical risks on the local population, thus threatening the attempts to balance investment protection and host country regulatory space.[37]

Some IIAs define 'investor' to include companies controlled either by their nationals or by companies organized under their laws. As a result, parent companies are often able to assert rights relating to an investment held through a subsidiary or holding company, even where that entity is organized under another country's laws.[38] This carries with it the risk of treaty shopping[39] and exposes the host state to more liability claims, while also heightening legal risk for investors.

[34] *Sempra v Argentina* (n 21) para 300.

[35] P Bekker and A Ogawa 'The Impact of Bilateral Investment Treaty (BIT) Proliferation on Demand for Investment Insurance: Reassessing Political Risk Insurance After the 'BIT Bang'' (2013) 28(2) *ICSID Review* 314, 331–332. See also J Hoyos, 'The Role of Bilateral Investment Treaties' (n2) 26–27. There is an extensive list of instances where all types of governmental conduct—legislative, administrative, and judicial alike—can be found to breach the FET obligation: *Impregilo SpA v Argentina* (ICSID Case No ARB/07/17, Award, 21 June 2011) para 331; *El Paso Energy v Argentina* (ICSID Case No ARB/03/15, Award, 31 October 2011) paras 518–19; *Suez* et al *v Argentina* (ICSID Case No ARB/03/19, Decision on Liability, 30 July 2010) para 246; *AWG Group v Argentina* (UNCITRAL, Decision on Liability, 30 July 2010) paras 247–48 <http://www.italaw.com/cases/106> accessed 6 June 2016; *Metalclad v Mexico* (ICSID Case No ARB(AF)/97/1, Award, 30 August 2000) paras 97–101; *SD Myers v Canada* (UNCITRAL, Partial Award, 13 November 2000) paras 266–68 <http://www.italaw.com/cases/969> accessed 6 June 2016.

[36] K Yannaca-Small, 'Improving the System of Investor–State Dispute Settlement', *OECD Working Papers on International Investment*, 2006/01 (OECD Publishing) 4–14. See also R Geiger, 'Multilateral Approaches to Investment: The Way Forward' in JE Alvarez et al (eds) *The Evolving International Investment Regime: Expectations, Realities, Options* (OUP 2011) 165.

[37] C Henckels, 'Balancing Investment Protection and Sustainable Development in Investor–State Arbitration: The Role of Deference' in AK Bjorklund (ed), *Yearbook on International Investment Law & Policy 2012–2013* (OUP 2014) 307.

[38] Eg, in *Waste Management (II) v Mexico* (ICSID Case No ARB(AF)/00/3, Award, 30 April 2004), paras 77–79) the US parent company was able to assert a NAFTA claim against Mexico even though the investment was structured through a Cayman Islands holding company.

[39] *Saluka v Czech Republic* (UNCITRAL, Partial Award, 17 March 2006) paras 240–41 <http://www.italaw.com/cases/961> accessed 6 June 2016.

Another type of legal risk arises from the operation of MFN clauses included in most IIAs. MFN clauses provide the foreign investor the opportunity to import more favourable provisions of a third-party investment treaty into the scope of application of its home state agreement with the host state (the basic treaty), thereby nullifying the efforts of the quid pro quo bargains.[40] Particularly, when the foreign investor demands more favourable treatment through the establishment of a subsidiary in a third state whose IIA protects the company regardless of the nationality of its owners or shareholders, the MFN clause can be easily invoked to modify the treatment of the investor.[41] The risk for the host state lies in the fact that changes in corporate ownership and control could lead to potential inadvertent breaches of IIAs.

13.3.2 Inconsistent awards concerning host state regulatory measures

13.3.2.1 Expropriation

Most investment disputes between the foreign investor and the host state relating to indirect expropriation concern the question of whether the measure taken is compensable or whether it served a legitimate public policy purpose. The tribunals' approaches can be categorized into three different interpretations.

First, the measure constitutes indirect expropriation due to a substantial deprivation of the foreign investor's benefit of its investment. Thus, compensation for indirect expropriation depends on the actual effect of the host state's measures rather than the intent of the host state.[42] Some tribunals have expanded the scope of indirect takings to include any covert or incidental interference with the foreign investor's use of property, which has the effect of depriving the owner, in whole or in significant part, of the use or reasonably-to-be-expected economic benefit of the property.[43]

This 'sole-effect' doctrine is contrasted with a second approach that determines whether the non-discriminatory, bona fide, and legitimate public purpose measure was proportionate—despite the adverse impact on the foreign investment.[44] If the

[40] SW Schill, 'Enhancing International Investment Law's Legitimacy: Conceptual and Methodological Foundations of a New Public Law Approach' (2011) 52(1) *Virginia Journal of International Law* 57, 94. See also SW Schill, *The Multilateralization of International Investment Law* (CUP 2009) 9–10, 16–18.

[41] Eg, in *Tokio Tokeles v Ukraine* (ICSID Case No ARB/02/18, Decision of Jurisdiction, 20 April 2004), paras 68–69 the tribunal upheld jurisdiction over claims against Ukraine notwithstanding that the Lithuanian claimant was 99% owned by Ukrainian nationals. In *CMS v Argentina* (n 21) paras 47–48, a single, and even minority shareholder, was entitled to bring a claim against the host state.

[42] *Occidental v Ecuador* (UNCITRAL/LCIA Case No UN3467, Final Award, 1 July 2004) paras 85, 92 <http://www.italaw.com/cases/761> accessed 6 June 2016; *Siemens v Argentina* (ICSID Case No ARB/02/8, Award, 17 January 2007) para 270. In *Santa Elena*, the tribunal found that expropriatory environmental measures—no matter how laudable and beneficial to society as a whole—are compensable (ICSID Case No ARB/96/1, Final Award, 17 February 2000) para 72.

[43] *AES v Hungary* (ICSID Case No ARB/07/22, Award, 23 September 2010) paras 14.3.1–14.3.4; *Metalclad v Mexico* (n 35) paras 103 and 107.

[44] *Azurix v Argentina* (ICSID Case No ARB/01/12, Award, 14 July 2006) paras 309–12; *Tecmed v Mexico* (ICSID Case No ARB(AF)/00/2, Award, 28 May 2003) paras 121–22.

tribunal considers host state's public policy reasons proportionate, the measure is not expropriatory.[45]

Third, some tribunals have attempted to find a balance between the host state's right to regulate in the public interest and the protection of the investor's rights. In *Methanex v United States*, the tribunal held that as a matter of general international law, a non-discriminatory regulation for a public purpose, which is enacted in accordance with due process and which affects a foreign investment, is not deemed expropriatory and compensable unless specific commitments were given by the government to the foreign investor to refrain from such regulation.[46]

These different approaches belie different framings of risk; the effects-based approach tends to insulate investors from business risks, while the approach in *Methanex*, *Azurix*, *Tecmed*, and *LG&E* focuses on reasonable, pareto-efficient risk imposition, enabling the avoidance of physical risks. The differences also lead to legal uncertainty for both investors and host states because investment activities diversify over time and economies develop, thereby increasing the need for regulatory diversity and intensity to respond to rapidly and dramatically shifting political and economic dynamics in host countries, the region, and globally. By way of example, when a developing host country develops economically the key regulatory concerns of securing food and providing healthcare may extend to include protection of the environment and the provision of safer and healthier labour standards. Consequently, as the economies of developing host states develop, they are likely to encounter more liability under IIAs. As *Ethyl Corporation v Canada* shows, host states may become reluctant to regulate in the field of environment and public health when they fear liability.[47]

13.3.2.2 Fair and equitable treatment

The fair and equitable treatment obligation in IIAs was created primarily to protect the foreign investor against unfair practices by the host state, such as arbitrary cancellation of licences, harassment of an investor through unjustified fines and penalties, or creation of other barriers to disrupt a business.[48]

Despite different formulations and diverging interpretations by investment tribunals, there is a general consensus that the fair and equitable treatment clause is a broad, overarching standard.[49] Lacking in more specific content, FET has variously

[45] KN Schefer, *International Investment Law: Text, Cases and Materials* (Edward Elgar 2013) 208–10.

[46] *Methanex v United States* (UNCITRAL/NAFTA, Final Award, 3 August 2005) Part IV-Chapter D, paras 7–9 <http://www.italaw.com/cases/683> accessed 6 June 2016.

[47] *Ethyl v Canada* (UNCITRAL/NAFTA, Award on Jurisdiction, 24 June 1998) paras 82 and 86–88 <http://www.italaw.com/cases/409> accessed 6 June 2016. Finally, the government of Canada settled the dispute and agreed to reverse the ban on the additive, to pay $19 million to Ethyl Corporation, and to issue a statement confirming that MMT does not affect health or the environment.

[48] *UNCTAD*, 'Fair and Equitable Treatment', UNCTAD Series on Issues in International Investment Agreements II (United Nations 2012) 7.

[49] B Kingsbury and SW Schill, 'Investor–State Arbitration as Governance: Fair and Equitable Treatment, Proportionality and the Emerging Global Administrative Law' (September 2, 2009), NYU School of Law, Public Law Research Paper No 09-46 <http://dx.doi.org/10.2139/ssrn.1466980> accessed 19 December 2016.

been interpreted as encompassing: (i) stability, predictability, and consistency with the host state's legal framework; (ii) protection of legitimate expectations; (iii) denial of justice and administrative due process; (iv) transparency; and (v) reasonableness and proportionality in relation to the host state's governmental action.[50] Two different framings of risk are implicated: on the one hand, an attempt to reconcile the investor's ability to reduce political risk with the ability of the host state to regulate risks of externalities from investments through concepts such as proportionality and due process rights; on the other hand, a less regulation-friendly framing which views a change in the status through governmental intervention as a source of risk, as such, against which investors should be protected and which has the potential to insulate investors from business risks if FET is interpreted broadly.

The contemporary and most cited definition of the FET standard requires the host state authorities to act consistently, without ambiguity, and transparently, making sure the investor knows in advance the regulatory and administrative policies and practices to which it will be subject so that it may comply.[51] This interpretation by the *Tecmed* tribunal has, however, been criticized by the Annulment Committee in *MTD v Chile* for deriving the host state's obligations—with regard to the FET standard—from the investor's expectations instead of from an independent interpretation of the terms of the applicable investment treaty in accordance with the general interpretative approach of the Vienna Convention on the Law of Treaties (VCLT).[52] We suggest that *Tecmed* was also too focused on reducing business risk for investors.

Moreover, many arbitral tribunals have interpreted the FET standard expansively, especially in cases concerning the legitimate expectations of the investors. Legitimate expectations of the foreign investor can arise from: (i) reliance on specific host state conduct in the form of oral or written representations or commitments and specific assurances;[53] (ii) the host state's obligation to maintain a stable and predictable legal and administrative framework, including consistency and transparency in decision-making;[54] and (iii) the foreign investor's reasonable expectation that the host state will comply with its obligations under IIAs.[55]

[50] KJ Vandevelde, 'A Unified Theory of Fair and Equitable Treatment' (2010) 43(1) *New York Journal of International Law and Politics* 43, 104–06.

[51] *Tecmed v Mexico* (n 44) para 163; *PSEG v Turkey* (ICSID Case No ARB/02/5, Award, 19 January 2007) para 240; *MTD v Chile* (ICSID Case No ARB/01/7, Award, 25 May 2004) paras 113–15. See also Schill, 'Enhancing International Investment Law's Legitimacy' (n 40) 82–83.

[52] *MTD v Chile*, ibid, Decision on Annulment, 21 March 2007, para 67. See also A Newcombe and L Paradell, *Law and Practice of Investment Treaties: Standards of Treatment* (Kluwer Law International 2009) 264–68.

[53] *ADF v United States* (ICSID Case No ARB(AF)/00/1, Award, 9 January 2003) para 189; *Wena Hotels Ltd v Egypt* (ICSID Case No ARB/98/4, Award, 8 December 2000) paras 85–87; *Parkerings v Lithuania* (ICSID Case No ARB/05/8, Award, 11 September 2007) para 331; *National Grid v Argentina* (UNCITRAL Award, 3 November 2008) para 173 <http://www.italaw.com/cases/732> accessed 6 June 2016; *Waste Management Inc (I) v Mexico* (ICSID Case No ARB(AF)/98/2, Award, 2 June 2000) para 98.

[54] *Occidental v Ecuador* (n 42) paras 183–86 and 190–91; *MTD v Chile* (n 51) paras 109–15; *Eureko v Poland* (Ad Hoc Arbitration, Partial Award, 19 August 2005) paras 231–32 <http://www.italaw.com/cases/412> accessed 6 June 2016; *CME v Czech Republic* (n 11) para 611; *Bayindir v Pakistan* (ICSID Case No ARB/03/29, Award, 27 August 2009) paras 231–32.

[55] The reasonableness in this regard refers to the foreign investor's behaviour and whether the host state interference was in response to the malpractices of the foreign investor.

In a number of cases, arbitral tribunals have found a breach of the fair and equitable treatment standard in situations in which the host state did not necessarily act in bad faith but, rather, in an improper and discreditable or unreasonable way.[56] These high standards of procedural reasonableness seem to have created an independent obligation without considering the circumstances in which the host state's bona fide regulation was taken. Other tribunals have, however, taken all circumstances, including the political and socioeconomic conditions of the host state as well as the host state's legitimate regulatory interests into consideration when assessing the reasonableness of investor's legitimate expectation.[57]

The question arises, however, whether exemptions should be made with regard to the foreign investor's legitimate expectations at the time of the investment. In *Total v Argentina*, the tribunal found that a basis for legitimate expectations could be found in the legal order of the host state if the relevant laws would have been prospective in nature.[58] In Dolzer's view, this approach undermines the stability and predictability of a host state's laws at the time of the investment and it creates indeterminacy about which laws can be classified as prospective.[59]

Due to the lack of clarity and predictability of the FET standard, as well as divergent case law, the host states struggle to organize their regulatory and administrative framework in a way that is compatible with the FET standard, which in turn creates legal uncertainty and a liability risk for host states. In particular, developing host states are likely to encounter difficulties in this regard due to lack of available legal expertise, access to facts, scientific evidence, and a well-developed regulatory apparatus. This increased liability risk may in turn have negative implications such as regulatory chill or positive discrimination in favour of foreign investors against domestic investors.[60] Further, the lack of clarity and of an objective benchmark for FET leaves to investment arbitration tribunals a wide margin of discretion in the balancing of investors' political risk protection as against host states' rights to regulate risks.[61] There is a danger that investment tribunals expect too much regulatory

[56] Eg, the tribunal in *Occidental v Ecuador* (n 42) (paras 183–86 and 190–91) seems to limit the host state's sovereign power to make changes in tax rates. Likewise, in a series of disputes the changes in gas tariff rates to provide public utility service were found in breach of the fair and equitable treatment standard, such as *Suez* et al *v Argentina* (n 35) para 226; *LG&E v Argentina* (n 23) paras 129 and 158; *Enron v Argentina* (n 21) para 263. In *Metalclad v Mexico* (n 35) paras 74 and 79–86 Mexico was found liable inter alia because there was uncertainty in Mexico's domestic law about whether the municipality or only the state and federal government had competence to issue permits for hazardous landfills in a situation where the investor was assured by federal government officials that the federal and state-level permits would suffice.

[57] *Parkerings v Lithuania* (n 53) paras 331–32; *Duke Energy v Ecuador* (ICSID Case No ARB/04/19, Award, 18 August 2008) para 320; *Saluka v Czech Republic* (n 39) paras 304–08.

[58] *Total v Argentina* (ICSID Case No ARB/04/01, Decision on Liability, 27 December 2010) para 122.

[59] R Dolzer, 'Fair and Equitable Treatment: Today's Contours' (2013) 12(1) *Santa Clara Journal of International Law* 7, 23–24.

[60] Haynes, 'The Evolving Nature of Fair and Equitable Treatment' (n 28) 120.

[61] F Ortino, 'Redefining the Content and Role of Investment "Rules" and "Standards": A New Approach to International Investment Treaty Making' (2013) 28(1) *ICSID Review* 152, 157. See also SW Schill, 'Deference in Investment Treaty Arbitration: Re-conceptualizing the Standard of Review' (2012) 3(3) *Journal of International Dispute Settlement* 577, 579.

perfectionism from host states, thereby chilling particularly the ability of developing countries to regulate risks.

Moreover, the disparate framings of risk are problematic not only when they only occur through different interpretations of the same provision in different awards of investment tribunals, but also when they occur across several provisions in an IIA, unless the text clearly requires it. If the purpose of IIAs were to insure investors against a unique category of business risk by looking solely at the existence and effects of governmental intervention by likening the interpretation of FET to stabilization clauses, it would be irrelevant also to require reasonableness and proportionality in respect of that same intervention under the expropriation provision. Conversely, the purpose of IIAs might be to balance the political risk of investors with the need for host states to regulate risks through standards of reasonableness and proportionality. Assuming that a host state regulation with significant business impact treats the foreign investor fairly and equitably because it is proportionate, it would be incongruent if that very conduct could give rise to a right to compensation under a broad, effects-based expropriation standard. These inconsistencies in the framing of risk are problematic for the very authority of law because they offer incompatible reasons for upholding IIAs and therefore ultimately no reason at all.

This raises the question as to which framing of risk is the doctrinally appropriate one for IIAs. If FET is a residual provision for the whole IIA, and since its very terms set the benchmark for what is fair and equitable, it must inform the interpretation of the other provisions; it would be inconceivable and inconsistent to interpret these other provisions as contrary to fairness and equity and yet consider FET to be a residual provision. Put differently, the other provisions should be seen as more specific enunciations of what fairness and equity require. Section 13.4 advances an account of fairness in the distribution of risk which, given the purpose of IIAs to frame, allocate, and manage risks, is the conception of fairness that is most logically doctrinally implicated by FET.

13.4 Fairness in Distribution of Risk as FET

13.4.1 What fairness in risk distribution requires

Risk and responsibility are ultimately connected to agency[62] in an abstract way; when an individual has knowledge of the possibly ensuing consequences of their voluntary act they are appropriately to be held responsible for those consequences because they acted freely. The imposition of an important risk onto us through the acts of another reduces our agency because we are now no longer completely free to go about our plans in quite the same way we would have done before the

[62] The connection between risk, responsibility, and agency is well illustrated in the distinction between brute and option luck in the work of Ronald Dworkin. Option luck points to the notion of a risk that is fully voluntarily undertaken and Dworkin argues individuals are responsible for any consequences. See R Dworkin, 'What Is Equality? Part 2: Equality of Resources' (1981) 10(4) *Philosophy and Public Affairs* 283, 292–304.

imposition of risk occurred. We are therefore entitled to some adjustment. What we are interested in for the purpose of delimiting the contours of the FET obligation is a distinct class of risk termed 'systemic risks' which, being no-fault risks, raise the most difficult questions about the allocation of responsibility for this risk. 'Systemic risks' sit between a voluntarily assumed and an externally imposed risk in that they are risks generally known to exist in a rule-governed practice for which no one agent or group of agents can be held responsible[63] because their realization hinges crucially on the convergence of actions in a large-scale, weakly coordinated interaction. Aaron James has argued that responsibility for systemic risks is collective and that a morally acceptable distribution of systemic risks must therefore be equal.[64] Systemic risks become morally acceptable only, James has argued, if expected *ex ante* benefits exceed expected *ex ante* losses for everyone regardless of starting positions *and* no less risky alternative is available at a reasonable cost to anyone else.[65]

Is the multilateral system of IIAs an example of a systemic risk? The first observation is that developing countries very often *do* assume the risks of liability and legal uncertainty of IIAs out of necessity, both because foreign direct investment (FDI) is a crucial tool by which they can develop and meet essential human interests of their own population and because bilateral IIAs set in motion a competitive dynamic between prospective host countries seeking to be the first among other competing countries to sign an IIA and attract FDI.[66] It has been argued that the result of the competitive dynamic is that developing countries are willing to sign IIAs containing more and more provisions constraining their regulatory freedom,[67] thereby augmenting the risk of legal liability. The second observation is that the decision of investors to invest in a particular host country hinges on growth of *per capita* gross domestic product (GDP), openness of the economy, and available infrastructure, all of which ensures that the return on investment (in other words, the profit) is higher, or materializes faster, relative to the amount invested than what the investor could obtain elsewhere.[68] We may think of these independent variables as indicators of the development potential of a host economy. Where these variables point in the right direction, political risk has little influence on investment location decisions. In the words of Demirhan and Masca:

> When the host countries present high returns, firms may ignore political risk. As long as the foreign company is confident of being able to operate profitably without excessive risk to its capital and personnel, it may continue to invest.[69]

[63] A James, 'The Distinctive Significance of Systemic Risks' (forthcoming) *Ratio Juris*, on file with the authors, 6, 13–14, 23.

[64] ibid, 13–14, 25.

[65] ibid. An illustrative example put forth in the literature and discussed also by James would be the practice of authorizing ambulances to speed on the way to hospital notwithstanding the risk of accident to bystanders this creates.

[66] A Guzman, 'Why Do LDCs Sign Treaties that Hurt Them? Explaining the Popularity of Bilateral Investment Treaties' (1997) 38 *Vanderbilt Journal of International Law* 639, 670–71, 676.

[67] ibid.

[68] E Demirhan and M Masca, 'Determinants of Foreign Direct Investment Flows to Developing Countries: A Cross-Sectional Analysis' (2008) 17(4) *Prague Economic Papers* 356, 365 <https://www.vse.cz/pep/337> accessed 12 December 2015.

[69] ibid, 366.

This finding suggests that economic growth, infrastructure, and openness of the economy often provide enough expected benefits to make the expected loss through political risk, which includes regulation of their activities by the host government, worthwhile. In other words, they yield a favourable *ex ante* ratio of benefits over costs for investors.

A second observation is that IIAs hold out the promise of economic development for their developing country signatories, which can reasonably be expected to lead to a change in regulations in the host country as, for example, new risks become relevant or governments increase their regulatory capacity (both procedurally and substantially). The strengthening of the previously weak regulatory environment may unavoidably proceed with some trial and error before a developing host country becomes well governed. This is particularly so because development is a broad concept covering economic growth and institutional and social development, each of which may be in possible tension with the other. It is thus a complex and variable process rather than one involving pre-determined, precise, and calculable shifts from one stage to another. This economic development is triggered by the concurrence of individual business decisions. The economic development process set in motion by IIAs may therefore give rise to a category of regulatory risks that are unavoidable, and therefore no-fault risks, and which are not perfectly foreseeable for investors either. In other words, the risk of a host country being found liable for a breach of an IIA due to regulatory imperfection linked to an ongoing process of development (but not bad faith or wilful breach) appears to be a systemic one.

Since IIAs create systemic risks, the way IIAs impose legal risks of uncompensated harm and legal liability must meet more demanding standards of equal concern in the sense that expected benefits must exceed losses for all individuals and no other safer alternative can be available at a reasonable cost to anyone. In essence, this means that the investment activity in question needs to be more likely than any other alternative to create a positive externality on both each individual in the host economy and also the investor. Based on the theory of fair distribution of systemic risks, the benchmark for determining what FET requires must be whether every stakeholder can expect net benefits. If everyone derives net benefits, the creation of risk can be reasonably assented to and thus presumptively fair.

We submit that sensitivity to these deontological considerations about risk and responsibility is what a doctrinally correct interpretation of the term 'fair and equitable' treatment requires. We thus agree with Kläger, who points out that 'fair' and 'equitable' requires a substantive theory of justice to articulate the content of the obligation.[70] The ordinary meaning of the term 'fair' refers to 'rightness or acceptability as well as treatment in a non-discriminatory manner; to being marked by impartiality and being free from self-interest'.[71] The term 'equitable' in turn is

[70] R Kläger, 'Fair and Equitable Treatment: A Look at the Theoretical Underpinnings of Legitimacy and Fairness' (2010) 11(3) *Journal of World Investment & Trade* 435, 437–38.

[71] <http://www.merriam-webster.com/dictionary/fair> accessed 22 November 2016.

defined as just or fair or as dealing equally with everyone.[72] Deontological standards of fairness in risk imposition fulfil exactly this requirement of being rightful in the sense of being free from self-interest because they meet tests of reciprocal acceptability and therefore tend towards equality.

Fairness in systemic risk imposition provides an objective end-point, which is arguably missing from Kläger's account of FET. Kläger enumerates various elements that undoubtedly have some relevance to questions of fairness, such as the procedural quality of judicial decisions rendered in terms of having considered a broad set of reasons and using coherent interpretative principles, redistributive fairness, the balancing of determinacy, and thus limited judicial discretion and situational appropriateness of a norm, which can call for greater indeterminacy.[73] He admits that these can be in tension and that 'it is ultimately the quality of the discourse balancing these tensions, which determines the perceived fairness of the outcome'.[74]

However, his list still remains much too indeterminate to fix the content of FET. Kläger only comes up with the vague—and not terribly enlightening—statement that fair procedure, non-discrimination, legitimate expectations, transparency, and proportionality 'may have an impact on the shaping of the standard or the outcome of a particular case', even if they are neither an exclusive list nor relevant in each case.[75] However, to know whether tribunals have correctly interpreted and applied the FET provision we not only need to know that these elements are relevant *pro tanto* but how much they are relevant in relation to each other *ceteris paribus* and *mutatis mutandis*.

We should also briefly discuss a rival position that sets forth a substantive conception of fairness and equity. Hirsch submits that investment awards have found breaches of FET obligations resulting from legal change on two grounds: either because specific governmental representations, assurances, or contractual obligations pre-existed changed circumstances; or because a legislative change was accompanied by procedural defects.[76] No legitimate expectations can thus derive solely from the previous legislative framework.[77] He further argues that a contractualist or semi-contractualist framing of FET in terms of statements detrimentally relied on is suitable for allocating the risks involved in long-term investment relations and the protection of expectations.[78] Our main objection to Hirsch's normative framing of the risk as a risk of a contractualist breach is that such framing (and its outcomes) would be fair only if the object of the 'contract' is rightfully owned by the contracting parties. Interests of the population in physical safety and other human rights necessary to create legitimate political authority are not objects the state can dispose of through a contract because they reside with the population with the state

[72] <https://www.merriam-webster.com/dictionary/equitable> accessed 26 January 2016.

[73] Kläger, 'Fair and Equitable Treatment' (n 70) 444, 447, 449, 451.

[74] ibid, 448. He also evokes balancing stability and change, 453.

[75] ibid, 452.

[76] Hirsch, 'Between Fair and Equitable Treatment and Stabilization Clause' (n 13) 784, 790, 792–99.

[77] ibid, 790, 792.

[78] ibid, 784, 801–05.

merely being an agent for their realization. Consequently, the government cannot abrogate them by means of a contract because doing so would be unfair and hence inconsistent with the FET standard.

A government might, of course, grant immunity to investors from legislative change on such matters, or a right to compensation through a stabilization clause that gets elevated to the level of an IIA obligation by an umbrella clause which incorporates a host state's contractual commitments of regulatory stability.[79] In such circumstances, the FET standard should still be considered as part of a contextual interpretation of IIAs, but there would obviously be less scope *de lege lata* to develop an interpretation that fully incorporates fairness, even if the result could nevertheless be criticized *de lege ferenda* as non-rightful abrogation.

13.4.2 What would fair systemic risk distribution under the FET standard precisely require?

One way in which host economies ensure that there is a likely net benefit for each individual is through social regulation of investment activities to reduce the risk of negative physical externalities on their population (eg, through environmental pollution). The benchmark for fairness and equity is hence how a host state *ought to* regulate to ensure that each citizen of the local population as well as the investor are more likely to be net beneficiaries rather than net losers. The question as to what the law of the host state provides and what assurances were made to the investor at the time the investment was made is immaterial to this benchmark. Assurances cannot amount to an expectation that the government will continue to permit investment activities that are harmful to its own population or that violate their human rights. No fair treatment claim by the investor in relation to risk imposition can arise here because this would essentially amount to asking for the imposition of a concentrated, serious risk on the host state's population without the risk bearers having had any expectation of concentrated high benefits to outweigh the risk imposition. Put differently, an expectation that a country would continue harming essential human interests of its own population can never be legitimate, even if the host country had done so in the past.

Our interpretation of FET is bolstered by the legal context of the positive law. As a treaty, an IIA is to be interpreted in accordance with Articles 31 and 32 of the VCLT. Article 31(1) mentions three interpretative elements: ordinary meaning, context, and object and purpose of the treaty. Context includes 'relevant rules of international law applicable in the relations between the parties'.[80] The body of positive law that expressly deals with standards of social justice (and thus fairness

[79] On the freezing effect of stabilization clauses concerning regulatory change and their legal status in investment arbitration, see K Gehne and R Brillo, 'Stabilization Clauses in International Investment Law: Beyond Balancing and Fair and Equitable Treatment', NCCR Working Paper, No 2013/46, 11–17 <http://www.nccr-trade.org/publication/stabilization-clauses-in-international-investment-law-beyond-balancing-and-fair-and-equitable-treat/> accessed 26 January 2016.

[80] VCLT, 23 May 1969, 1155 UNTS 331, art 31(3)(c).

and equity) is international human rights law.[81] It is hence a 'relevant' rule, even under a predominantly textual approach to Article 31(1), which would consider context and purpose to be merely elements to be used in ascertaining the ordinary meaning of the terms 'fairness' and 'equity'. International human rights law stipulates duties to respect, protect, and fulfil human rights. The last two elements particularly encompass positive duties of the state to take action, including through passing laws. Context hence supports the interpretation argued for, namely that it can never be fair and equitable, nor legitimately expected, that the host state violates its international human rights law obligations. Additionally, some IIAs like the US model BIT, note in their preamble the desire to maintain protection of health, safety, and the environment and the promotion of internationally recognized labour rights.[82] The preamble is relevant for the interpretation of FET as evidence of object and purpose of the IIA. Investors are thus on notice, not only ideally but also actually, through the human rights obligations countries have accepted that they cannot legitimately expect a host state not to take any action necessary for the full realization of human rights.

Where the institutional environment of a host state is weak and this factors into the investor's decision to seek out a developing country as a specific destination for investment (because low levels of development and high political risk correspond with higher anticipated returns), tribunals should take this factor into account in determining whether regulatory change amounts to a breach of the fair and equitable treatment standard. In fact, if the investor expects economic gains because of anticipated local economic development, which will typically be accompanied by regulatory changes, the current lower level of development and weak institutional structure are necessary elements for yielding the favourable cost–benefit ratio of the investment *ex ante*. The investor should then not be able to complain about a lack of fairness *ex post* even if bona fide regulatory change suffers from some degree of disproportion, lack of evidence base, or lack of full transparency due to the less developed nature of the host country, since this fact was both known and determined the decision of the investor to invest *ex ante*. What this generally means is that developing country host economies must be given a greater margin of policy space regarding the proportionality and reasonableness of their risk regulation under FET than developed host economies.[83]

In *SD Myers*, the tribunal acknowledged that a tribunal applying the FET standard does not have an open-ended mandate to second-guess government decision-making. Governments have to make many potentially controversial choices. In doing so, they may appear to have made mistakes, to have misjudged the facts, proceeded on the basis of a misguided economic or sociological theory, placed too much emphasis on some social values over others, and adopted solutions that are

[81] Universal Declaration of Human Rights (adopted 10 December 1948 UNGA Res 217 A(III), Preamble; International Covenant on Economic, Social and Cultural Rights, 16 December 1966, 993 UNTS 3, Preamble, arts 2.1 and 23.

[82] US Model BIT <http://www.state.gov/documents/organization/188371.pdf> accessed 22 November 2016.

[83] In a similar vein, see Hayes, 'The Evolving Nature of Fair and Equitable Treatment' (n 29) 115.

ultimately ineffective or counterproductive. The tribunal acknowledged that the ordinary remedy, if there were one, for errors in modern governments is through internal political and legal processes, including elections.[84]

The approach of the tribunal in *SD Myers* is a welcome one. It recognizes that a certain margin of error must be left to the host state government in how it regulates. For developing countries, such errors are likely to be more and greater precisely because they are less developed, while economic development (potential) is a reason for why investors are likely to generate comparatively higher levels of profit. As we have argued, the fair distribution of risk requires that each person had higher expected benefits than losses. What investment tribunals should do in their interpretation and application of FET is to ensure first that the regulatory measure is effective at regulating physical externalities, and second that the risks of regulatory imperfection remain calibrated (or proportionate) to the levels of profit that an investor can expect. Moreover, if economic development increases investors' profit, but profits (and growth rates) level off once a certain stage of development has been reached, then the margin of error that tribunals may permit should shrink quite naturally as host economies develop. Interpreted this way, FET would contain a built-in special and differential treatment provision, which piggy-backs on the concept of fairness it enshrines. A normative 'ought' (FET) implies an empirical 'can' but, as Haynes has argued, it is unrealistic to expect developing countries to have in place the kinds of institutions which would allow for full transparency and good governance envisaged by the tribunal in *Tecmed*.[85]

13.5 Conclusion

We have argued that IIAs can be viewed as an instrument to frame, allocate, and manage risks, but that case law has articulated different and conflicting framings of risk. Some of it has suggested that political risk and the right of the host country to regulate are reconciled by focusing on the reasonableness of the regulation. However, other awards have gone in the direction of insulating investors against business risk. These inconsistencies in the framing of risk become a source of legal risk and undermine the authority of IIAs. This applies in particular to the FET provision because it has emerged as a default provision to try and hold host states liable for conduct that does not infringe the other IIA provisions. We have argued that the principle underpinning the FET provision should inform the litmus test for when compensation is due under the whole IIA. To give objective content to its open-ended terms, we propose theories of fairness in risk distribution. These deontological theories require evaluating fairness from the point of view of individuals as the audience at risk. They require that each individual must enjoy greater *ex ante* prospects of benefits over losses and that no mechanism must be available to make

[84] *SD Myers v Canada* (n 35) para 261.

[85] Haynes, 'The Evolving Nature of Fair and Equitable Treatment' (n 28) 130, 132–33, 135–36.

the activity safer at a reasonable cost to anyone. We have argued that public interest regulation of host economies ensures that investment is adequately safe and yields a net expected benefit compared to losses. As a consequence of development, new regulatory needs may emerge, yet developing countries cannot realistically jump to a procedurally and substantively perfect regulatory system immediately. Inasmuch as it is the expectation of development that determines investment location decisions and not political risk, investors have not only reckoned with political risk, but the risk may also be outweighed by the anticipated profits *ex ante.* As long as this is the case, and the political risk is not the result of deliberate wrongful conduct on the part of the host economy, we suggest that such investors are treated fairly and should therefore not derive compensation under FET.

Author Index

Index